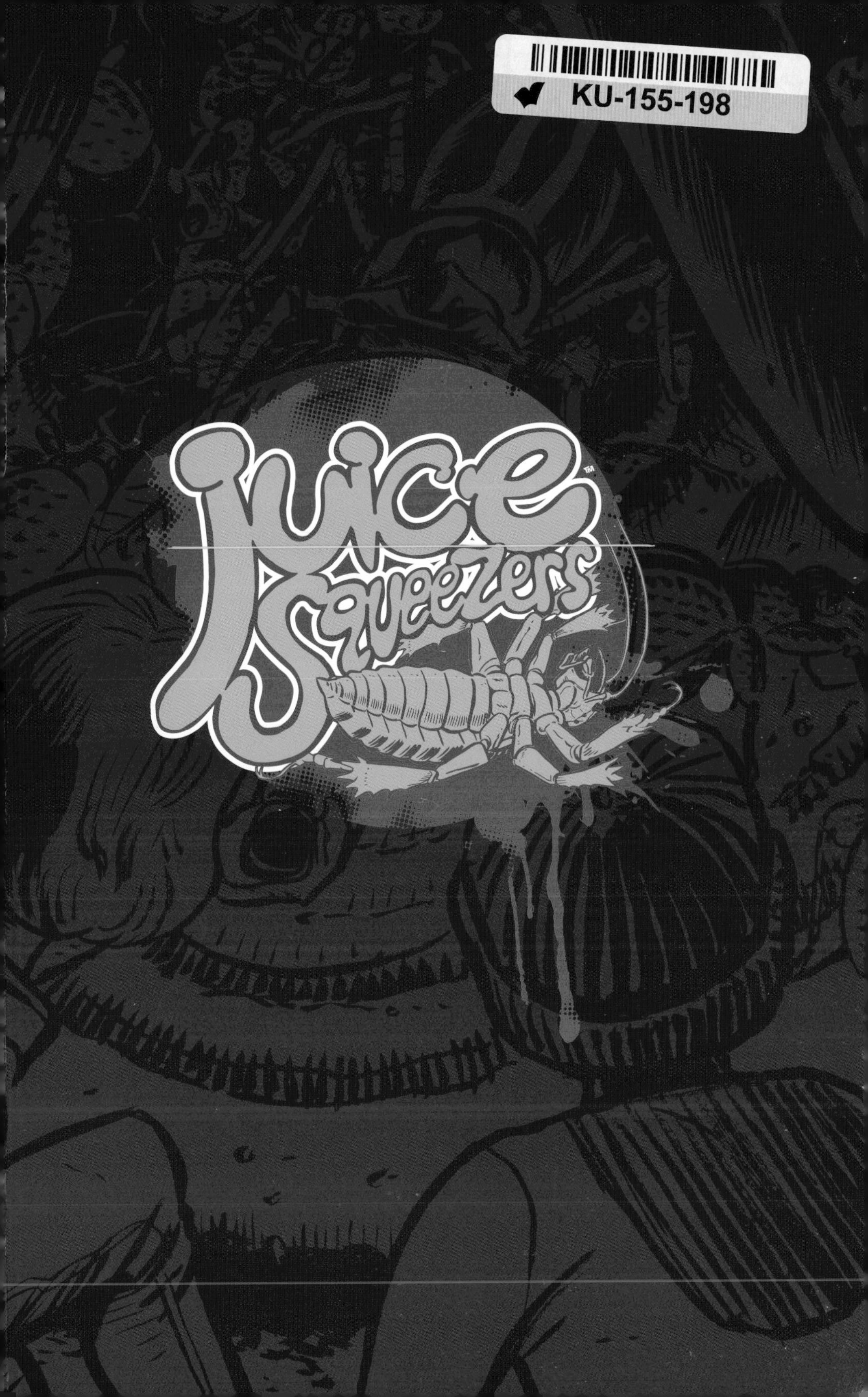
Juice Squeezers™

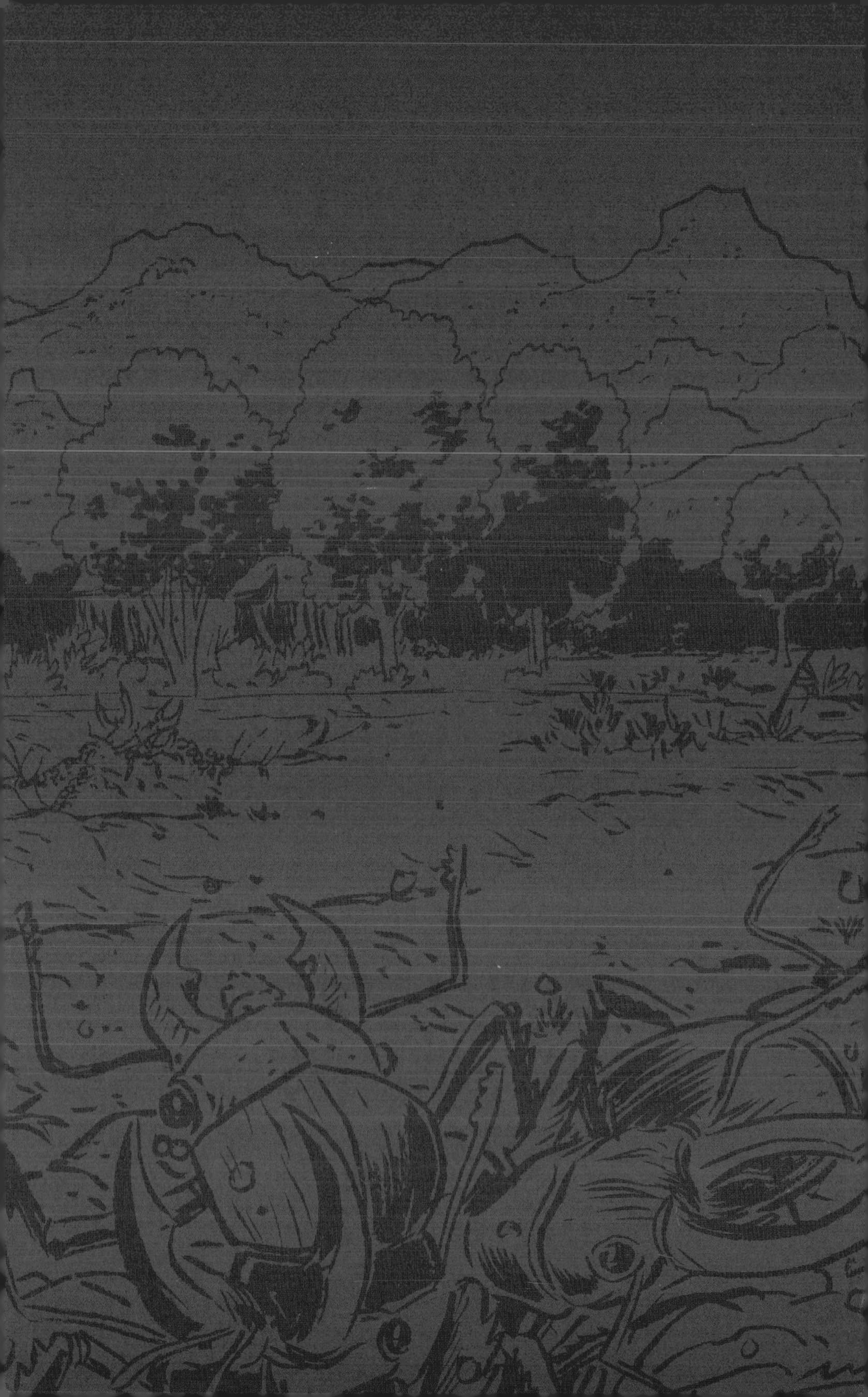

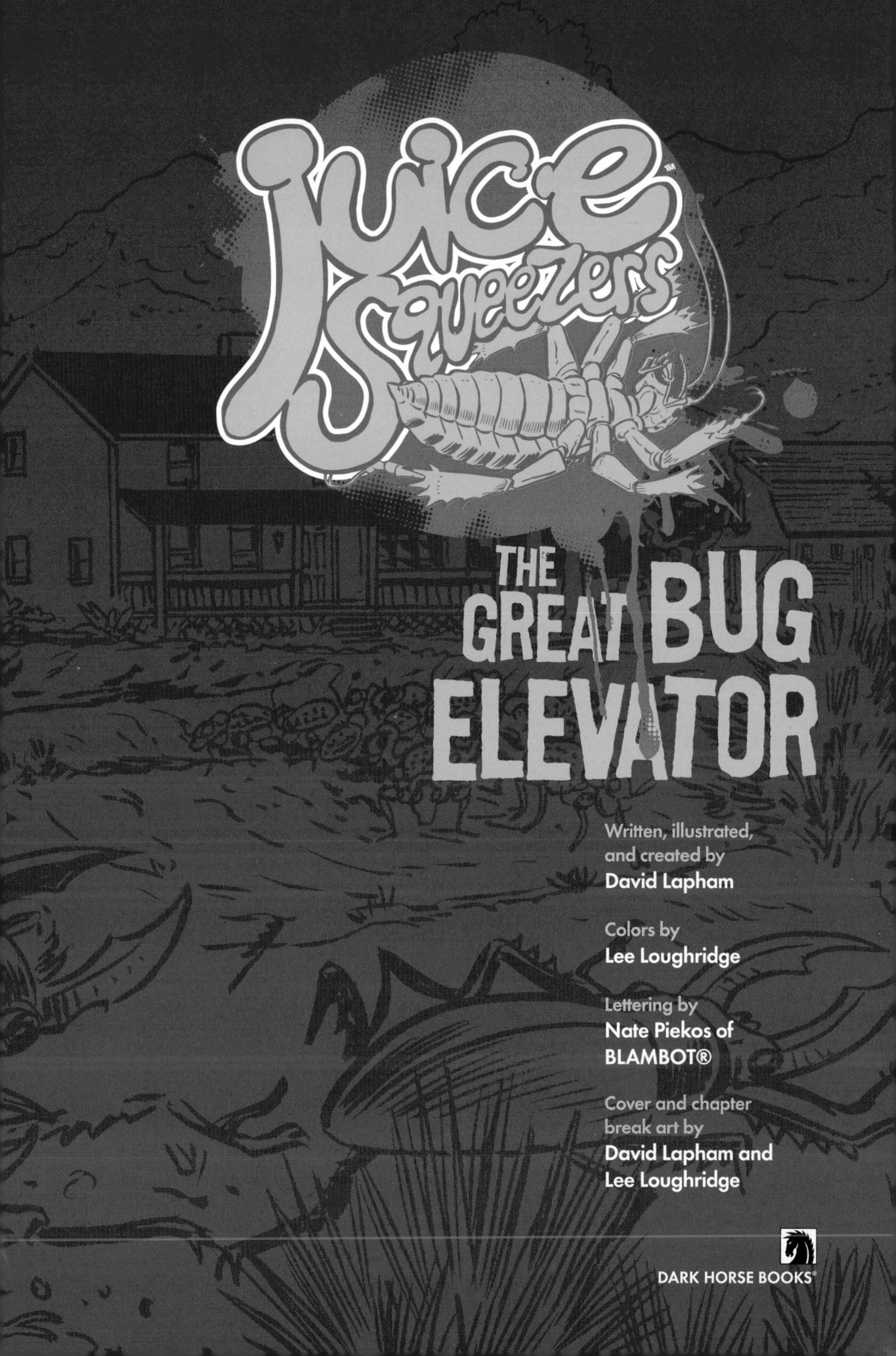

Juice Squeezers™

THE GREAT BUG ELEVATOR

Written, illustrated, and created by
David Lapham

Colors by
Lee Loughridge

Lettering by
Nate Piekos of BLAMBOT®

Cover and chapter break art by
David Lapham and Lee Loughridge

DARK HORSE BOOKS®

Publisher
Mike Richardson

Editor
Jim Gibbons

Digital Production
Christianne Goudreau

Collection Design
Rick DeLucco

Logo Design
Irina Beffa and David Lapham

Special thanks to
Sierra Hahn and Spencer Cushing

NEIL HANKERSON Executive Vice President | TOM WEDDLE Chief
Financial Officer | RANDY STRADLEY Vice President of Publishing
| MICHAEL MARTENS Vice President of Book Trade Sales | ANITA
NELSON Vice President of Business Affairs | SCOTT ALLIE Editor in
Chief | MATT PARKINSON Vice President of Marketing | DAVID
SCROGGY Vice President of Product Development | DALE
LaFOUNTAIN Vice President of Information Technology | DARLENE
VOGEL Senior Director of Print, Design, and Production | KEN LIZZI
General Counsel | DAVEY ESTRADA Editorial Director | CHRIS
WARNER Senior Books Editor | DIANA SCHUTZ Executive Editor
| CARY GRAZZINI Director of Print and Development | LIA
RIBACCHI Art Director | CARA NIECE Director of Scheduling | TIM
WIESCH Director of International Licensing | MARK BERNARDI
Director of Digital Publishing

Published by Dark Horse Books
A division of Dark Horse Comics, Inc.
10956 SE Main Street
Milwaukie, OR 97222

First edition: August 2014
ISBN 978-1-61655-438-5

10 9 8 7 6 5 4 3 2 1
Printed in China

International Licensing: (503) 905-2377
Comic Shop Locator Service: (888) 266-4226

This volume collects the Juice Squeezers: Squish *one-shot,* Juice
Squeezers *#1–#4, and* Juice Squeezers: Ants in Your Pants *from*
Free Comic Book Day 2014, *published by Dark Horse Comics.*

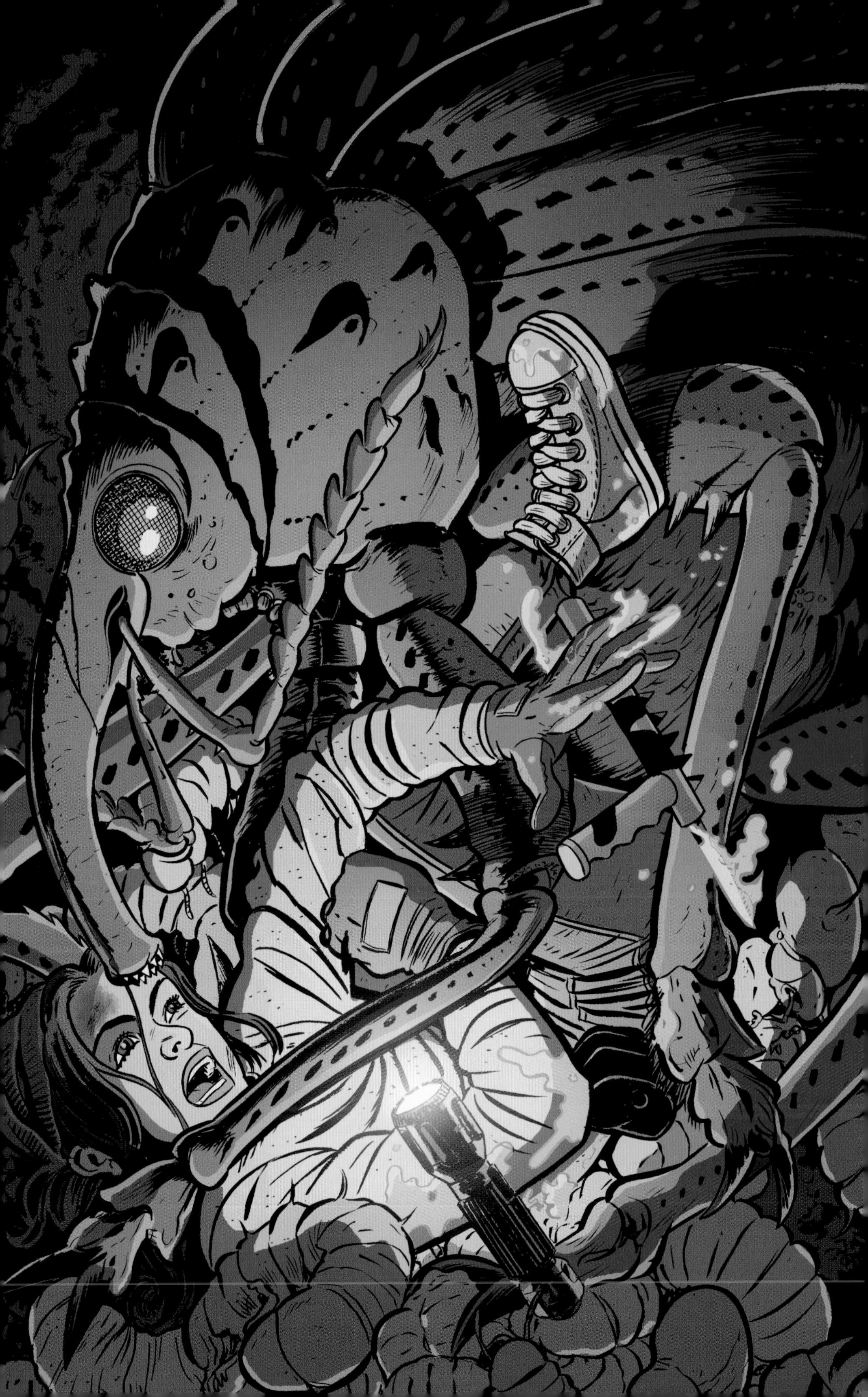

SQUISH: A JUICE SQUEEZERS TALE

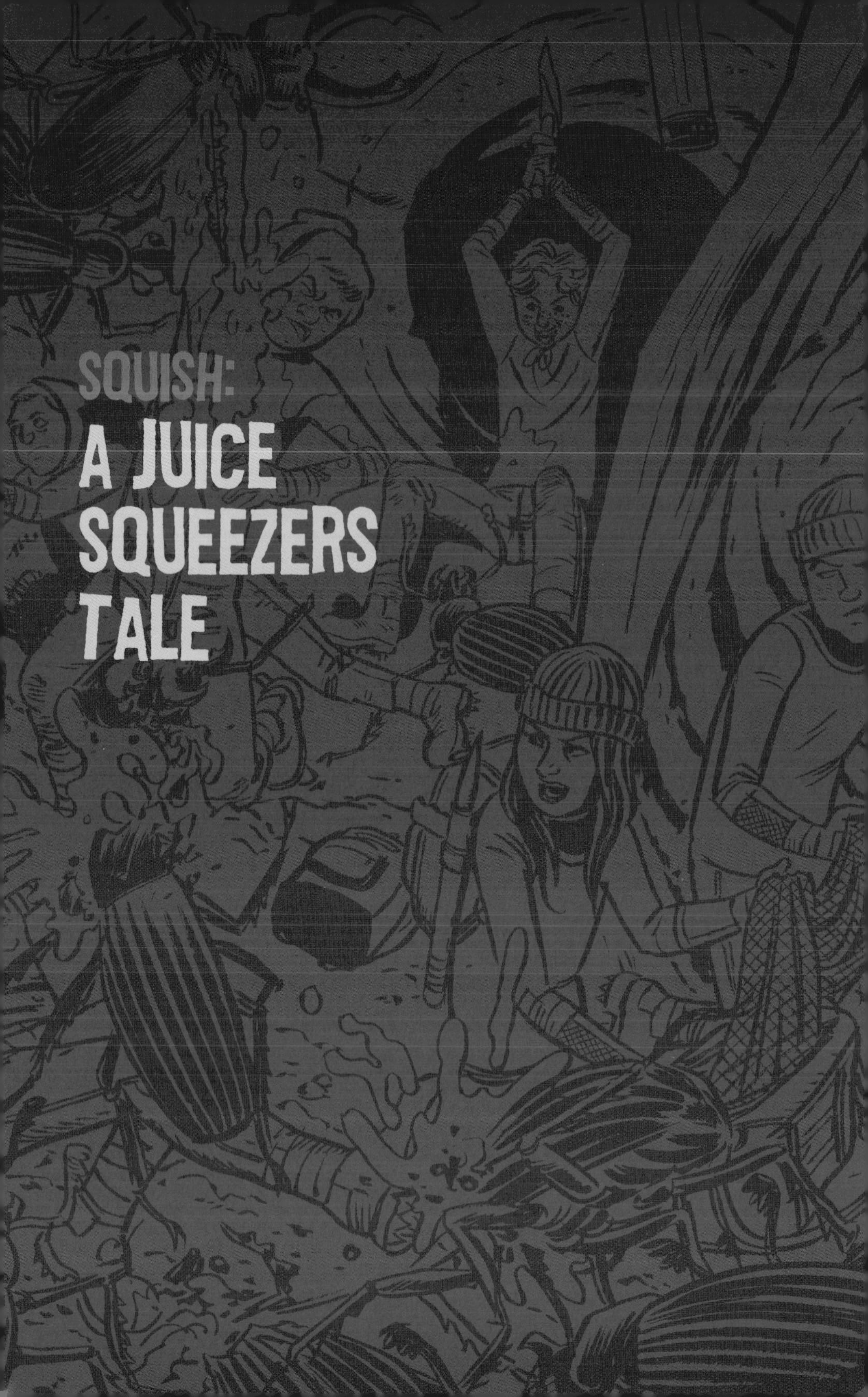

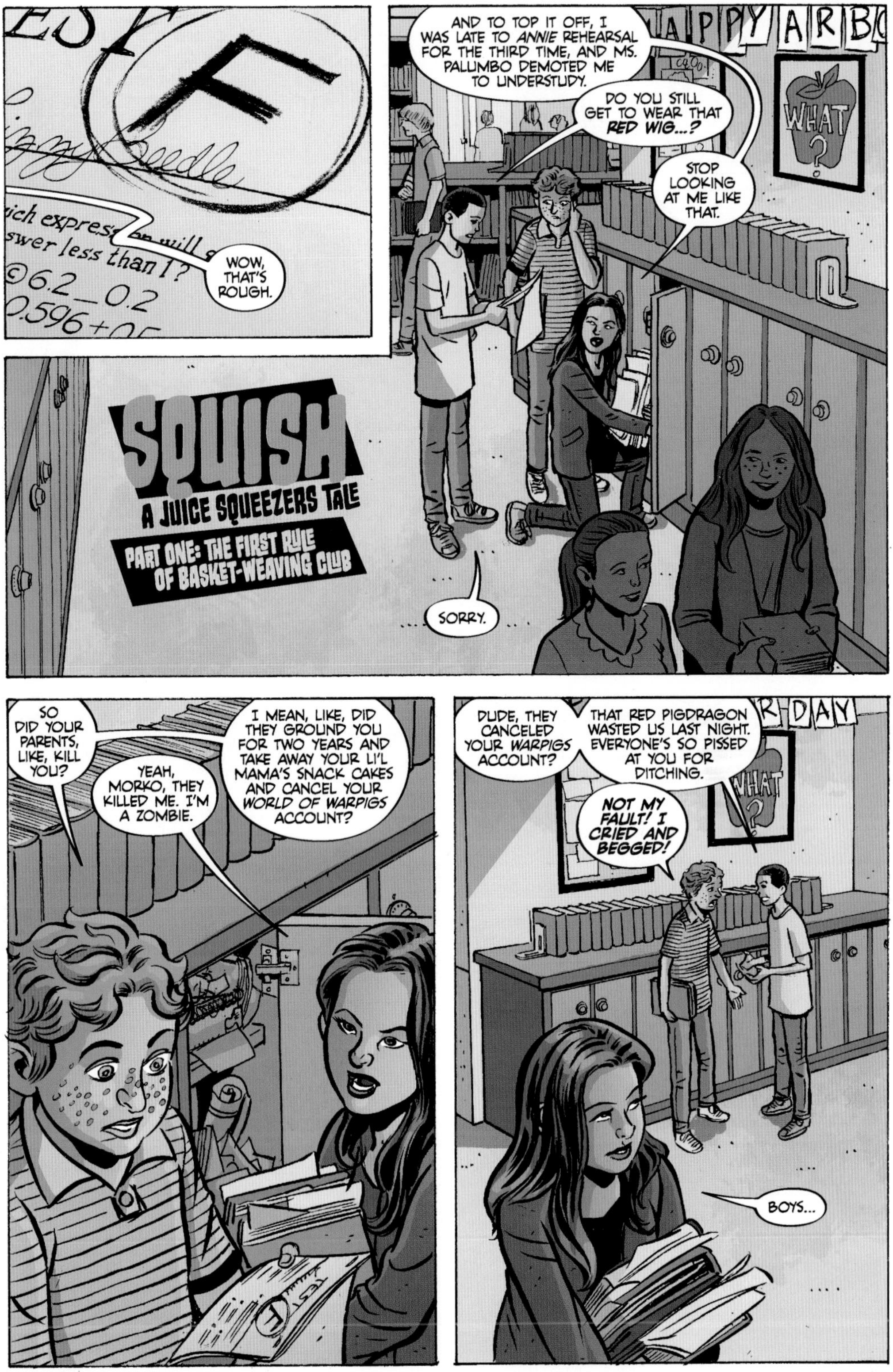
WOW, THAT'S ROUGH.
AND TO TOP IT OFF, I WAS LATE TO ANNIE REHEARSAL FOR THE THIRD TIME, AND MS. PALUMBO DEMOTED ME TO UNDERSTUDY.
DO YOU STILL GET TO WEAR THAT RED WIG...?
STOP LOOKING AT ME LIKE THAT.
WHAT ?
SQUISH
A JUICE SQUEEZERS TALE
PART ONE: THE FIRST RULE OF BASKET-WEAVING CLUB
SORRY.
SO DID YOUR PARENTS, LIKE, KILL YOU?
YEAH, MORKO, THEY KILLED ME. I'M A ZOMBIE.
I MEAN, LIKE, DID THEY GROUND YOU FOR TWO YEARS AND TAKE AWAY YOUR LI'L MAMA'S SNACK CAKES AND CANCEL YOUR WORLD OF WARPIGS ACCOUNT?
DUDE, THEY CANCELED YOUR WARPIGS ACCOUNT?
THAT RED PIGDRAGON WASTED US LAST NIGHT. EVERYONE'S SO PISSED AT YOU FOR DITCHING.
NOT MY FAULT! I CRIED AND BEGGED!
BOYS...

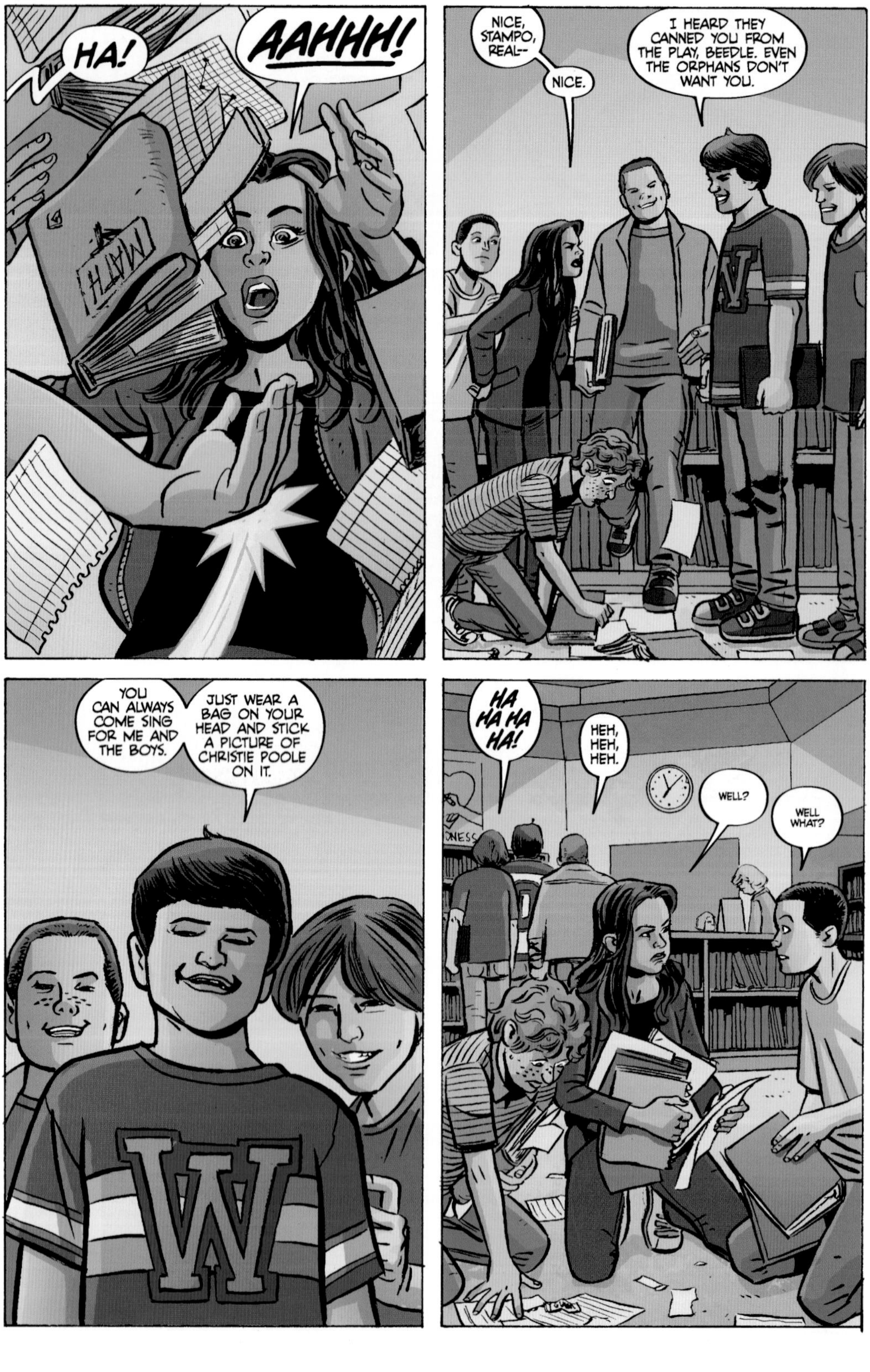
HA!
AAHHH!
NICE, STAMPO, REAL--
NICE.
I HEARD THEY CANNED YOU FROM THE PLAY, BEEDLE. EVEN THE ORPHANS DON'T WANT YOU.
YOU CAN ALWAYS COME SING FOR ME AND THE BOYS.
JUST WEAR A BAG ON YOUR HEAD AND STICK A PICTURE OF CHRISTIE POOLE ON IT.
HA HA HA HA!
HEH, HEH, HEH.
WELL?
WELL WHAT?

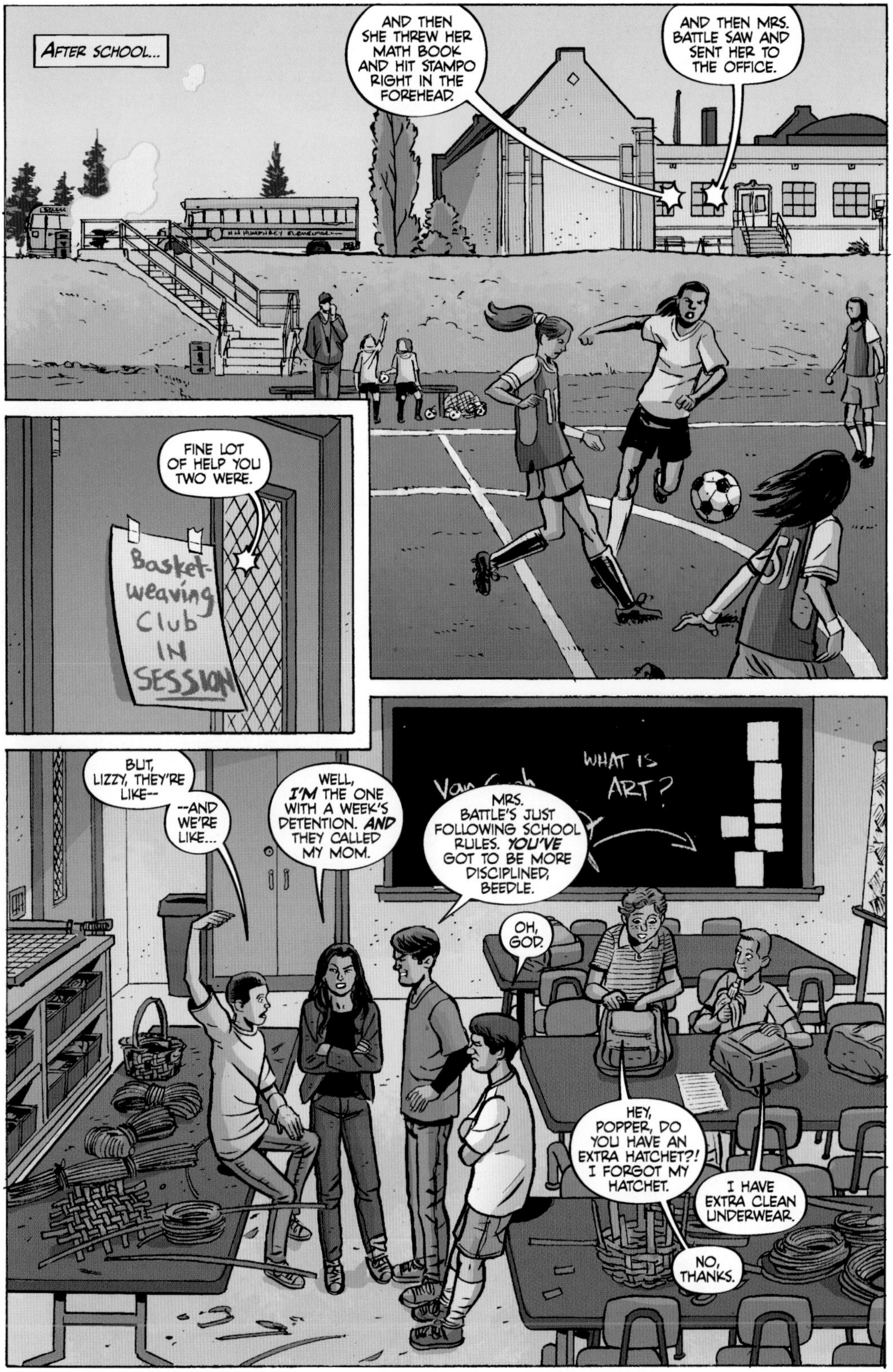
After school...
AND THEN SHE THREW HER MATH BOOK AND HIT STAMPO RIGHT IN THE FOREHEAD.
AND THEN MRS. BATTLE SAW AND SENT HER TO THE OFFICE.
FINE LOT OF HELP YOU TWO WERE.
Basket-weaving Club IN SESSION
WHAT IS ART?
Van Gogh
BUT, LIZZY, THEY'RE LIKE--
--AND WE'RE LIKE...
WELL, *I'M* THE ONE WITH A WEEK'S DETENTION. *AND* THEY CALLED MY MOM.
MRS. BATTLE'S JUST FOLLOWING SCHOOL RULES. *YOU'VE* GOT TO BE MORE DISCIPLINED, BEEDLE.
OH, GOD.
HEY, POPPER, DO YOU HAVE AN EXTRA HATCHET?! I FORGOT MY HATCHET.
I HAVE EXTRA CLEAN UNDERWEAR.
NO, THANKS.

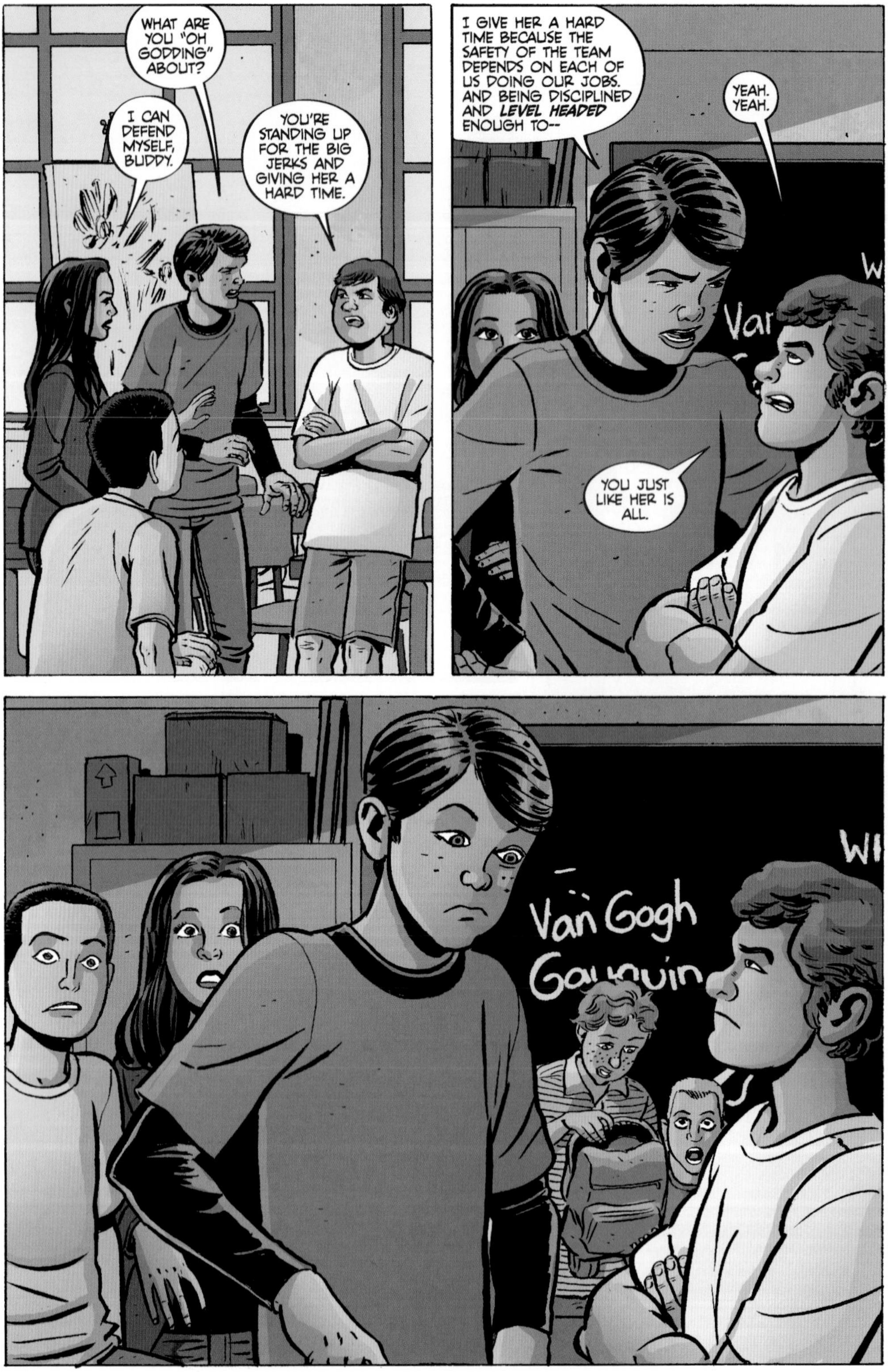

WHAT ARE YOU "OH GODDING" ABOUT?
I CAN DEFEND MYSELF, BUDDY.
YOU'RE STANDING UP FOR THE BIG JERKS AND GIVING HER A HARD TIME.
I GIVE HER A HARD TIME BECAUSE THE SAFETY OF THE TEAM DEPENDS ON EACH OF US DOING OUR JOBS. AND BEING DISCIPLINED AND *LEVEL HEADED* ENOUGH TO--
YEAH. YEAH.
YOU JUST LIKE HER IS ALL.
Van Gogh

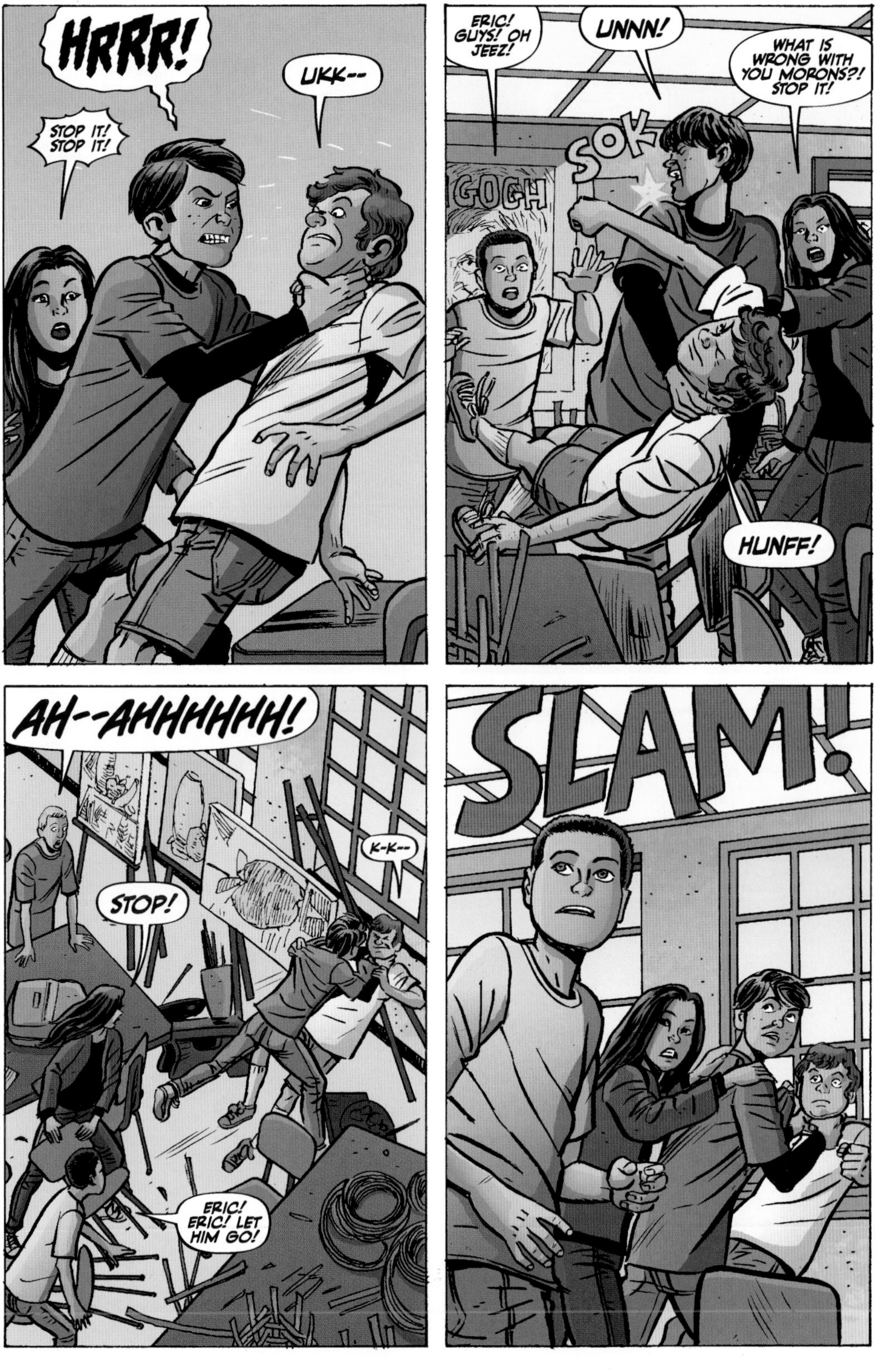
HRRR!
UKK--
STOP IT! STOP IT!
ERIC! GUYS! OH JEEZ!
UNNN!
WHAT IS WRONG WITH YOU MORONS?! STOP IT!
SOK
GOGH
HUNFF!
AH--AHHHHHH!
K-K--
STOP!
ERIC! ERIC! LET HIM GO!
SLAM!

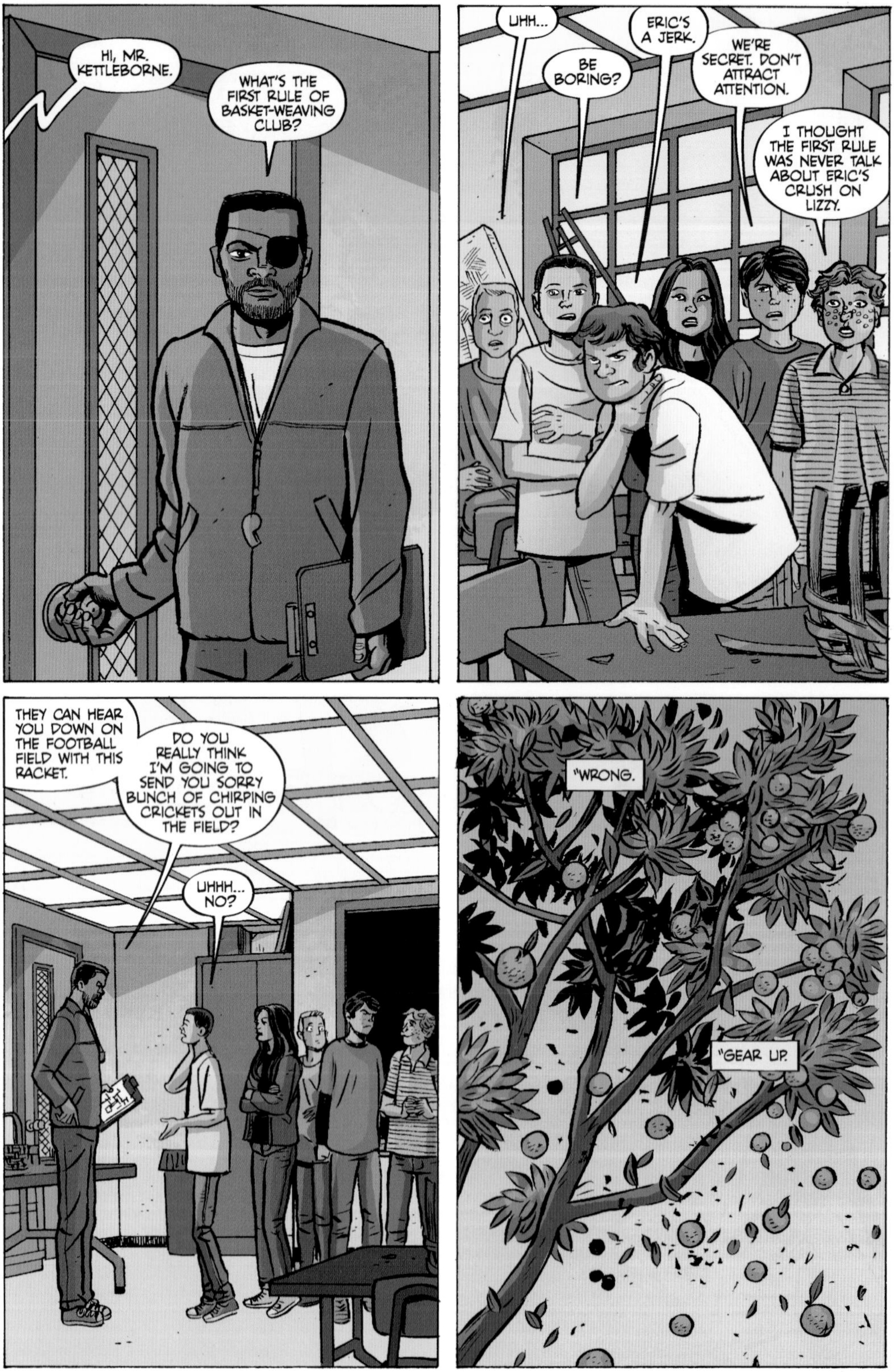
HI, MR. KETTLEBORNE.
WHAT'S THE FIRST RULE OF BASKET-WEAVING CLUB?
UHH...
BE BORING?
ERIC'S A JERK.
WE'RE SECRET. DON'T ATTRACT ATTENTION.
I THOUGHT THE FIRST RULE WAS NEVER TALK ABOUT ERIC'S CRUSH ON LIZZY.
THEY CAN HEAR YOU DOWN ON THE FOOTBALL FIELD WITH THIS RACKET.
DO YOU REALLY THINK I'M GOING TO SEND YOU SORRY BUNCH OF CHIRPING CRICKETS OUT IN THE FIELD?
UHHH... NO?
"WRONG.
"GEAR UP.

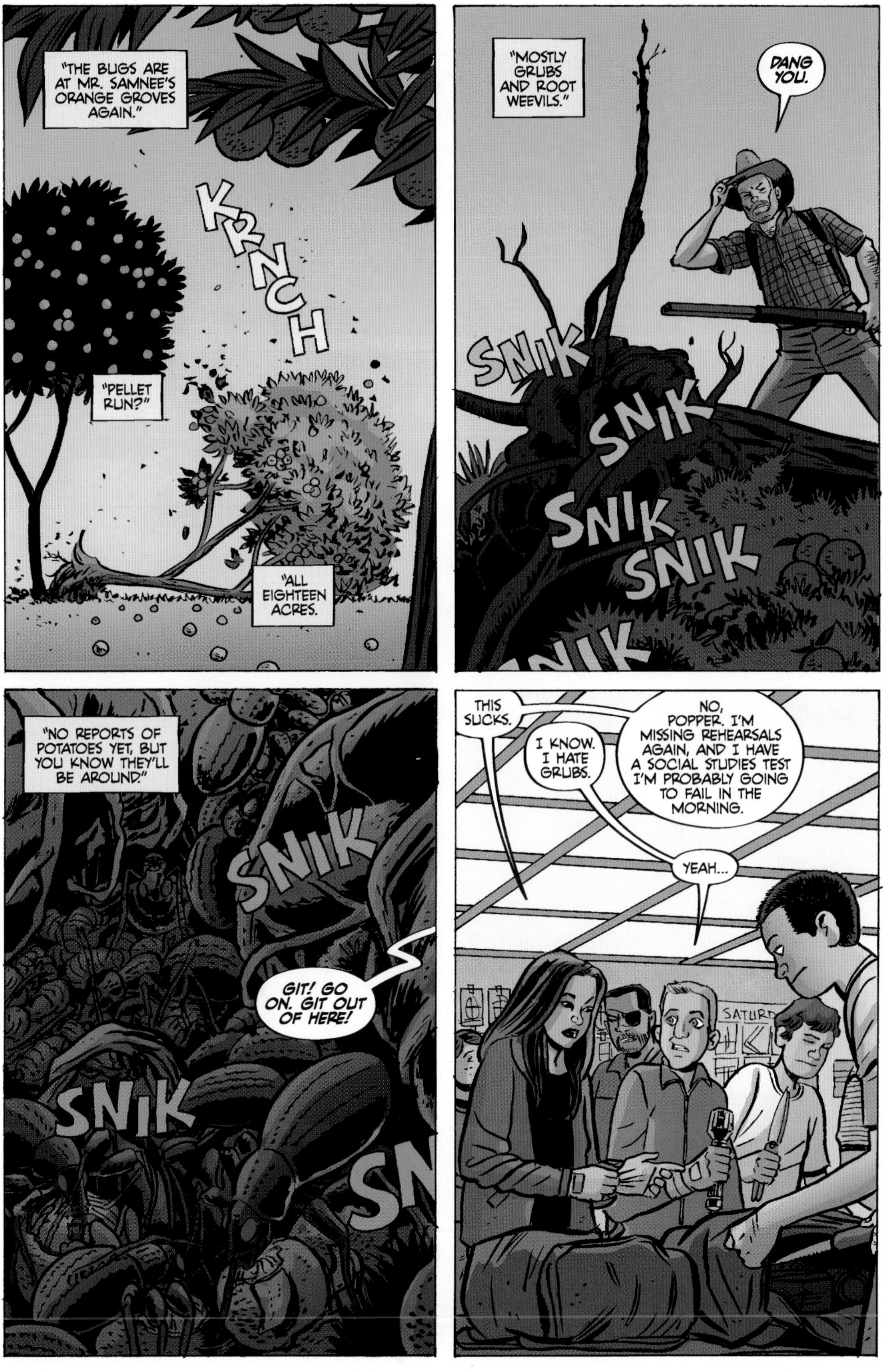
"THE BUGS ARE AT MR. SAMNEE'S ORANGE GROVES AGAIN."
KRNCH
"PELLET RUN?"
"ALL EIGHTEEN ACRES.
"MOSTLY GRUBS AND ROOT WEEVILS."
DANG YOU.
SNIK
SNIK
SNIK
SNIK
"NO REPORTS OF POTATOES YET, BUT YOU KNOW THEY'LL BE AROUND."
SNIK
GIT! GO ON. GIT OUT OF HERE!
SNIK
THIS SUCKS.
I KNOW. I HATE GRUBS.
NO, POPPER. I'M MISSING REHEARSALS AGAIN, AND I HAVE A SOCIAL STUDIES TEST I'M PROBABLY GOING TO FAIL IN THE MORNING.
YEAH...

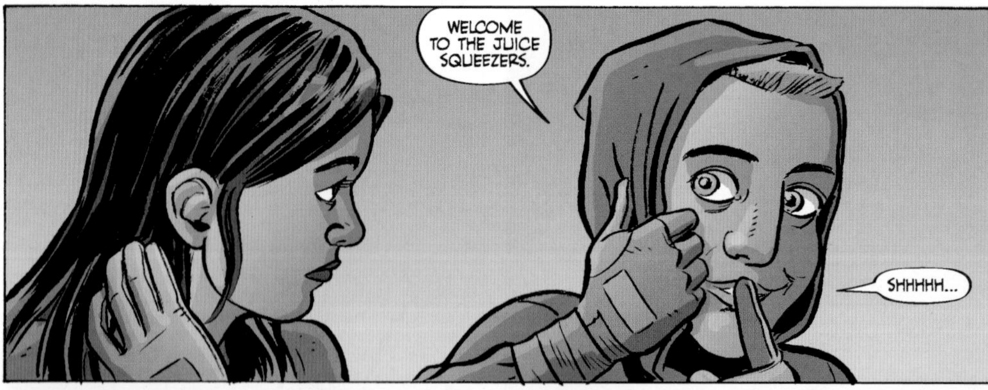
WELCOME TO THE JUICE SQUEEZERS.
SHHHHH...

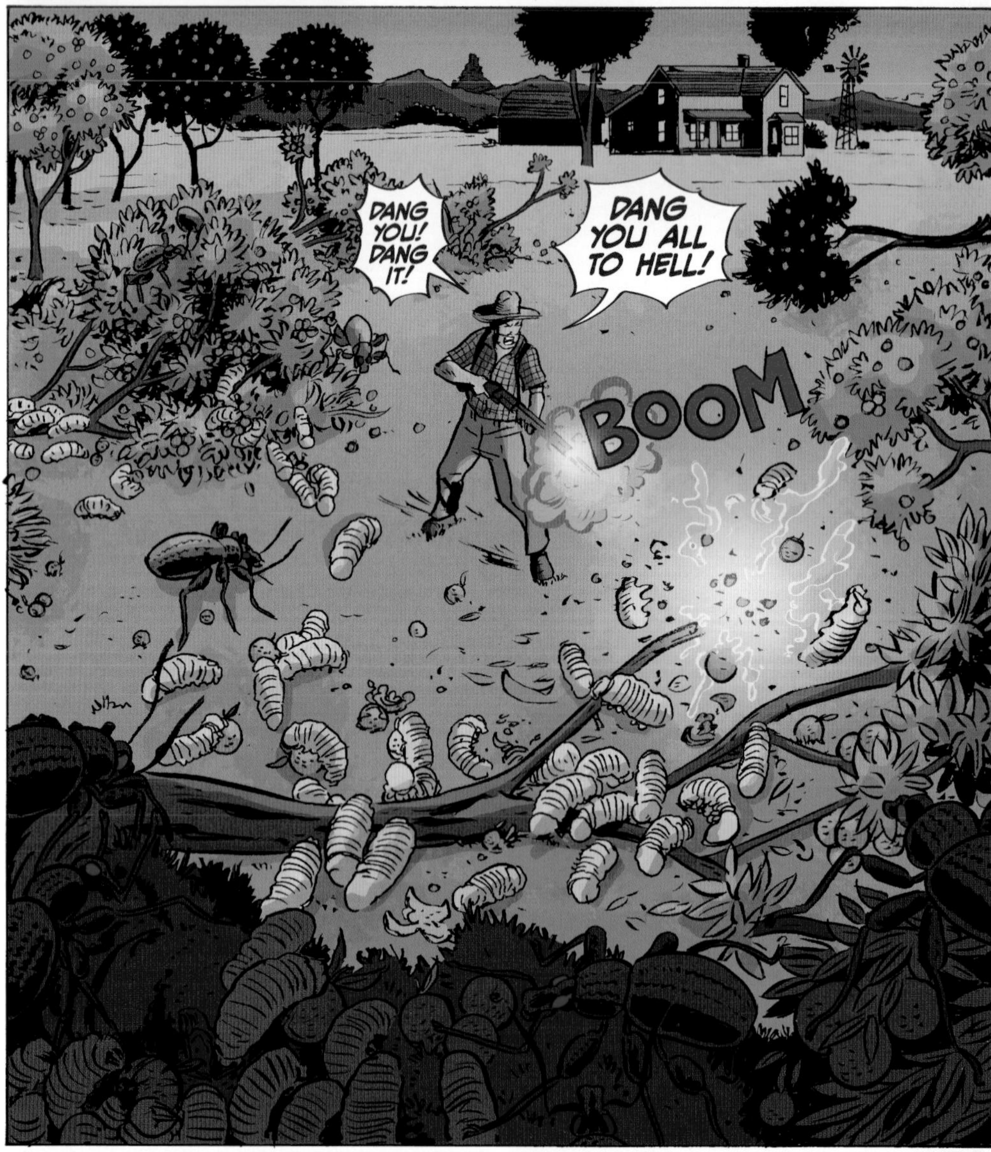
DANG YOU! DANG IT!
DANG YOU ALL TO HELL!
BOOM

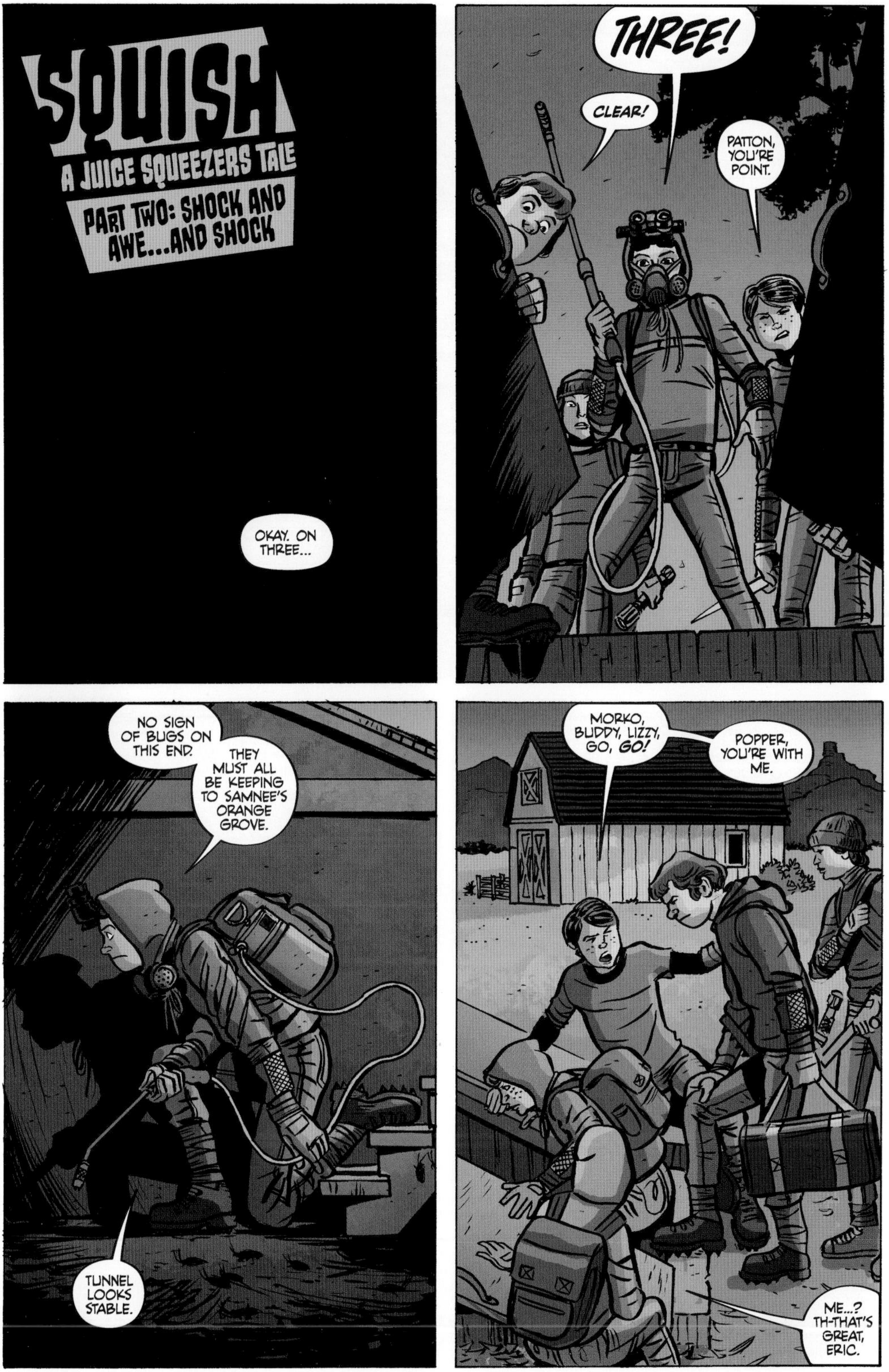
SQUISH
A JUICE SQUEEZERS TALE
PART TWO: SHOCK AND AWE...AND SHOCK
OKAY. ON THREE...
THREE!
CLEAR!
PATTON, YOU'RE POINT.
NO SIGN OF BUGS ON THIS END.
THEY MUST ALL BE KEEPING TO SAMNEE'S ORANGE GROVE.
TUNNEL LOOKS STABLE.
MORKO, BUDDY, LIZZY, GO, GO!
POPPER, YOU'RE WITH ME.
ME...? TH-THAT'S GREAT, ERIC.

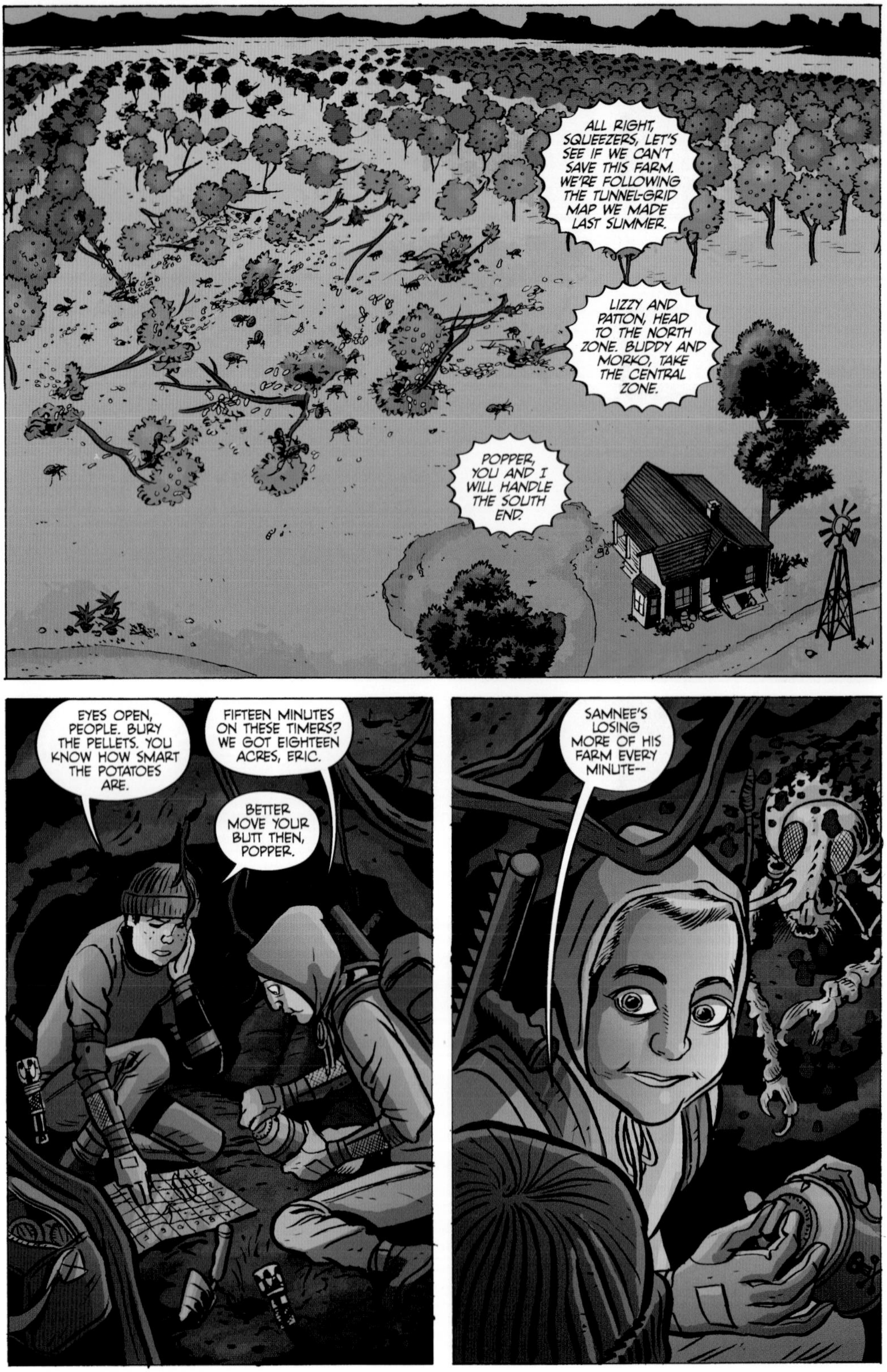
ALL RIGHT, SQUEEZERS, LET'S SEE IF WE CAN'T SAVE THIS FARM. WE'RE FOLLOWING THE TUNNEL-GRID MAP WE MADE LAST SUMMER.
LIZZY AND PATTON, HEAD TO THE NORTH ZONE. BUDDY AND MORKO, TAKE THE CENTRAL ZONE.
POPPER, YOU AND I WILL HANDLE THE SOUTH END.
EYES OPEN, PEOPLE. BURY THE PELLETS. YOU KNOW HOW SMART THE POTATOES ARE.
FIFTEEN MINUTES ON THESE TIMERS? WE GOT EIGHTEEN ACRES, ERIC.
BETTER MOVE YOUR BUTT THEN, POPPER.
SAMNEE'S LOSING MORE OF HIS FARM EVERY MINUTE--

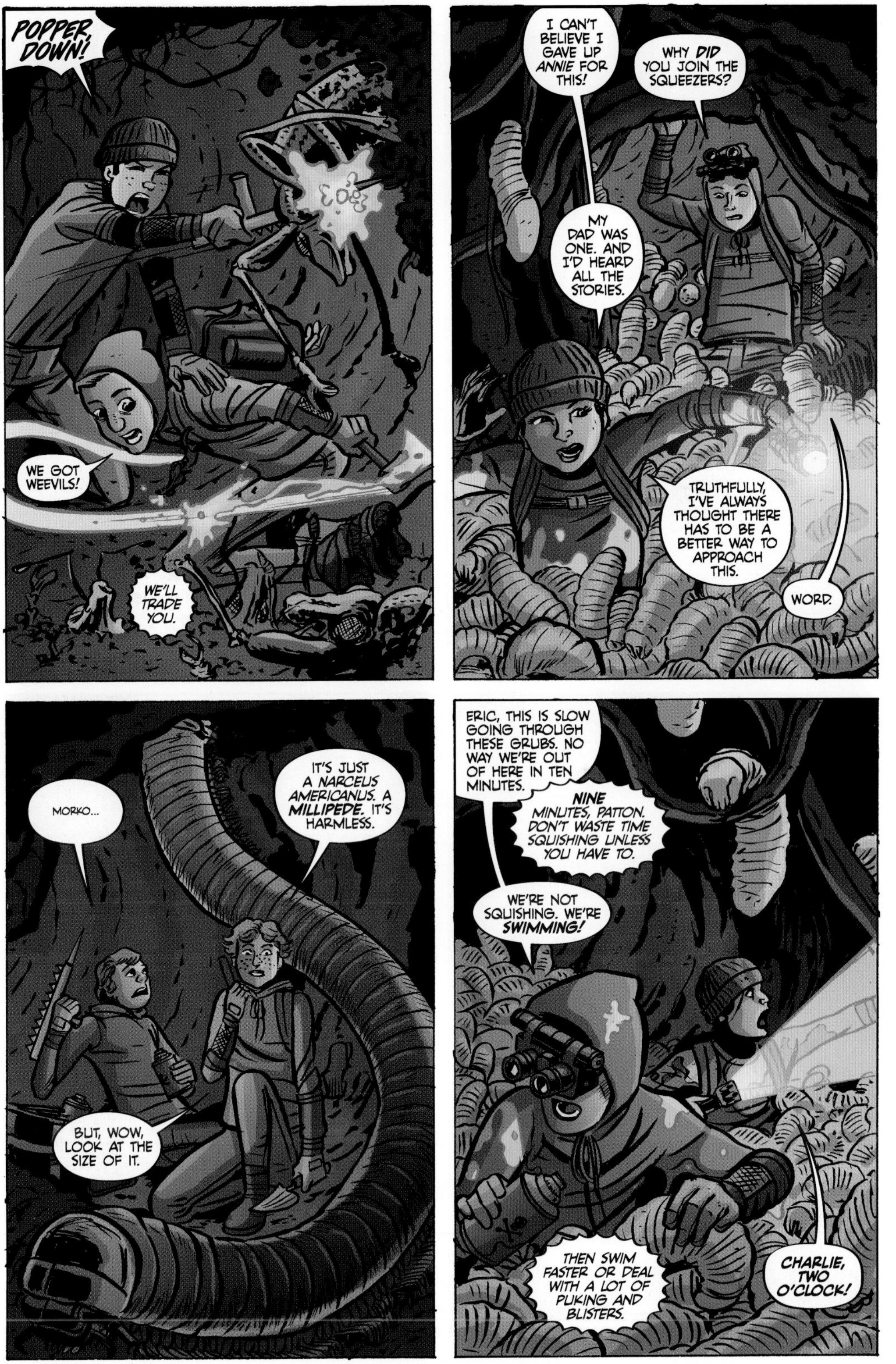
POPPER, DOWN!
WE GOT WEEVILS!
WE'LL TRADE YOU.
I CAN'T BELIEVE I GAVE UP *ANNIE* FOR THIS!
WHY *DID* YOU JOIN THE SQUEEZERS?
MY DAD WAS ONE. AND I'D HEARD ALL THE STORIES.
TRUTHFULLY, I'VE ALWAYS THOUGHT THERE HAS TO BE A BETTER WAY TO APPROACH THIS.
WORD.
MORKO...
IT'S JUST A *NARCEUS AMERICANUS*. A **MILLIPEDE.** IT'S HARMLESS.
BUT, WOW, LOOK AT THE SIZE OF IT.
ERIC, THIS IS SLOW GOING THROUGH THESE GRUBS. NO WAY WE'RE OUT OF HERE IN TEN MINUTES.
NINE MINUTES, PATTON. DON'T WASTE TIME SQUISHING UNLESS YOU HAVE TO.
WE'RE NOT SQUISHING. WE'RE ***SWIMMING!***
THEN SWIM FASTER OR DEAL WITH A LOT OF PUKING AND BLISTERS.
CHARLIE, TWO O'CLOCK!

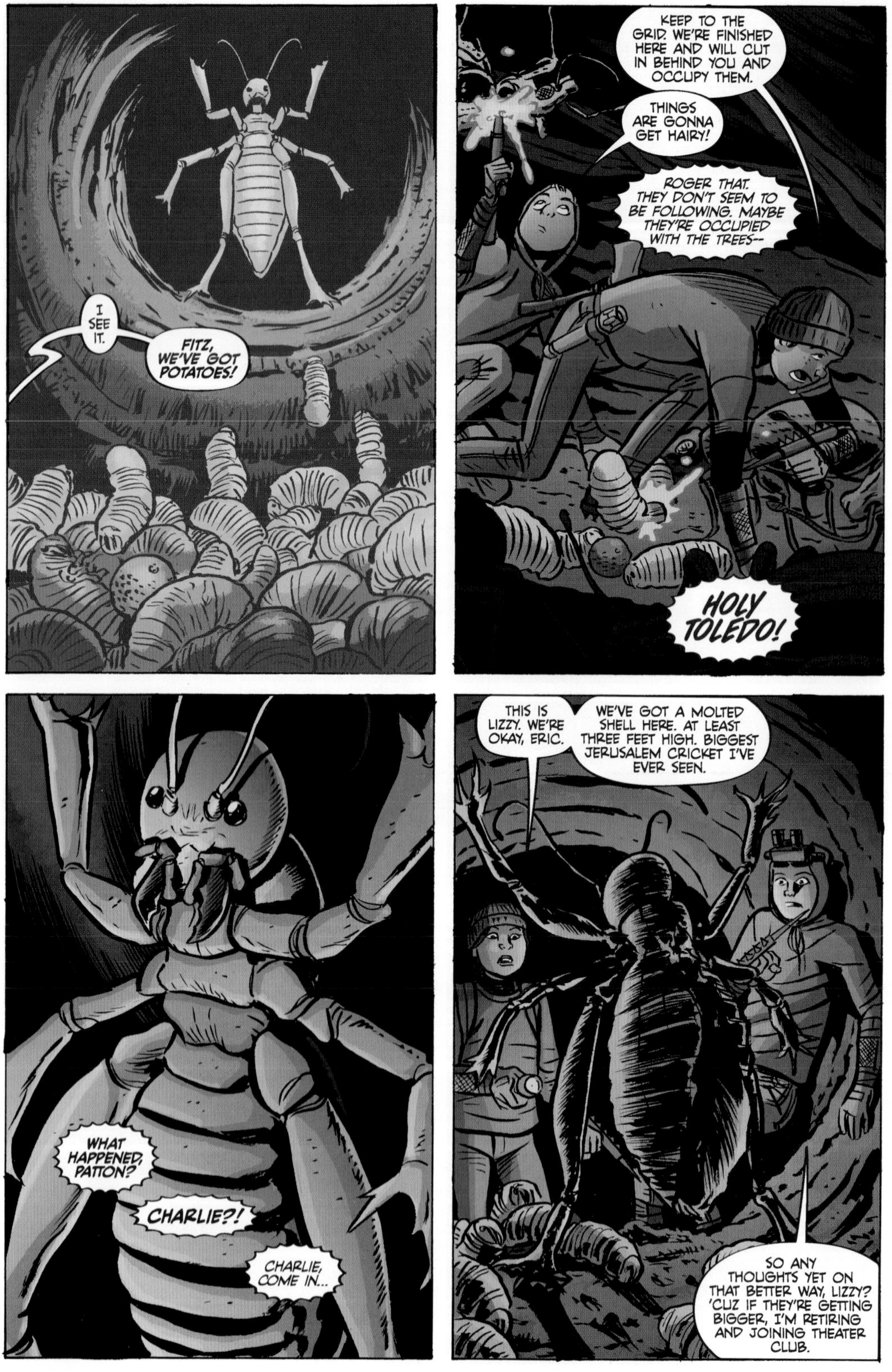

I SEE IT.
FITZ, WE'VE GOT POTATOES!
KEEP TO THE GRID. WE'RE FINISHED HERE AND WILL CUT IN BEHIND YOU AND OCCUPY THEM.
THINGS ARE GONNA GET HAIRY!
ROGER THAT. THEY DON'T SEEM TO BE FOLLOWING. MAYBE THEY'RE OCCUPIED WITH THE TREES--
HOLY TOLEDO!
WHAT HAPPENED, PATTON?
CHARLIE?!
CHARLIE, COME IN...
THIS IS LIZZY. WE'RE OKAY, ERIC.
WE'VE GOT A MOLTED SHELL HERE. AT LEAST THREE FEET HIGH. BIGGEST JERUSALEM CRICKET I'VE EVER SEEN.
SO ANY THOUGHTS YET ON THAT BETTER WAY, LIZZY? 'CUZ IF THEY'RE GETTING BIGGER, I'M RETIRING AND JOINING THEATER CLUB.

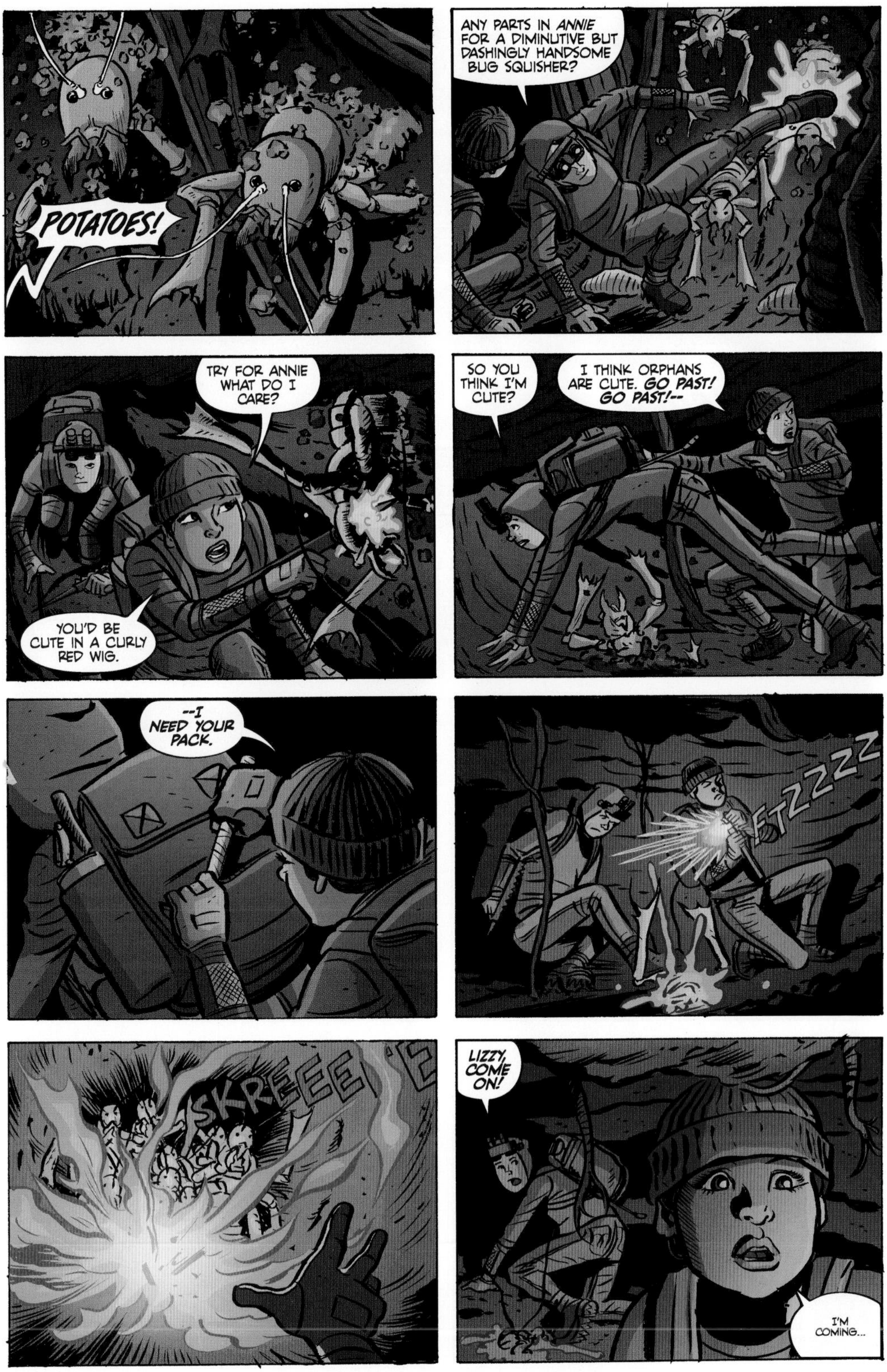
POTATOES!
ANY PARTS IN ANNIE FOR A DIMINUTIVE BUT DASHINGLY HANDSOME BUG SQUISHER?
TRY FOR ANNIE WHAT DO I CARE?
YOU'D BE CUTE IN A CURLY RED WIG.
SO YOU THINK I'M CUTE?
I THINK ORPHANS ARE CUTE. GO PAST! GO PAST!--
--I NEED YOUR PACK.
FTZZZZ
SKREEEE
LIZZY, COME ON!
I'M COMING...

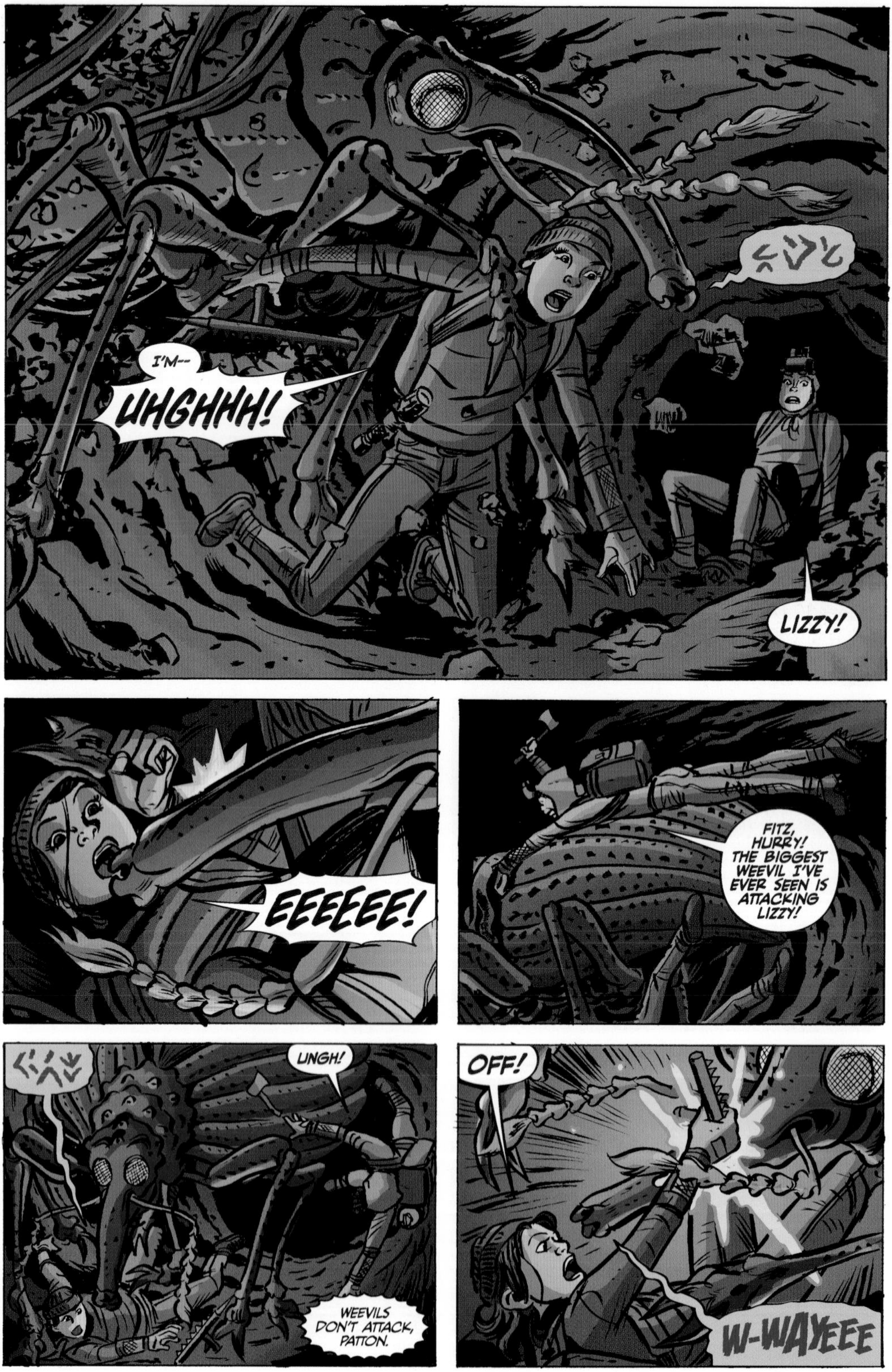
I'M--
UHGHHH!
LIZZY!
EEEEEE!
FITZ, HURRY! THE BIGGEST WEEVIL I'VE EVER SEEN IS ATTACKING LIZZY!
UNGH!
WEEVILS DON'T ATTACK, PATTON.
OFF!
W-WAYEEE

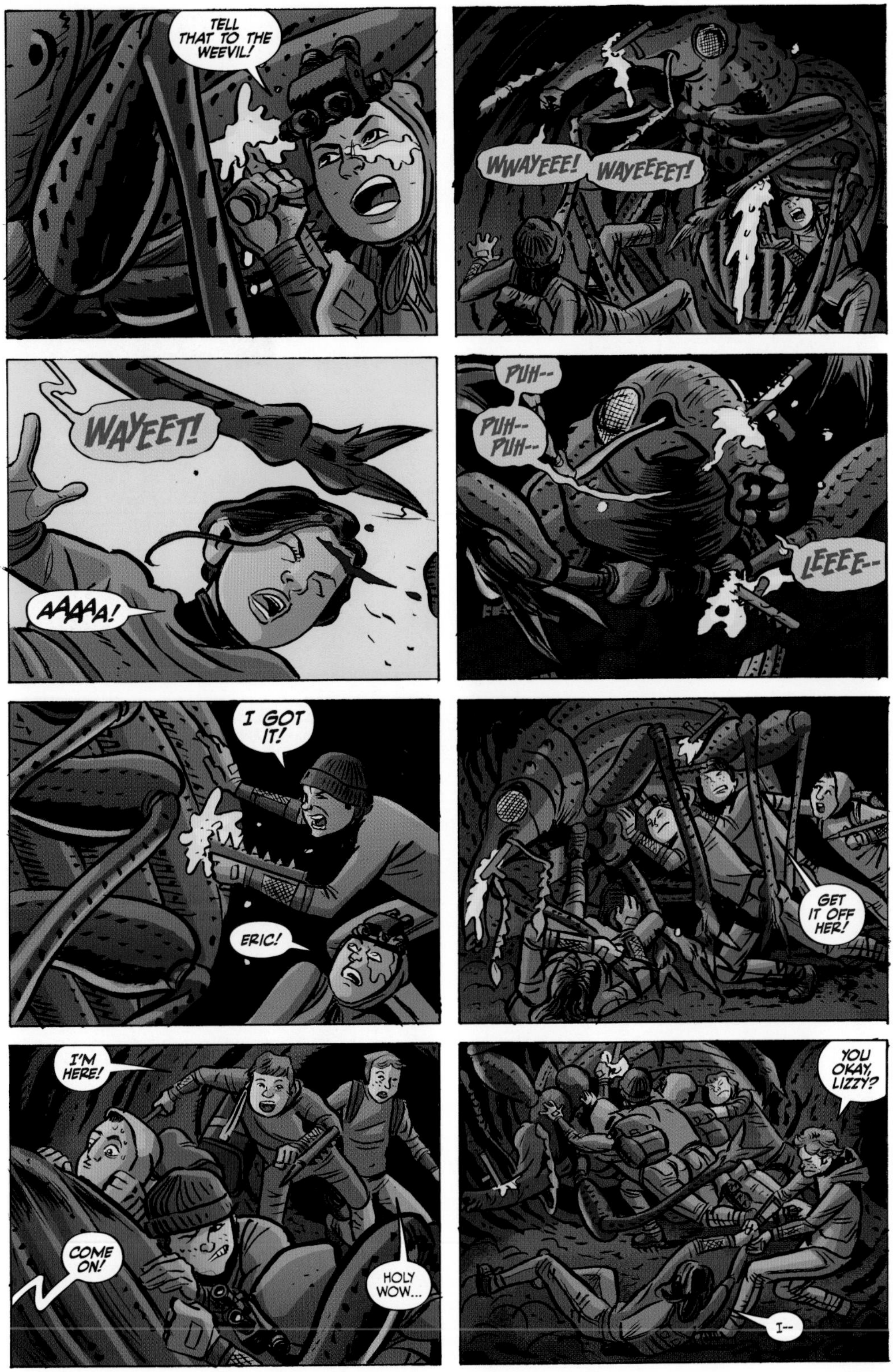
TELL THAT TO THE WEEVIL!
WWAYEEE!
WAYEEEET!
WAYEET!
AAAAA!
PUH--
PUH-- PUH--
LEEEE--
I GOT IT!
ERIC!
GET IT OFF HER!
I'M HERE!
COME ON!
HOLY WOW...
YOU OKAY, LIZZY?
I--

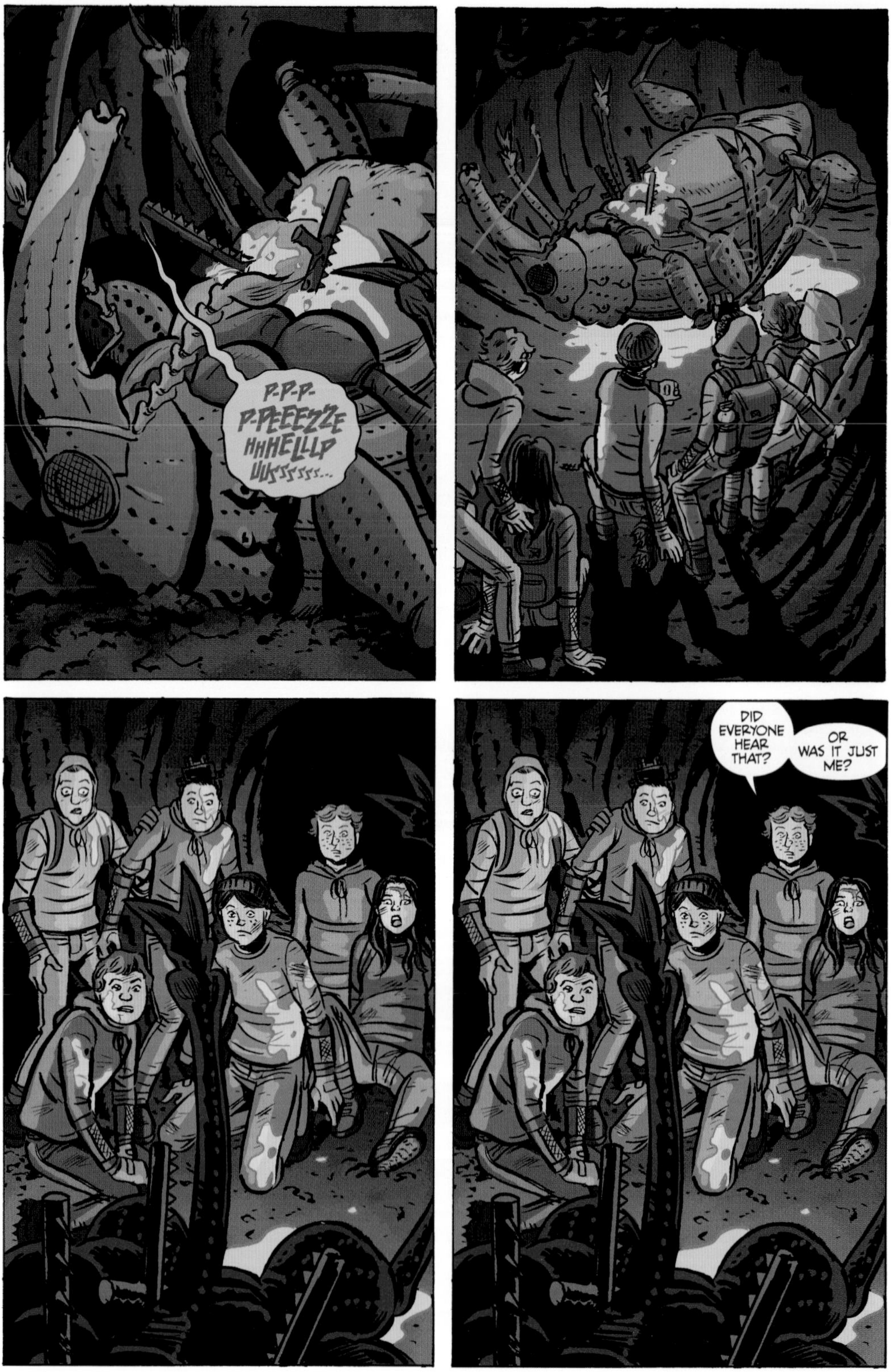
P-P-P- P-PEEEZZE HHHELLLP UUSSSSS...
DID EVERYONE HEAR THAT?
OR WAS IT JUST ME?

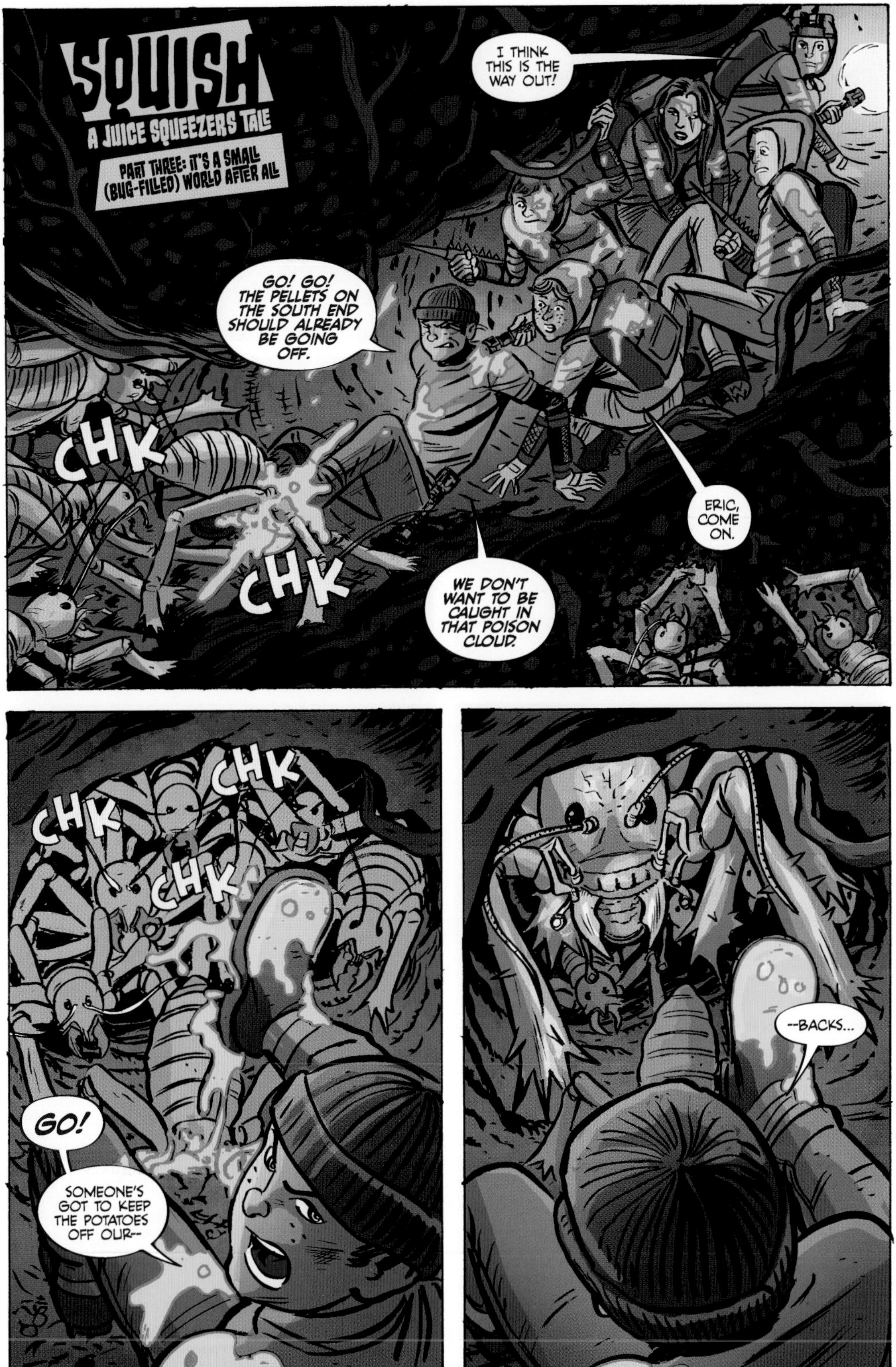
SQUISCH
A JUICE SQUEEZERS TALE
PART THREE: IT'S A SMALL (BUG-FILLED) WORLD AFTER ALL
I THINK THIS IS THE WAY OUT!
GO! GO! THE PELLETS ON THE SOUTH END SHOULD ALREADY BE GOING OFF.
CHK
CHK
WE DON'T WANT TO BE CAUGHT IN THAT POISON CLOUD.
ERIC, COME ON.
CHK
CHK
CHK
GO!
SOMEONE'S GOT TO KEEP THE POTATOES OFF OUR--
--BACKS...

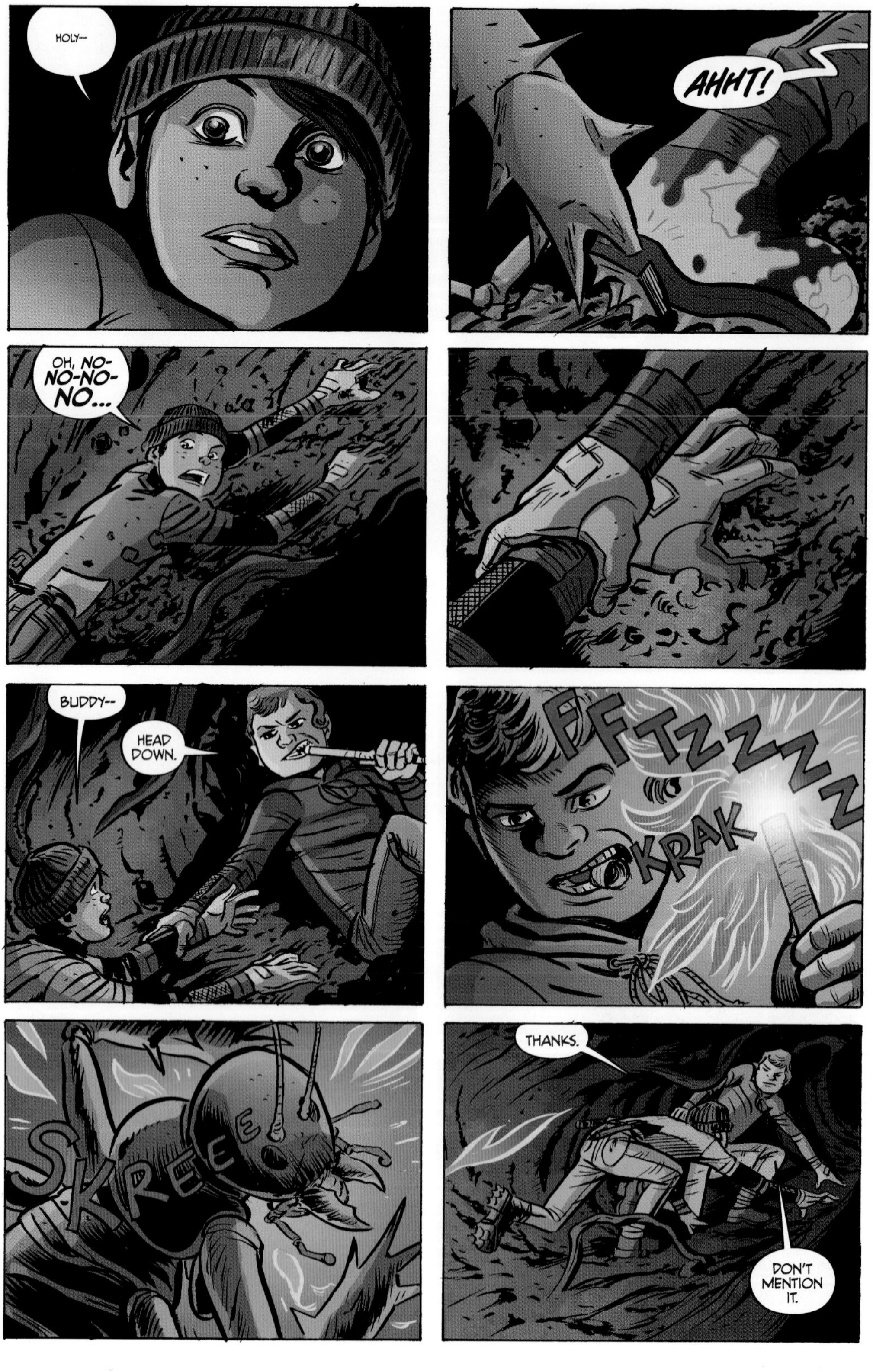
HOLY--
AHHT!
OH, NO-NO-NO-NO...
BUDDY--
HEAD DOWN.
FFTZZZZN
KRAK
SKREEE
THANKS.
DON'T MENTION IT.

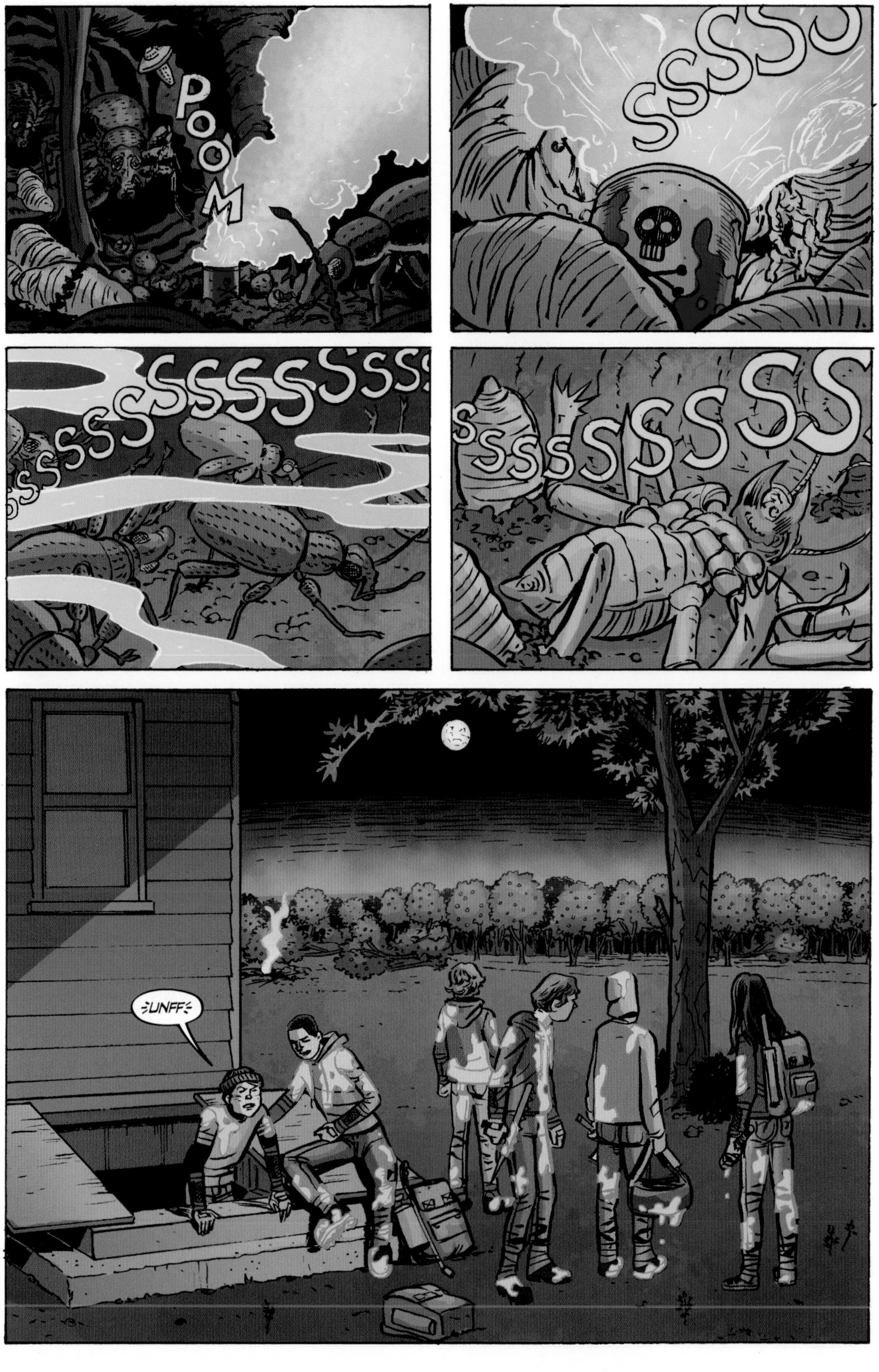
POOM
SSSSS
SSSSSSSSSSSSS
SSSSSSSSS
UNFF

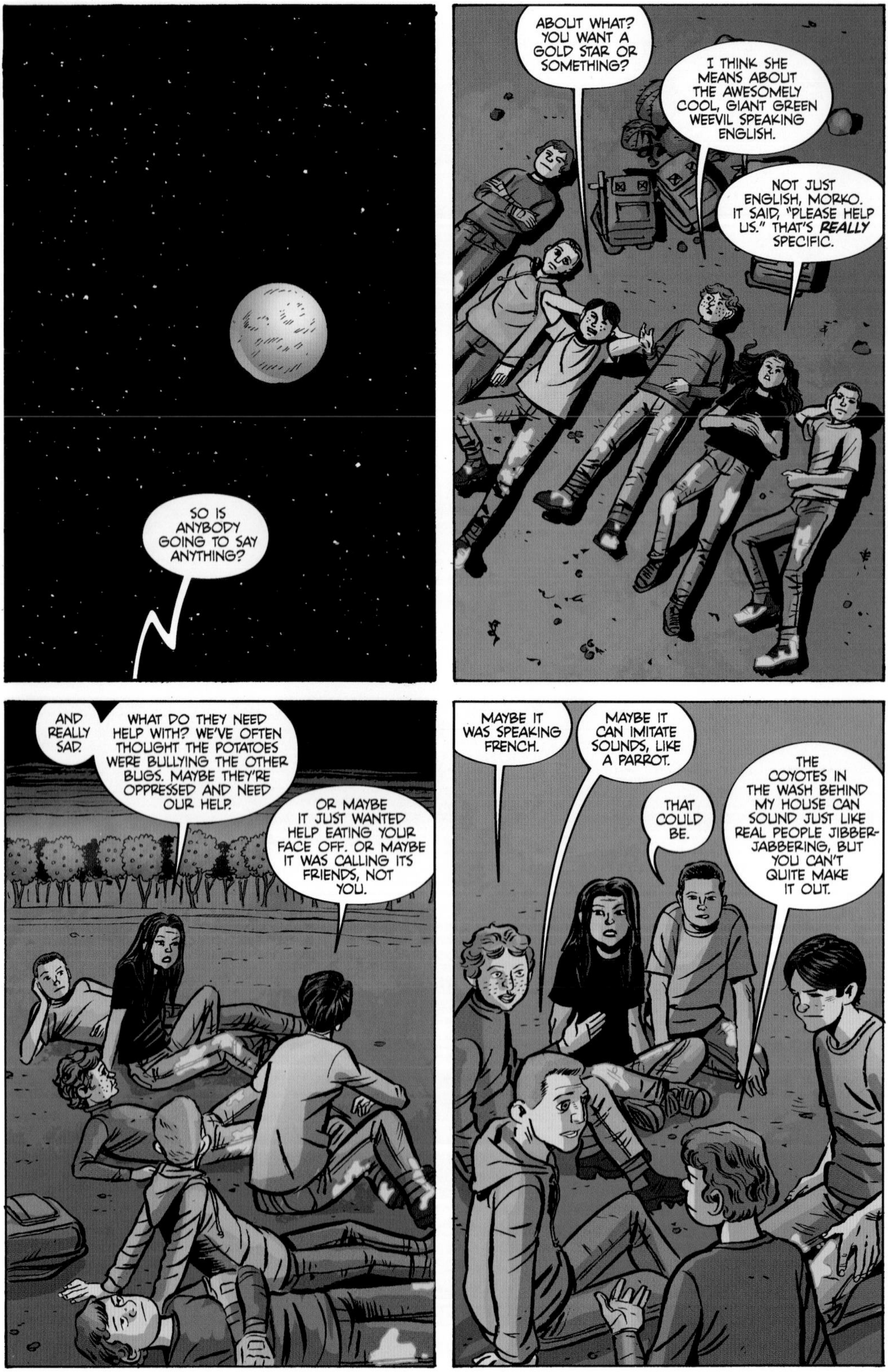
SO IS ANYBODY GOING TO SAY ANYTHING?
ABOUT WHAT? YOU WANT A GOLD STAR OR SOMETHING?
I THINK SHE MEANS ABOUT THE AWESOMELY COOL, GIANT GREEN WEEVIL SPEAKING ENGLISH.
NOT JUST ENGLISH, MORKO. IT SAID, "PLEASE HELP US." THAT'S *REALLY* SPECIFIC.
AND REALLY SAD.
WHAT DO THEY NEED HELP WITH? WE'VE OFTEN THOUGHT THE POTATOES WERE BULLYING THE OTHER BUGS. MAYBE THEY'RE OPPRESSED AND NEED OUR HELP.
OR MAYBE IT JUST WANTED HELP EATING YOUR FACE OFF. OR MAYBE IT WAS CALLING ITS FRIENDS, NOT YOU.
MAYBE IT WAS SPEAKING FRENCH.
MAYBE IT CAN IMITATE SOUNDS, LIKE A PARROT.
THAT COULD BE.
THE COYOTES IN THE WASH BEHIND MY HOUSE CAN SOUND JUST LIKE REAL PEOPLE JIBBER-JABBERING, BUT YOU CAN'T QUITE MAKE IT OUT.

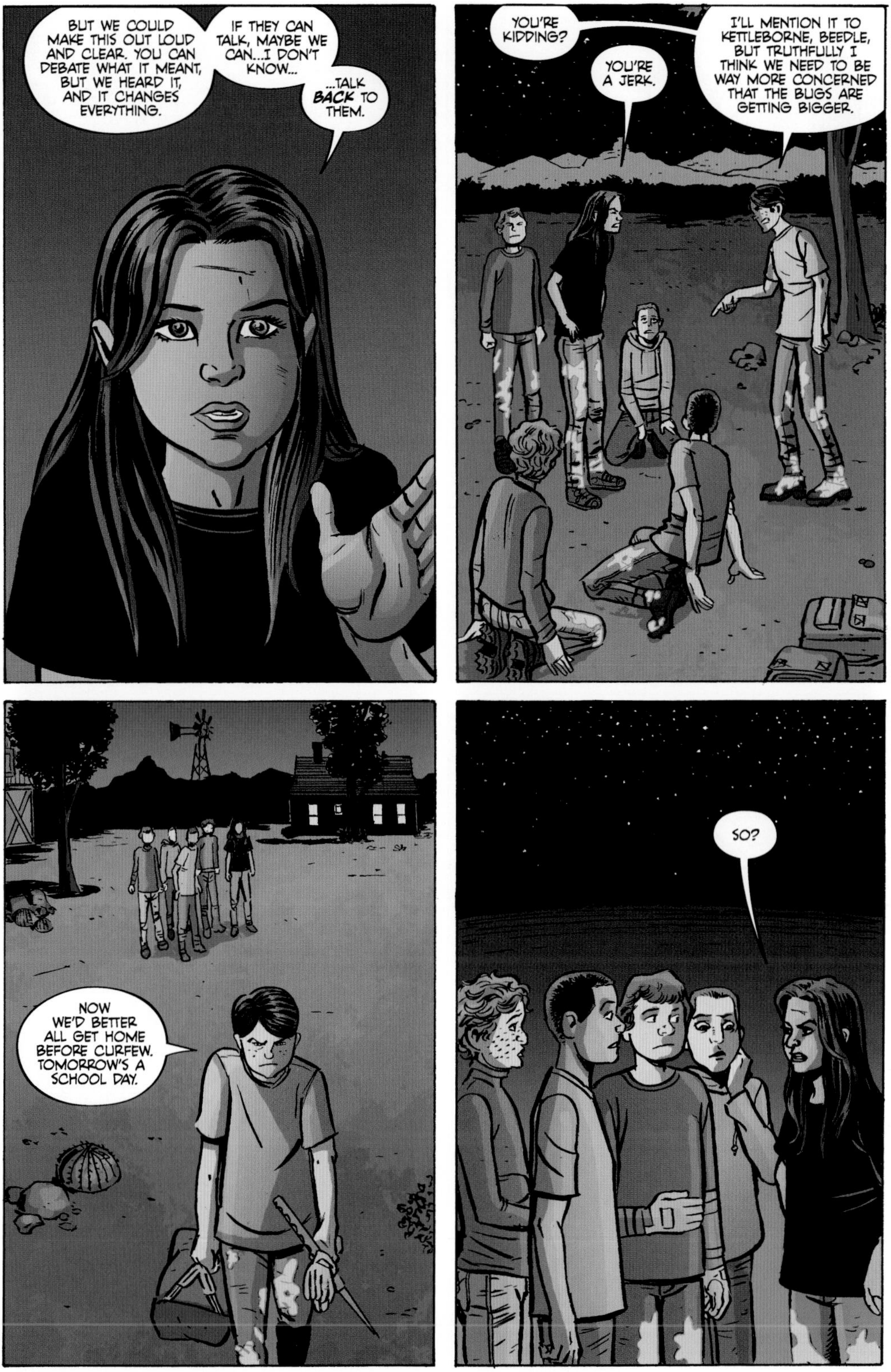
BUT WE COULD MAKE THIS OUT LOUD AND CLEAR. YOU CAN DEBATE WHAT IT MEANT, BUT WE HEARD IT, AND IT CHANGES EVERYTHING.
IF THEY CAN TALK, MAYBE WE CAN...I DON'T KNOW...
...TALK BACK TO THEM.
YOU'RE KIDDING?
YOU'RE A JERK.
I'LL MENTION IT TO KETTLEBORNE, BEEDLE, BUT TRUTHFULLY I THINK WE NEED TO BE WAY MORE CONCERNED THAT THE BUGS ARE GETTING BIGGER.
NOW WE'D BETTER ALL GET HOME BEFORE CURFEW. TOMORROW'S A SCHOOL DAY.
SO?

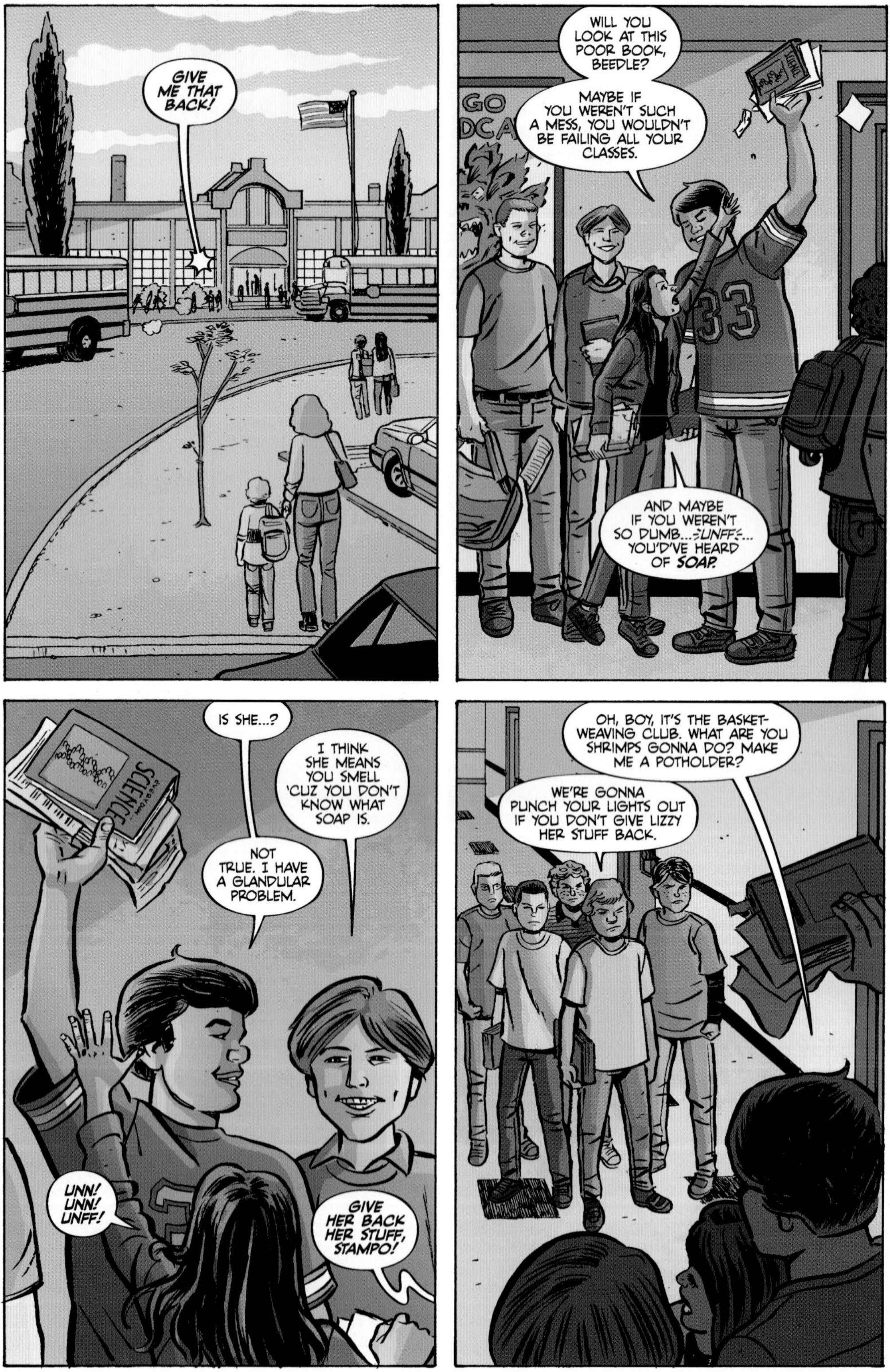
GIVE ME THAT BACK!
WILL YOU LOOK AT THIS POOR BOOK, BEEDLE?
MAYBE IF YOU WEREN'T SUCH A MESS, YOU WOULDN'T BE FAILING ALL YOUR CLASSES.
AND MAYBE IF YOU WEREN'T SO DUMB... UNFF... YOU'D'VE HEARD OF SOAP.
IS SHE...?
I THINK SHE MEANS YOU SMELL 'CUZ YOU DON'T KNOW WHAT SOAP IS.
NOT TRUE. I HAVE A GLANDULAR PROBLEM.
UNN! UNN! UNFF!
GIVE HER BACK HER STUFF, STAMPO!
OH, BOY, IT'S THE BASKET-WEAVING CLUB. WHAT ARE YOU SHRIMPS GONNA DO? MAKE ME A POTHOLDER?
WE'RE GONNA PUNCH YOUR LIGHTS OUT IF YOU DON'T GIVE LIZZY HER STUFF BACK.

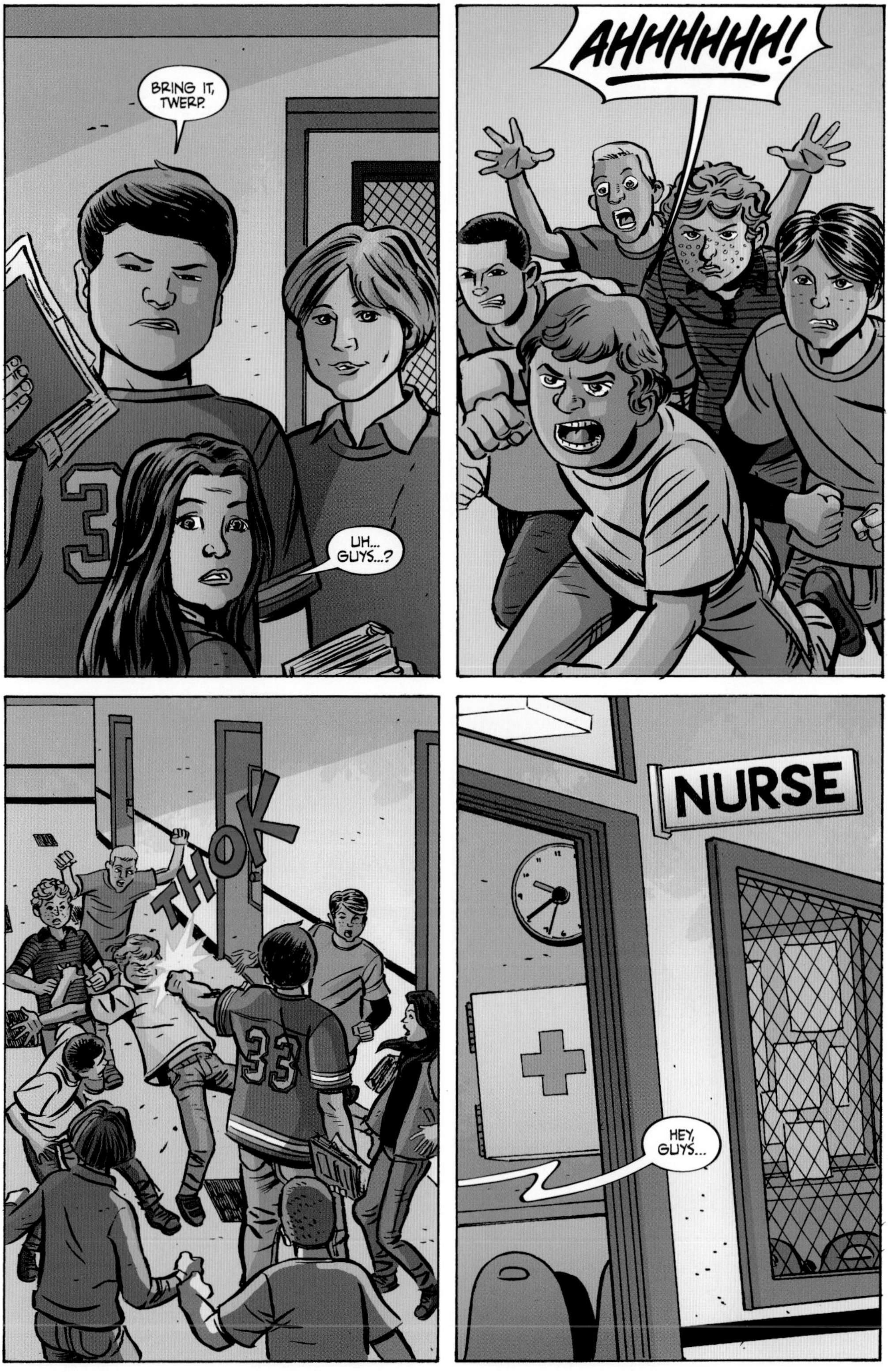
BRING IT, TWERP.
UH... GUYS...?
AHHHHHH!
THOK
NURSE
HEY, GUYS...

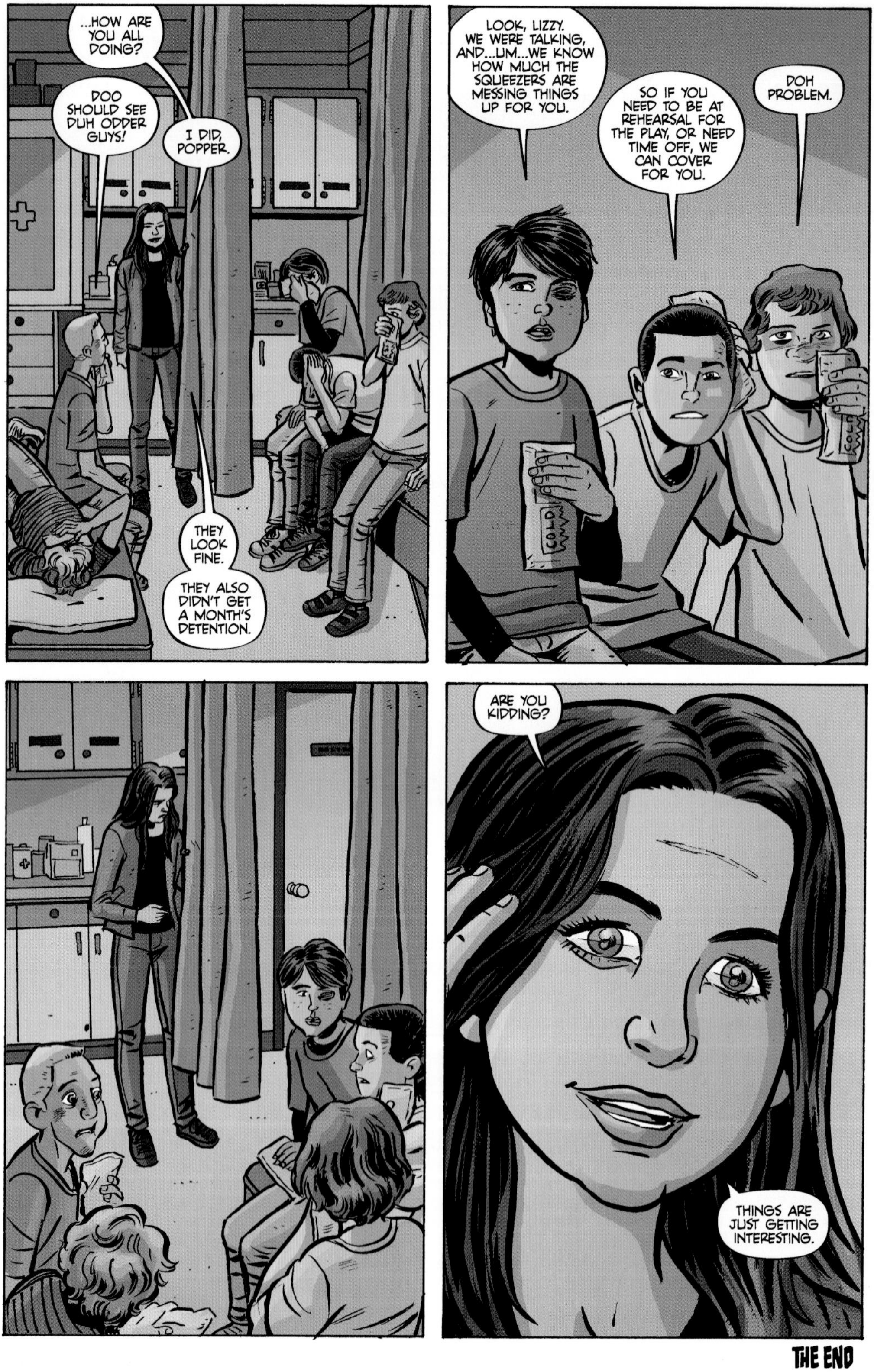
...HOW ARE YOU ALL DOING?
DOO SHOULD SEE DUH ODDER GUYS!
I DID, POPPER.
THEY LOOK FINE.
THEY ALSO DIDN'T GET A MONTH'S DETENTION.
LOOK, LIZZY. WE WERE TALKING, AND...UM...WE KNOW HOW MUCH THE SQUEEZERS ARE MESSING THINGS UP FOR YOU.
SO IF YOU NEED TO BE AT REHEARSAL FOR THE PLAY, OR NEED TIME OFF, WE CAN COVER FOR YOU.
DOH PROBLEM.
ARE YOU KIDDING?
THINGS ARE JUST GETTING INTERESTING.
THE END

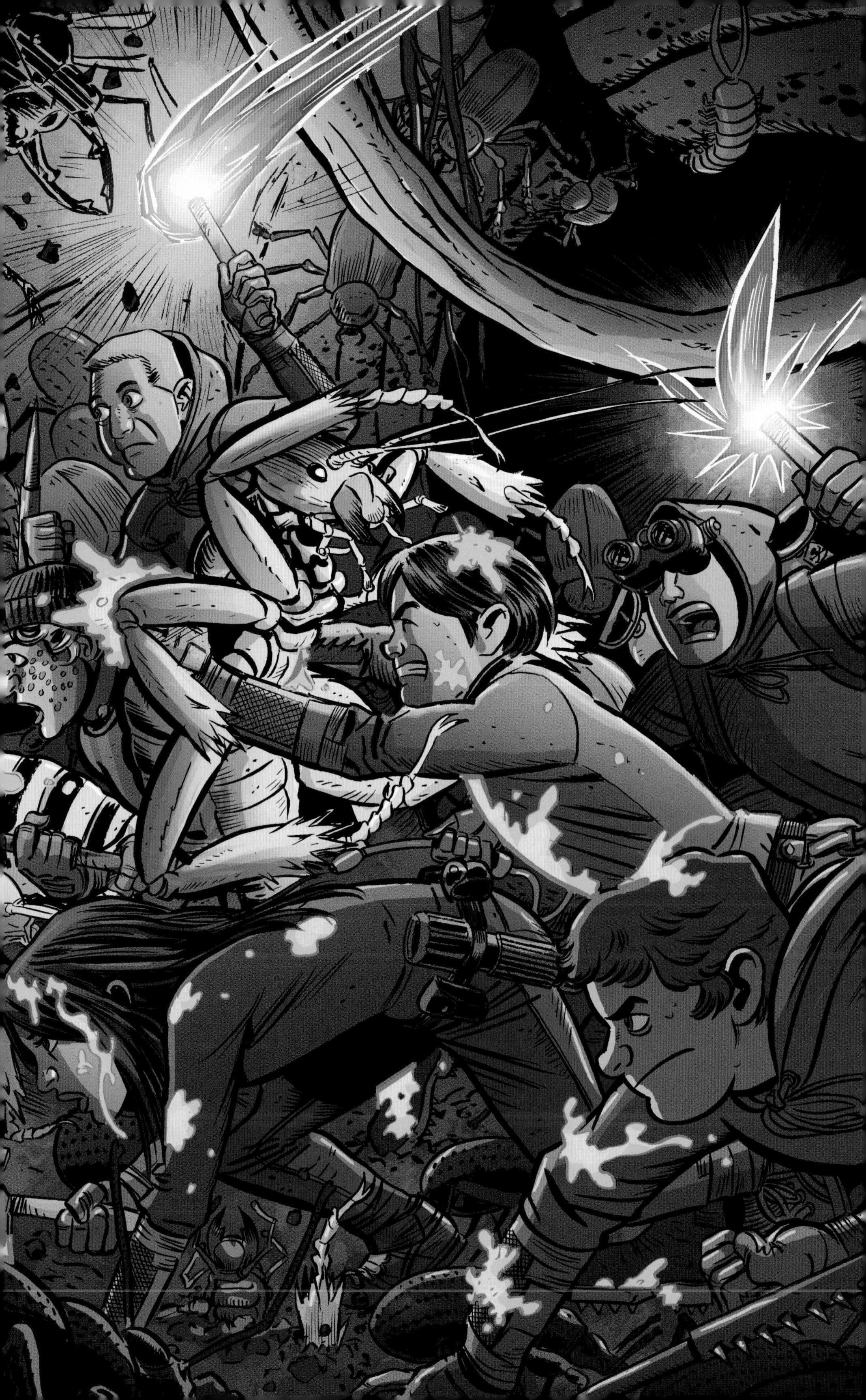

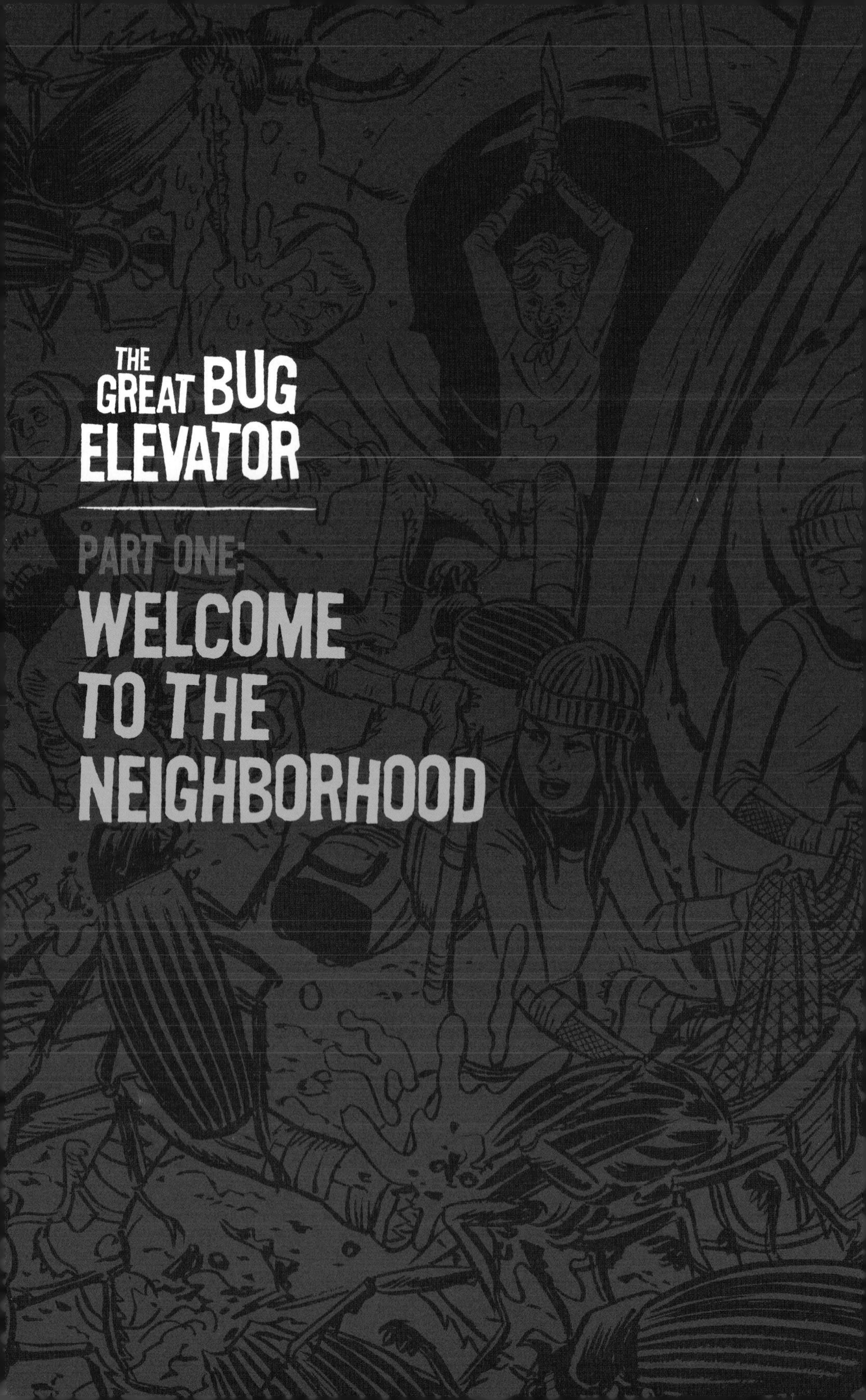

THE GREAT BUG ELEVATOR

PART ONE:
WELCOME TO THE NEIGHBORHOOD

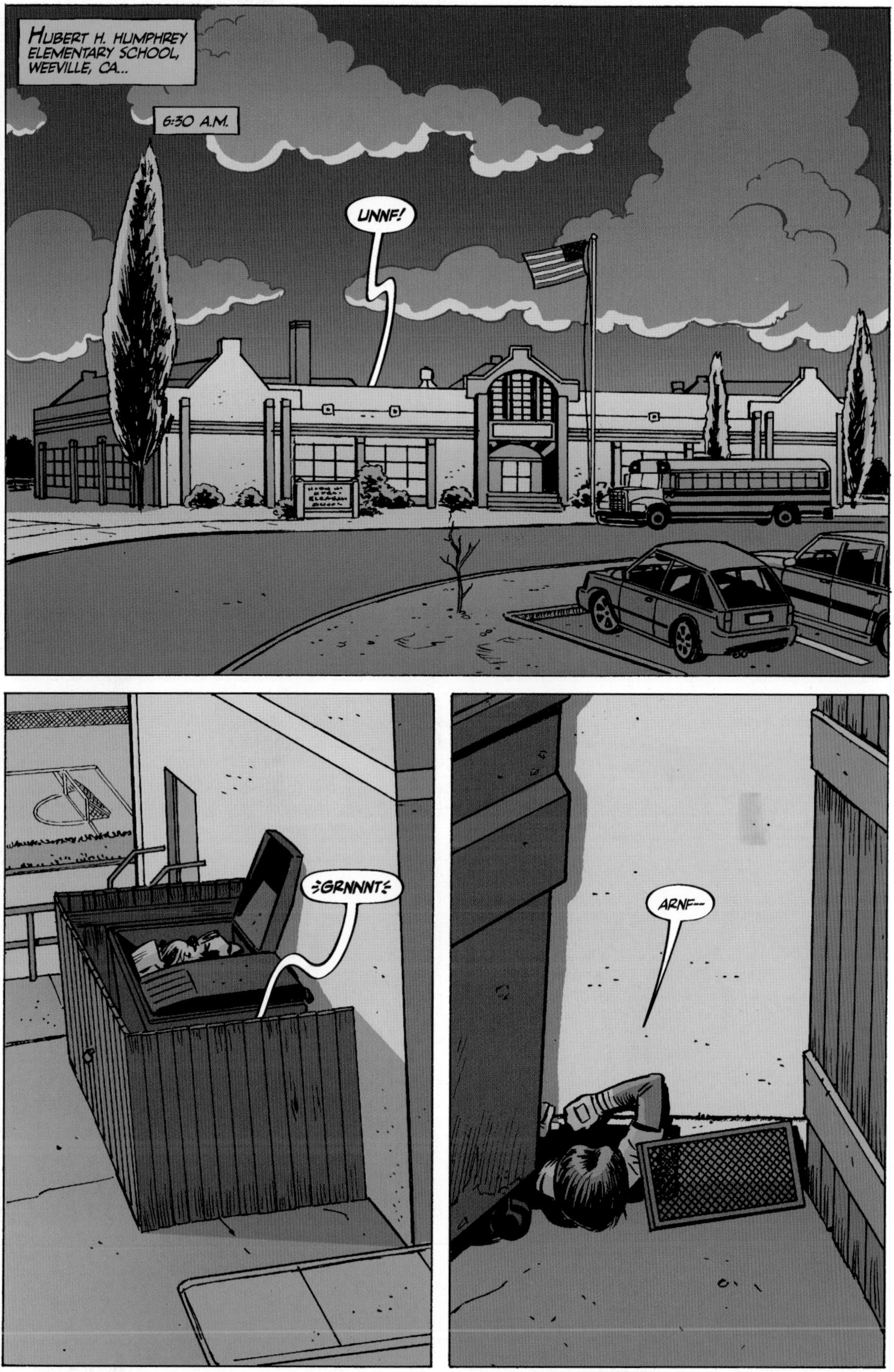
HUBERT H. HUMPHREY ELEMENTARY SCHOOL, WEEVILLE, CA...
6:30 A.M.
UNNF!
GRNNNT
ARNF--

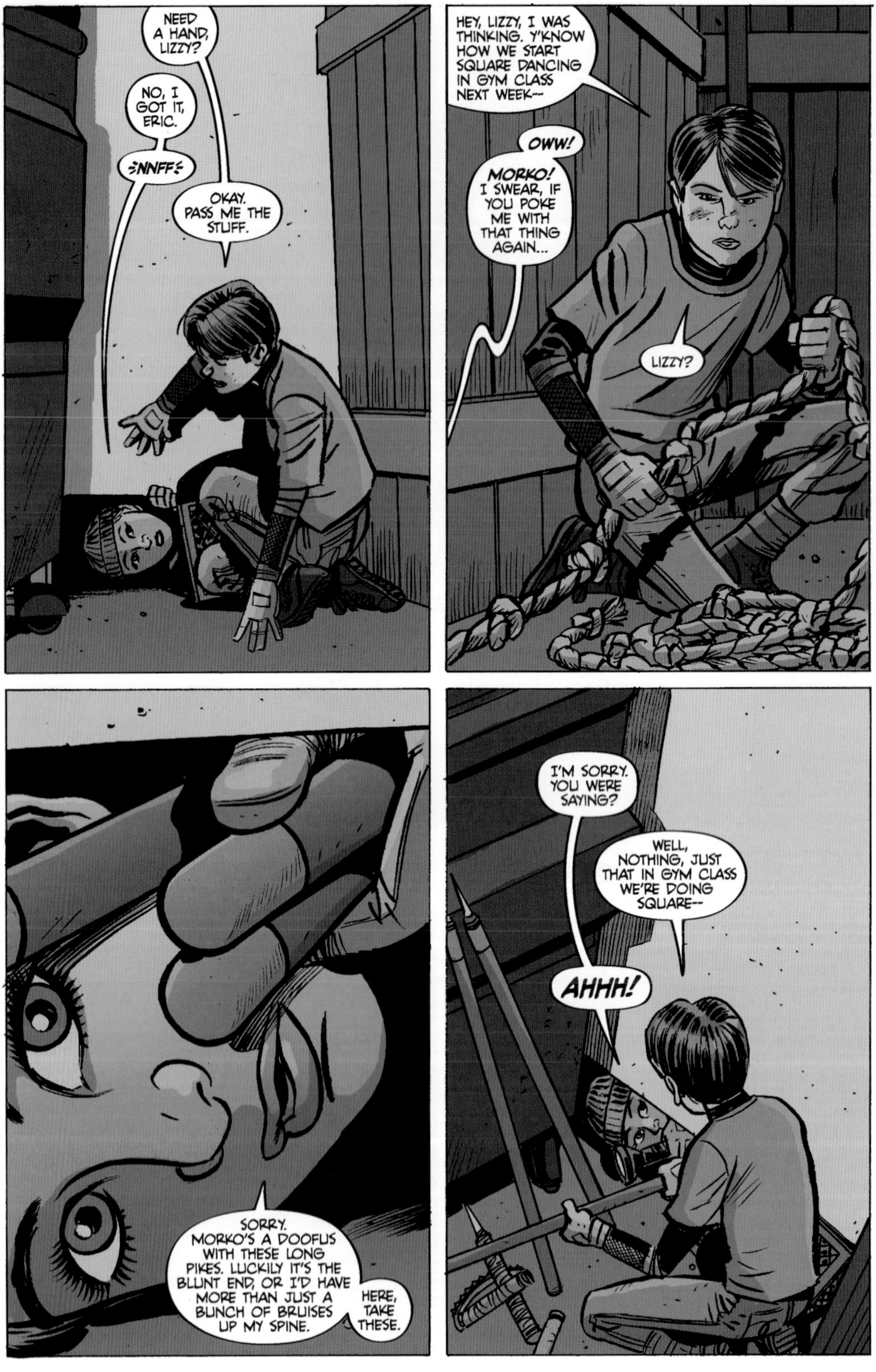
NEED A HAND, LIZZY?
NO, I GOT IT, ERIC.
NNFF
OKAY. PASS ME THE STUFF.
HEY, LIZZY, I WAS THINKING. Y'KNOW HOW WE START SQUARE DANCING IN GYM CLASS NEXT WEEK--
OWW!
MORKO! I SWEAR, IF YOU POKE ME WITH THAT THING AGAIN...
LIZZY?
SORRY. MORKO'S A DOOFUS WITH THESE LONG PIKES. LUCKILY IT'S THE BLUNT END, OR I'D HAVE MORE THAN JUST A BUNCH OF BRUISES UP MY SPINE.
HERE, TAKE THESE.
I'M SORRY. YOU WERE SAYING?
WELL, NOTHING, JUST THAT IN GYM CLASS WE'RE DOING SQUARE--
AHHH!

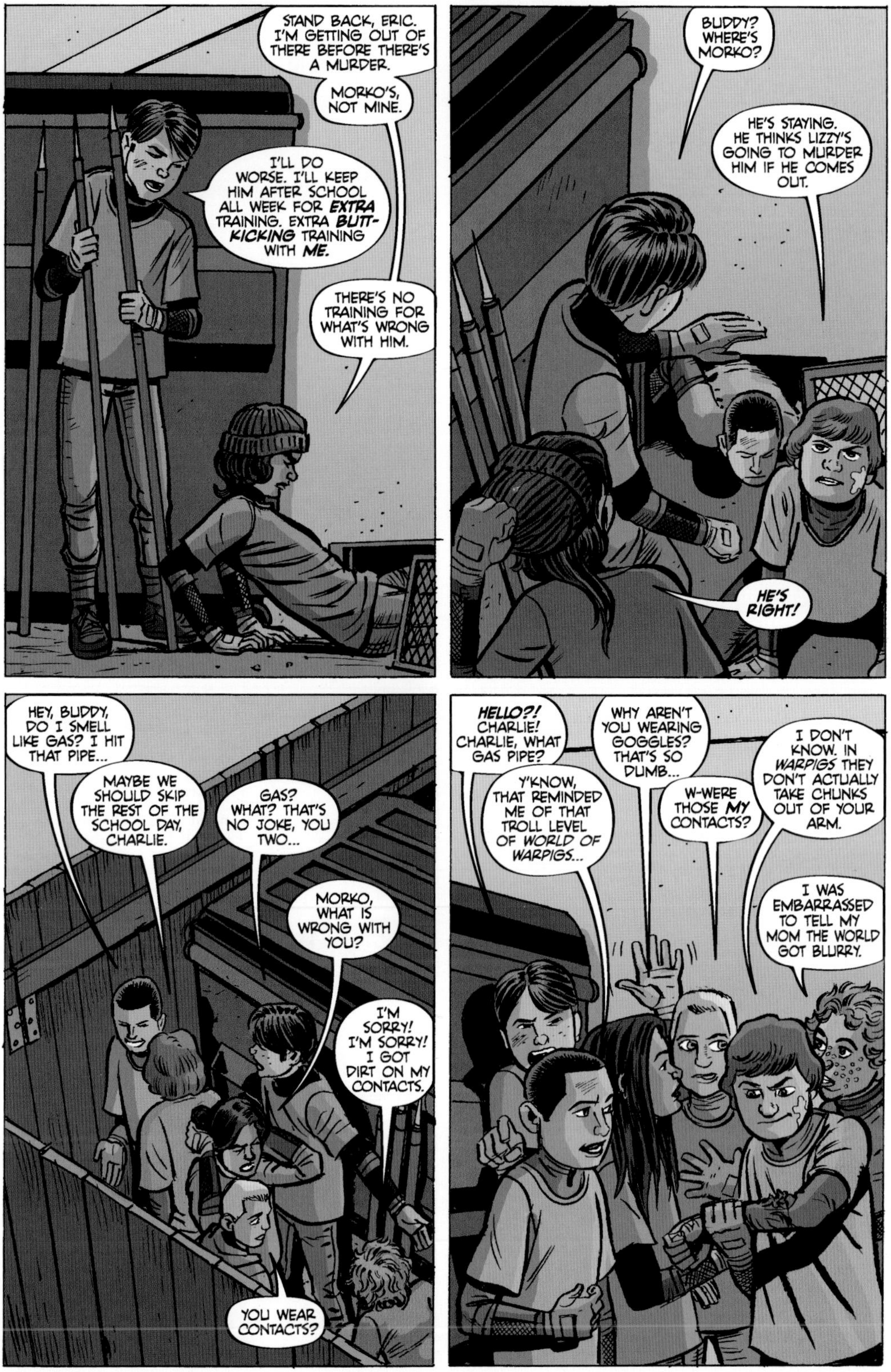
STAND BACK, ERIC. I'M GETTING OUT OF THERE BEFORE THERE'S A MURDER.
MORKO'S, NOT MINE.
I'LL DO WORSE. I'LL KEEP HIM AFTER SCHOOL ALL WEEK FOR EXTRA TRAINING. EXTRA BUTT-KICKING TRAINING WITH ME.
THERE'S NO TRAINING FOR WHAT'S WRONG WITH HIM.
BUDDY? WHERE'S MORKO?
HE'S STAYING. HE THINKS LIZZY'S GOING TO MURDER HIM IF HE COMES OUT.
HE'S RIGHT!
HEY, BUDDY, DO I SMELL LIKE GAS? I HIT THAT PIPE...
MAYBE WE SHOULD SKIP THE REST OF THE SCHOOL DAY, CHARLIE.
GAS? WHAT? THAT'S NO JOKE, YOU TWO...
MORKO, WHAT IS WRONG WITH YOU?
I'M SORRY! I'M SORRY! I GOT DIRT ON MY CONTACTS.
YOU WEAR CONTACTS?
HELLO?! CHARLIE! CHARLIE, WHAT GAS PIPE?
Y'KNOW, THAT REMINDED ME OF THAT TROLL LEVEL OF WORLD OF WARPIGS...
WHY AREN'T YOU WEARING GOGGLES? THAT'S SO DUMB...
W-WERE THOSE MY CONTACTS?
I DON'T KNOW. IN WARPIGS THEY DON'T ACTUALLY TAKE CHUNKS OUT OF YOUR ARM.
I WAS EMBARRASSED TO TELL MY MOM THE WORLD GOT BLURRY.

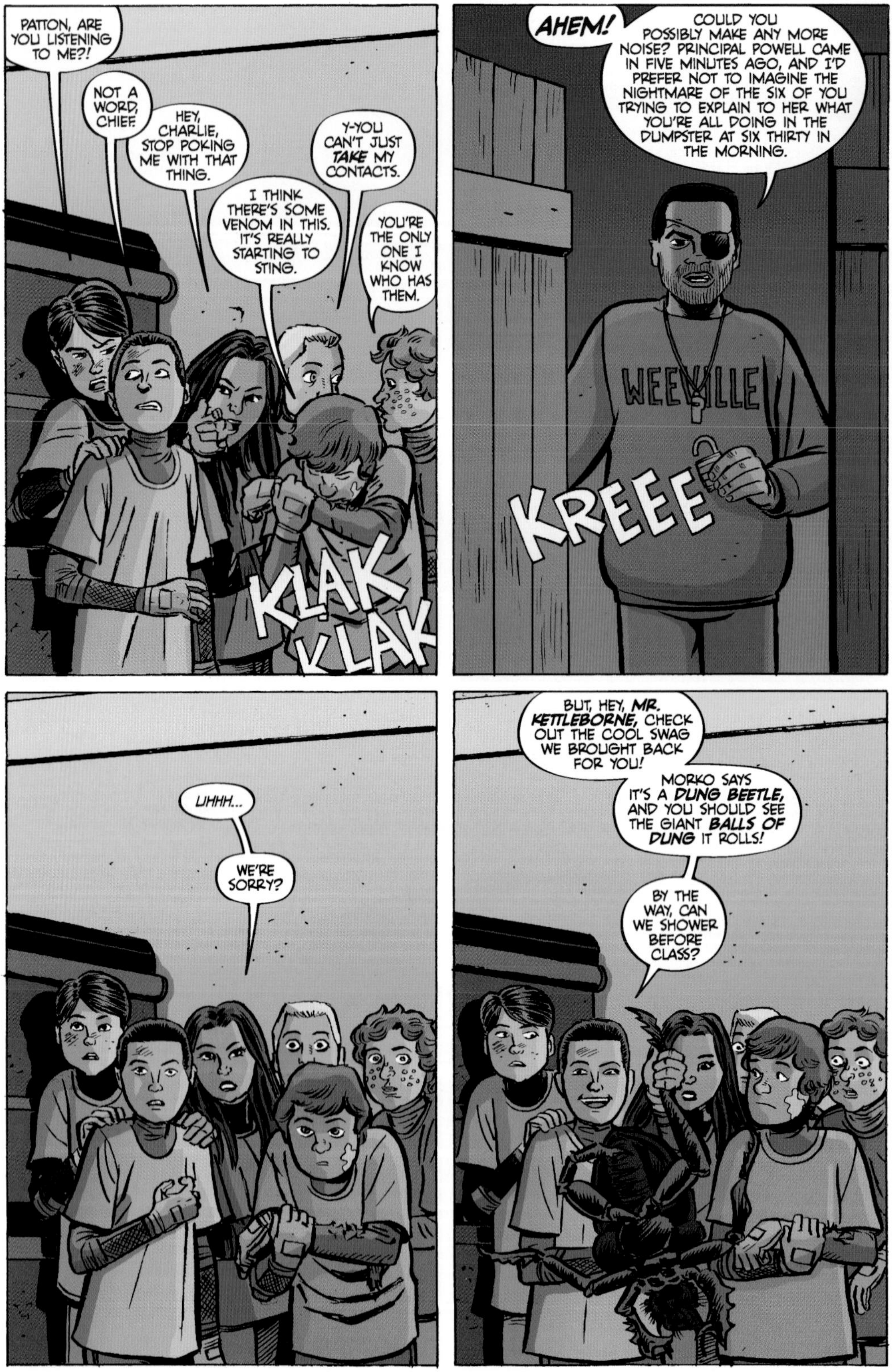

PATTON, ARE YOU LISTENING TO ME?!
NOT A WORD, CHIEF.
HEY, CHARLIE, STOP POKING ME WITH THAT THING.
I THINK THERE'S SOME VENOM IN THIS. IT'S REALLY STARTING TO STING.
Y-YOU CAN'T JUST TAKE MY CONTACTS.
YOU'RE THE ONLY ONE I KNOW WHO HAS THEM.
KLAK KLAK
AHEM!
COULD YOU POSSIBLY MAKE ANY MORE NOISE? PRINCIPAL POWELL CAME IN FIVE MINUTES AGO, AND I'D PREFER NOT TO IMAGINE THE NIGHTMARE OF THE SIX OF YOU TRYING TO EXPLAIN TO HER WHAT YOU'RE ALL DOING IN THE DUMPSTER AT SIX THIRTY IN THE MORNING.
KREEE
WEEVILLE
UHHH...
WE'RE SORRY?
BUT, HEY, MR. KETTLEBORNE, CHECK OUT THE COOL SWAG WE BROUGHT BACK FOR YOU!
MORKO SAYS IT'S A DUNG BEETLE, AND YOU SHOULD SEE THE GIANT BALLS OF DUNG IT ROLLS!
BY THE WAY, CAN WE SHOWER BEFORE CLASS?

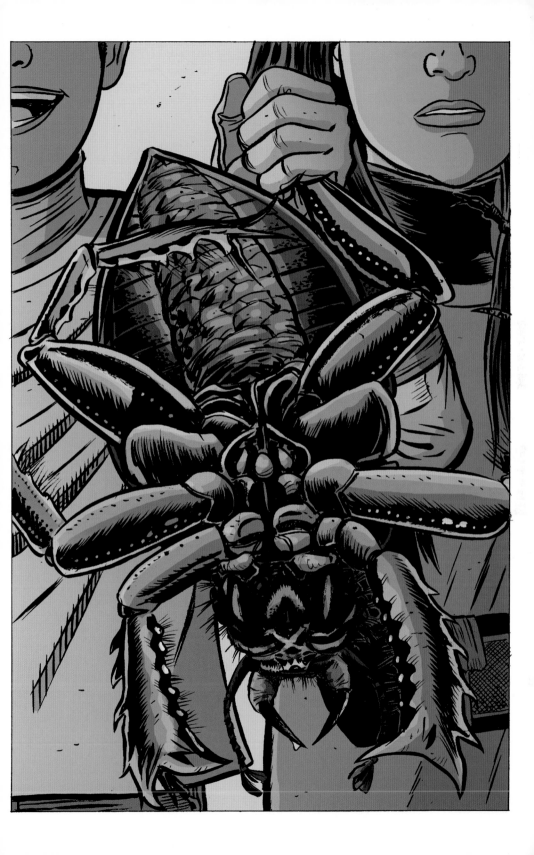

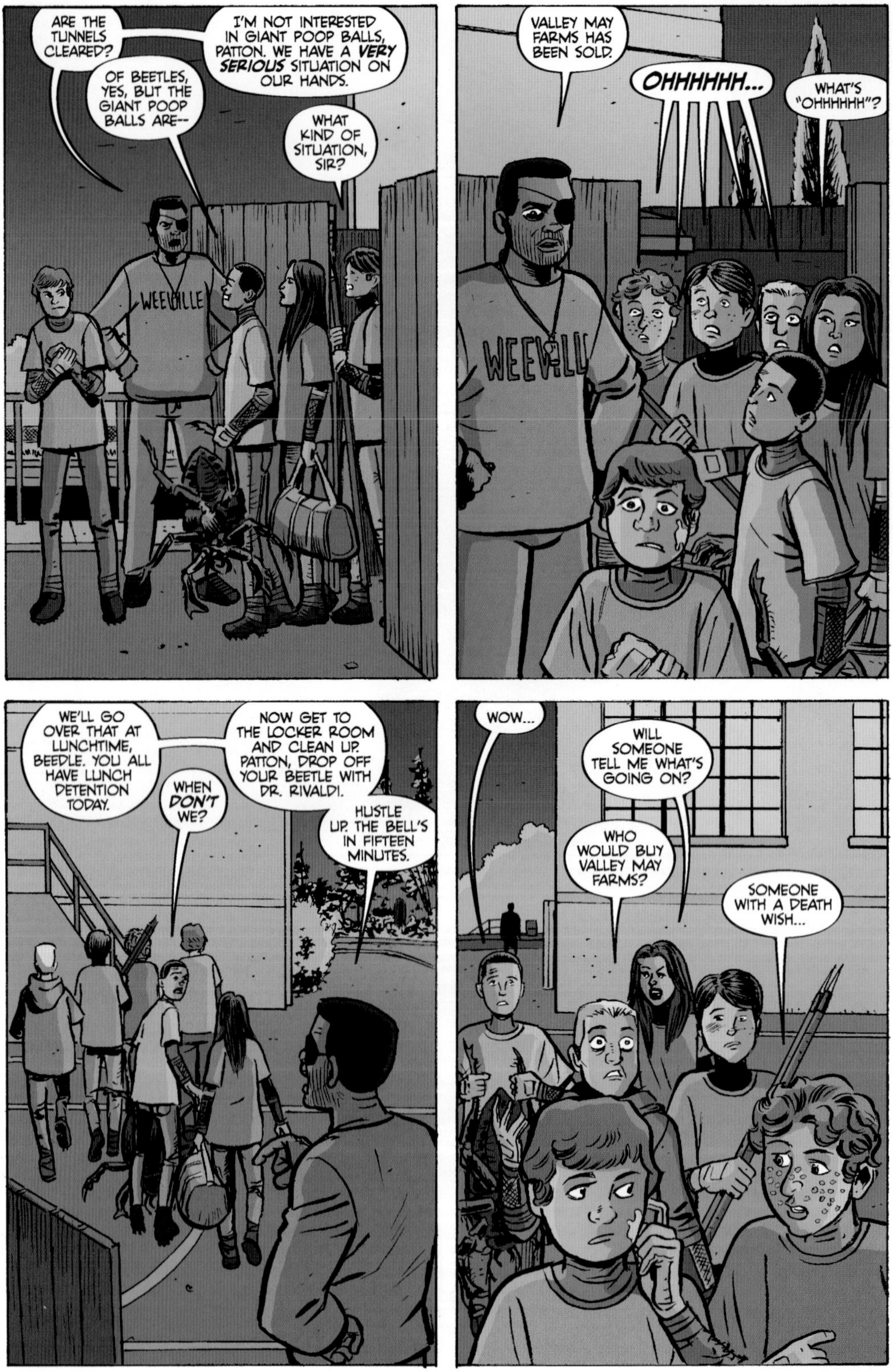
ARE THE TUNNELS CLEARED?
OF BEETLES, YES, BUT THE GIANT POOP BALLS ARE--
I'M NOT INTERESTED IN GIANT POOP BALLS, PATTON. WE HAVE A VERY SERIOUS SITUATION ON OUR HANDS.
WHAT KIND OF SITUATION, SIR?
WEEVILLE
VALLEY MAY FARMS HAS BEEN SOLD.
OHHHHHH...
WHAT'S "OHHHHHH"?
WEEVILLE
WE'LL GO OVER THAT AT LUNCHTIME, BEEDLE. YOU ALL HAVE LUNCH DETENTION TODAY.
NOW GET TO THE LOCKER ROOM AND CLEAN UP. PATTON, DROP OFF YOUR BEETLE WITH DR. RIVALDI.
WHEN DON'T WE?
HUSTLE UP. THE BELL'S IN FIFTEEN MINUTES.
WOW...
WILL SOMEONE TELL ME WHAT'S GOING ON?
WHO WOULD BUY VALLEY MAY FARMS?
SOMEONE WITH A DEATH WISH...

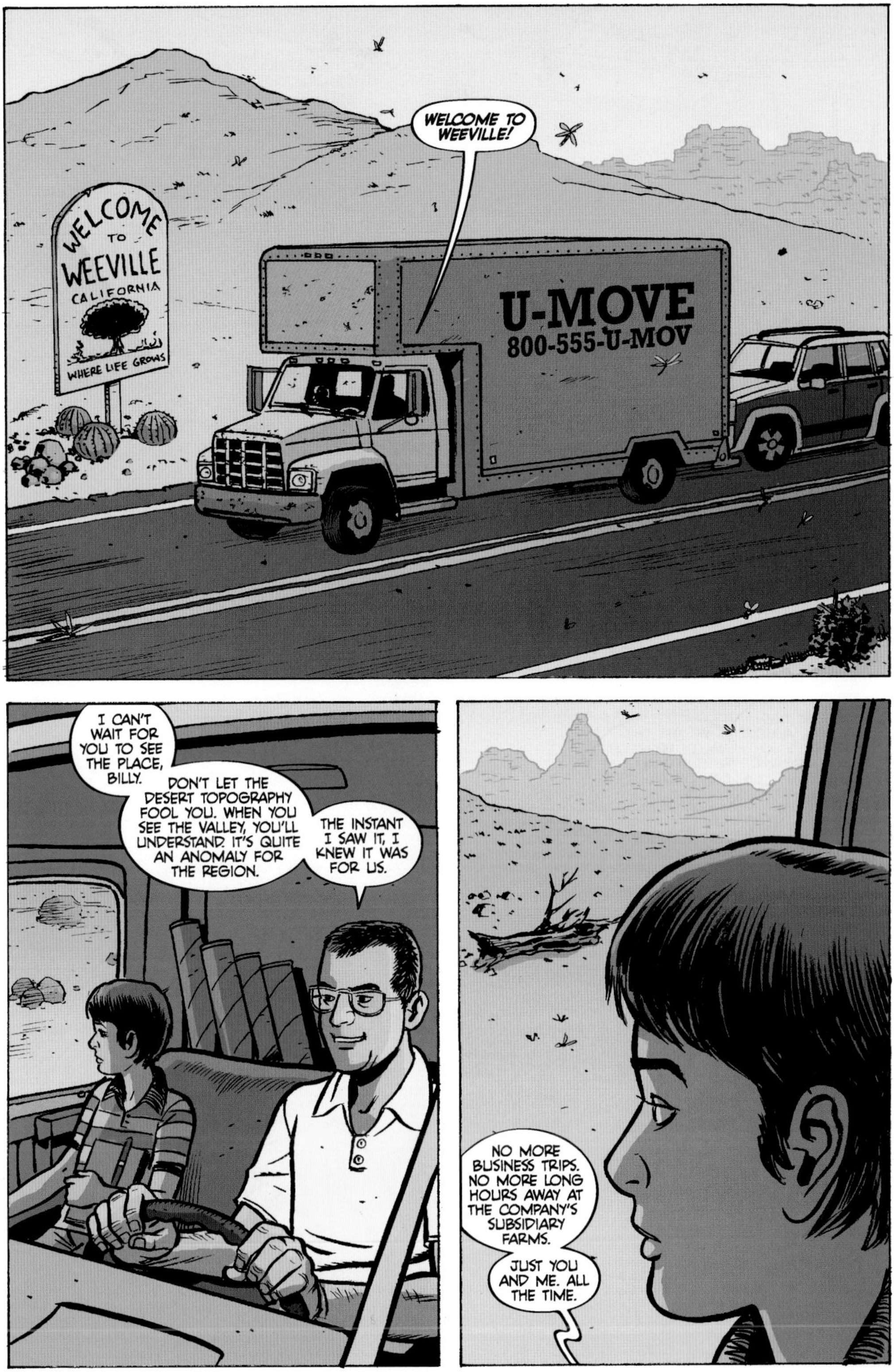
WELCOME TO WEEVILLE CALIFORNIA
WHERE LIFE GROWS
WELCOME TO WEEVILLE!
U-MOVE
800-555-U-MOV
I CAN'T WAIT FOR YOU TO SEE THE PLACE, BILLY.
DON'T LET THE DESERT TOPOGRAPHY FOOL YOU. WHEN YOU SEE THE VALLEY, YOU'LL UNDERSTAND. IT'S QUITE AN ANOMALY FOR THE REGION.
THE INSTANT I SAW IT, I KNEW IT WAS FOR US.
NO MORE BUSINESS TRIPS. NO MORE LONG HOURS AWAY AT THE COMPANY'S SUBSIDIARY FARMS.
JUST YOU AND ME. ALL THE TIME.

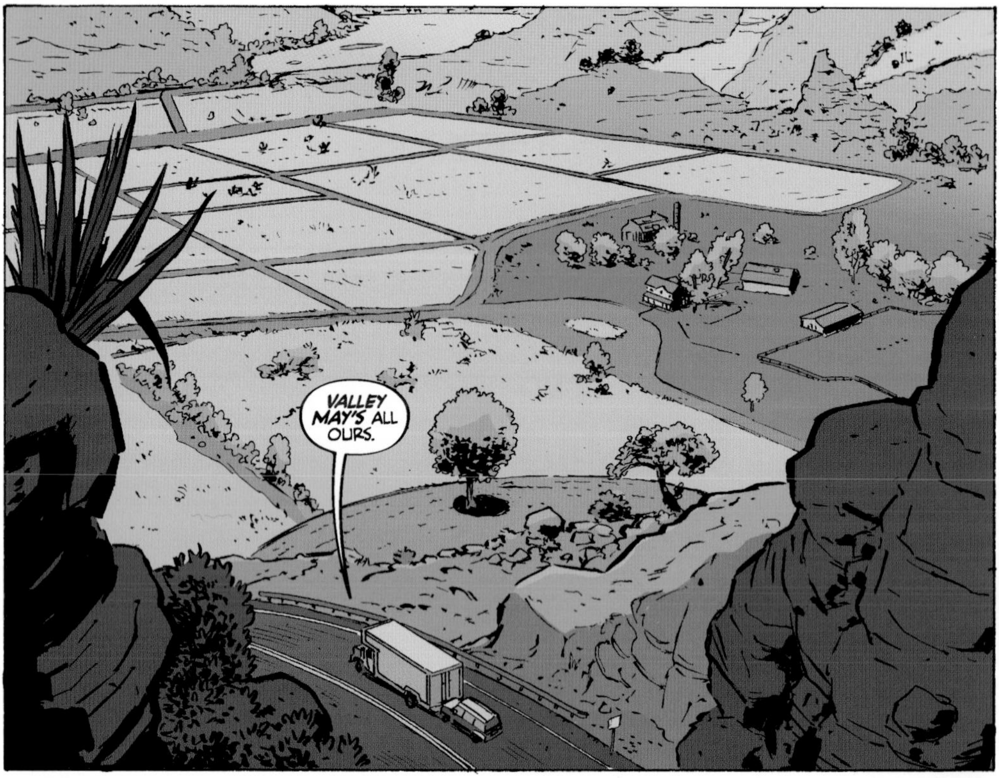
VALLEY MAY'S ALL OURS.

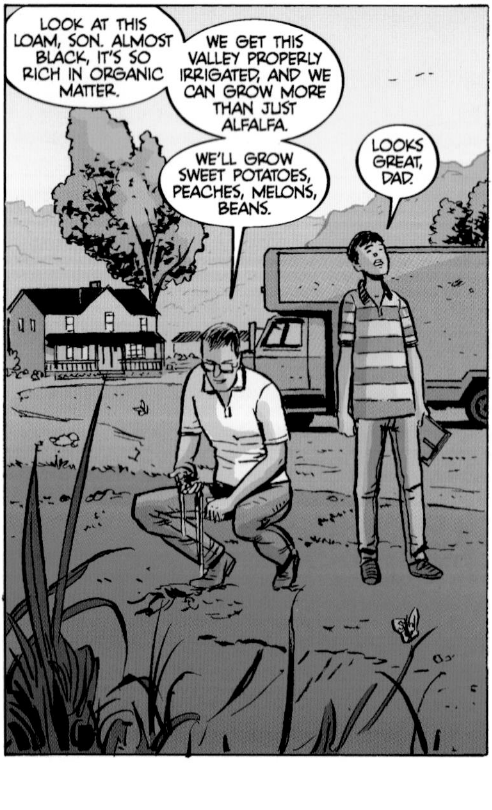
LOOK AT THIS LOAM, SON. ALMOST BLACK, IT'S SO RICH IN ORGANIC MATTER.
WE GET THIS VALLEY PROPERLY IRRIGATED, AND WE CAN GROW MORE THAN JUST ALFALFA.
WE'LL GROW SWEET POTATOES, PEACHES, MELONS, BEANS.
LOOKS GREAT, DAD.

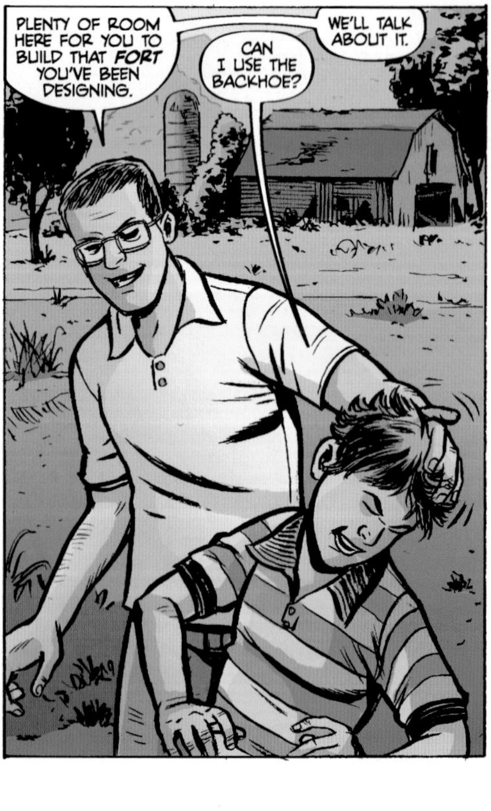
PLENTY OF ROOM HERE FOR YOU TO BUILD THAT FORT YOU'VE BEEN DESIGNING.
CAN I USE THE BACKHOE?
WE'LL TALK ABOUT IT.

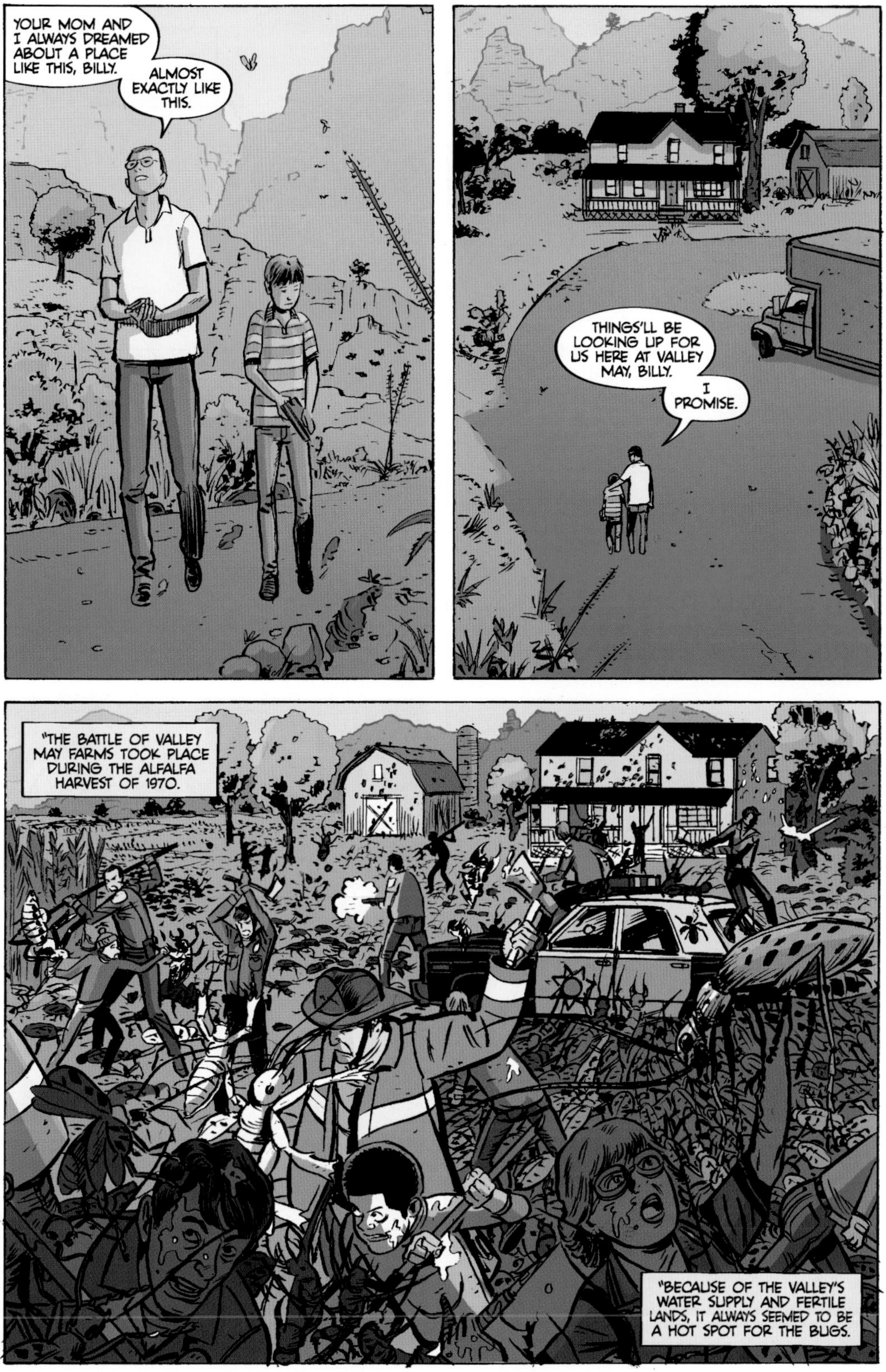
YOUR MOM AND I ALWAYS DREAMED ABOUT A PLACE LIKE THIS, BILLY.
ALMOST EXACTLY LIKE THIS.
THINGS'LL BE LOOKING UP FOR US HERE AT VALLEY MAY, BILLY.
I PROMISE.
"THE BATTLE OF VALLEY MAY FARMS TOOK PLACE DURING THE ALFALFA HARVEST OF 1970.
"BECAUSE OF THE VALLEY'S WATER SUPPLY AND FERTILE LANDS, IT ALWAYS SEEMED TO BE A HOT SPOT FOR THE BUGS.

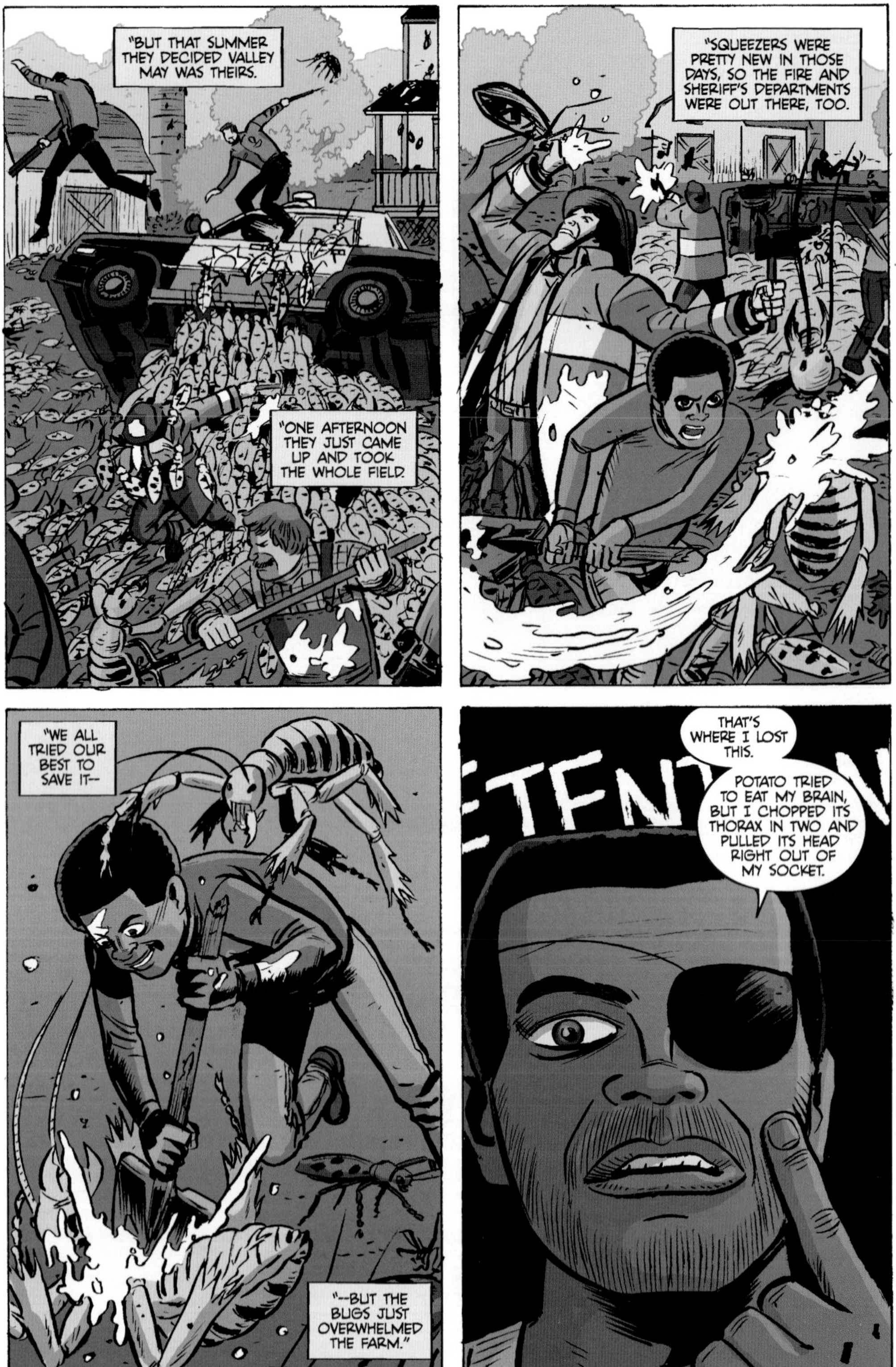
"BUT THAT SUMMER THEY DECIDED VALLEY MAY WAS THEIRS.
"ONE AFTERNOON THEY JUST CAME UP AND TOOK THE WHOLE FIELD.
"SQUEEZERS WERE PRETTY NEW IN THOSE DAYS, SO THE FIRE AND SHERIFF'S DEPARTMENTS WERE OUT THERE, TOO.
"WE ALL TRIED OUR BEST TO SAVE IT--
"--BUT THE BUGS JUST OVERWHELMED THE FARM."
THAT'S WHERE I LOST THIS.
POTATO TRIED TO EAT MY BRAIN, BUT I CHOPPED ITS THORAX IN TWO AND PULLED ITS HEAD RIGHT OUT OF MY SOCKET.

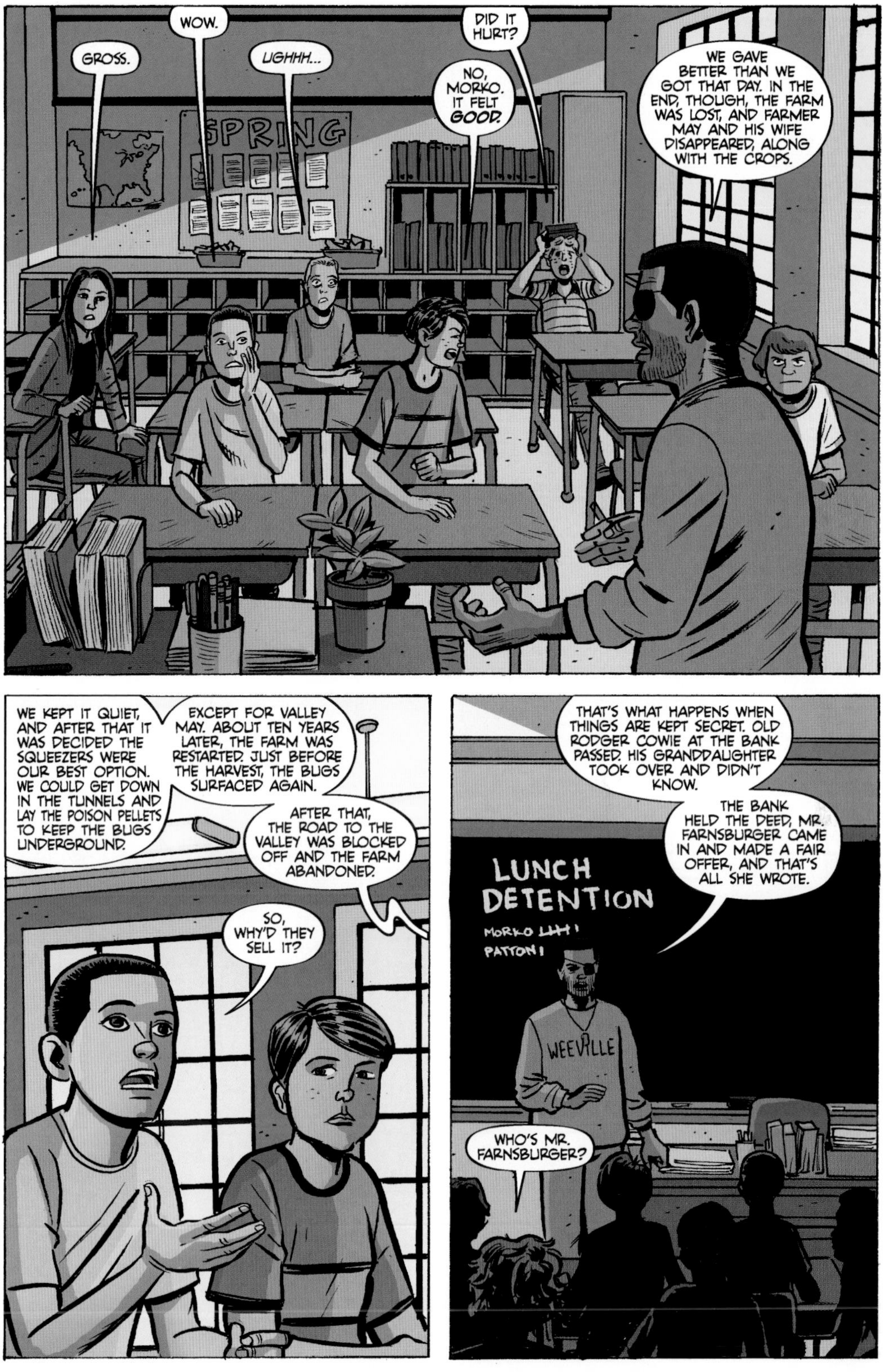
GROSS.
WOW.
UGHHH...
SPRING
DID IT HURT?
NO, MORKO. IT FELT **GOOD.**
WE GAVE BETTER THAN WE GOT THAT DAY. IN THE END, THOUGH, THE FARM WAS LOST, AND FARMER MAY AND HIS WIFE DISAPPEARED, ALONG WITH THE CROPS.
WE KEPT IT QUIET, AND AFTER THAT IT WAS DECIDED THE SQUEEZERS WERE OUR BEST OPTION. WE COULD GET DOWN IN THE TUNNELS AND LAY THE POISON PELLETS TO KEEP THE BUGS UNDERGROUND.
EXCEPT FOR VALLEY MAY. ABOUT TEN YEARS LATER, THE FARM WAS RESTARTED. JUST BEFORE THE HARVEST, THE BUGS SURFACED AGAIN.
AFTER THAT, THE ROAD TO THE VALLEY WAS BLOCKED OFF AND THE FARM ABANDONED.
SO, WHY'D THEY SELL IT?
THAT'S WHAT HAPPENS WHEN THINGS ARE KEPT SECRET. OLD RODGER COWIE AT THE BANK PASSED. HIS GRANDDAUGHTER TOOK OVER AND DIDN'T KNOW.
THE BANK HELD THE DEED, MR. FARNSBURGER CAME IN AND MADE A FAIR OFFER, AND THAT'S ALL SHE WROTE.
LUNCH DETENTION
MORKO
PATTON
WEEVILLE
WHO'S MR. FARNSBURGER?

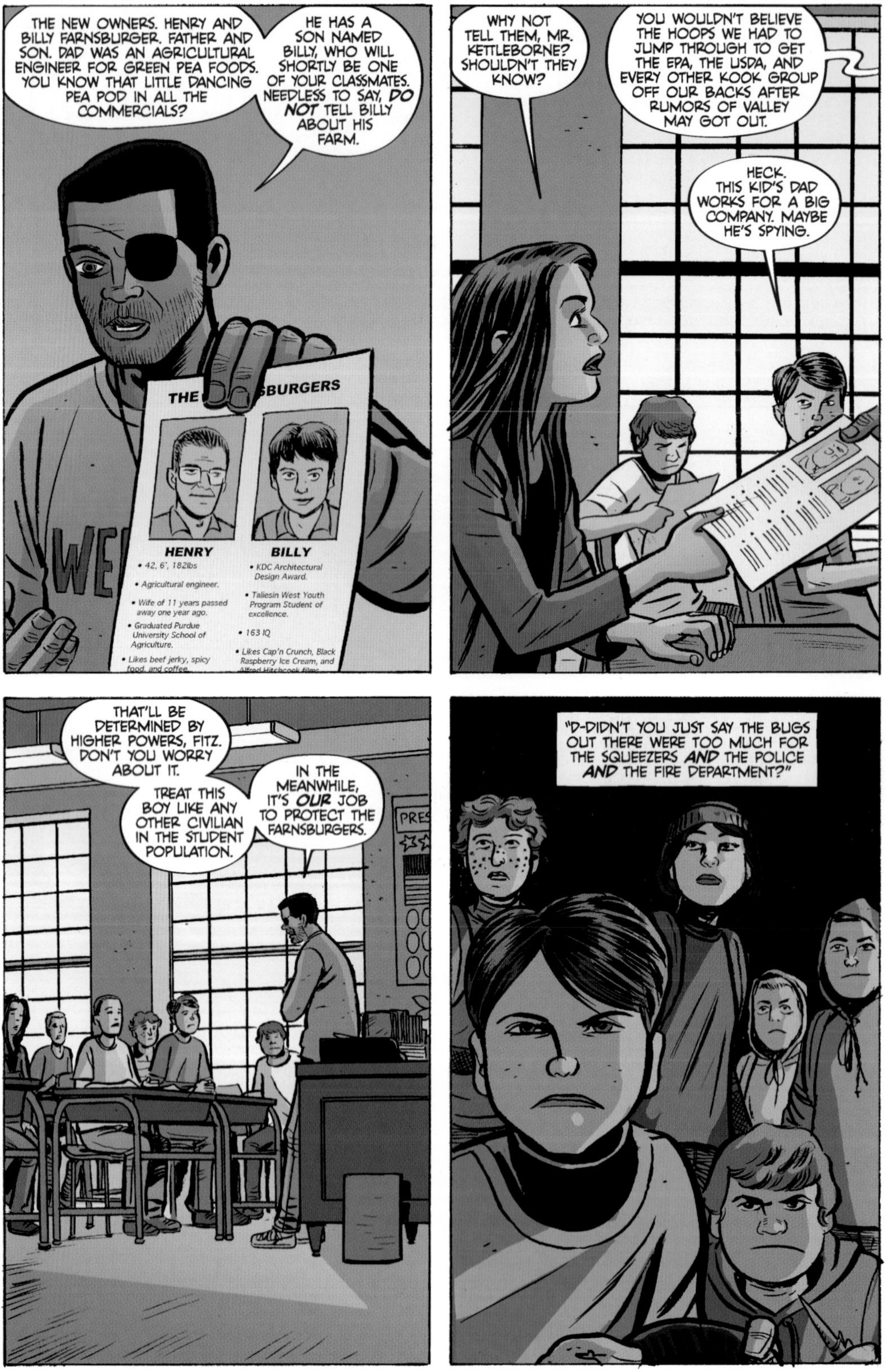
THE NEW OWNERS. HENRY AND BILLY FARNSBURGER. FATHER AND SON. DAD WAS AN AGRICULTURAL ENGINEER FOR GREEN PEA FOODS. YOU KNOW THAT LITTLE DANCING PEA POD IN ALL THE COMMERCIALS?
HE HAS A SON NAMED BILLY, WHO WILL SHORTLY BE ONE OF YOUR CLASSMATES. NEEDLESS TO SAY, *DO NOT* TELL BILLY ABOUT HIS FARM.
HENRY
• 42, 6', 182lbs
• Agricultural engineer.
• Wife of 11 years passed away one year ago.
• Graduated Purdue University School of Agriculture.
• Likes beef jerky, spicy
BILLY
• KDC Architectural Design Award.
• Taliesin West Youth Program Student of excellence.
• 163 IQ
• Likes Cap'n Crunch, Black Raspberry Ice Cream, and
WHY NOT TELL THEM, MR. KETTLEBORNE? SHOULDN'T THEY KNOW?
YOU WOULDN'T BELIEVE THE HOOPS WE HAD TO JUMP THROUGH TO GET THE EPA, THE USDA, AND EVERY OTHER KOOK GROUP OFF OUR BACKS AFTER RUMORS OF VALLEY MAY GOT OUT.
HECK. THIS KID'S DAD WORKS FOR A BIG COMPANY. MAYBE HE'S SPYING.
THAT'LL BE DETERMINED BY HIGHER POWERS, FITZ. DON'T YOU WORRY ABOUT IT.
TREAT THIS BOY LIKE ANY OTHER CIVILIAN IN THE STUDENT POPULATION.
IN THE MEANWHILE, IT'S *OUR* JOB TO PROTECT THE FARNSBURGERS.
"D-DIDN'T YOU JUST SAY THE BUGS OUT THERE WERE TOO MUCH FOR THE SQUEEZERS *AND* THE POLICE *AND* THE FIRE DEPARTMENT?"

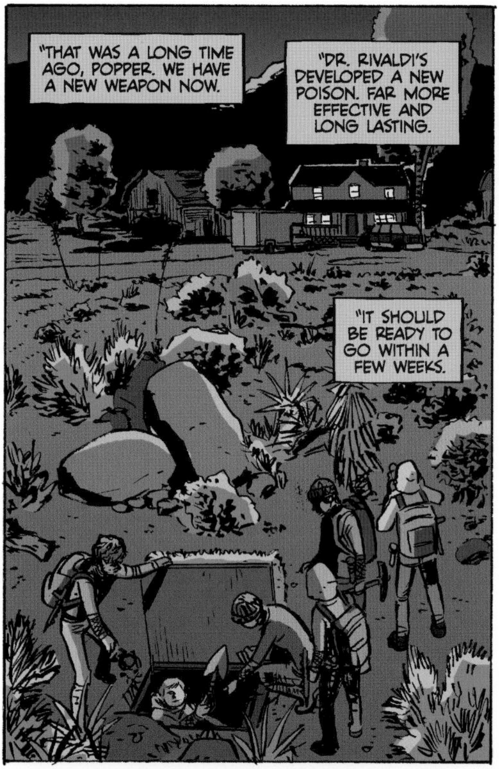
"THAT WAS A LONG TIME AGO, POPPER. WE HAVE A NEW WEAPON NOW.
"DR. RIVALDI'S DEVELOPED A NEW POISON. FAR MORE EFFECTIVE AND LONG LASTING.
"IT SHOULD BE READY TO GO WITHIN A FEW WEEKS.

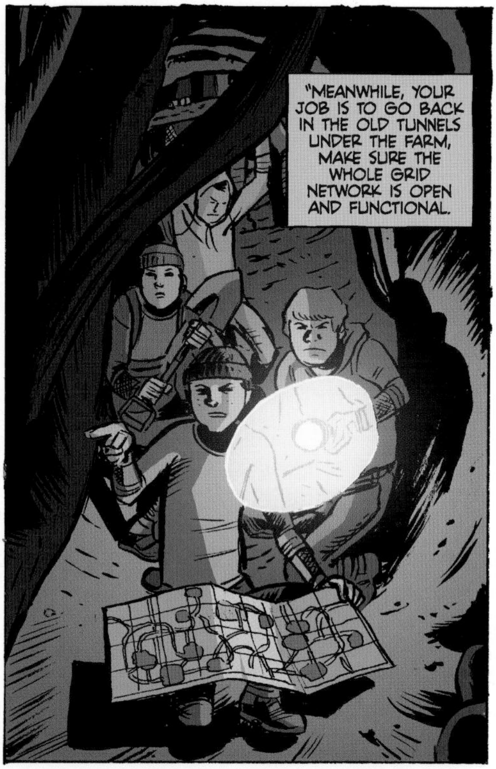
"MEANWHILE, YOUR JOB IS TO GO BACK IN THE OLD TUNNELS UNDER THE FARM, MAKE SURE THE WHOLE GRID NETWORK IS OPEN AND FUNCTIONAL.

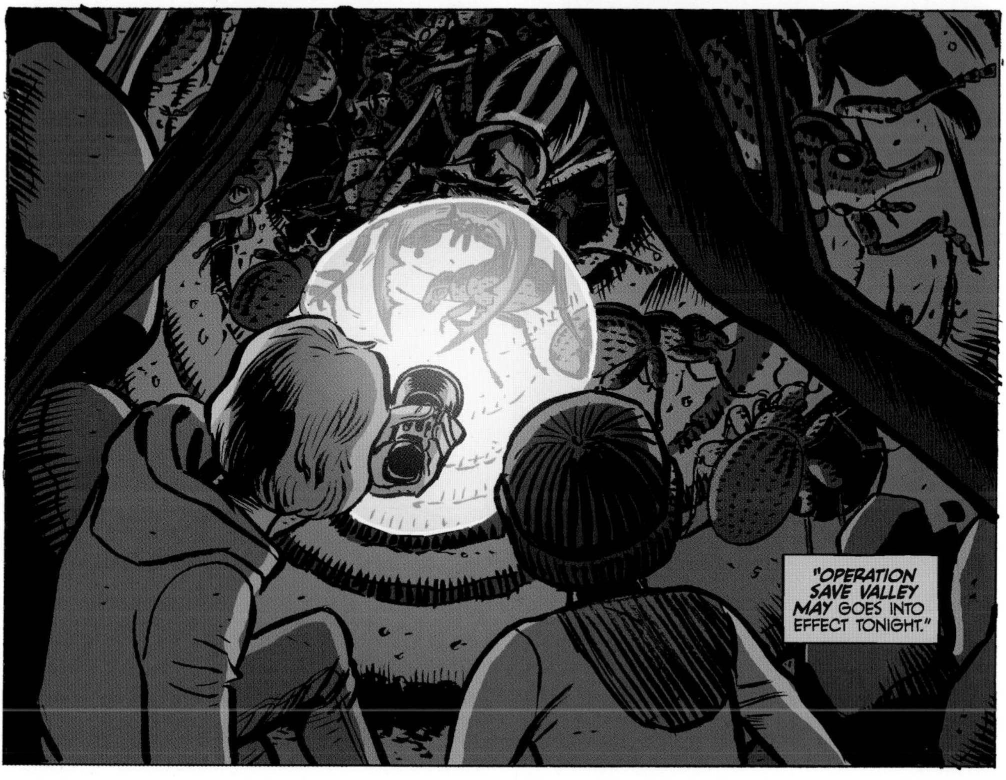
"OPERATION SAVE VALLEY MAY GOES INTO EFFECT TONIGHT."

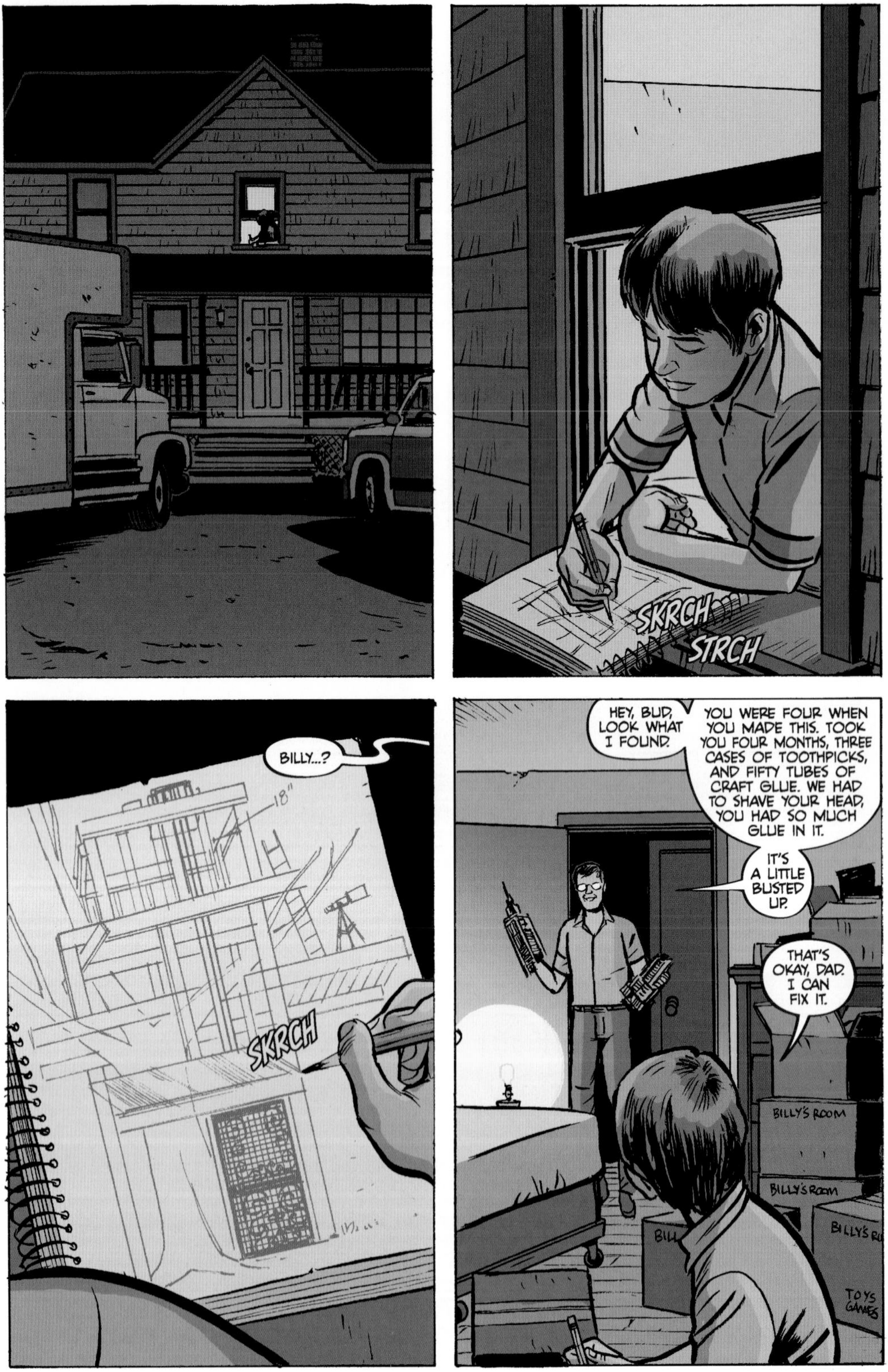
SKRCH
STRCH
BILLY...?
18"
SKRCH
HEY, BUD, LOOK WHAT I FOUND.
YOU WERE FOUR WHEN YOU MADE THIS. TOOK YOU FOUR MONTHS, THREE CASES OF TOOTHPICKS, AND FIFTY TUBES OF CRAFT GLUE. WE HAD TO SHAVE YOUR HEAD, YOU HAD SO MUCH GLUE IN IT.
IT'S A LITTLE BUSTED UP.
THAT'S OKAY, DAD. I CAN FIX IT.
BILLY'S ROOM
BILLY'S ROOM
TOYS GAMES

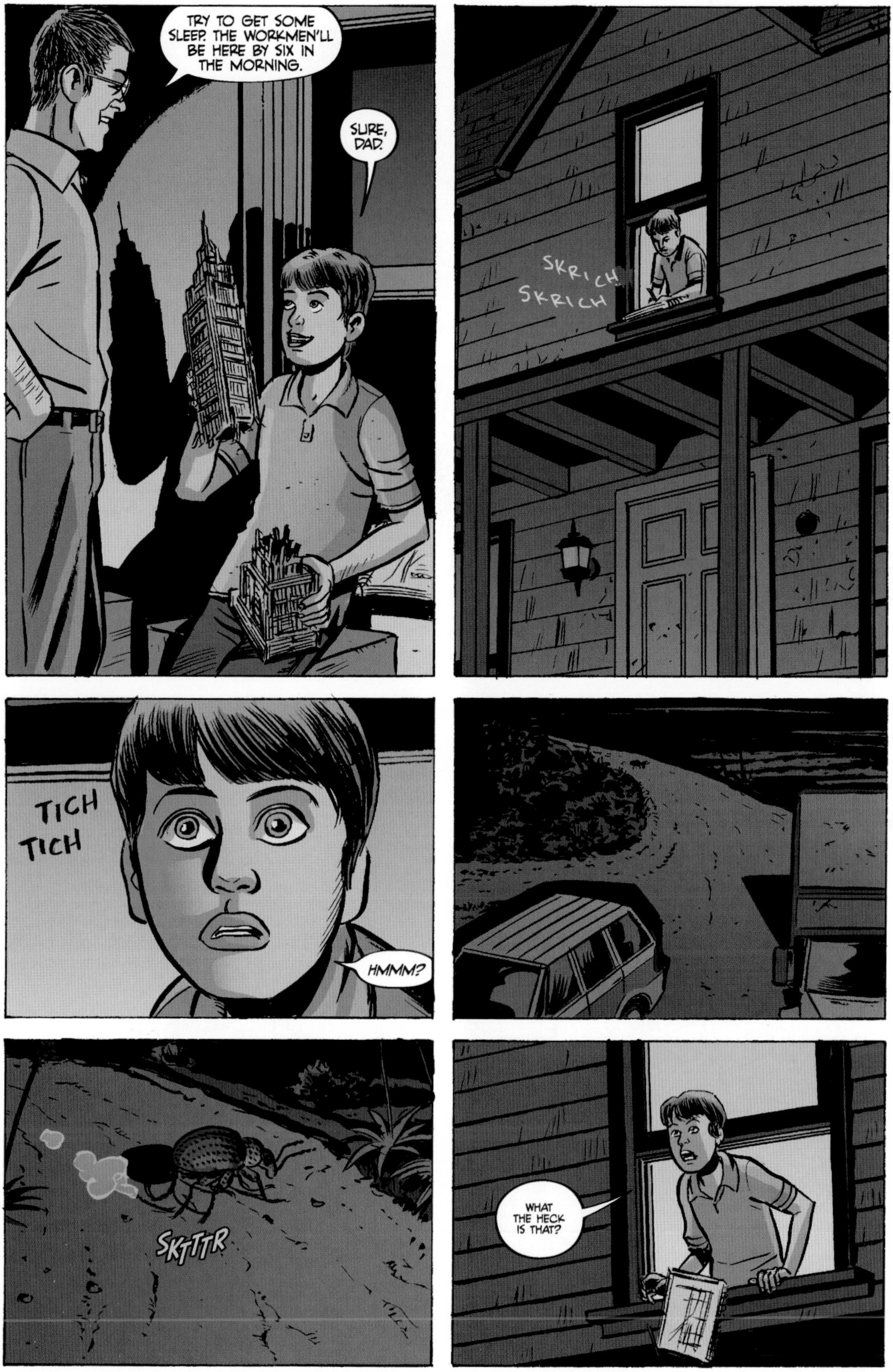
TRY TO GET SOME SLEEP. THE WORKMEN'LL BE HERE BY SIX IN THE MORNING.
SURE, DAD.
SKRICH
SKRICH
TICH
TICH
HMMM?
SKTTTR
WHAT THE HECK IS THAT?

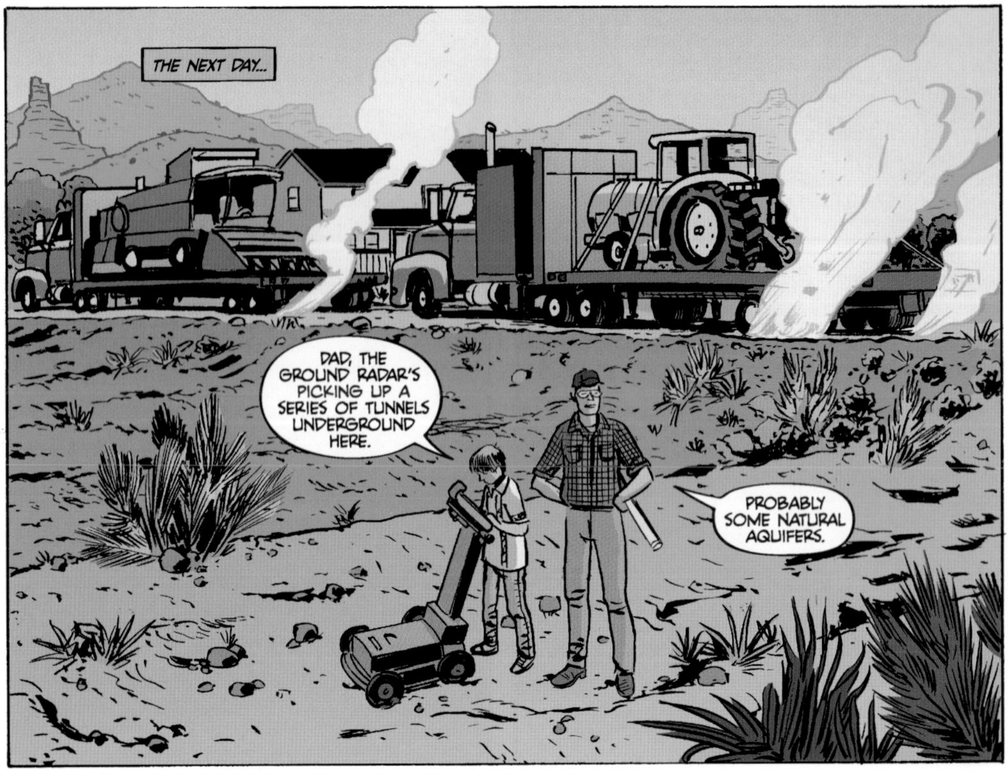
THE NEXT DAY...
DAD, THE GROUND RADAR'S PICKING UP A SERIES OF TUNNELS UNDERGROUND HERE.
PROBABLY SOME NATURAL AQUIFERS.

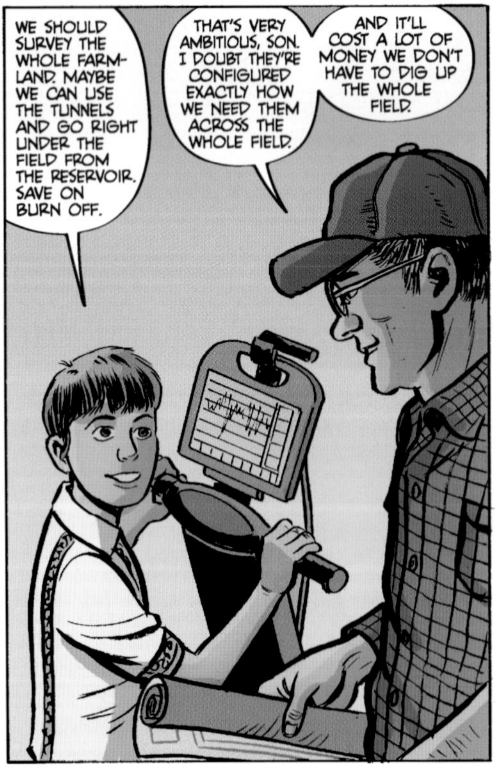
WE SHOULD SURVEY THE WHOLE FARMLAND. MAYBE WE CAN USE THE TUNNELS AND GO RIGHT UNDER THE FIELD FROM THE RESERVOIR. SAVE ON BURN OFF.
THAT'S VERY AMBITIOUS, SON. I DOUBT THEY'RE CONFIGURED EXACTLY HOW WE NEED THEM ACROSS THE WHOLE FIELD.
AND IT'LL COST A LOT OF MONEY WE DON'T HAVE TO DIG UP THE WHOLE FIELD.

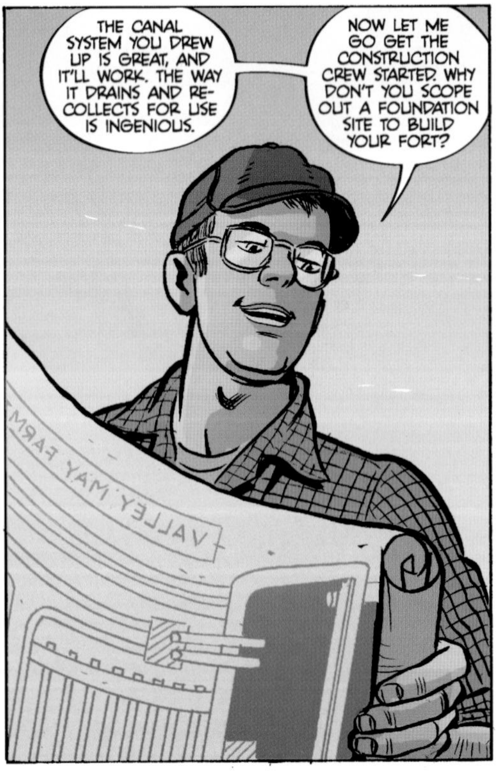
THE CANAL SYSTEM YOU DREW UP IS GREAT, AND IT'LL WORK. THE WAY IT DRAINS AND RECOLLECTS FOR USE IS INGENIOUS.
NOW LET ME GO GET THE CONSTRUCTION CREW STARTED. WHY DON'T YOU SCOPE OUT A FOUNDATION SITE TO BUILD YOUR FORT?
VALLEY MAY FARM

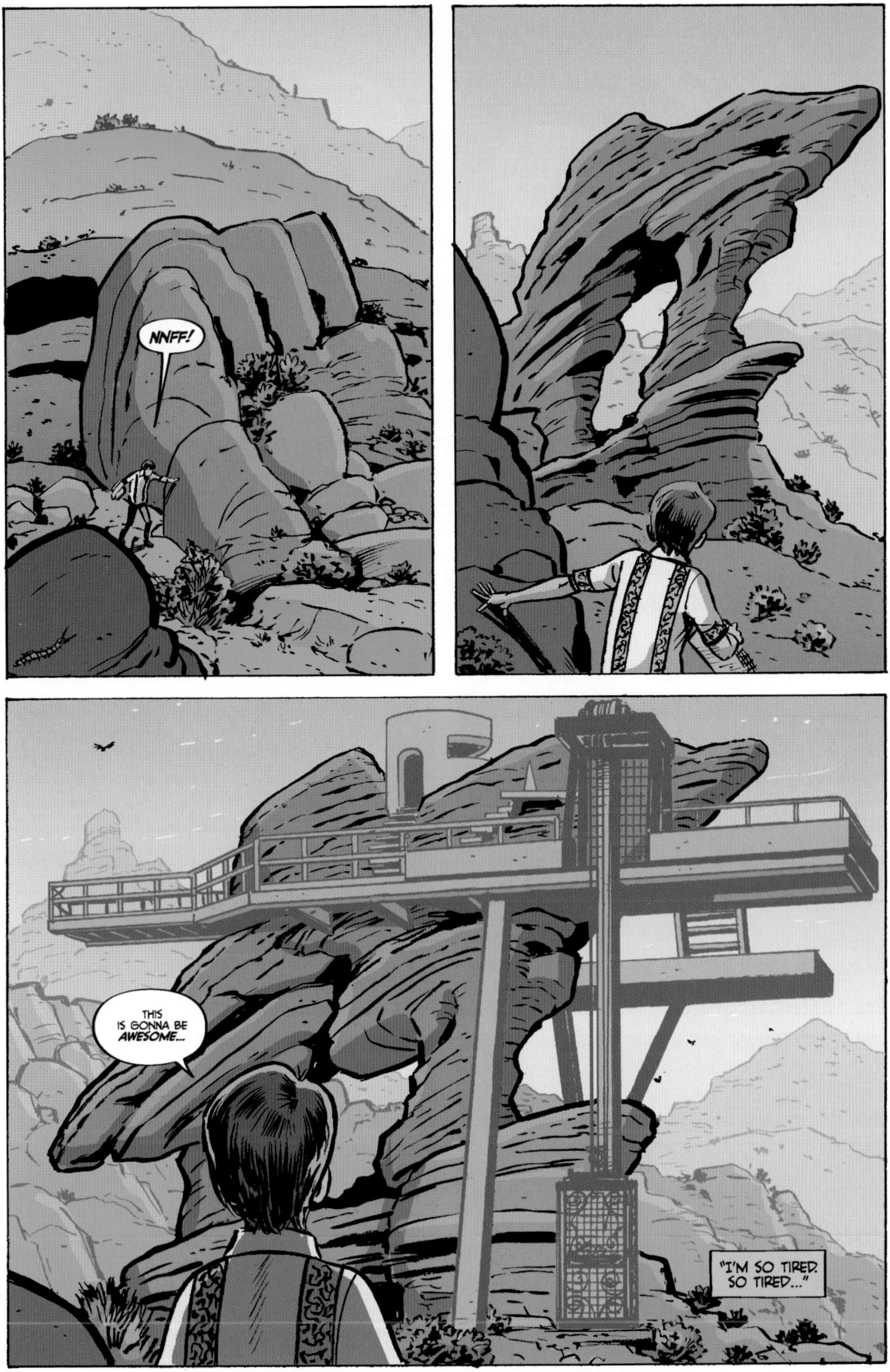
NNFF!
THIS IS GONNA BE AWESOME...
"I'M SO TIRED. SO TIRED..."

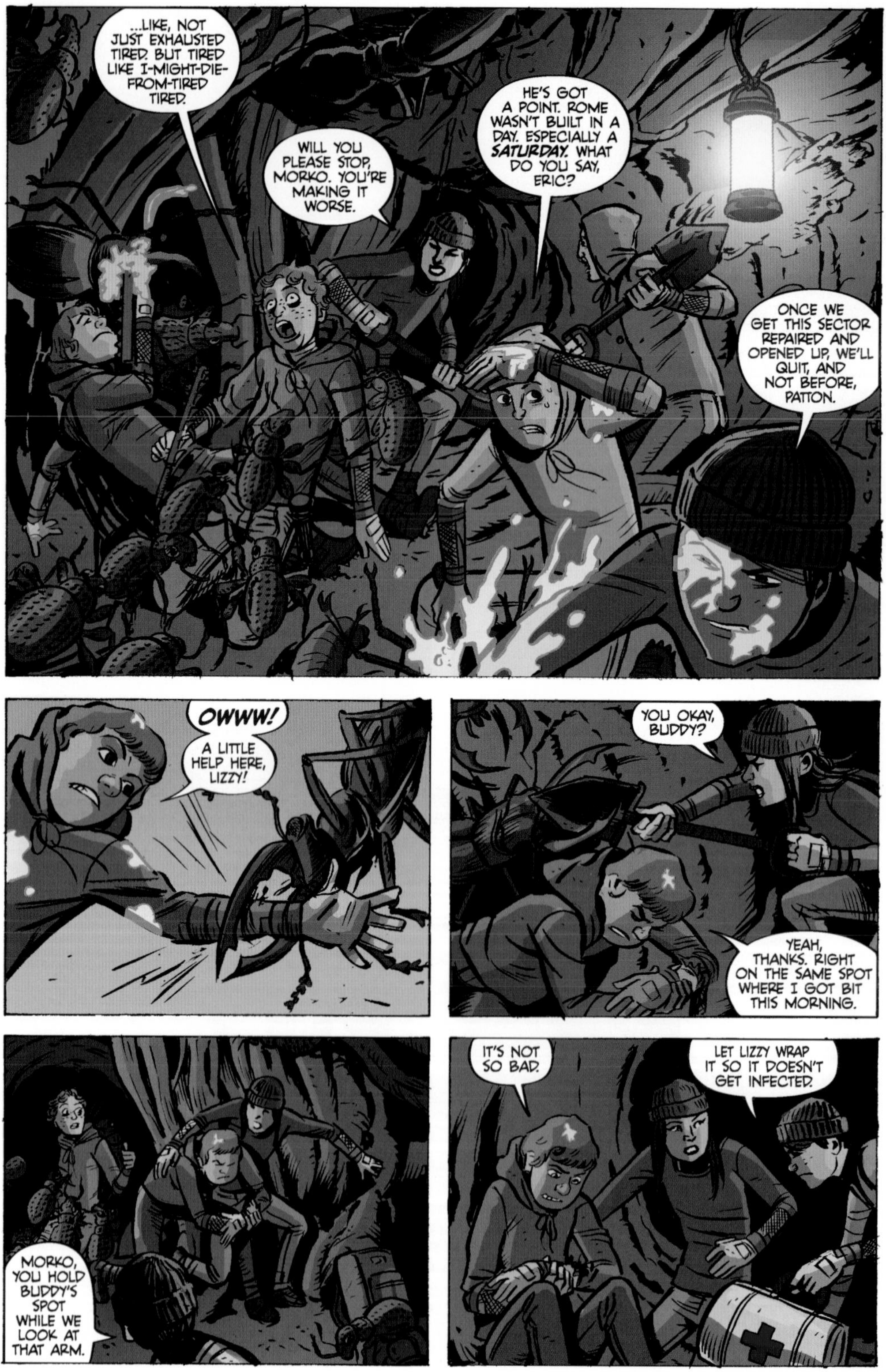
...LIKE, NOT JUST EXHAUSTED TIRED. BUT TIRED LIKE I-MIGHT-DIE-FROM-TIRED TIRED.
WILL YOU PLEASE STOP, MORKO. YOU'RE MAKING IT WORSE.
HE'S GOT A POINT. ROME WASN'T BUILT IN A DAY. ESPECIALLY A SATURDAY. WHAT DO YOU SAY, ERIC?
ONCE WE GET THIS SECTOR REPAIRED AND OPENED UP, WE'LL QUIT, AND NOT BEFORE, PATTON.
OWWW!
A LITTLE HELP HERE, LIZZY!
YOU OKAY, BUDDY?
YEAH, THANKS. RIGHT ON THE SAME SPOT WHERE I GOT BIT THIS MORNING.
MORKO, YOU HOLD BUDDY'S SPOT WHILE WE LOOK AT THAT ARM.
IT'S NOT SO BAD.
LET LIZZY WRAP IT SO IT DOESN'T GET INFECTED.

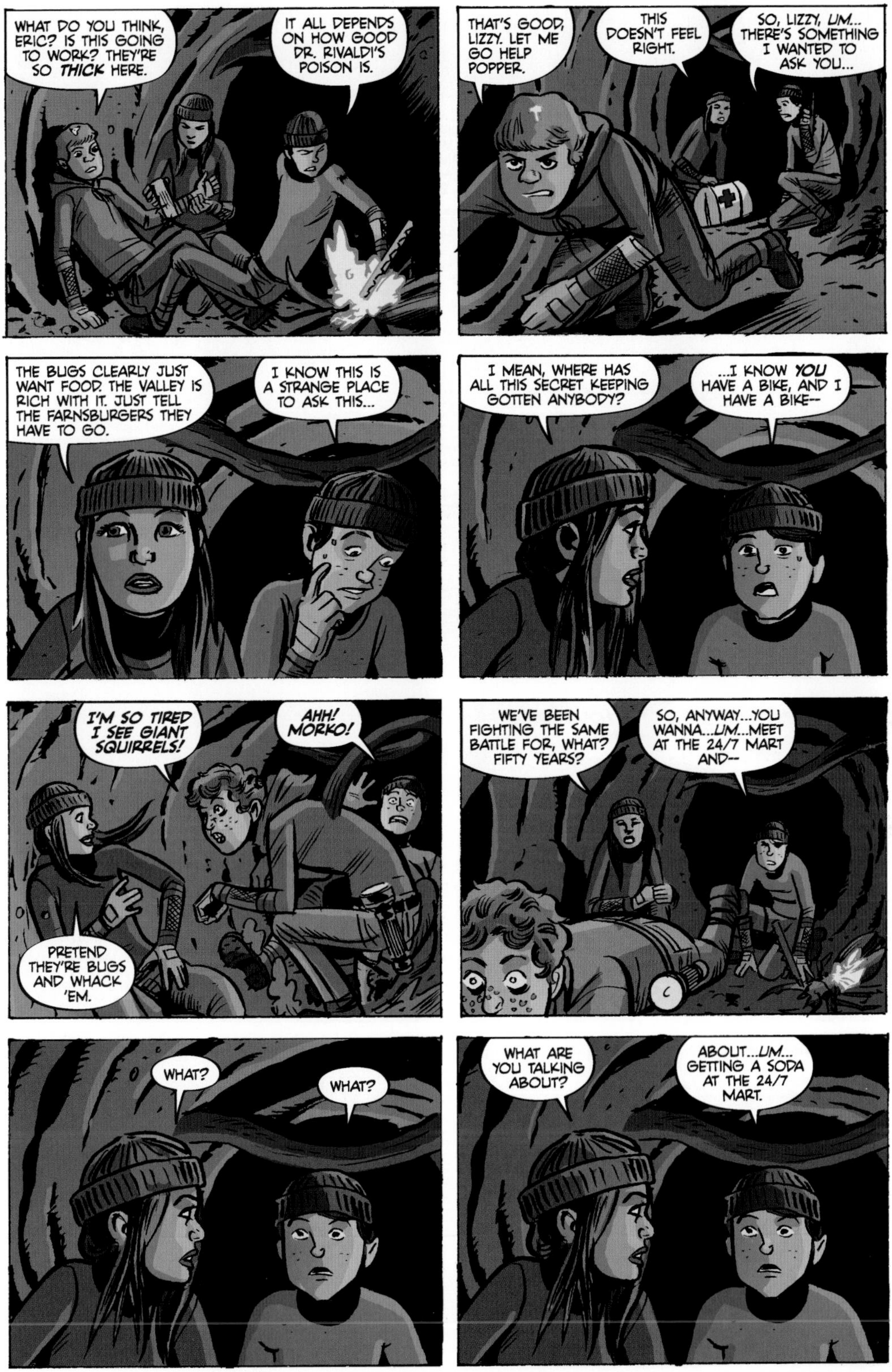
WHAT DO YOU THINK, ERIC? IS THIS GOING TO WORK? THEY'RE SO *THICK* HERE.
IT ALL DEPENDS ON HOW GOOD DR. RIVALDI'S POISON IS.
THAT'S GOOD, LIZZY. LET ME GO HELP POPPER.
THIS DOESN'T FEEL RIGHT.
SO, LIZZY, *UM*... THERE'S SOMETHING I WANTED TO ASK YOU...
THE BUGS CLEARLY JUST WANT FOOD. THE VALLEY IS RICH WITH IT. JUST TELL THE FARNSBURGERS THEY HAVE TO GO.
I KNOW THIS IS A STRANGE PLACE TO ASK THIS...
I MEAN, WHERE HAS ALL THIS SECRET KEEPING GOTTEN ANYBODY?
...I KNOW *YOU* HAVE A BIKE, AND I HAVE A BIKE--
I'M SO TIRED I SEE GIANT SQUIRRELS!
AHH! MORKO!
PRETEND THEY'RE BUGS AND WHACK 'EM.
WE'VE BEEN FIGHTING THE SAME BATTLE FOR, WHAT? FIFTY YEARS?
SO, ANYWAY...YOU WANNA...*UM*...MEET AT THE 24/7 MART AND--
WHAT?
WHAT?
WHAT ARE YOU TALKING ABOUT?
ABOUT...*UM*... GETTING A SODA AT THE 24/7 MART.

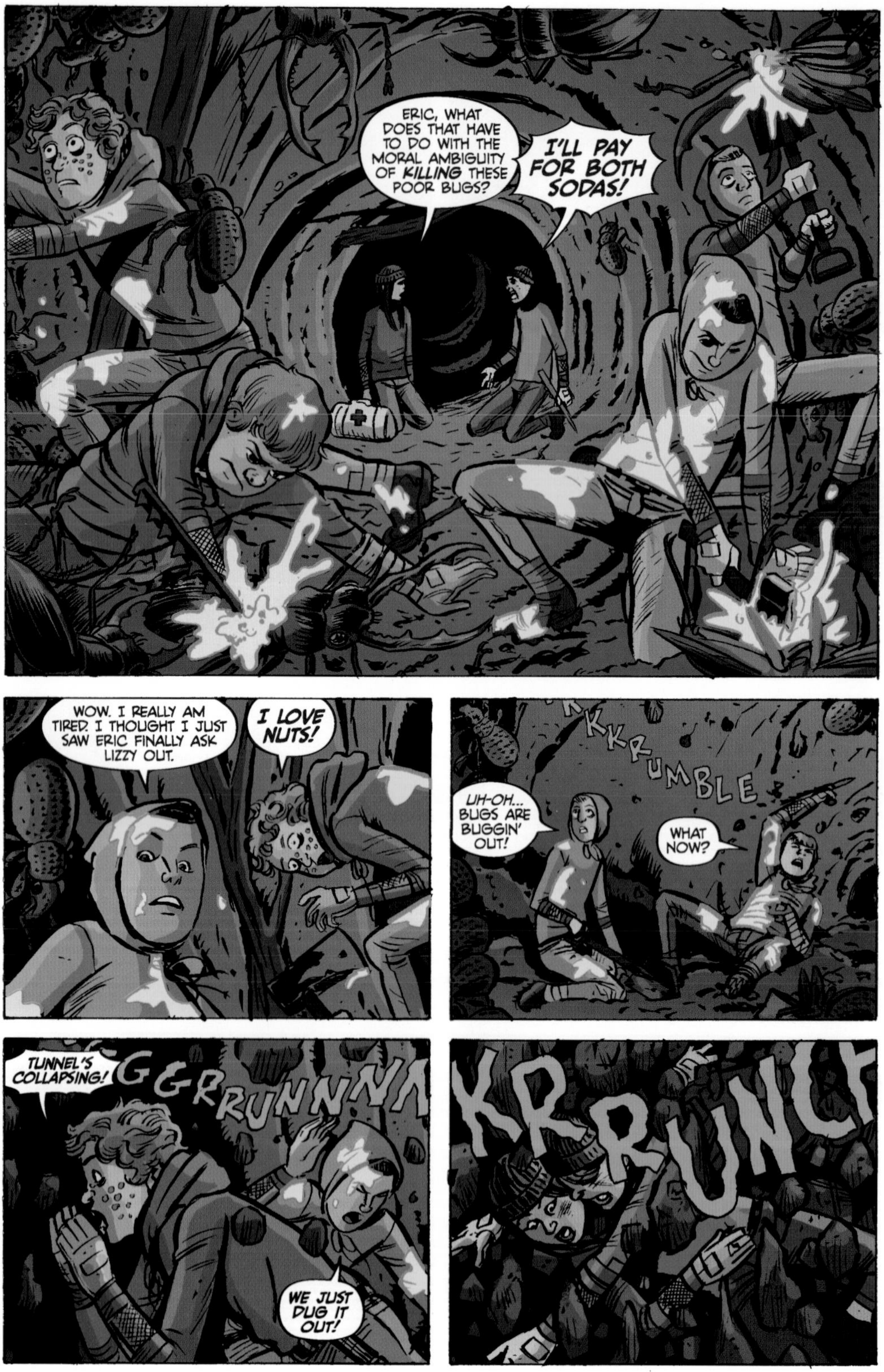
ERIC, WHAT DOES THAT HAVE TO DO WITH THE MORAL AMBIGUITY OF *KILLING* THESE POOR BUGS?
I'LL PAY FOR BOTH SODAS!
WOW. I REALLY AM TIRED. I THOUGHT I JUST SAW ERIC FINALLY ASK LIZZY OUT.
I LOVE NUTS!
KKRUMBLE
UH-OH... BUGS ARE BUGGIN' OUT!
WHAT NOW?
TUNNEL'S COLLAPSING!
GGRRUNNNN
WE JUST DUG IT OUT!
KRRUNC

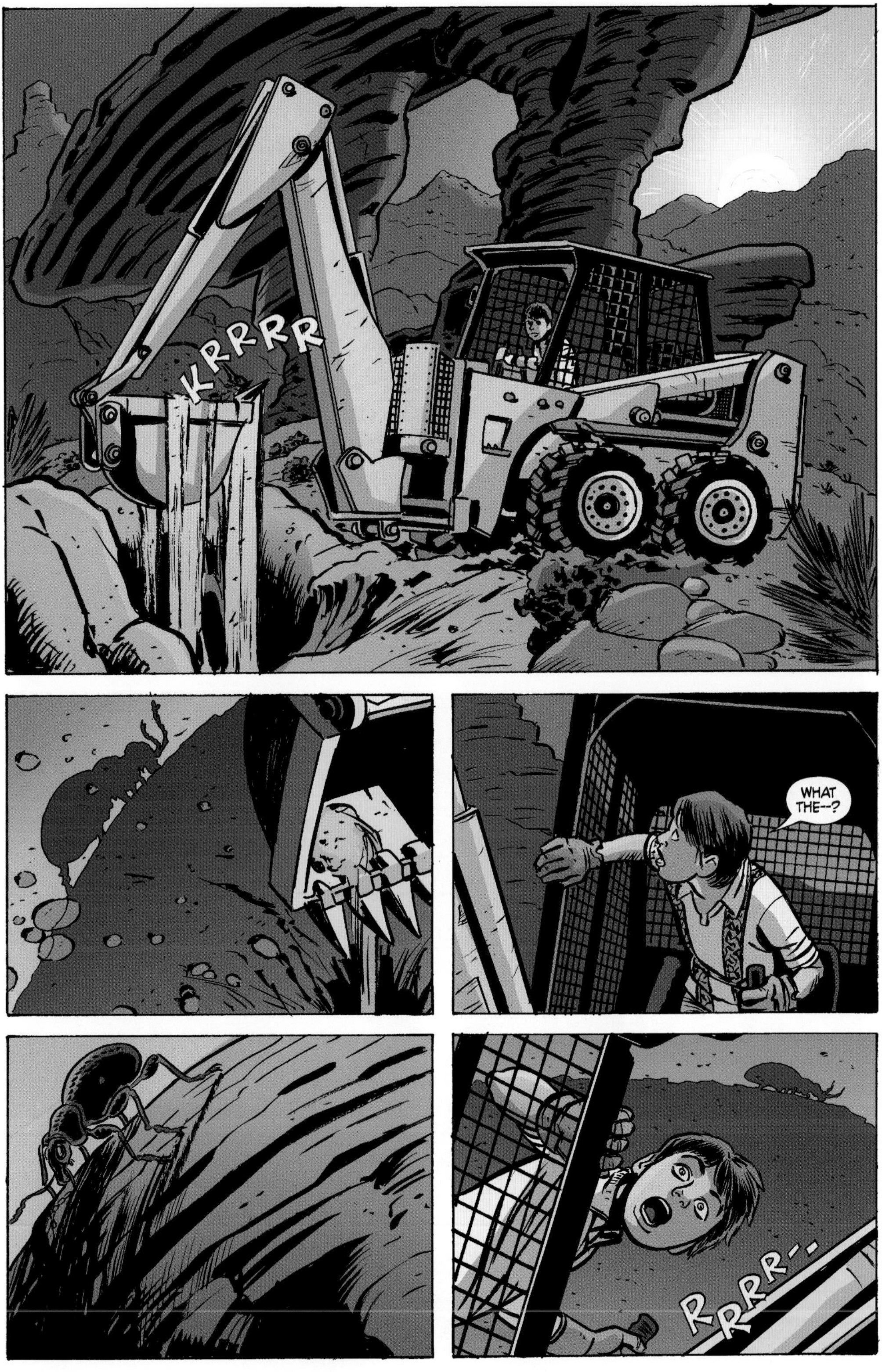
KRRRR
WHAT THE--?
RRRR--

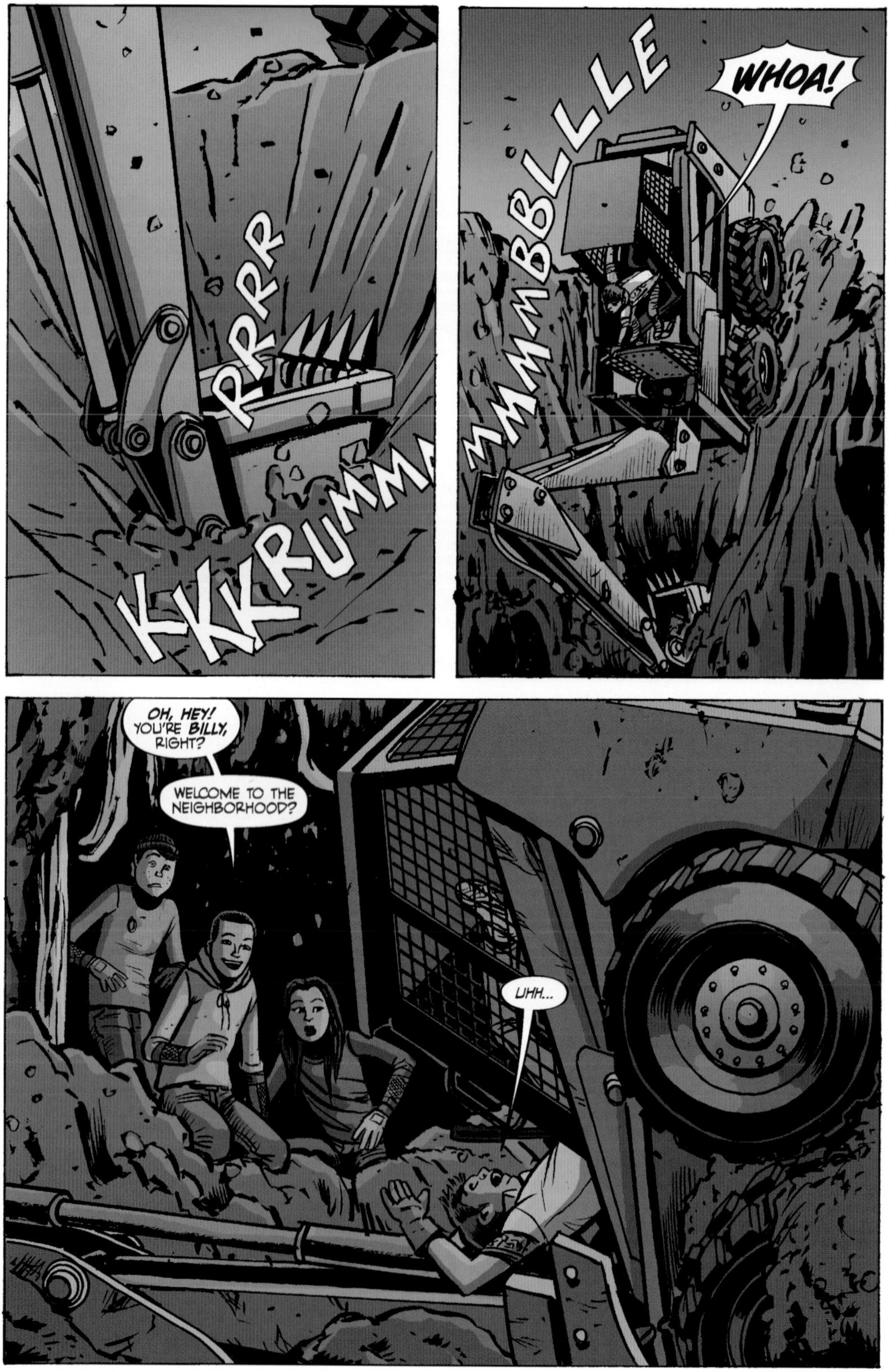
RRRR
KKRUMMM
MMMMMBBLLLE
WHOA!
OH, HEY! YOU'RE BILLY, RIGHT?
WELCOME TO THE NEIGHBORHOOD?
UHH...

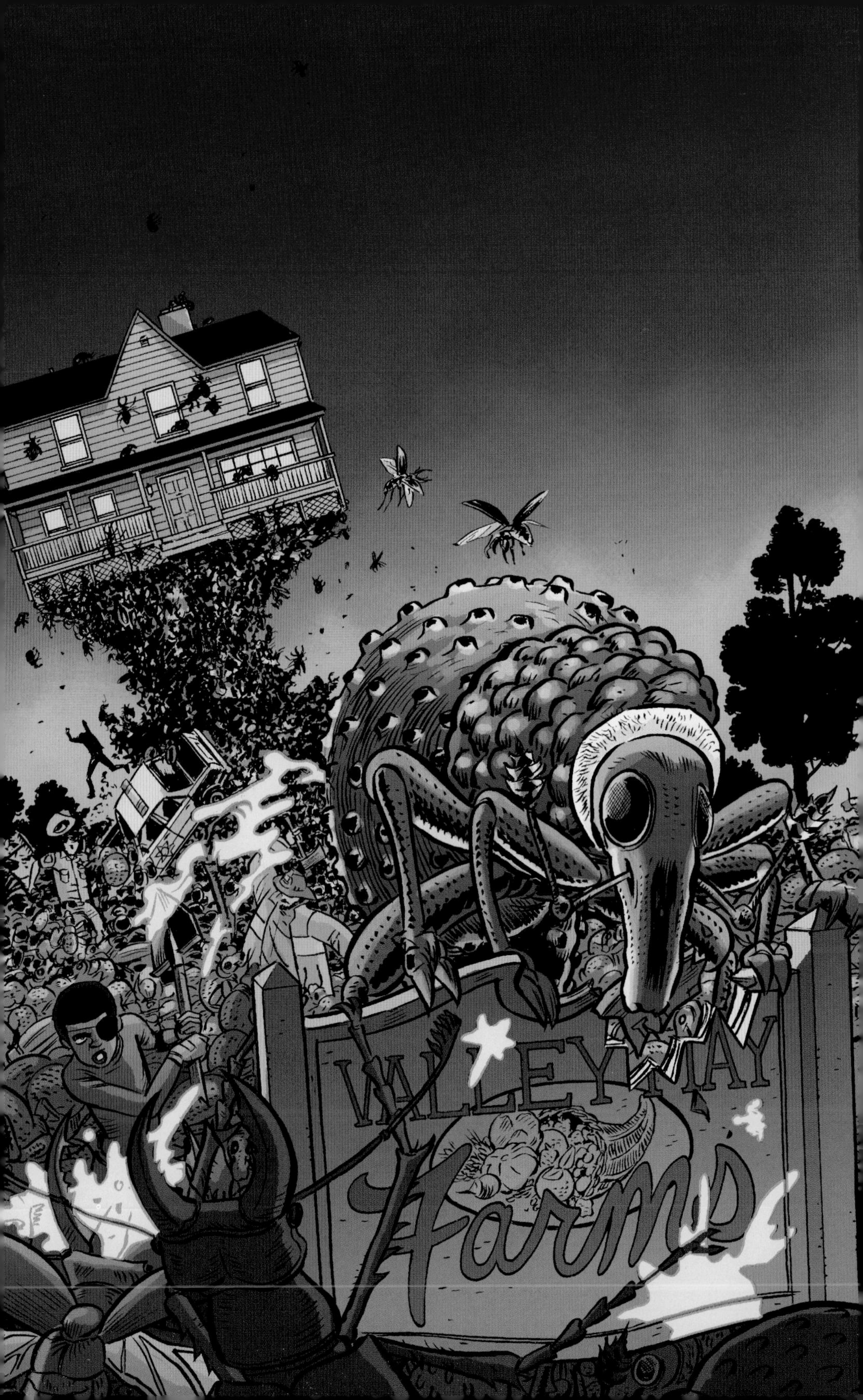
VALLEY MAY
Farms

THE GREAT BUG ELEVATOR

PART TWO:

THE BUG WHO CAME IN FROM THE COLD

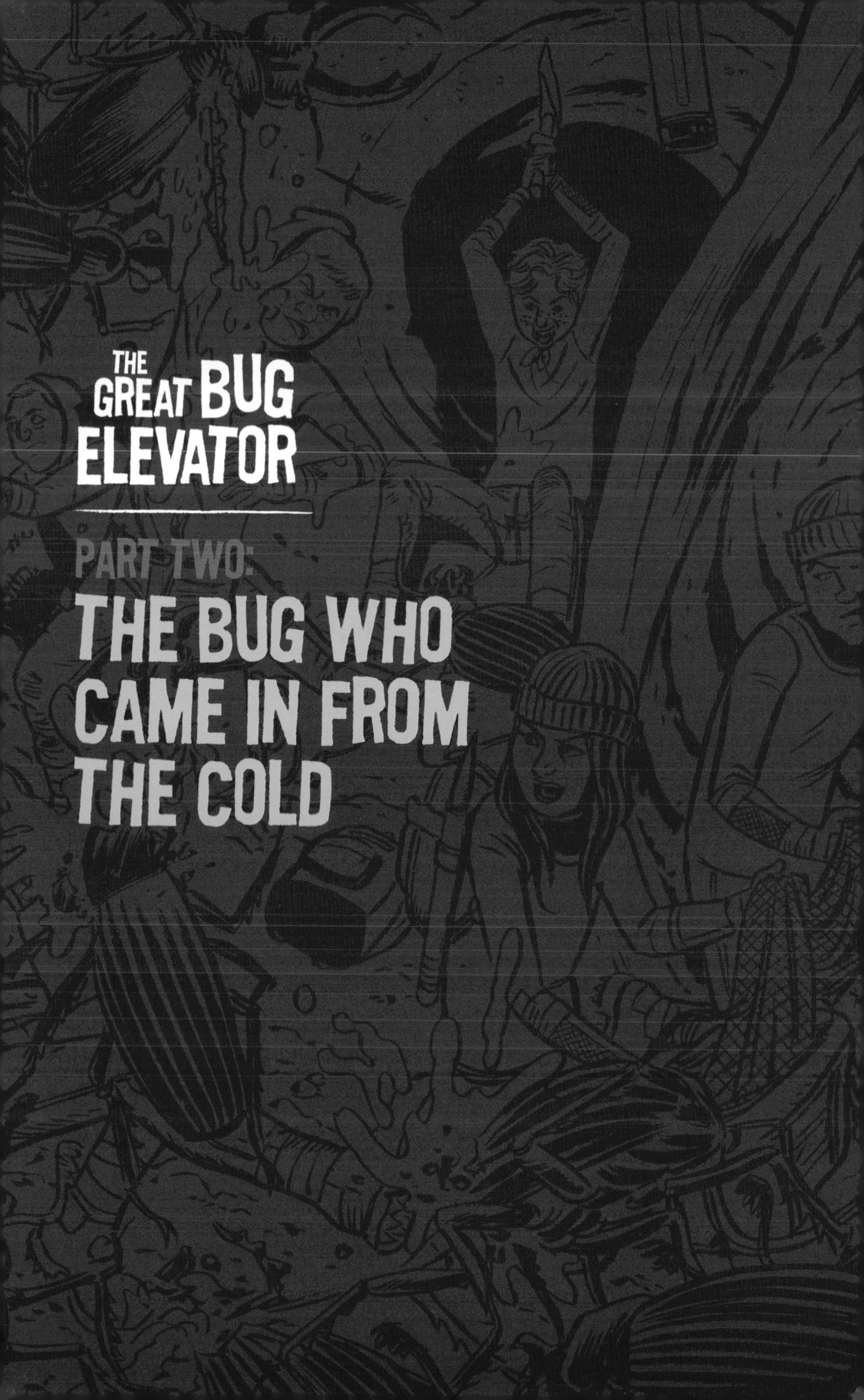

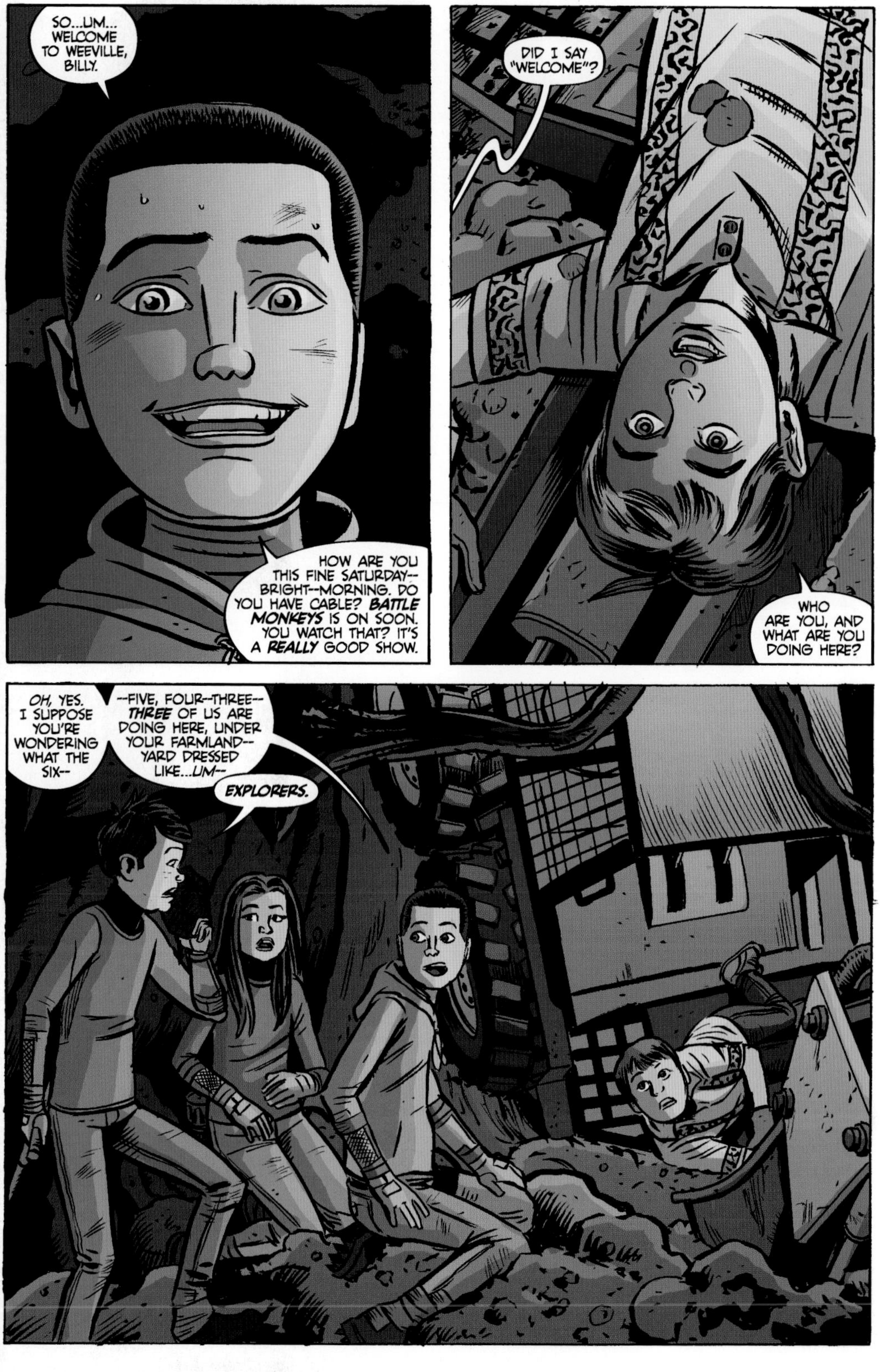
SO...UM... WELCOME TO WEEVILLE, BILLY.
HOW ARE YOU THIS FINE SATURDAY--BRIGHT--MORNING. DO YOU HAVE CABLE? BATTLE MONKEYS IS ON SOON. YOU WATCH THAT? IT'S A REALLY GOOD SHOW.
DID I SAY "WELCOME"?
WHO ARE YOU, AND WHAT ARE YOU DOING HERE?
OH, YES. I SUPPOSE YOU'RE WONDERING WHAT THE SIX--
--FIVE, FOUR--THREE--THREE OF US ARE DOING HERE, UNDER YOUR FARMLAND--YARD DRESSED LIKE...UM--
EXPLORERS.

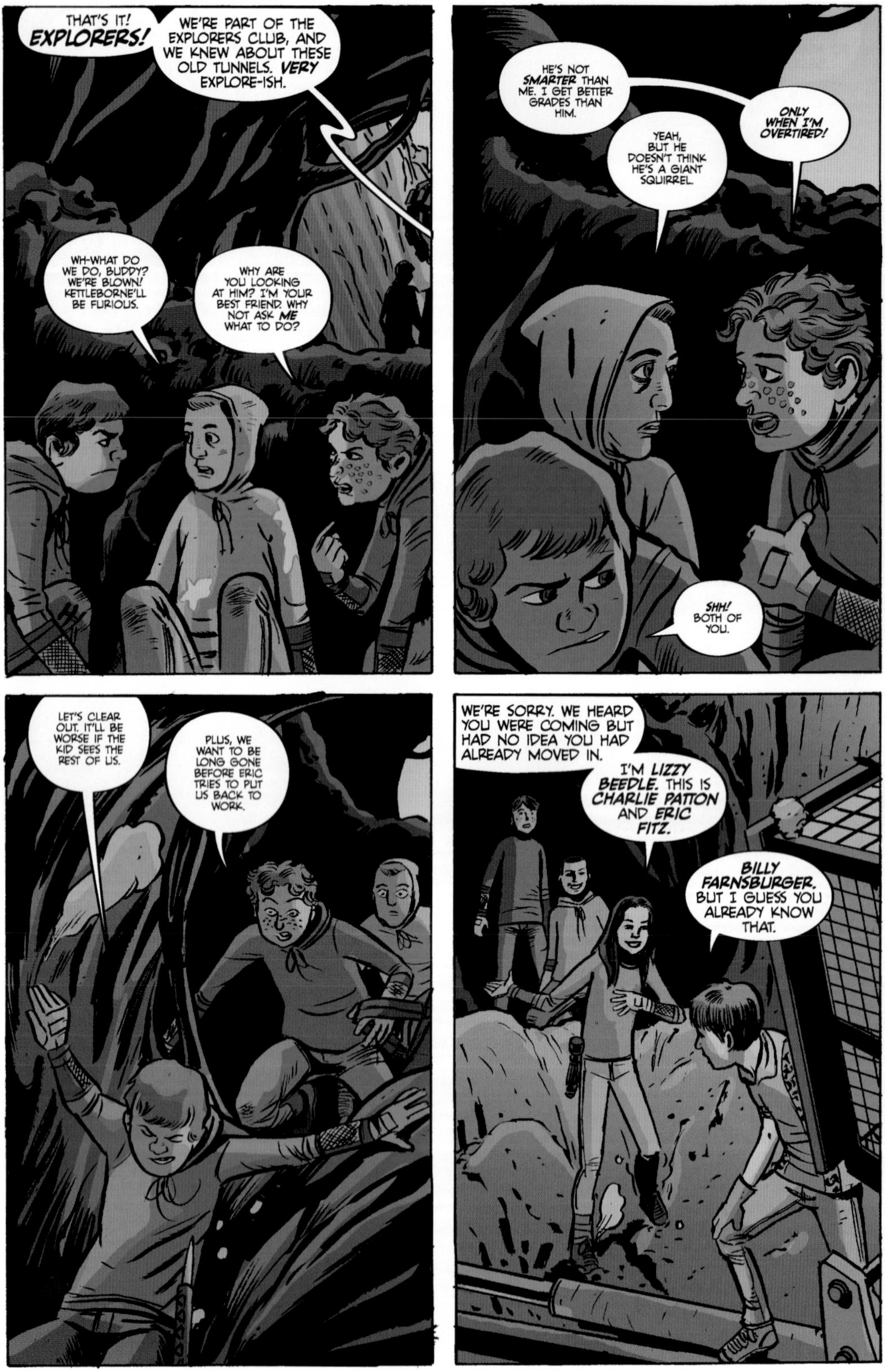
THAT'S IT! EXPLORERS!
WE'RE PART OF THE EXPLORERS CLUB, AND WE KNEW ABOUT THESE OLD TUNNELS. VERY EXPLORE-ISH.
WH-WHAT DO WE DO, BUDDY? WE'RE BLOWN! KETTLEBORNE'LL BE FURIOUS.
WHY ARE YOU LOOKING AT HIM? I'M YOUR BEST FRIEND. WHY NOT ASK ME WHAT TO DO?
HE'S NOT SMARTER THAN ME. I GET BETTER GRADES THAN HIM.
YEAH, BUT HE DOESN'T THINK HE'S A GIANT SQUIRREL.
ONLY WHEN I'M OVERTIRED!
SHH! BOTH OF YOU.
LET'S CLEAR OUT. IT'LL BE WORSE IF THE KID SEES THE REST OF US.
PLUS, WE WANT TO BE LONG GONE BEFORE ERIC TRIES TO PUT US BACK TO WORK.
WE'RE SORRY. WE HEARD YOU WERE COMING BUT HAD NO IDEA YOU HAD ALREADY MOVED IN.
I'M LIZZY BEEDLE. THIS IS CHARLIE PATTON AND ERIC FITZ.
BILLY FARNSBURGER. BUT I GUESS YOU ALREADY KNOW THAT.

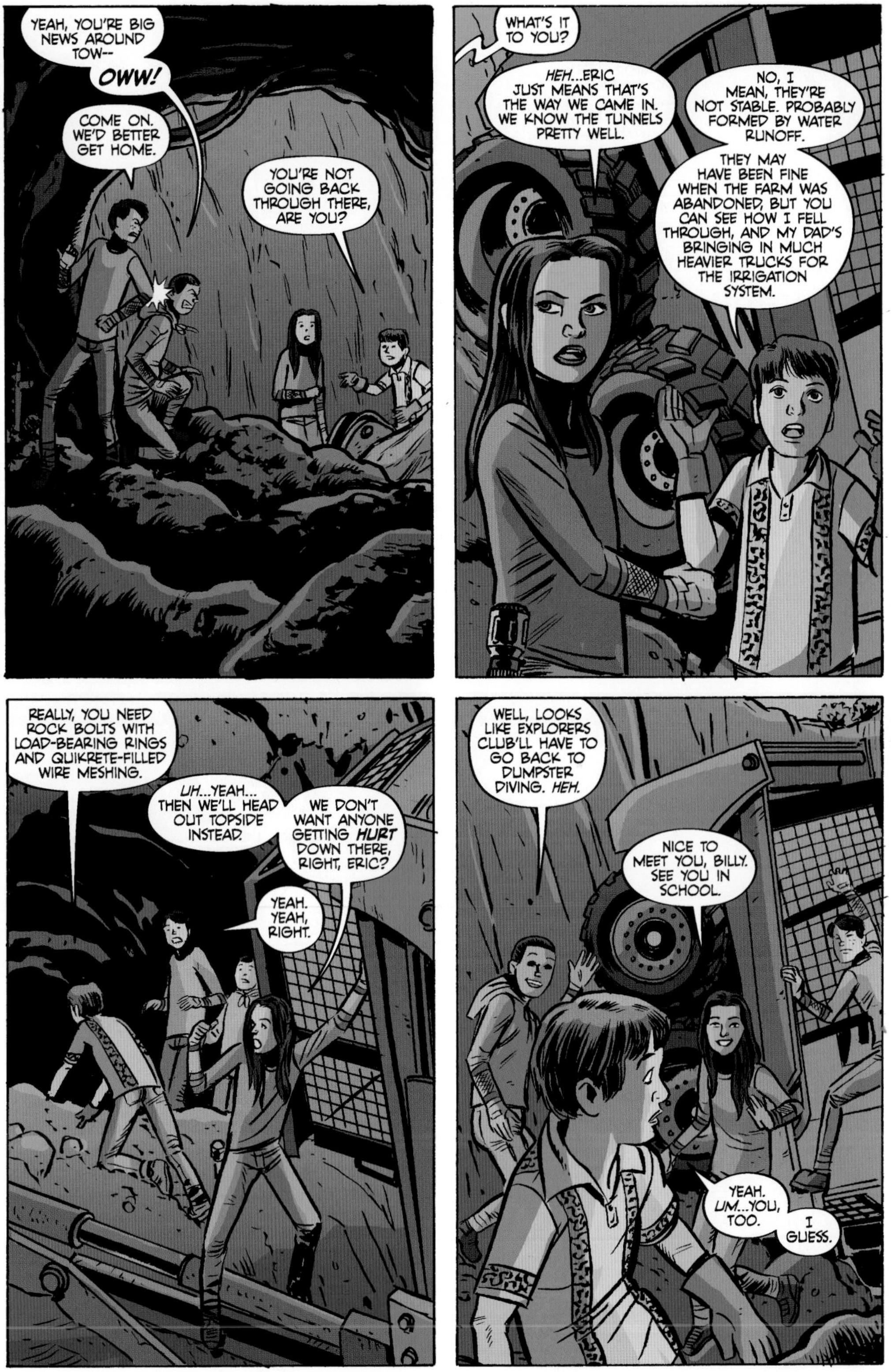
YEAH, YOU'RE BIG NEWS AROUND TOW--
OWW!
COME ON. WE'D BETTER GET HOME.
YOU'RE NOT GOING BACK THROUGH THERE, ARE YOU?
WHAT'S IT TO YOU?
HEH...ERIC JUST MEANS THAT'S THE WAY WE CAME IN. WE KNOW THE TUNNELS PRETTY WELL.
NO, I MEAN, THEY'RE NOT STABLE. PROBABLY FORMED BY WATER RUNOFF.
THEY MAY HAVE BEEN FINE WHEN THE FARM WAS ABANDONED, BUT YOU CAN SEE HOW I FELL THROUGH, AND MY DAD'S BRINGING IN MUCH HEAVIER TRUCKS FOR THE IRRIGATION SYSTEM.
REALLY, YOU NEED ROCK BOLTS WITH LOAD-BEARING RINGS AND QUIKRETE-FILLED WIRE MESHING.
UH...YEAH... THEN WE'LL HEAD OUT TOPSIDE INSTEAD.
WE DON'T WANT ANYONE GETTING HURT DOWN THERE, RIGHT, ERIC?
YEAH. YEAH, RIGHT.
WELL, LOOKS LIKE EXPLORERS CLUB'LL HAVE TO GO BACK TO DUMPSTER DIVING. HEH.
NICE TO MEET YOU, BILLY. SEE YOU IN SCHOOL.
YEAH. UM...YOU, TOO.
I GUESS.

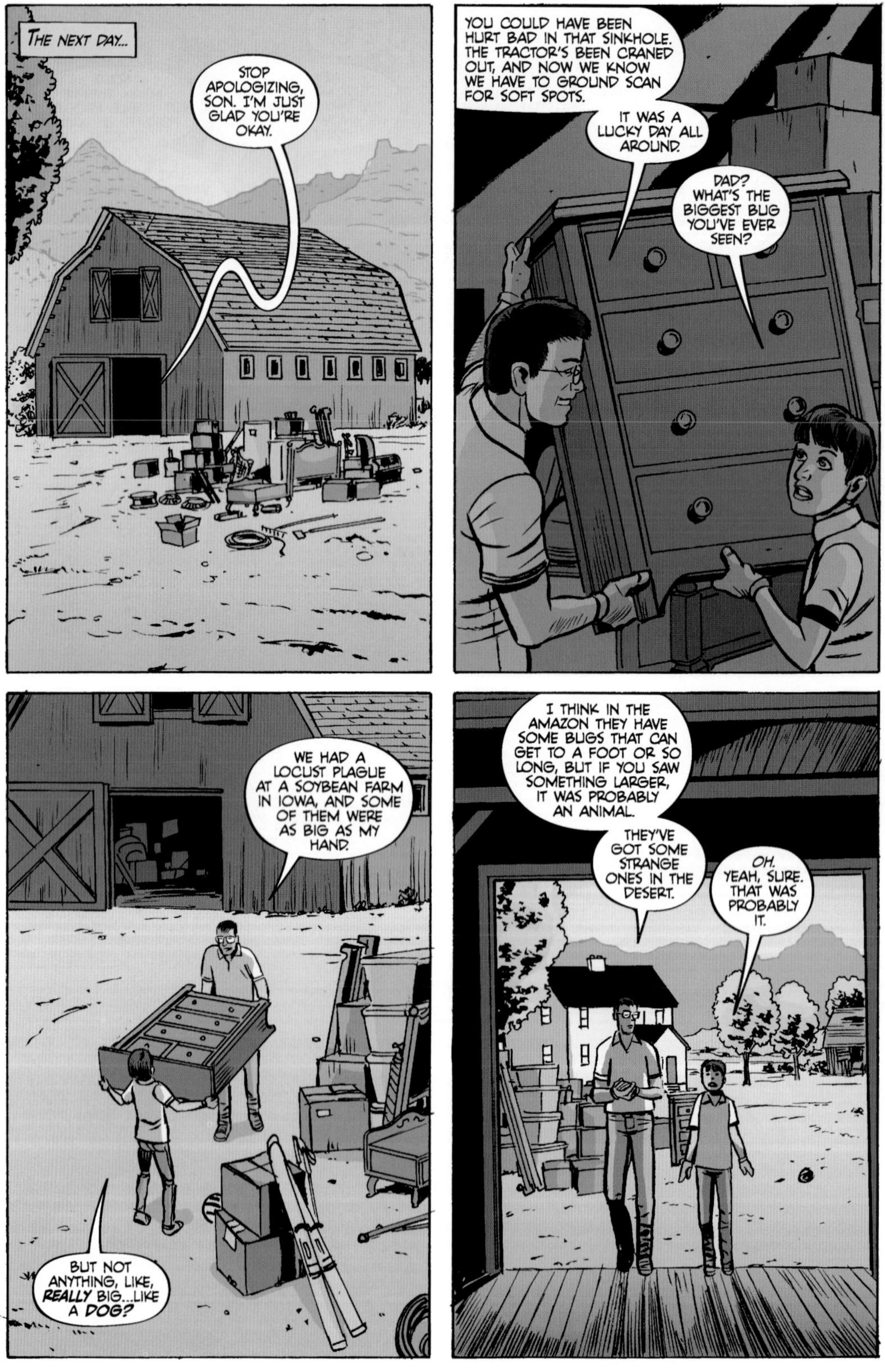
THE NEXT DAY...
STOP APOLOGIZING, SON. I'M JUST GLAD YOU'RE OKAY.
YOU COULD HAVE BEEN HURT BAD IN THAT SINKHOLE. THE TRACTOR'S BEEN CRANED OUT, AND NOW WE KNOW WE HAVE TO GROUND SCAN FOR SOFT SPOTS.
IT WAS A LUCKY DAY ALL AROUND.
DAD? WHAT'S THE BIGGEST BUG YOU'VE EVER SEEN?
WE HAD A LOCUST PLAGUE AT A SOYBEAN FARM IN IOWA, AND SOME OF THEM WERE AS BIG AS MY HAND.
BUT NOT ANYTHING, LIKE, *REALLY* BIG...LIKE A *DOG?*
I THINK IN THE AMAZON THEY HAVE SOME BUGS THAT CAN GET TO A FOOT OR SO LONG, BUT IF YOU SAW SOMETHING LARGER, IT WAS PROBABLY AN ANIMAL.
THEY'VE GOT SOME STRANGE ONES IN THE DESERT.
OH. YEAH, SURE. THAT WAS PROBABLY IT.

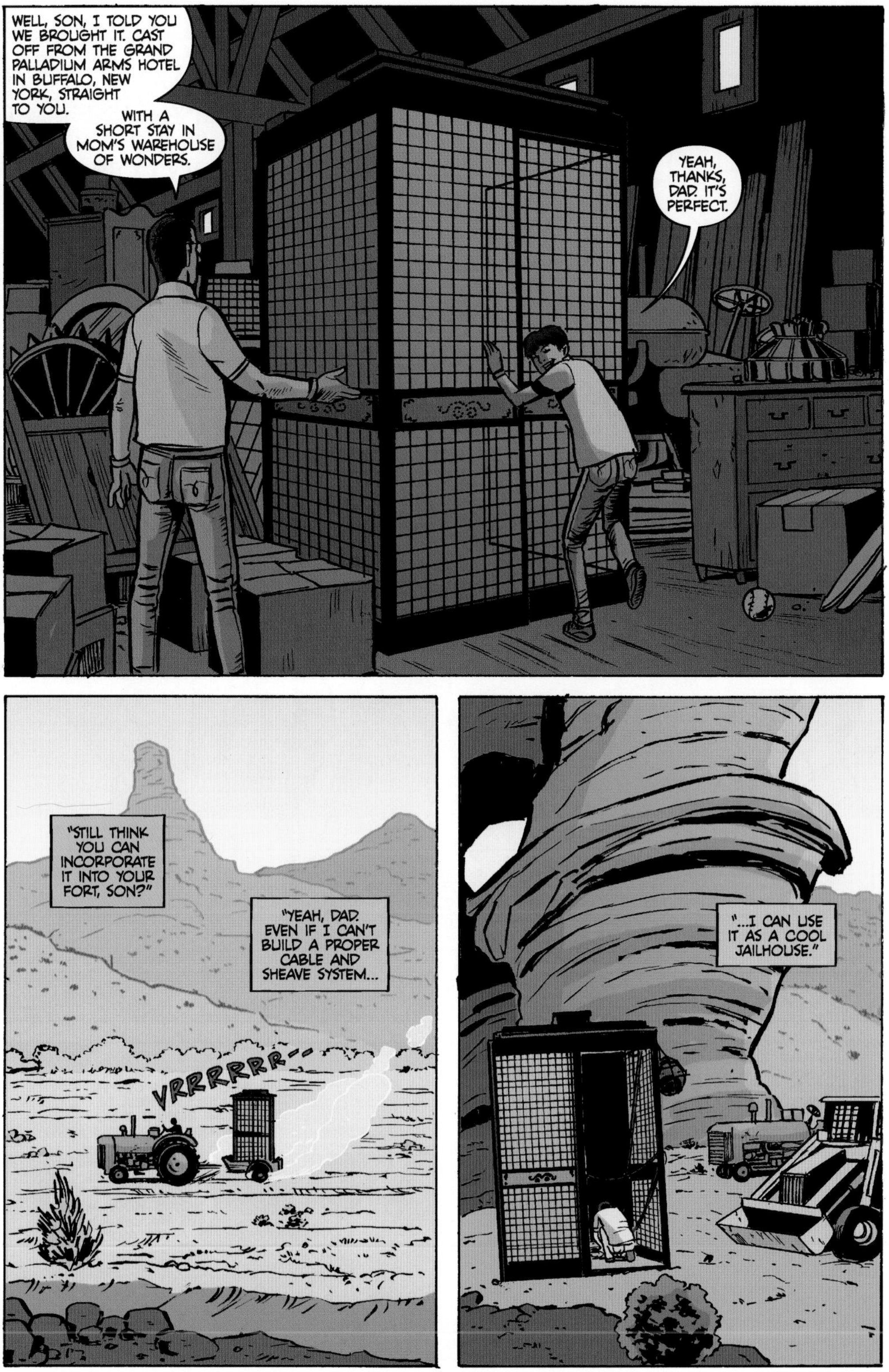
WELL, SON, I TOLD YOU WE BROUGHT IT. CAST OFF FROM THE GRAND PALLADIUM ARMS HOTEL IN BUFFALO, NEW YORK, STRAIGHT TO YOU.
WITH A SHORT STAY IN MOM'S WAREHOUSE OF WONDERS.
YEAH, THANKS, DAD. IT'S PERFECT.
"STILL THINK YOU CAN INCORPORATE IT INTO YOUR FORT, SON?"
"YEAH, DAD. EVEN IF I CAN'T BUILD A PROPER CABLE AND SHEAVE SYSTEM...
VRRRRRR--
"...I CAN USE IT AS A COOL JAILHOUSE."

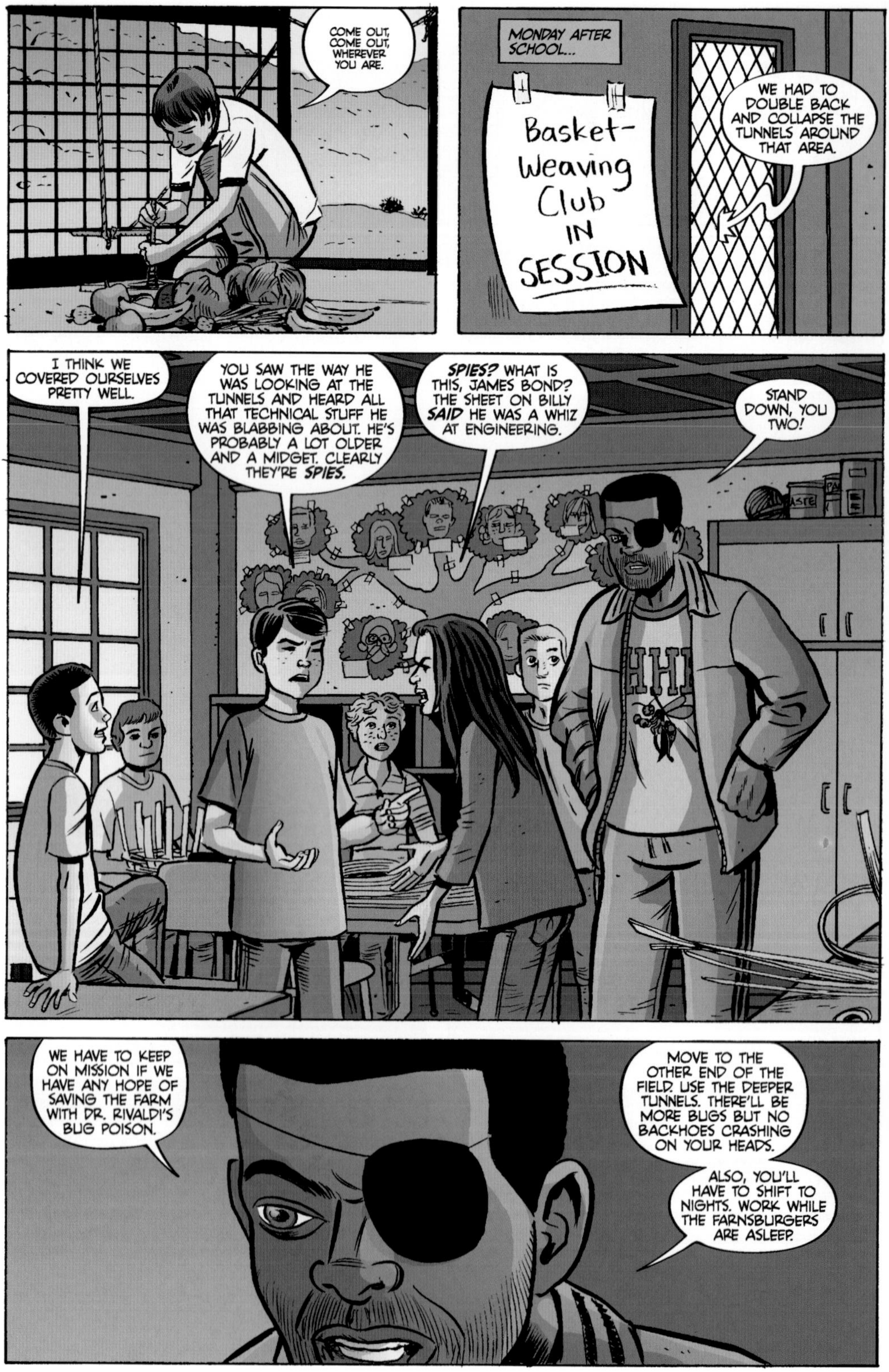
COME OUT, COME OUT, WHEREVER YOU ARE.
MONDAY AFTER SCHOOL...
Basket-Weaving Club IN SESSION
WE HAD TO DOUBLE BACK AND COLLAPSE THE TUNNELS AROUND THAT AREA.
I THINK WE COVERED OURSELVES PRETTY WELL.
YOU SAW THE WAY HE WAS LOOKING AT THE TUNNELS AND HEARD ALL THAT TECHNICAL STUFF HE WAS BLABBING ABOUT. HE'S PROBABLY A LOT OLDER AND A MIDGET. CLEARLY THEY'RE SPIES.
SPIES? WHAT IS THIS, JAMES BOND? THE SHEET ON BILLY SAID HE WAS A WHIZ AT ENGINEERING.
STAND DOWN, YOU TWO!
WE HAVE TO KEEP ON MISSION IF WE HAVE ANY HOPE OF SAVING THE FARM WITH DR. RIVALDI'S BUG POISON.
MOVE TO THE OTHER END OF THE FIELD. USE THE DEEPER TUNNELS. THERE'LL BE MORE BUGS BUT NO BACKHOES CRASHING ON YOUR HEADS.
ALSO, YOU'LL HAVE TO SHIFT TO NIGHTS. WORK WHILE THE FARNSBURGERS ARE ASLEEP.

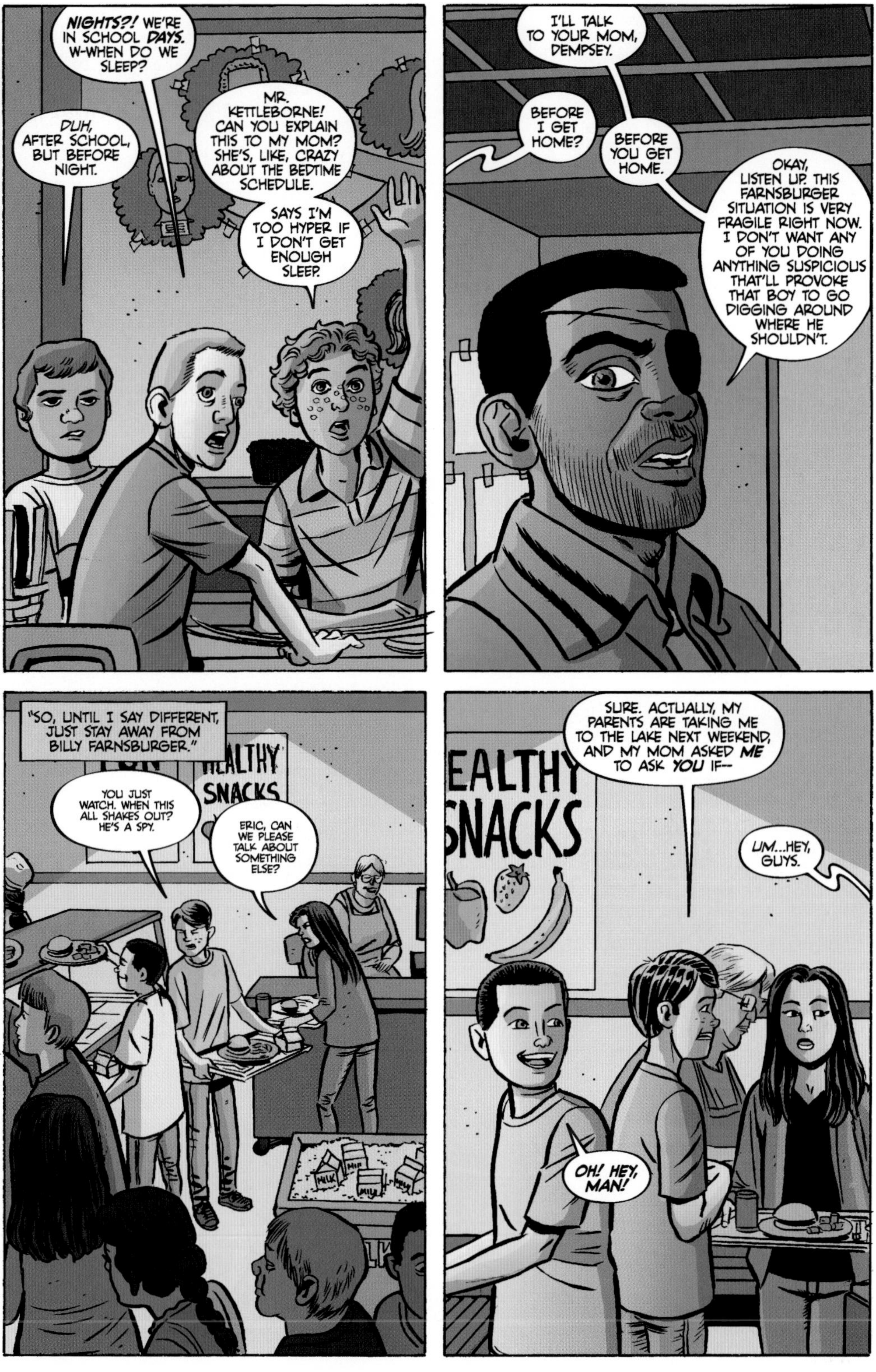

NIGHTS?! WE'RE IN SCHOOL DAYS. W-WHEN DO WE SLEEP?
DUH, AFTER SCHOOL, BUT BEFORE NIGHT.
MR. KETTLEBORNE! CAN YOU EXPLAIN THIS TO MY MOM? SHE'S, LIKE, CRAZY ABOUT THE BEDTIME SCHEDULE.
SAYS I'M TOO HYPER IF I DON'T GET ENOUGH SLEEP.
I'LL TALK TO YOUR MOM, DEMPSEY.
BEFORE I GET HOME?
BEFORE YOU GET HOME.
OKAY, LISTEN UP. THIS FARNSBURGER SITUATION IS VERY FRAGILE RIGHT NOW. I DON'T WANT ANY OF YOU DOING ANYTHING SUSPICIOUS THAT'LL PROVOKE THAT BOY TO GO DIGGING AROUND WHERE HE SHOULDN'T.
"SO, UNTIL I SAY DIFFERENT, JUST STAY AWAY FROM BILLY FARNSBURGER."
YOU JUST WATCH. WHEN THIS ALL SHAKES OUT? HE'S A SPY.
ERIC, CAN WE PLEASE TALK ABOUT SOMETHING ELSE?
SURE. ACTUALLY, MY PARENTS ARE TAKING ME TO THE LAKE NEXT WEEKEND, AND MY MOM ASKED ME TO ASK YOU IF--
UM...HEY, GUYS.
OH! HEY, MAN!

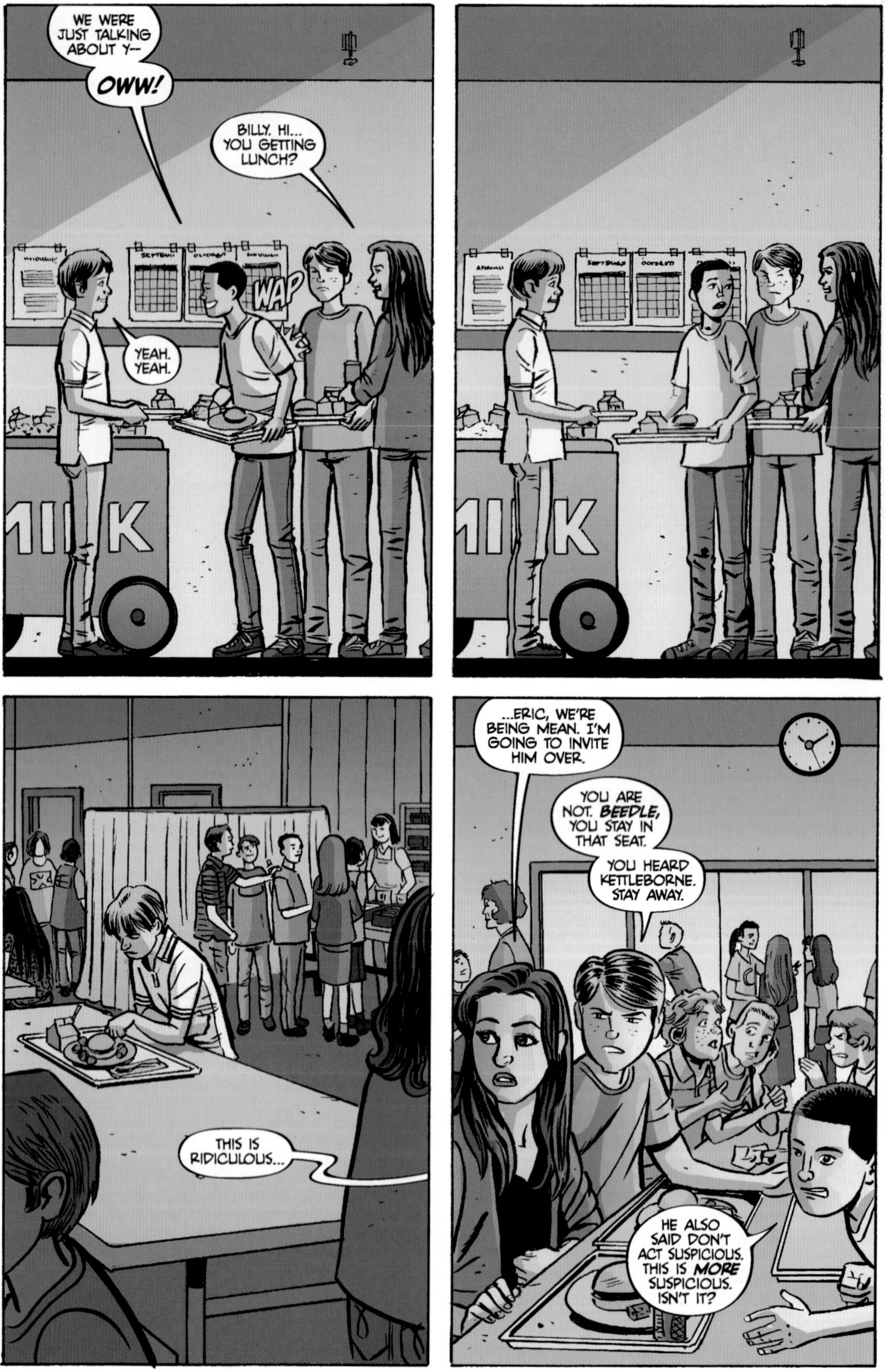

WE WERE JUST TALKING ABOUT Y--
OWW!
BILLY. HI... YOU GETTING LUNCH?
WAP
YEAH. YEAH.
MILK
MILK
THIS IS RIDICULOUS...
...ERIC, WE'RE BEING MEAN. I'M GOING TO INVITE HIM OVER.
YOU ARE NOT. BEEDLE, YOU STAY IN THAT SEAT.
YOU HEARD KETTLEBORNE. STAY AWAY.
HE ALSO SAID DON'T ACT SUSPICIOUS. THIS IS MORE SUSPICIOUS. ISN'T IT?

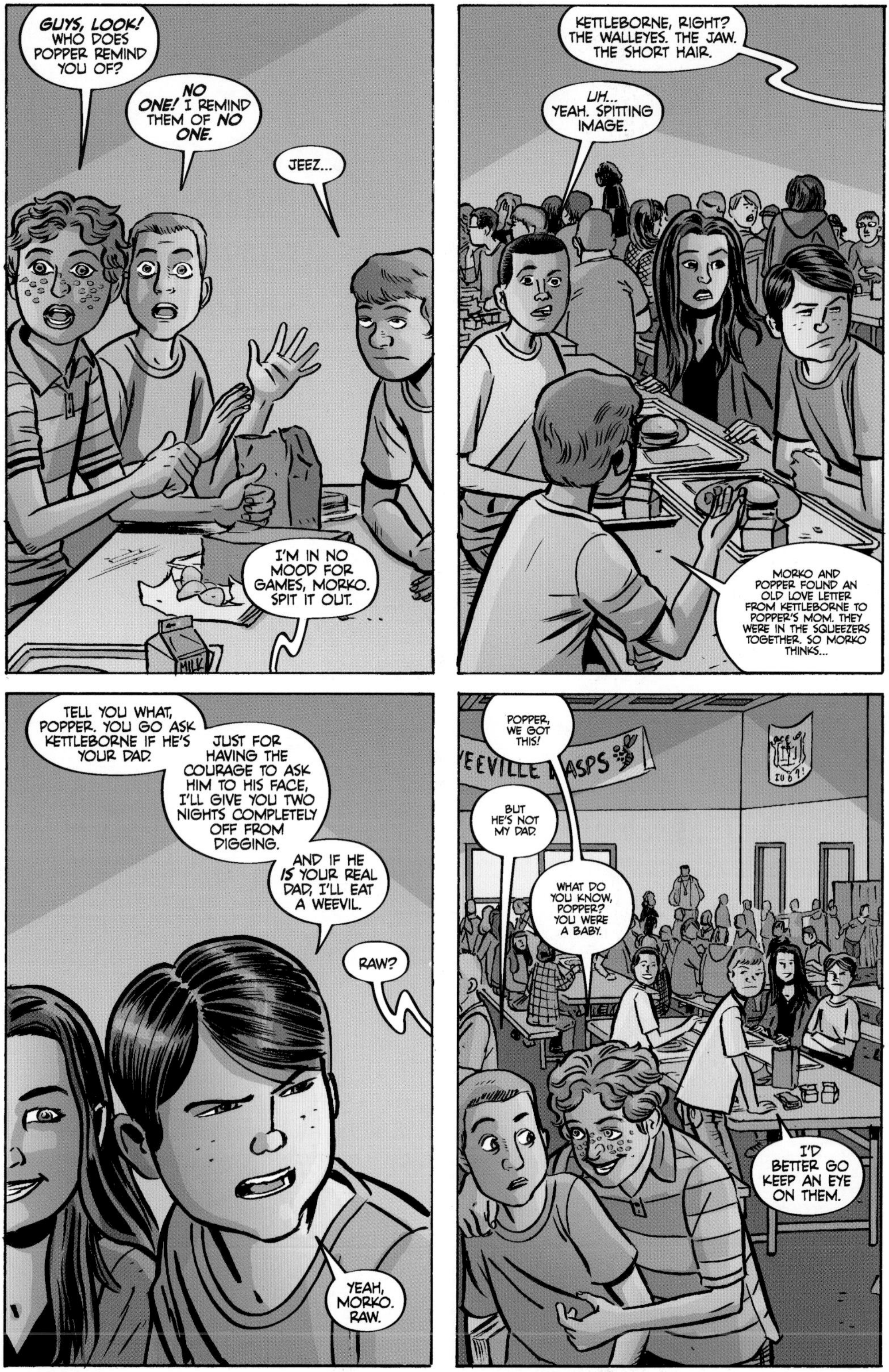
GUYS, LOOK! WHO DOES POPPER REMIND YOU OF?
NO ONE! I REMIND THEM OF NO ONE.
JEEZ...
I'M IN NO MOOD FOR GAMES, MORKO. SPIT IT OUT.
MILK
KETTLEBORNE, RIGHT? THE WALLEYES. THE JAW. THE SHORT HAIR.
UH... YEAH. SPITTING IMAGE.
MORKO AND POPPER FOUND AN OLD LOVE LETTER FROM KETTLEBORNE TO POPPER'S MOM. THEY WERE IN THE SQUEEZERS TOGETHER. SO MORKO THINKS...
TELL YOU WHAT, POPPER. YOU GO ASK KETTLEBORNE IF HE'S YOUR DAD.
JUST FOR HAVING THE COURAGE TO ASK HIM TO HIS FACE, I'LL GIVE YOU TWO NIGHTS COMPLETELY OFF FROM DIGGING.
AND IF HE IS YOUR REAL DAD, I'LL EAT A WEEVIL.
RAW?
YEAH, MORKO. RAW.
POPPER, WE GOT THIS!
BUT HE'S NOT MY DAD.
WHAT DO YOU KNOW, POPPER? YOU WERE A BABY.
I'D BETTER GO KEEP AN EYE ON THEM.

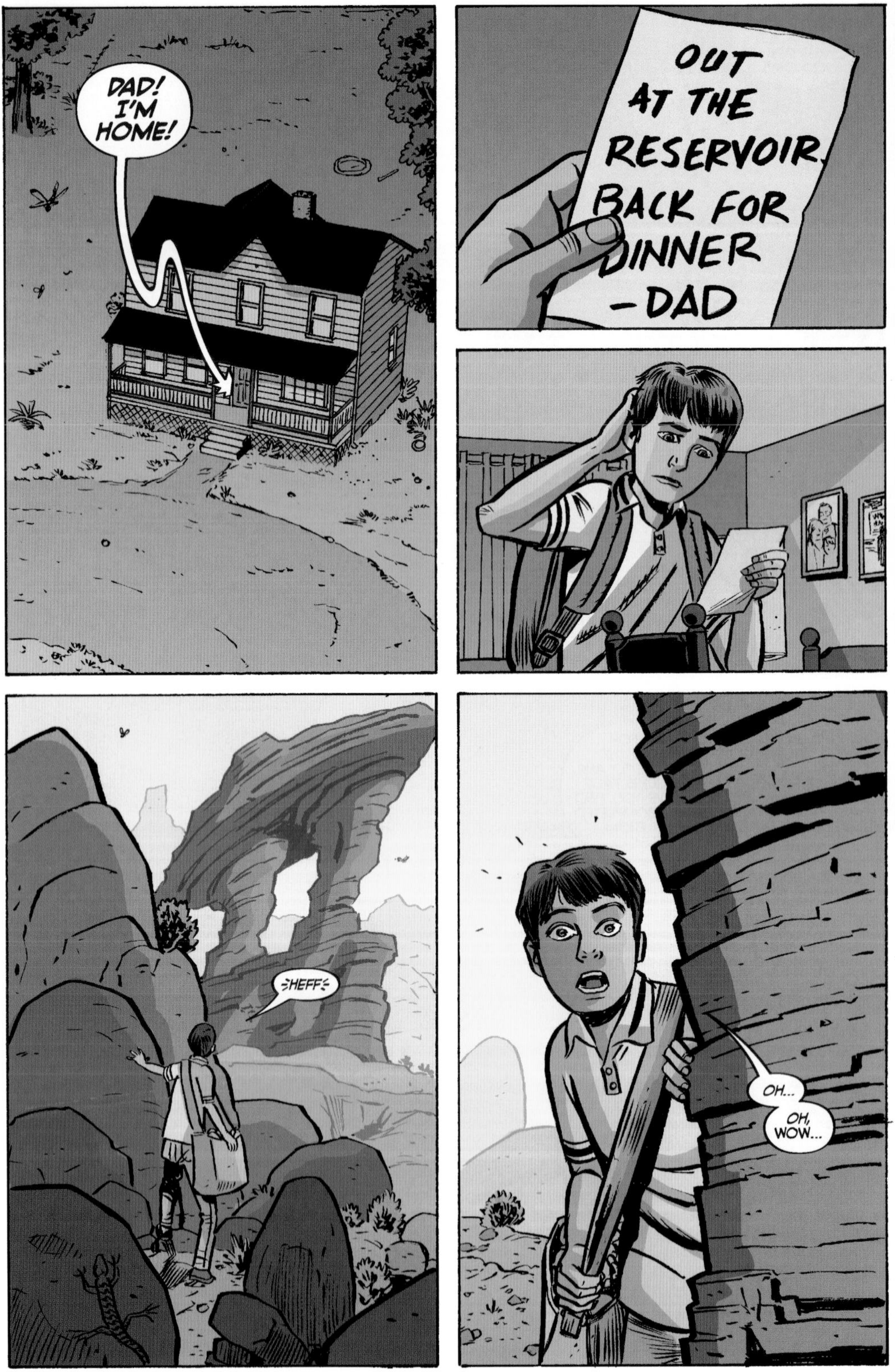
DAD! I'M HOME!
OUT AT THE RESERVOIR. BACK FOR DINNER -DAD
HEFF
OH...
OH, WOW...

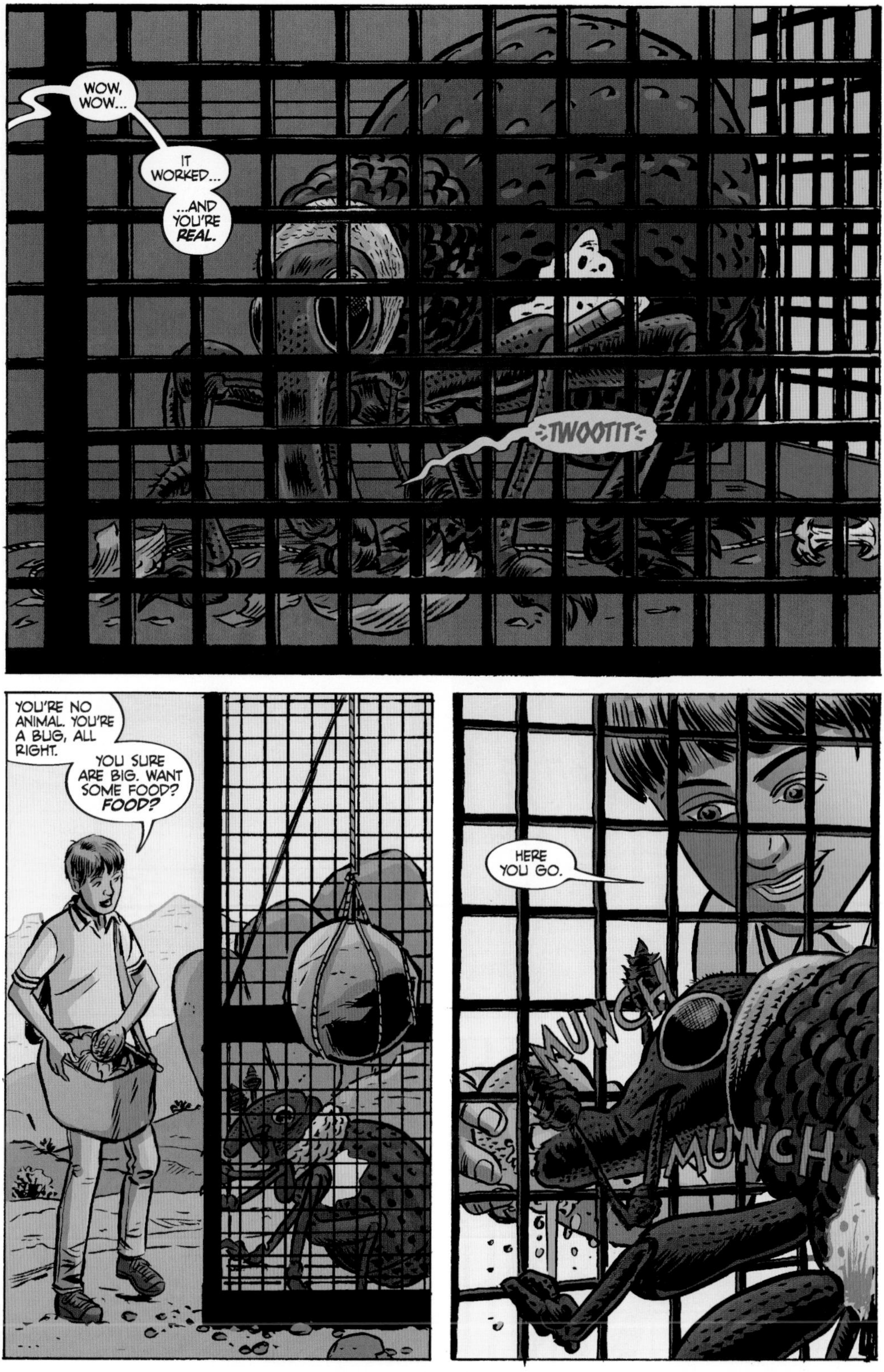
WOW, WOW...
IT WORKED...
...AND YOU'RE *REAL.*
TWOOTIT
YOU'RE NO ANIMAL. YOU'RE A BUG, ALL RIGHT.
YOU SURE ARE BIG. WANT SOME FOOD? *FOOD?*
HERE YOU GO.
MUNCH
MUNCH

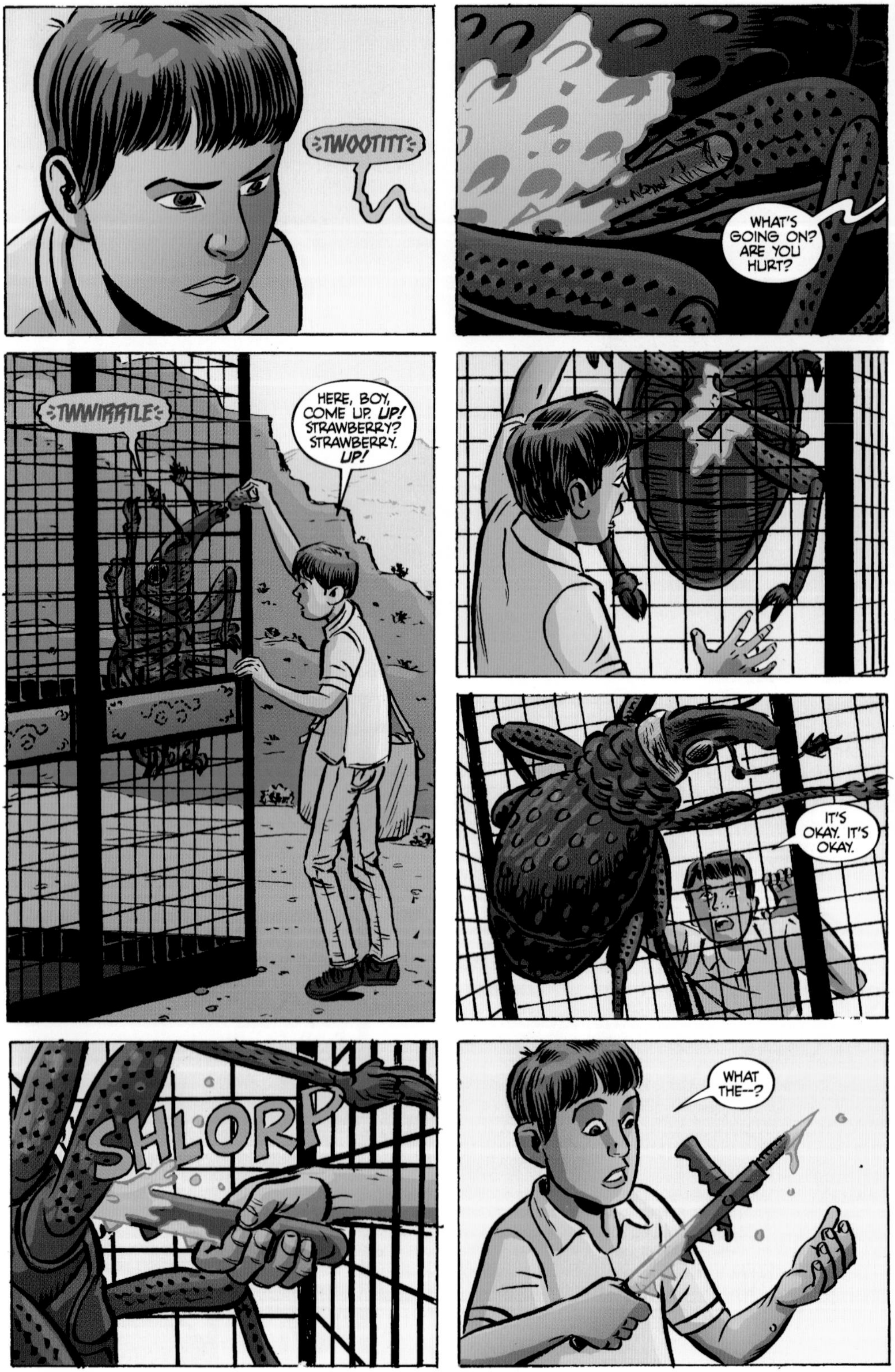
TWOOTITT
WHAT'S GOING ON? ARE YOU HURT?
TWWIRRTLE
HERE, BOY, COME UP. UP! STRAWBERRY? STRAWBERRY. UP!
IT'S OKAY. IT'S OKAY.
SHLORP
WHAT THE--?

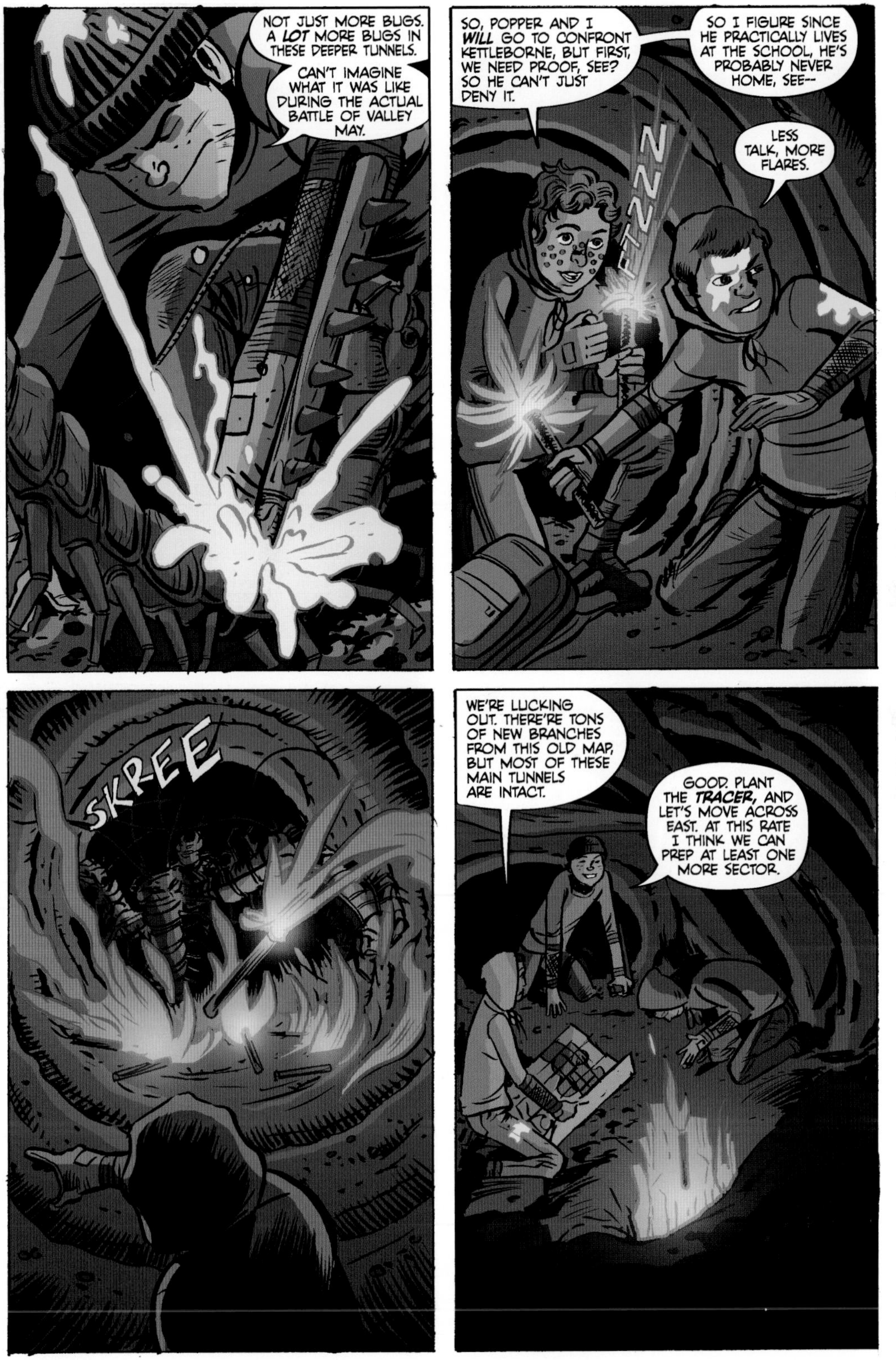
NOT JUST MORE BUGS. A LOT MORE BUGS IN THESE DEEPER TUNNELS.
CAN'T IMAGINE WHAT IT WAS LIKE DURING THE ACTUAL BATTLE OF VALLEY MAY.
SO, POPPER AND I WILL GO TO CONFRONT KETTLEBORNE, BUT FIRST, WE NEED PROOF, SEE? SO HE CAN'T JUST DENY IT.
SO I FIGURE SINCE HE PRACTICALLY LIVES AT THE SCHOOL, HE'S PROBABLY NEVER HOME, SEE--
FTZZNNN
LESS TALK, MORE FLARES.
SKREEE
WE'RE LUCKING OUT. THERE'RE TONS OF NEW BRANCHES FROM THIS OLD MAP, BUT MOST OF THESE MAIN TUNNELS ARE INTACT.
GOOD. PLANT THE TRACER, AND LET'S MOVE ACROSS EAST. AT THIS RATE I THINK WE CAN PREP AT LEAST ONE MORE SECTOR.

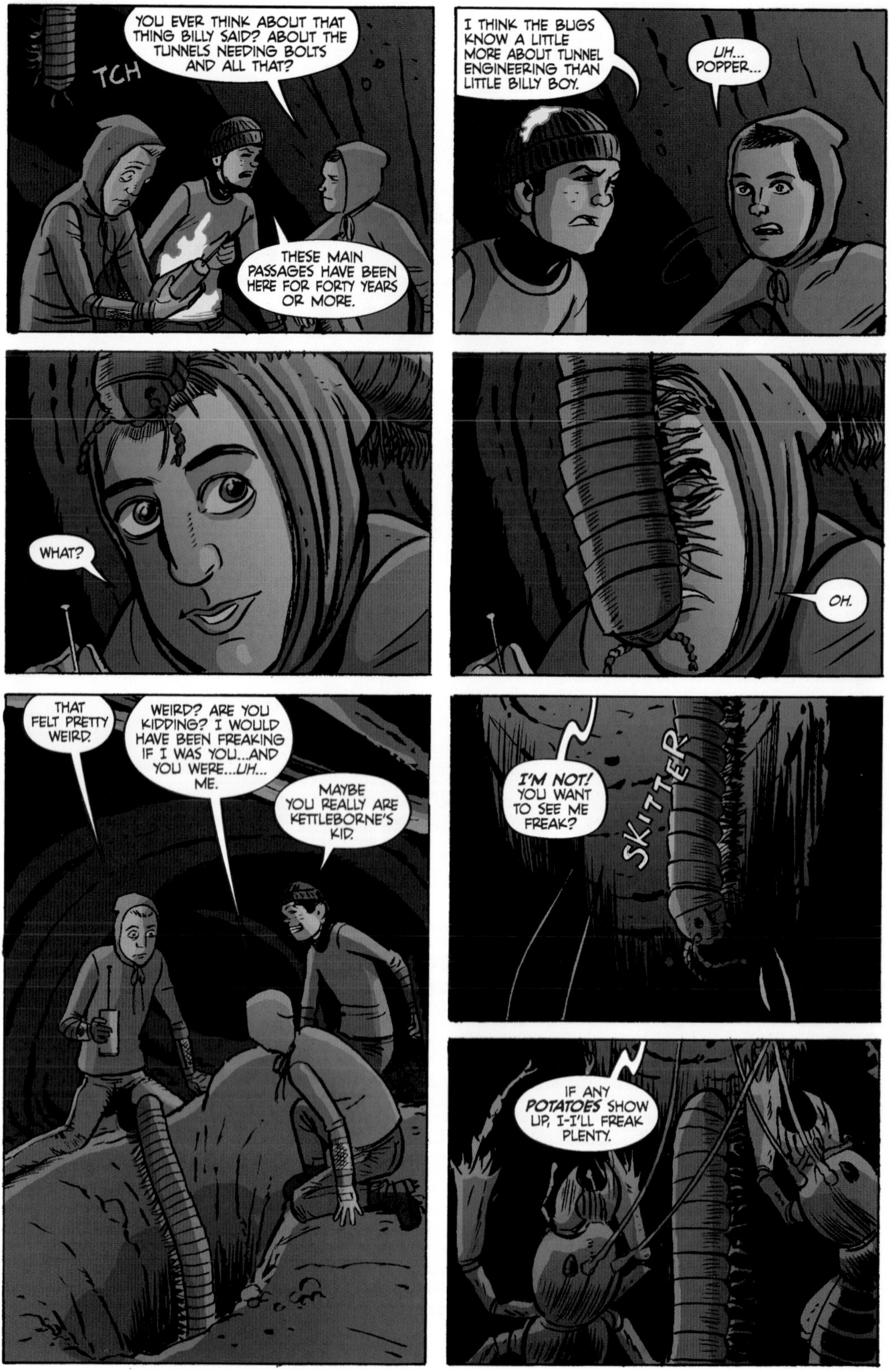
YOU EVER THINK ABOUT THAT THING BILLY SAID? ABOUT THE TUNNELS NEEDING BOLTS AND ALL THAT?
TCH
THESE MAIN PASSAGES HAVE BEEN HERE FOR FORTY YEARS OR MORE.
I THINK THE BUGS KNOW A LITTLE MORE ABOUT TUNNEL ENGINEERING THAN LITTLE BILLY BOY.
UH... POPPER...
WHAT?
OH.
THAT FELT PRETTY WEIRD.
WEIRD? ARE YOU KIDDING? I WOULD HAVE BEEN FREAKING IF I WAS YOU...AND YOU WERE...UH... ME.
MAYBE YOU REALLY ARE KETTLEBORNE'S KID.
I'M NOT! YOU WANT TO SEE ME FREAK?
SKITTER
IF ANY POTATOES SHOW UP, I-I'LL FREAK PLENTY.

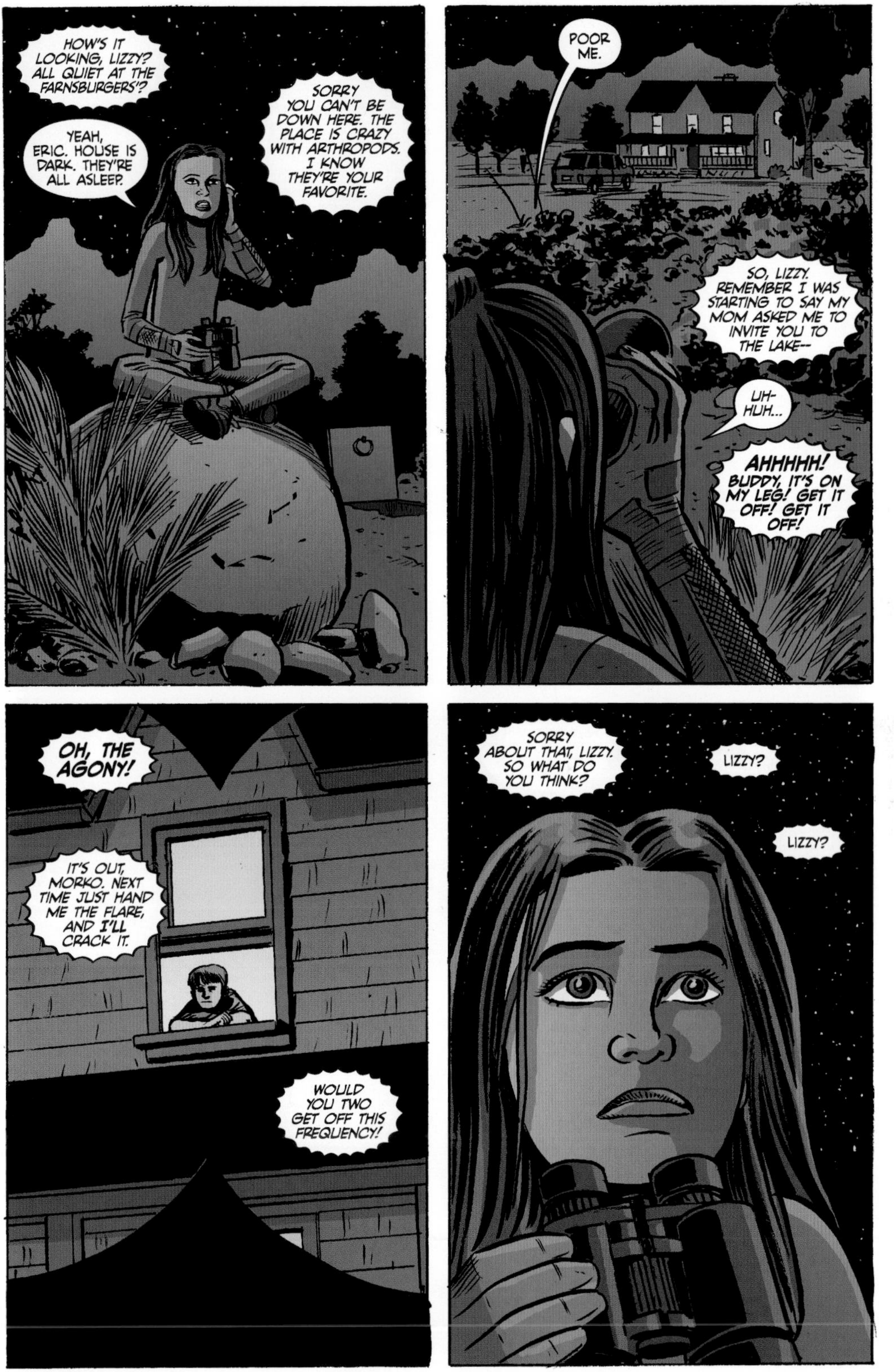
HOW'S IT LOOKING, LIZZY? ALL QUIET AT THE FARNSBURGERS'?
YEAH, ERIC. HOUSE IS DARK. THEY'RE ALL ASLEEP.
SORRY YOU CAN'T BE DOWN HERE. THE PLACE IS CRAZY WITH ARTHROPODS. I KNOW THEY'RE YOUR FAVORITE.
POOR ME.
SO, LIZZY. REMEMBER I WAS STARTING TO SAY MY MOM ASKED ME TO INVITE YOU TO THE LAKE--
UH-HUH...
AHHHHH! BUDDY, IT'S ON MY LEG! GET IT OFF! GET IT OFF!
OH, THE AGONY!
IT'S OUT, MORKO. NEXT TIME JUST HAND ME THE FLARE, AND I'LL CRACK IT.
WOULD YOU TWO GET OFF THIS FREQUENCY!
SORRY ABOUT THAT, LIZZY. SO WHAT DO YOU THINK?
LIZZY?
LIZZY?

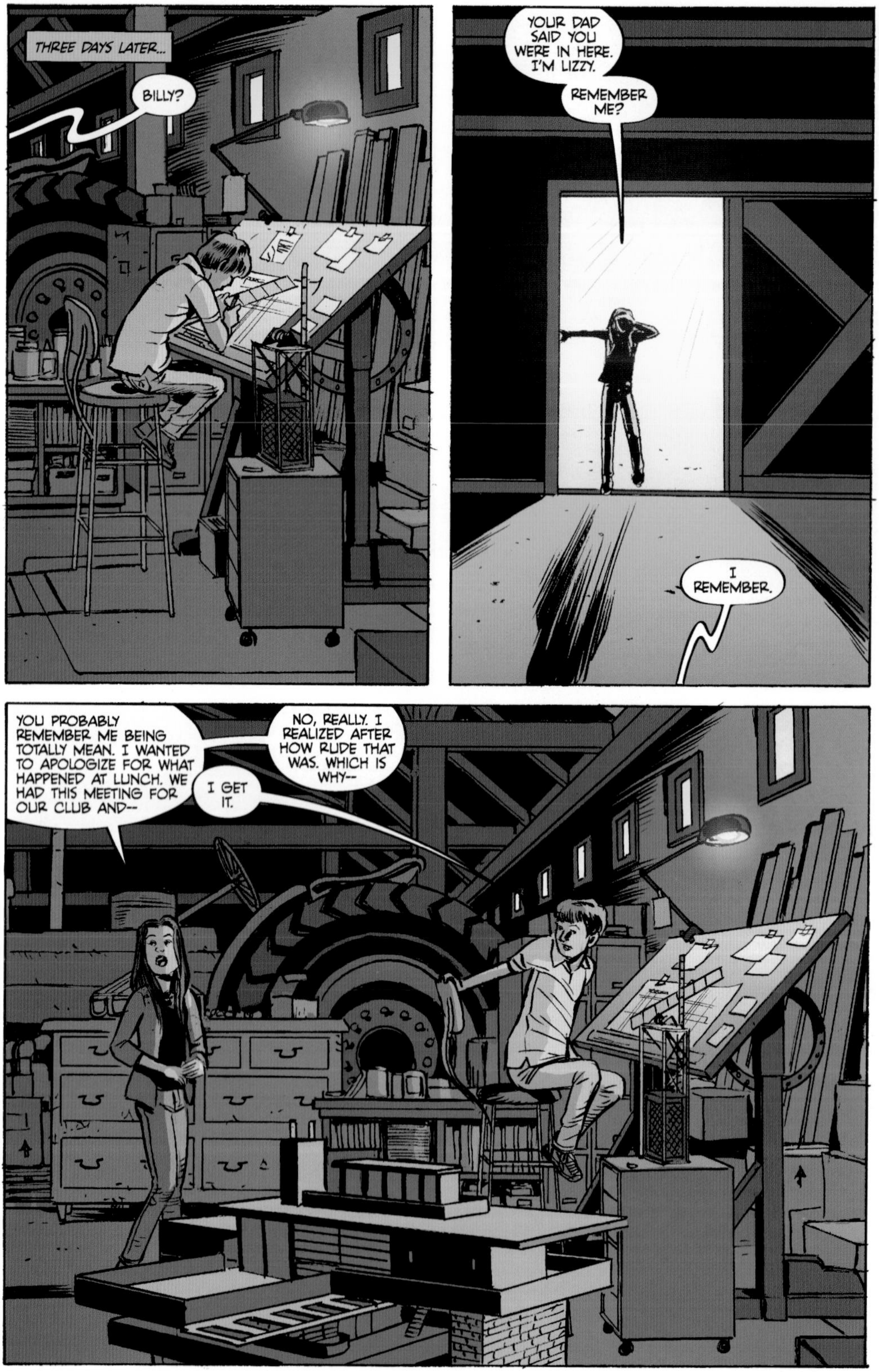
THREE DAYS LATER...
BILLY?
YOUR DAD SAID YOU WERE IN HERE. I'M LIZZY.
REMEMBER ME?
I REMEMBER.
YOU PROBABLY REMEMBER ME BEING TOTALLY MEAN. I WANTED TO APOLOGIZE FOR WHAT HAPPENED AT LUNCH. WE HAD THIS MEETING FOR OUR CLUB AND--
I GET IT.
NO, REALLY. I REALIZED AFTER HOW RUDE THAT WAS. WHICH IS WHY--

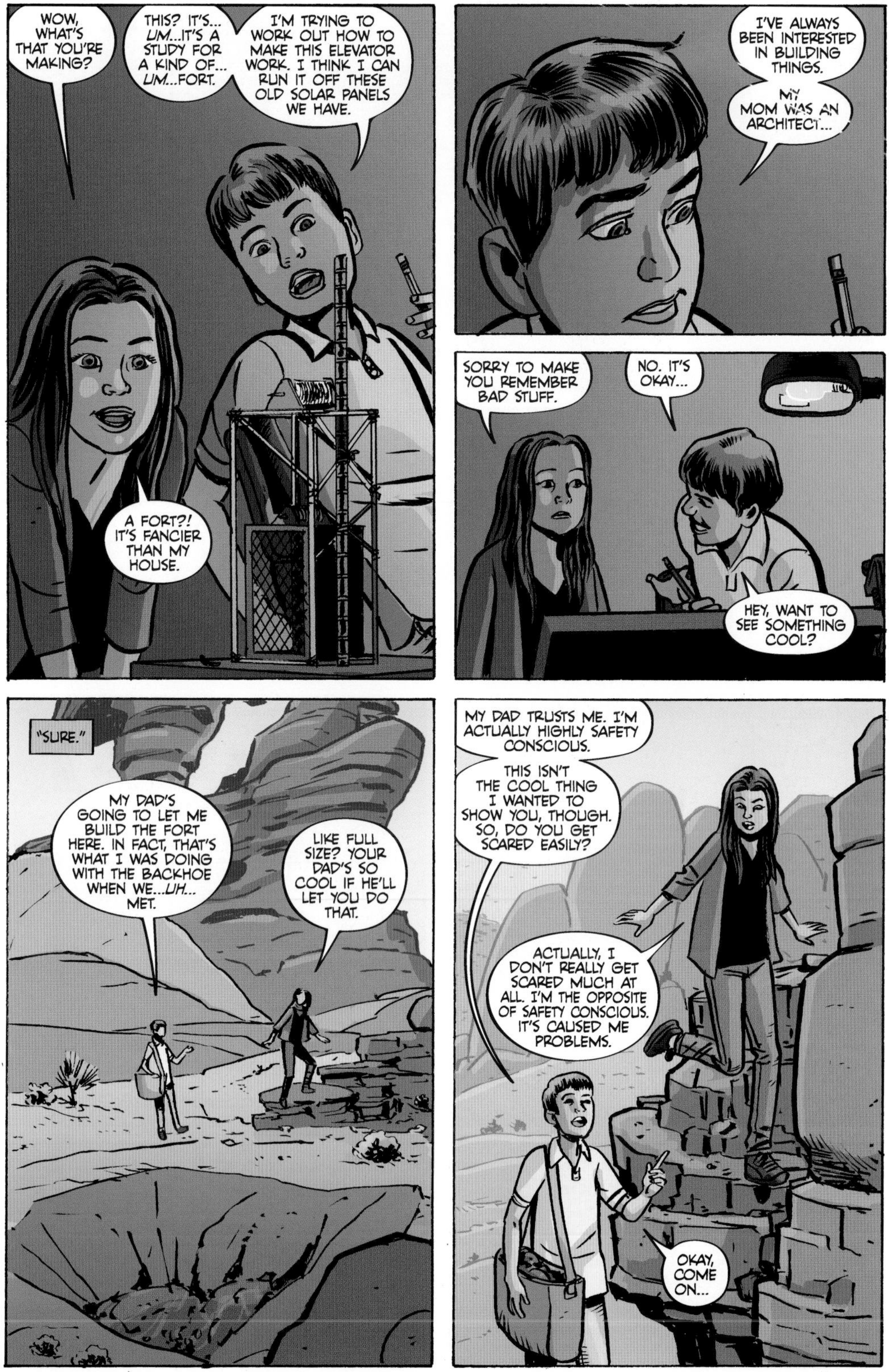
WOW, WHAT'S THAT YOU'RE MAKING?
THIS? IT'S... UM...IT'S A STUDY FOR A KIND OF... UM...FORT.
I'M TRYING TO WORK OUT HOW TO MAKE THIS ELEVATOR WORK. I THINK I CAN RUN IT OFF THESE OLD SOLAR PANELS WE HAVE.
A FORT?! IT'S FANCIER THAN MY HOUSE.
I'VE ALWAYS BEEN INTERESTED IN BUILDING THINGS.
MY MOM WAS AN ARCHITECT...
SORRY TO MAKE YOU REMEMBER BAD STUFF.
NO. IT'S OKAY...
HEY, WANT TO SEE SOMETHING COOL?
"SURE."
MY DAD'S GOING TO LET ME BUILD THE FORT HERE. IN FACT, THAT'S WHAT I WAS DOING WITH THE BACKHOE WHEN WE...UH... MET.
LIKE FULL SIZE? YOUR DAD'S SO COOL IF HE'LL LET YOU DO THAT.
MY DAD TRUSTS ME. I'M ACTUALLY HIGHLY SAFETY CONSCIOUS.
THIS ISN'T THE COOL THING I WANTED TO SHOW YOU, THOUGH. SO, DO YOU GET SCARED EASILY?
ACTUALLY, I DON'T REALLY GET SCARED MUCH AT ALL. I'M THE OPPOSITE OF SAFETY CONSCIOUS. IT'S CAUSED ME PROBLEMS.
OKAY, COME ON...

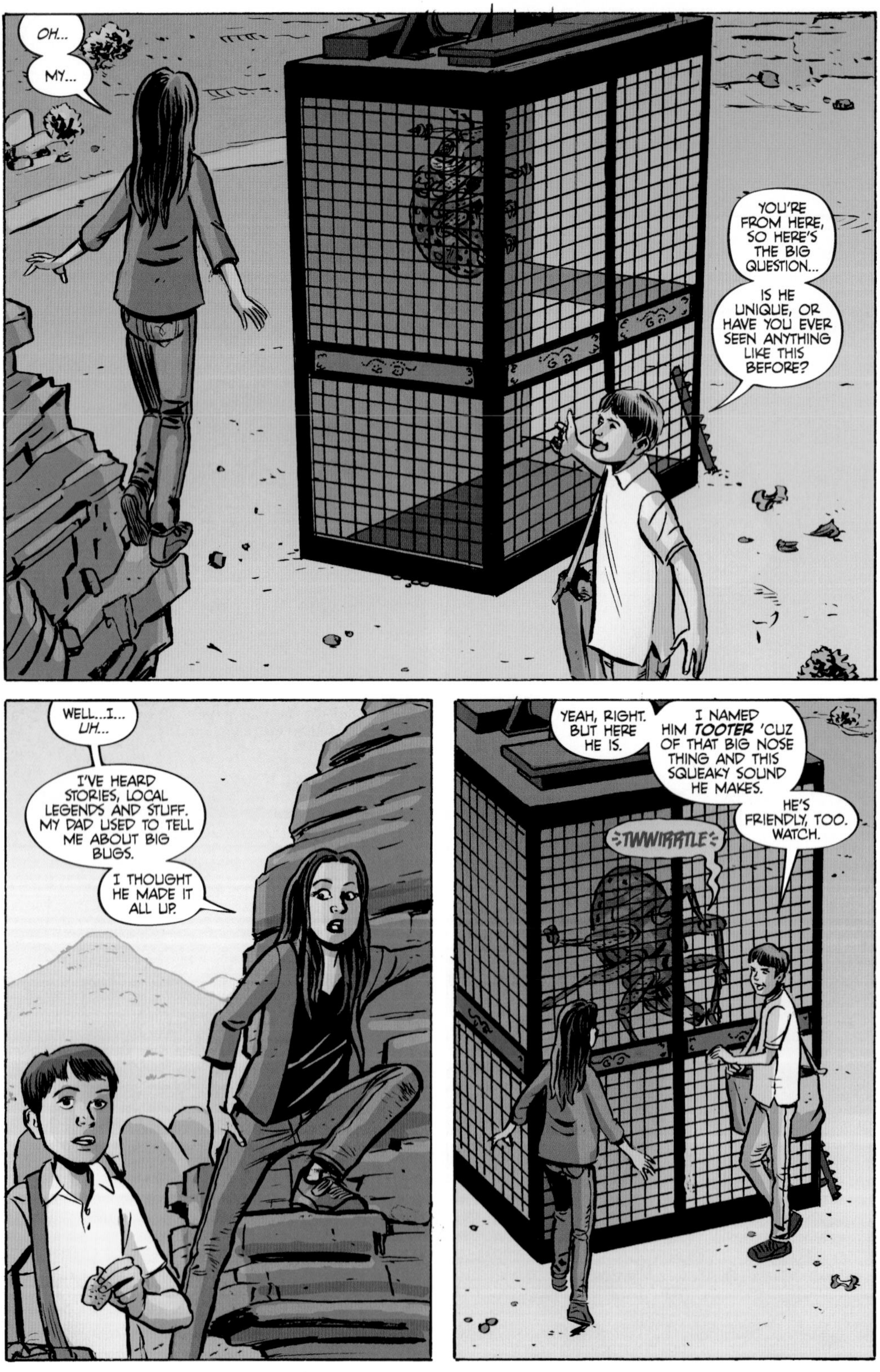
OH...
MY...
YOU'RE FROM HERE, SO HERE'S THE BIG QUESTION...
IS HE UNIQUE, OR HAVE YOU EVER SEEN ANYTHING LIKE THIS BEFORE?
WELL...I... UH...
I'VE HEARD STORIES, LOCAL LEGENDS AND STUFF. MY DAD USED TO TELL ME ABOUT BIG BUGS.
I THOUGHT HE MADE IT ALL UP.
YEAH, RIGHT. BUT HERE HE IS.
I NAMED HIM TOOTER 'CUZ OF THAT BIG NOSE THING AND THIS SQUEAKY SOUND HE MAKES.
TWWIRRTLE
HE'S FRIENDLY, TOO. WATCH.

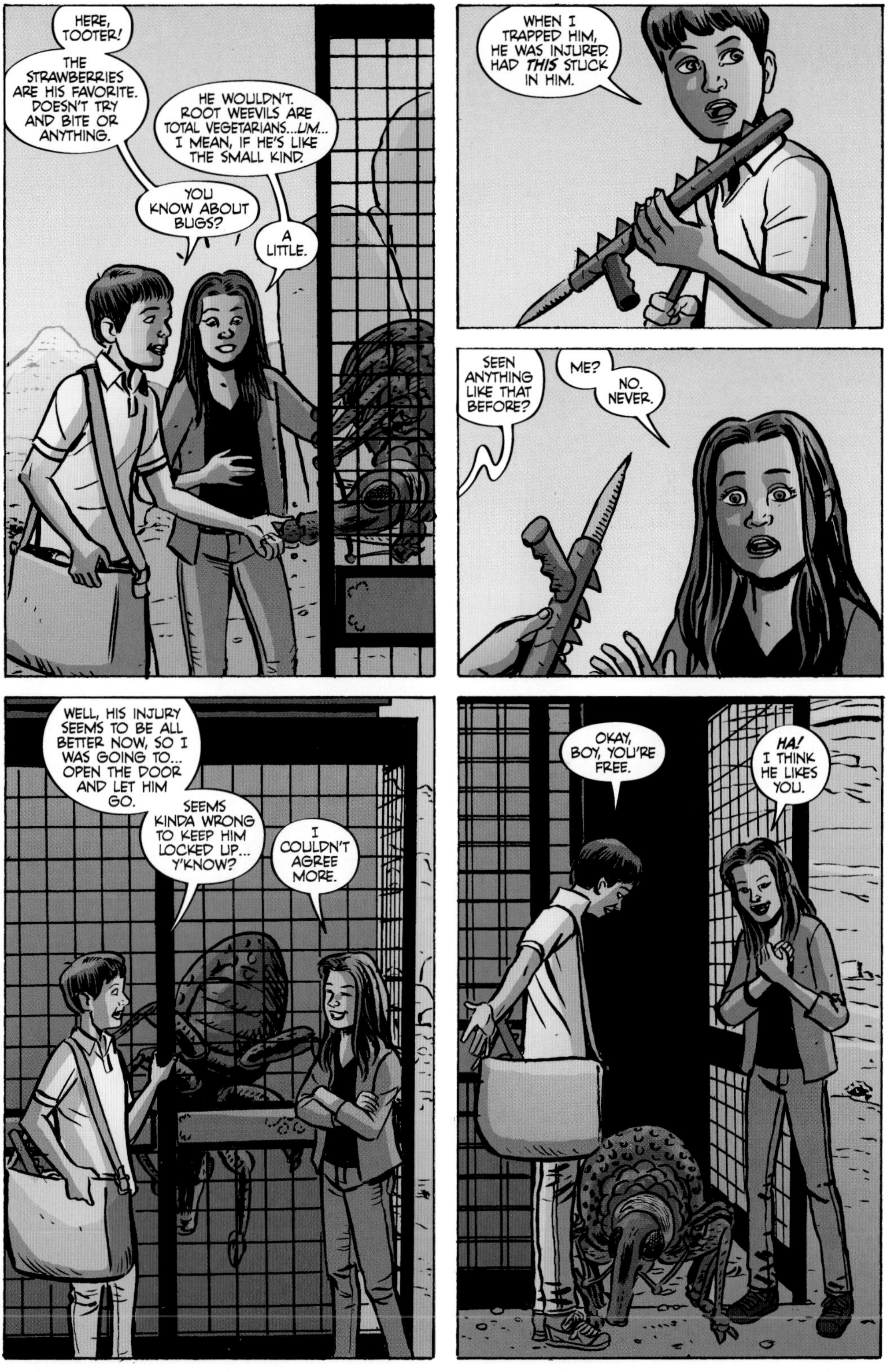
HERE, TOOTER!
THE STRAWBERRIES ARE HIS FAVORITE. DOESN'T TRY AND BITE OR ANYTHING.
HE WOULDN'T. ROOT WEEVILS ARE TOTAL VEGETARIANS...UM... I MEAN, IF HE'S LIKE THE SMALL KIND.
YOU KNOW ABOUT BUGS?
A LITTLE.
WHEN I TRAPPED HIM, HE WAS INJURED. HAD THIS STUCK IN HIM.
SEEN ANYTHING LIKE THAT BEFORE?
ME?
NO. NEVER.
WELL, HIS INJURY SEEMS TO BE ALL BETTER NOW, SO I WAS GOING TO... OPEN THE DOOR AND LET HIM GO.
SEEMS KINDA WRONG TO KEEP HIM LOCKED UP... Y'KNOW?
I COULDN'T AGREE MORE.
OKAY, BOY, YOU'RE FREE.
HA! I THINK HE LIKES YOU.

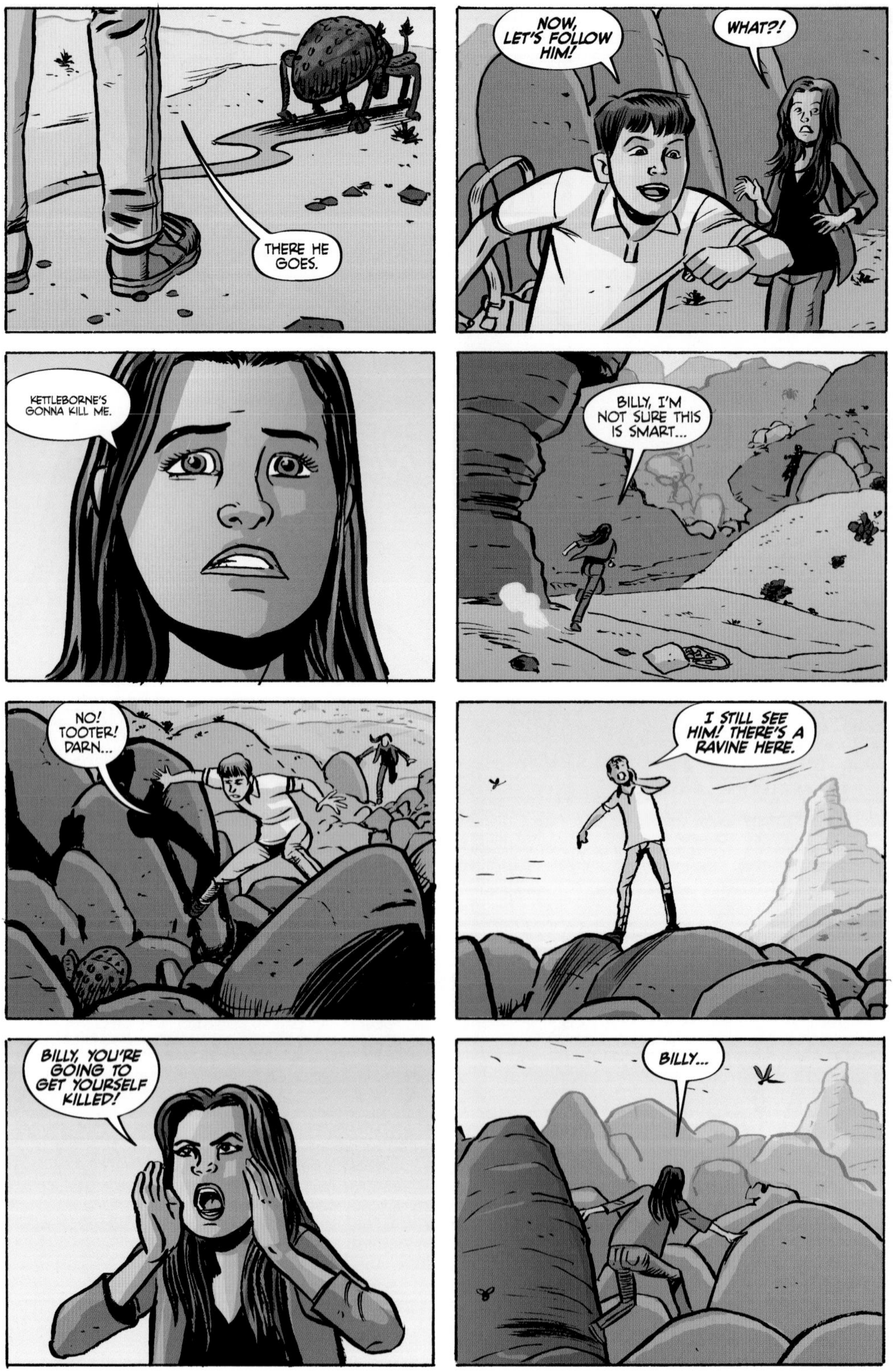
THERE HE GOES.
NOW, LET'S FOLLOW HIM!
WHAT?!
KETTLEBORNE'S GONNA KILL ME.
BILLY, I'M NOT SURE THIS IS SMART...
NO! TOOTER! DARN...
I STILL SEE HIM! THERE'S A RAVINE HERE.
BILLY, YOU'RE GOING TO GET YOURSELF KILLED!
BILLY...

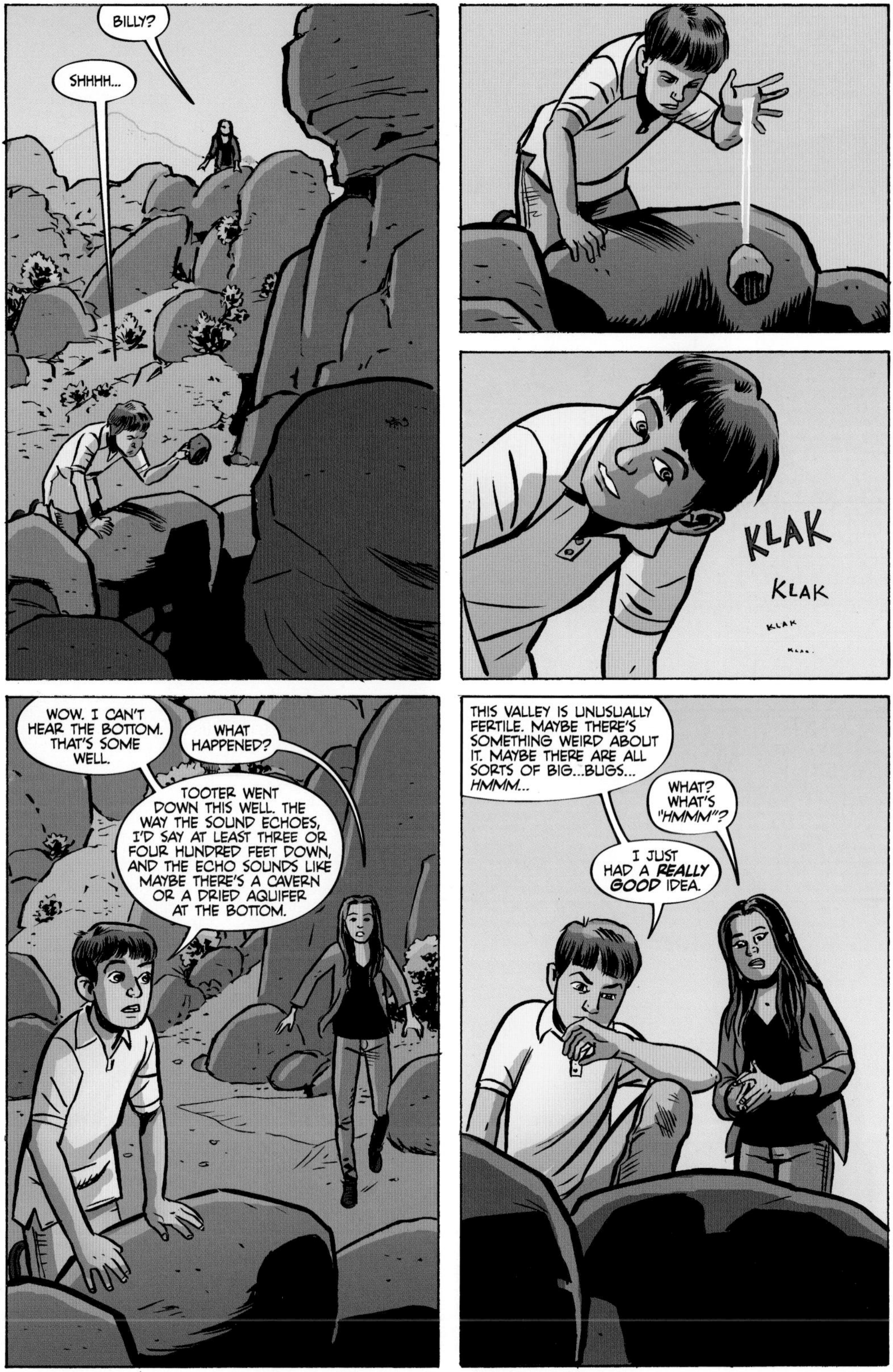

BILLY?
SHHHH...
KLAK
KLAK
KLAK
WOW. I CAN'T HEAR THE BOTTOM. THAT'S SOME WELL.
WHAT HAPPENED?
TOOTER WENT DOWN THIS WELL. THE WAY THE SOUND ECHOES, I'D SAY AT LEAST THREE OR FOUR HUNDRED FEET DOWN, AND THE ECHO SOUNDS LIKE MAYBE THERE'S A CAVERN OR A DRIED AQUIFER AT THE BOTTOM.
THIS VALLEY IS UNUSUALLY FERTILE. MAYBE THERE'S SOMETHING WEIRD ABOUT IT. MAYBE THERE ARE ALL SORTS OF BIG...BUGS... *HMMM...*
WHAT? WHAT'S *"HMMM"*?
I JUST HAD A ***REALLY GOOD*** IDEA.

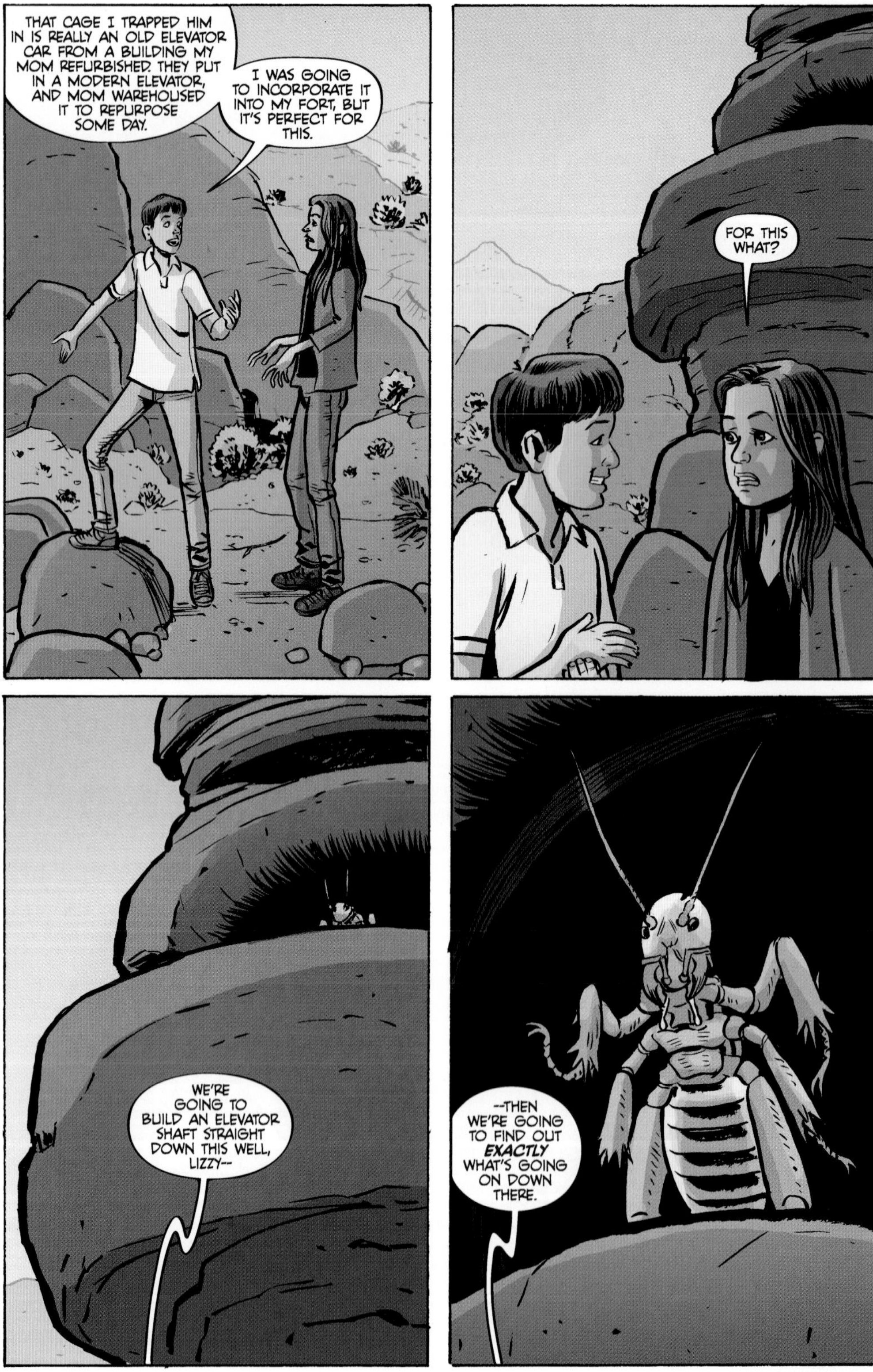
THAT CAGE I TRAPPED HIM IN IS REALLY AN OLD ELEVATOR CAR FROM A BUILDING MY MOM REFURBISHED. THEY PUT IN A MODERN ELEVATOR, AND MOM WAREHOUSED IT TO REPURPOSE SOME DAY.
I WAS GOING TO INCORPORATE IT INTO MY FORT, BUT IT'S PERFECT FOR THIS.
FOR THIS WHAT?
WE'RE GOING TO BUILD AN ELEVATOR SHAFT STRAIGHT DOWN THIS WELL, LIZZY--
--THEN WE'RE GOING TO FIND OUT *EXACTLY* WHAT'S GOING ON DOWN THERE.

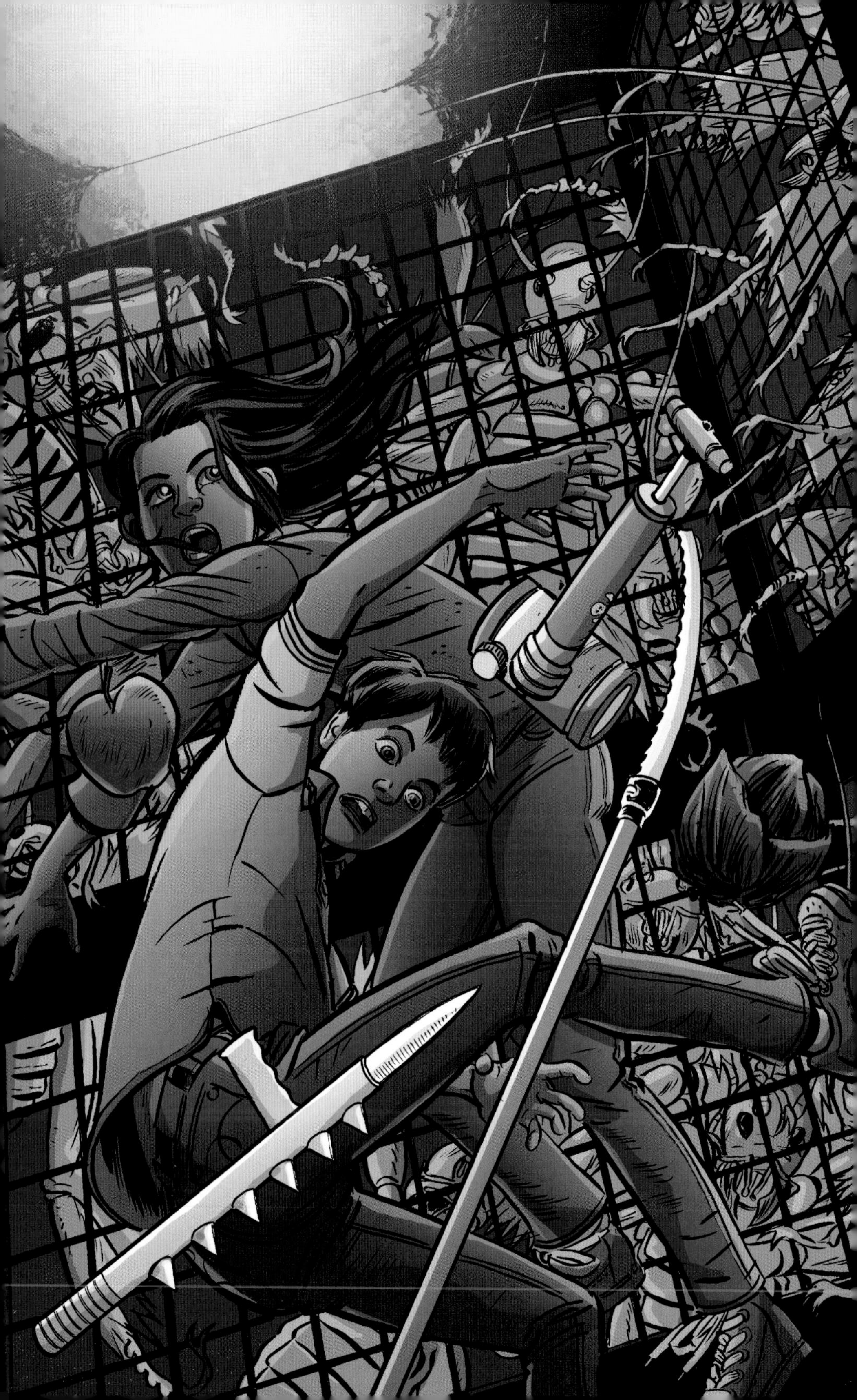

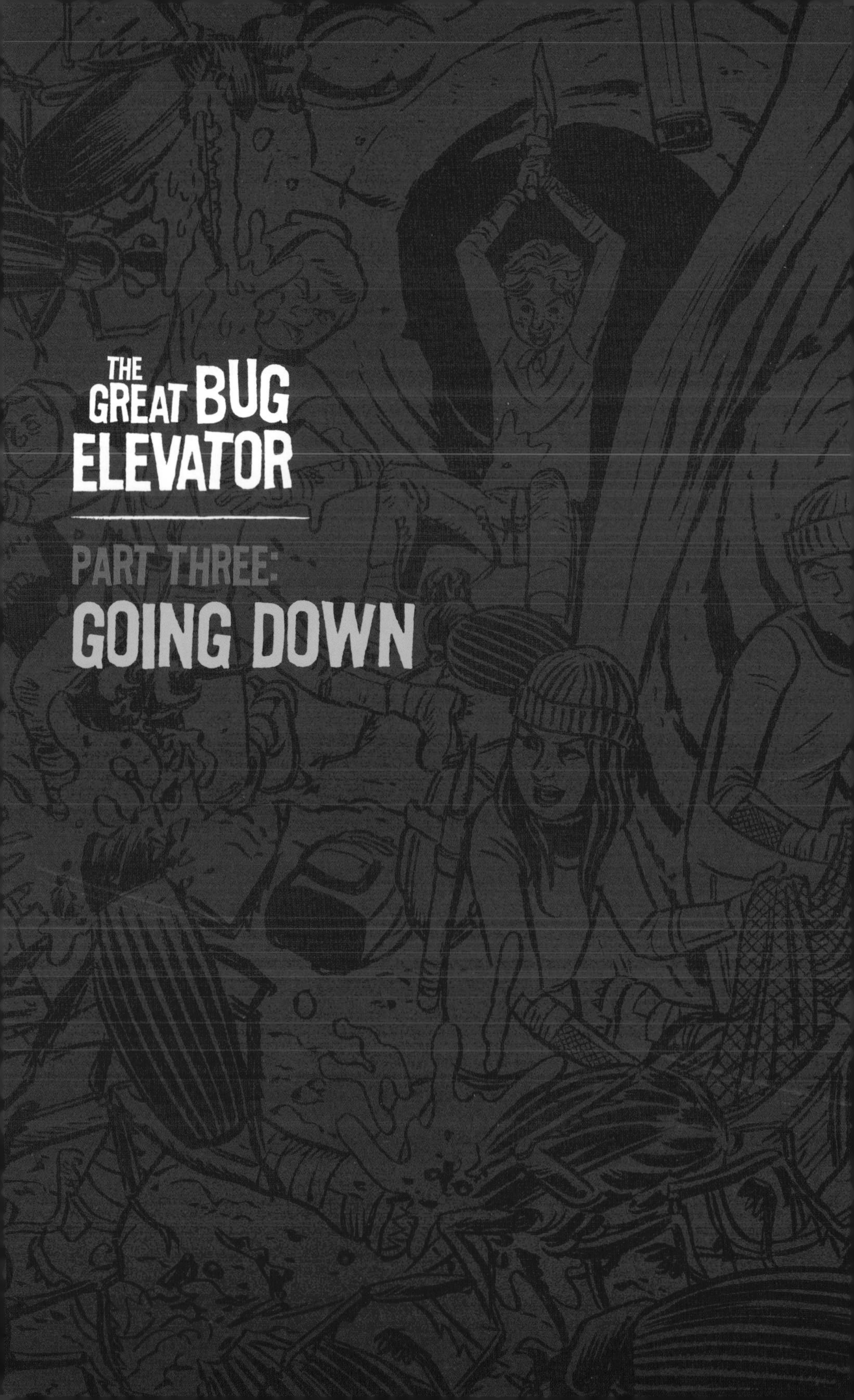

THE GREAT BUG ELEVATOR

PART THREE: GOING DOWN

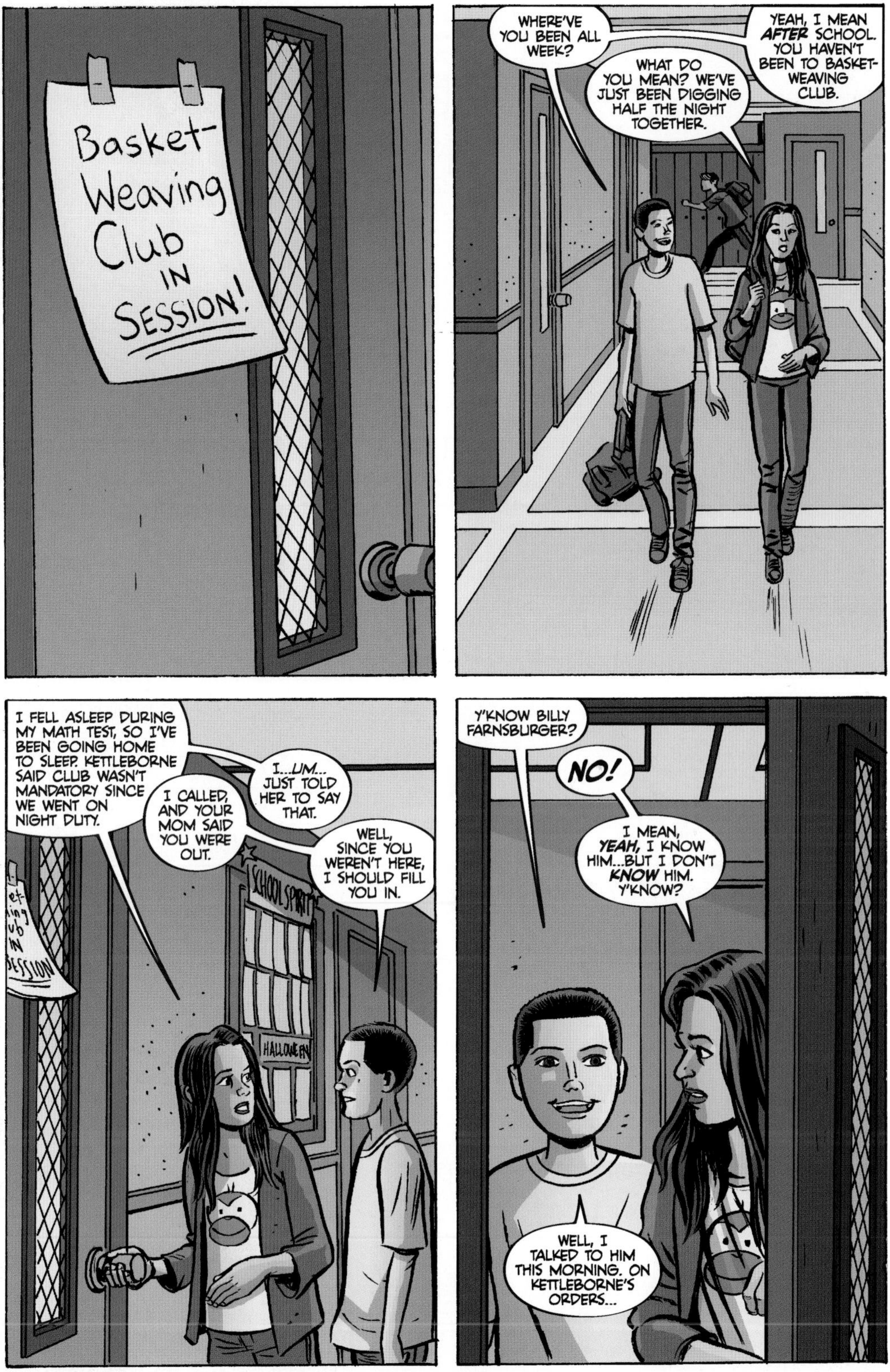
Basket-
Weaving
Club
IN
SESSION!
WHERE'VE YOU BEEN ALL WEEK?
WHAT DO YOU MEAN? WE'VE JUST BEEN DIGGING HALF THE NIGHT TOGETHER.
YEAH, I MEAN AFTER SCHOOL. YOU HAVEN'T BEEN TO BASKET-WEAVING CLUB.
I FELL ASLEEP DURING MY MATH TEST, SO I'VE BEEN GOING HOME TO SLEEP. KETTLEBORNE SAID CLUB WASN'T MANDATORY SINCE WE WENT ON NIGHT DUTY.
I CALLED, AND YOUR MOM SAID YOU WERE OUT.
I...UM... JUST TOLD HER TO SAY THAT.
WELL, SINCE YOU WEREN'T HERE, I SHOULD FILL YOU IN.
SCHOOL SPIRIT
HALLOWEEN
Y'KNOW BILLY FARNSBURGER?
NO!
I MEAN, YEAH, I KNOW HIM...BUT I DON'T KNOW HIM. Y'KNOW?
WELL, I TALKED TO HIM THIS MORNING. ON KETTLEBORNE'S ORDERS...

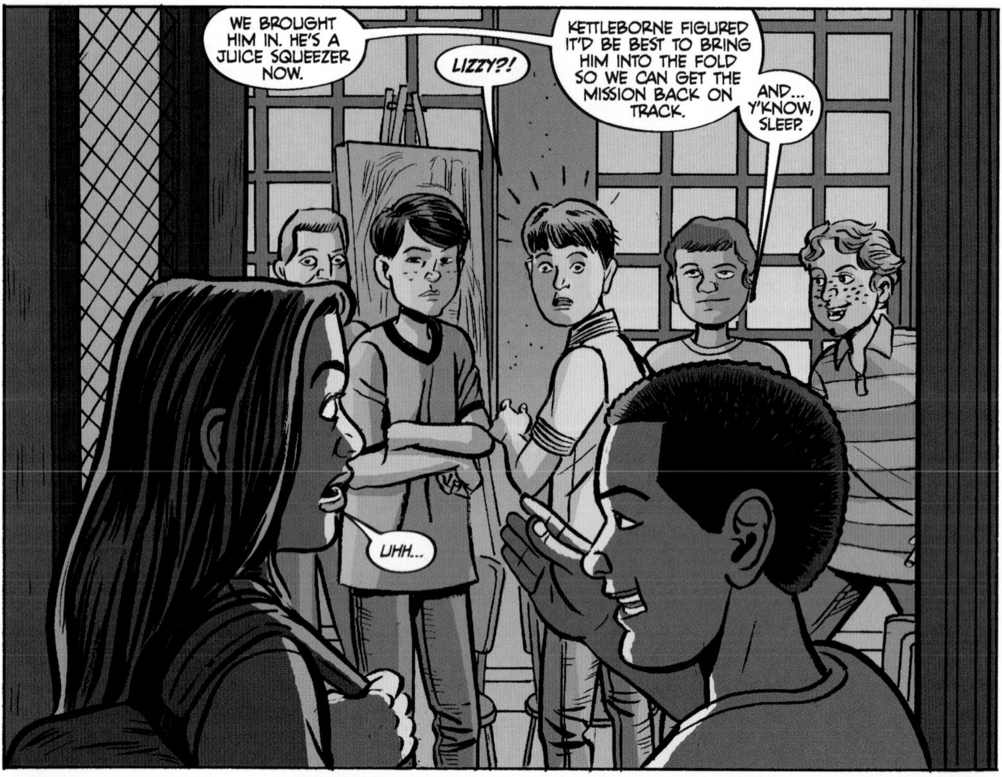
WE BROUGHT HIM IN. HE'S A JUICE SQUEEZER NOW.
LIZZY?!
KETTLEBORNE FIGURED IT'D BE BEST TO BRING HIM INTO THE FOLD SO WE CAN GET THE MISSION BACK ON TRACK.
AND... Y'KNOW, SLEEP.
UHH...

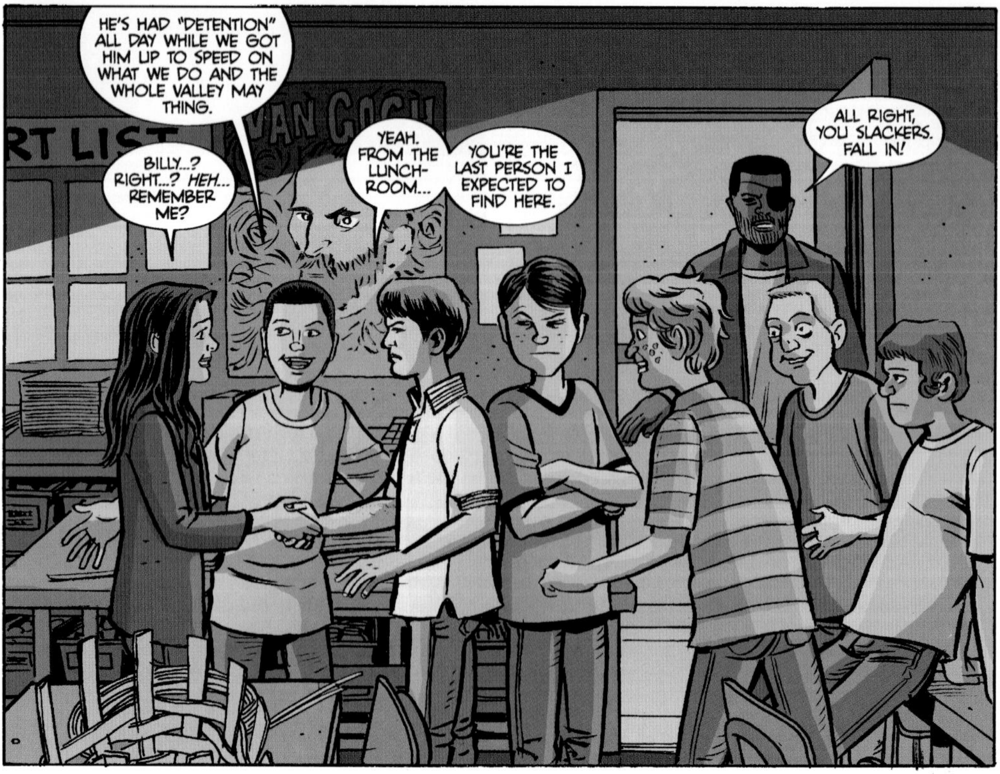
HE'S HAD "DETENTION" ALL DAY WHILE WE GOT HIM UP TO SPEED ON WHAT WE DO AND THE WHOLE VALLEY MAY THING.
VAN GOGH
RT LIST
BILLY...? RIGHT...? HEH... REMEMBER ME?
YEAH. FROM THE LUNCH-ROOM...
YOU'RE THE LAST PERSON I EXPECTED TO FIND HERE.
ALL RIGHT, YOU SLACKERS. FALL IN!

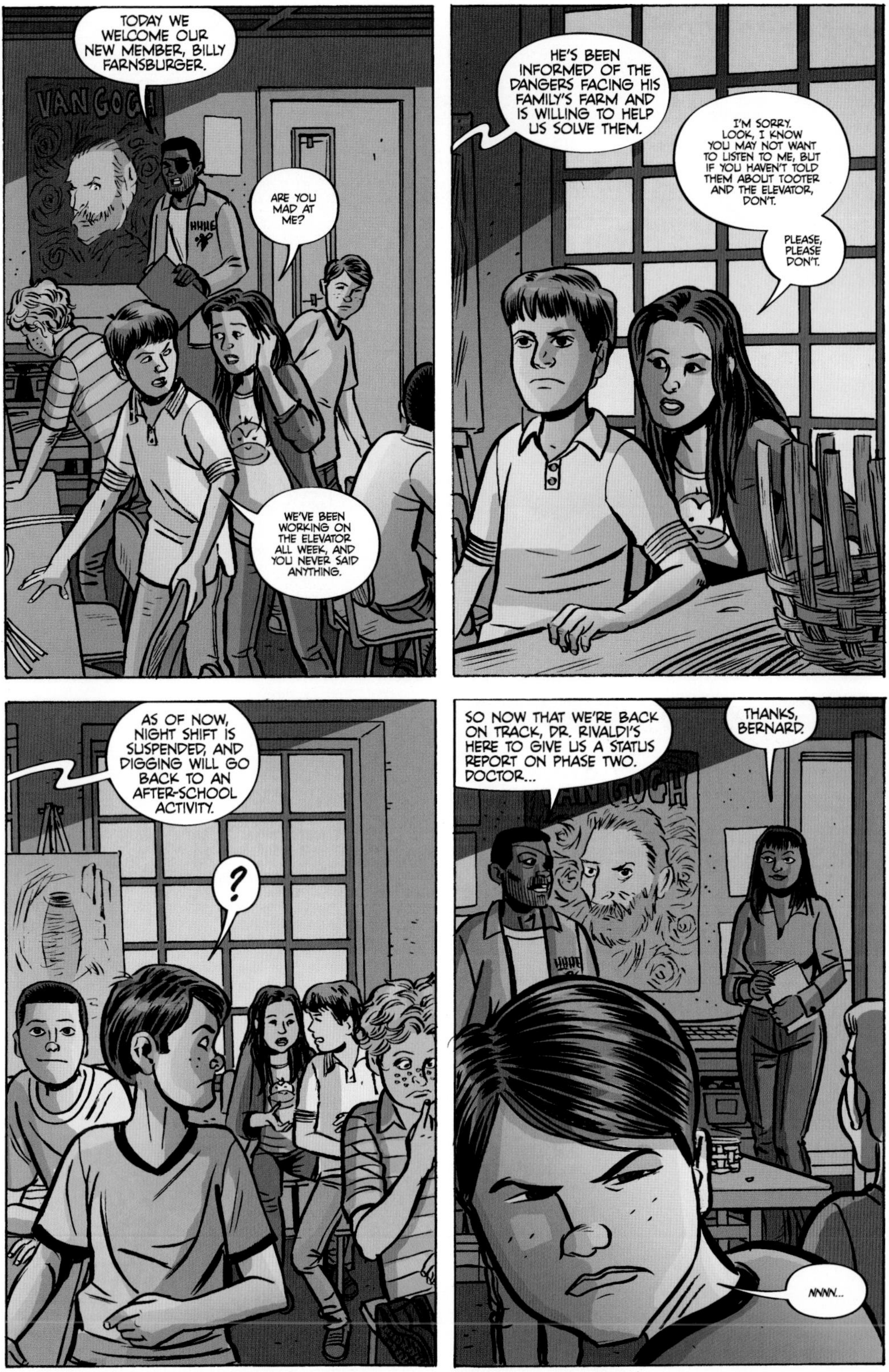
TODAY WE WELCOME OUR NEW MEMBER, BILLY FARNSBURGER.
VAN GOGH
ARE YOU MAD AT ME?
WE'VE BEEN WORKING ON THE ELEVATOR ALL WEEK, AND YOU NEVER SAID ANYTHING.
HE'S BEEN INFORMED OF THE DANGERS FACING HIS FAMILY'S FARM AND IS WILLING TO HELP US SOLVE THEM.
I'M SORRY. LOOK, I KNOW YOU MAY NOT WANT TO LISTEN TO ME, BUT IF YOU HAVEN'T TOLD THEM ABOUT TOOTER AND THE ELEVATOR, DON'T.
PLEASE, PLEASE DON'T.
AS OF NOW, NIGHT SHIFT IS SUSPENDED, AND DIGGING WILL GO BACK TO AN AFTER-SCHOOL ACTIVITY.
?
SO NOW THAT WE'RE BACK ON TRACK, DR. RIVALDI'S HERE TO GIVE US A STATUS REPORT ON PHASE TWO. DOCTOR...
THANKS, BERNARD.
NNNN...

HI, EVERYBODY. WELL, IT LOOKS LIKE THE NEW POISON IS A SUCCESS.
WE'RE CALLING IT *ORANGE SHIELD* BECAUSE OF ITS COLOR AND THE PROTECTION WE HOPE IT WILL GIVE.
IT'S EUTHANIZED EVERYTHING WE'VE THROWN AT IT SO FAR. EVEN THE LARGER ARTHROPODS.
ORANGE SHIELD
ORANGE SHIELD LASTS THREE TIMES LONGER THAN THE OLD PELLETS AND HAS DEEPER GROUND PENETRATION.
WE'RE HOPING IT'S DEEP ENOUGH TO FLOOD THE GRID NETWORK AND CREATE A BARRIER LAYER TO PROTECT VALLEY MAY FARMS.
CLEARLY THERE'S A CONCENTRATION OF BUGS UNDER THAT VALLEY. PERHAPS IT'S EVEN THEIR CENTRAL LOCATION. THAT MAY BE WHY THEY'VE BEEN SO PROPRIETARY ABOUT IT.
IT WOULD BE **HIGHLY BENEFICIAL** IF WE--AND BY ***WE,*** I MEAN ***YOU***--COULD DISCOVER SOME OF THE DOWNWARD ROUTES TO THESE DEEPER CHAMBERS.
IF WE COULD GET ORANGE SHIELD DOWN DEEP, WE MIGHT END THIS BUG PROBLEM ONCE AND FOR ALL.

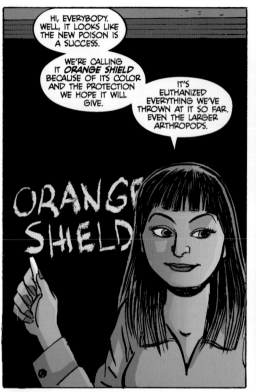

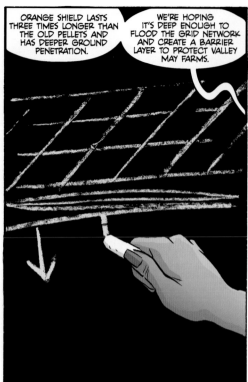

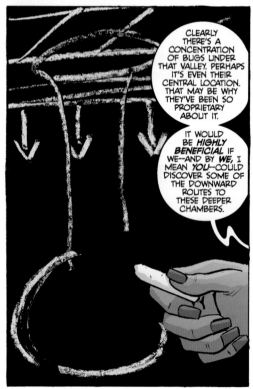

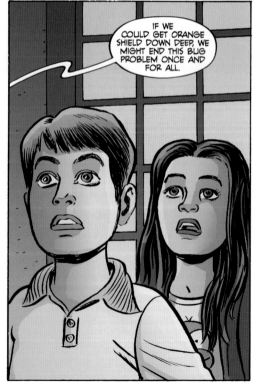

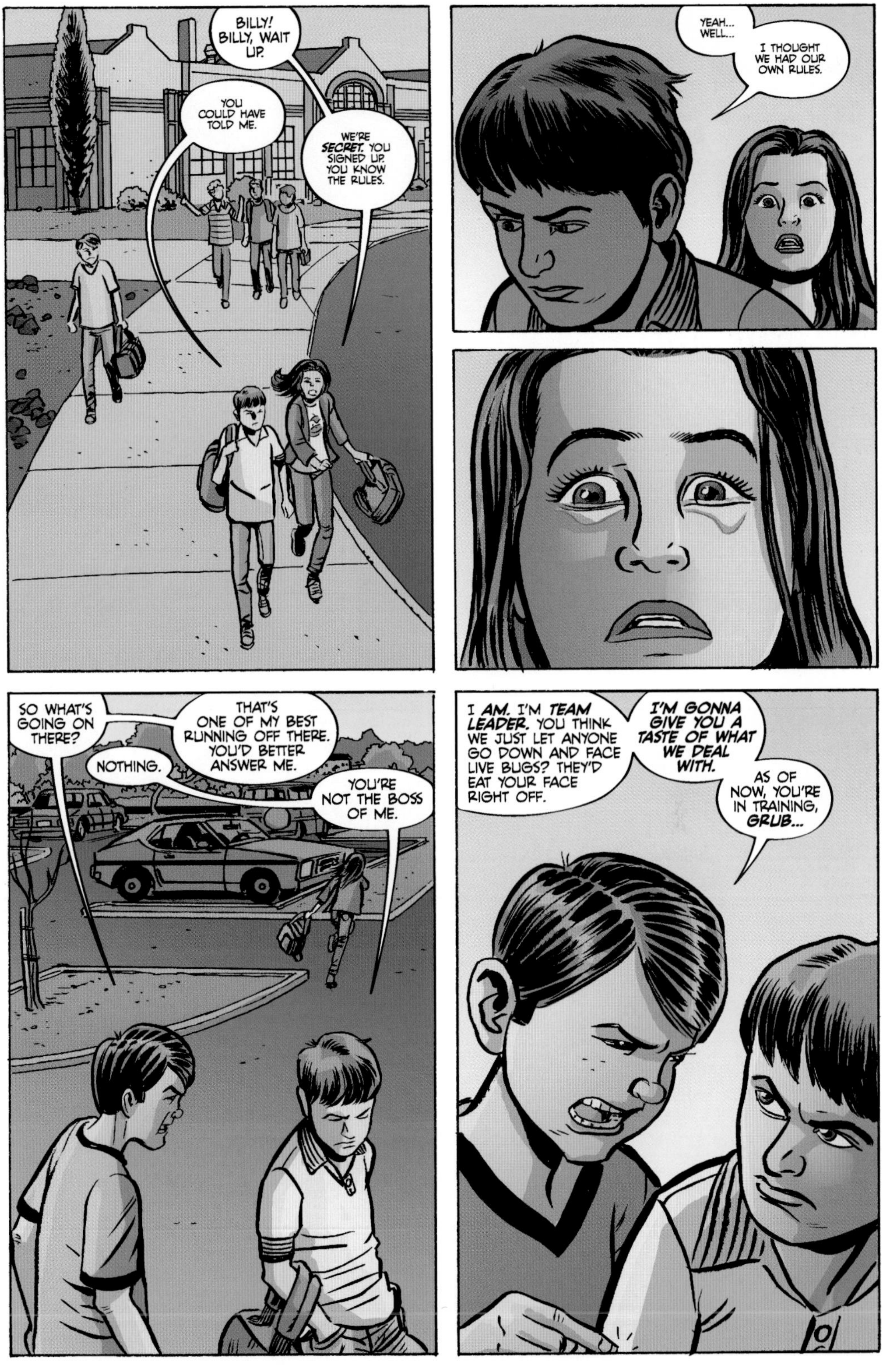
BILLY! BILLY, WAIT UP.
YOU COULD HAVE TOLD ME.
WE'RE SECRET. YOU SIGNED UP. YOU KNOW THE RULES.
YEAH... WELL...
I THOUGHT WE HAD OUR OWN RULES.
SO WHAT'S GOING ON THERE?
NOTHING.
THAT'S ONE OF MY BEST RUNNING OFF THERE. YOU'D BETTER ANSWER ME.
YOU'RE NOT THE BOSS OF ME.
I AM. I'M TEAM LEADER. YOU THINK WE JUST LET ANYONE GO DOWN AND FACE LIVE BUGS? THEY'D EAT YOUR FACE RIGHT OFF.
I'M GONNA GIVE YOU A TASTE OF WHAT WE DEAL WITH.
AS OF NOW, YOU'RE IN TRAINING, GRUB...

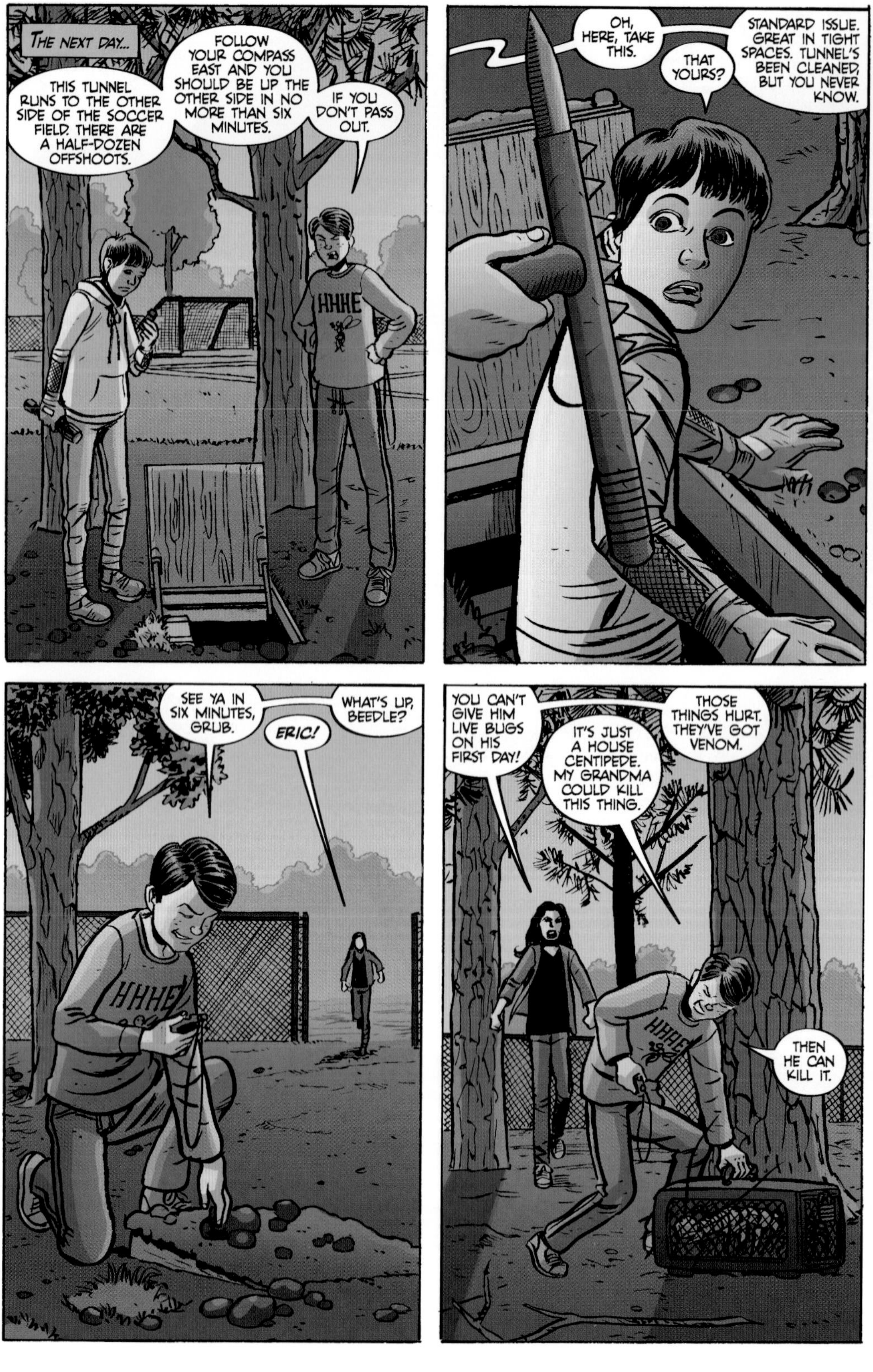
THE NEXT DAY...
THIS TUNNEL RUNS TO THE OTHER SIDE OF THE SOCCER FIELD. THERE ARE A HALF-DOZEN OFFSHOOTS.
FOLLOW YOUR COMPASS EAST AND YOU SHOULD BE UP THE OTHER SIDE IN NO MORE THAN SIX MINUTES.
IF YOU DON'T PASS OUT.
OH, HERE, TAKE THIS.
THAT YOURS?
STANDARD ISSUE. GREAT IN TIGHT SPACES. TUNNEL'S BEEN CLEANED, BUT YOU NEVER KNOW.
SEE YA IN SIX MINUTES, GRUB.
WHAT'S UP, BEEDLE?
ERIC!
YOU CAN'T GIVE HIM LIVE BUGS ON HIS FIRST DAY!
THOSE THINGS HURT. THEY'VE GOT VENOM.
IT'S JUST A HOUSE CENTIPEDE. MY GRANDMA COULD KILL THIS THING.
THEN HE CAN KILL IT.
HHHE

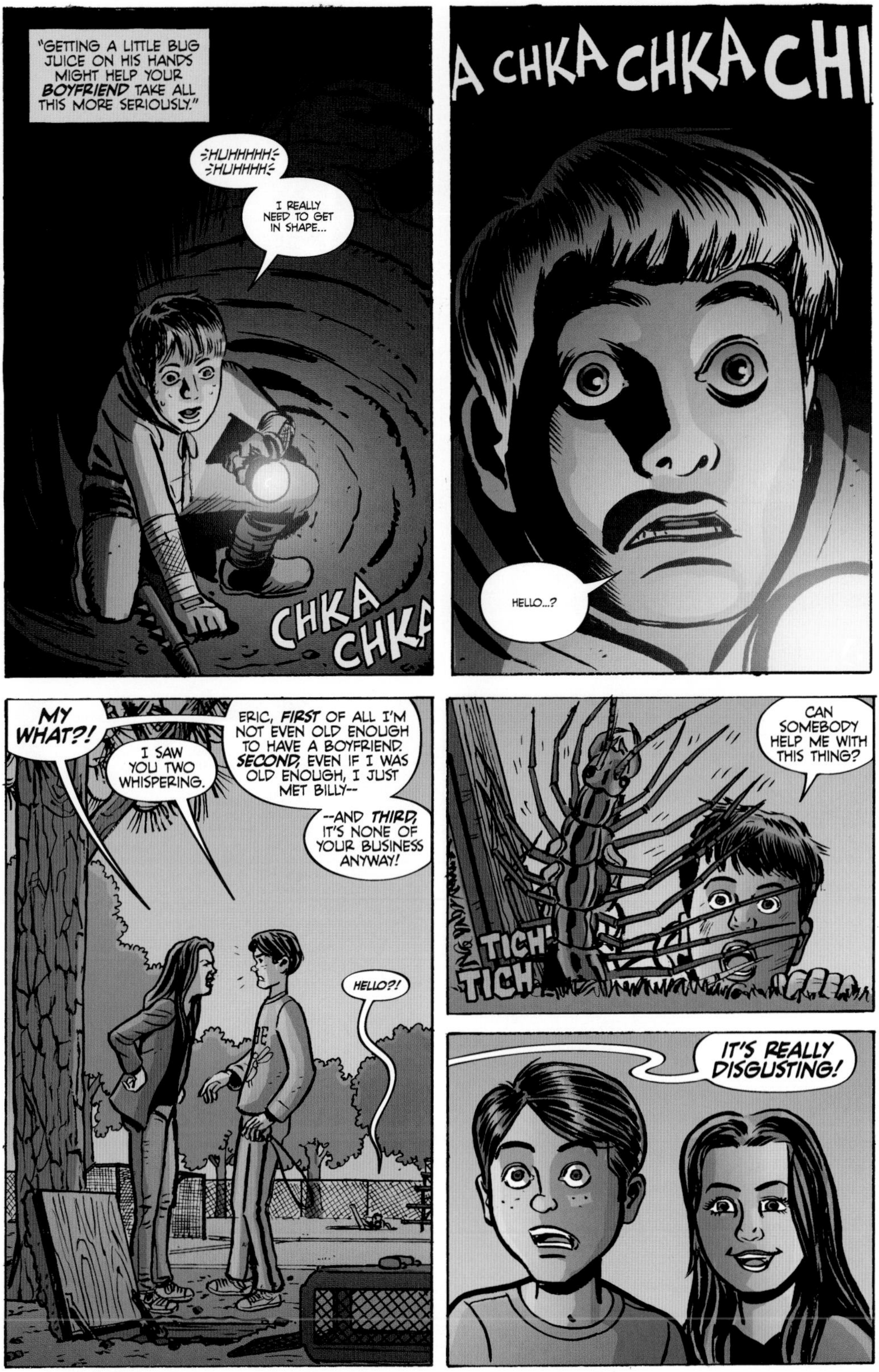
"GETTING A LITTLE BUG JUICE ON HIS HANDS MIGHT HELP YOUR BOYFRIEND TAKE ALL THIS MORE SERIOUSLY."
HUHHHHH HUHHHH
I REALLY NEED TO GET IN SHAPE...
CHKA CHKA
A CHKA CHKA CHI
HELLO...?
MY WHAT?!
I SAW YOU TWO WHISPERING.
ERIC, FIRST OF ALL I'M NOT EVEN OLD ENOUGH TO HAVE A BOYFRIEND. SECOND, EVEN IF I WAS OLD ENOUGH, I JUST MET BILLY--
--AND THIRD, IT'S NONE OF YOUR BUSINESS ANYWAY!
HELLO?!
CAN SOMEBODY HELP ME WITH THIS THING?
TICH TICH
IT'S REALLY DISGUSTING!

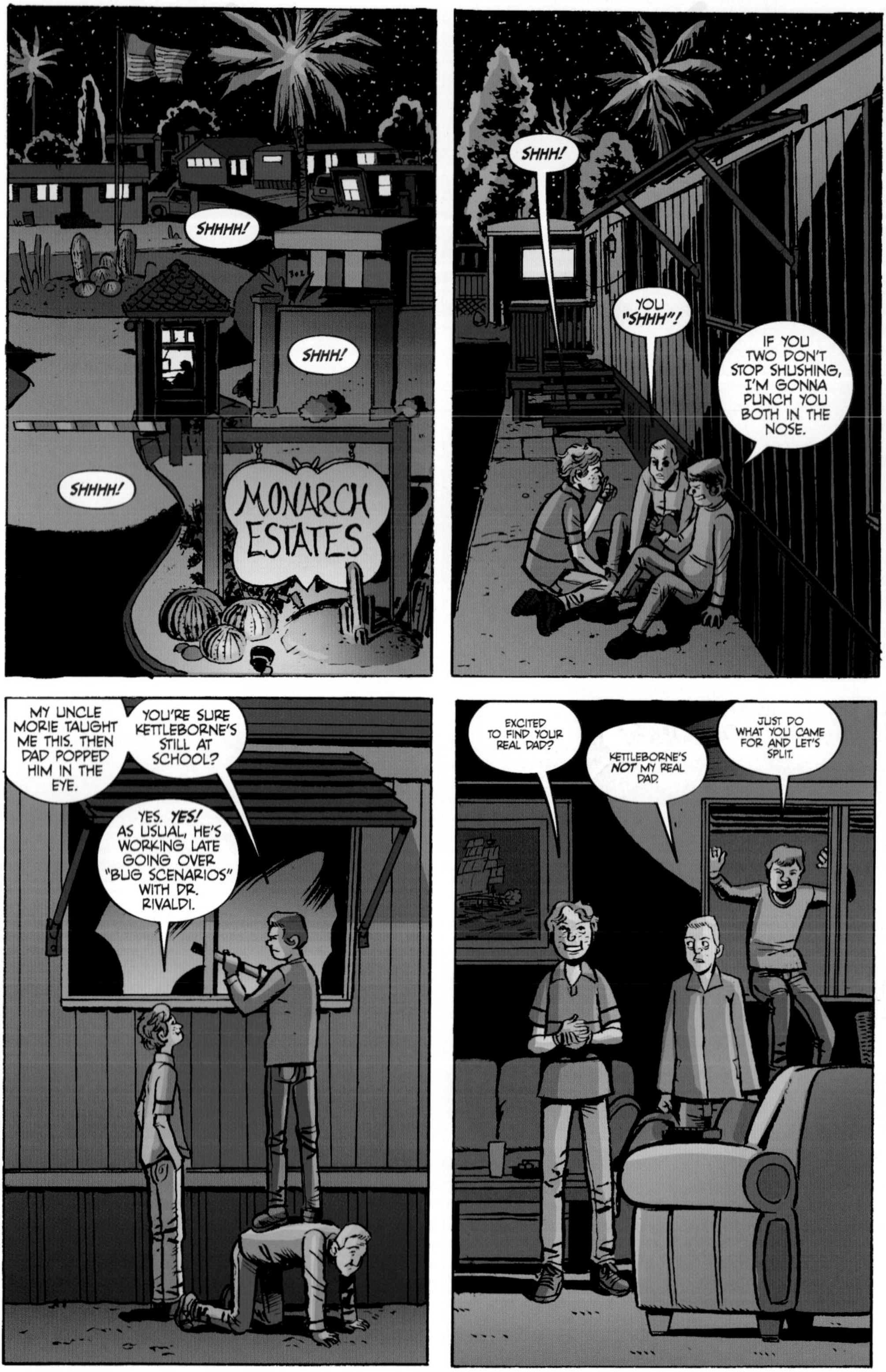
SHHHH!
SHHH!
SHHHH!
MONARCH ESTATES
SHHH!
YOU "SHHH"!
IF YOU TWO DON'T STOP SHUSHING, I'M GONNA PUNCH YOU BOTH IN THE NOSE.
MY UNCLE MORIE TAUGHT ME THIS. THEN DAD POPPED HIM IN THE EYE.
YOU'RE SURE KETTLEBORNE'S STILL AT SCHOOL?
YES. *YES!* AS USUAL, HE'S WORKING LATE GOING OVER "BUG SCENARIOS" WITH DR. RIVALDI.
EXCITED TO FIND YOUR REAL DAD?
KETTLEBORNE'S *NOT* MY REAL DAD.
JUST DO WHAT YOU CAME FOR AND LET'S SPLIT.

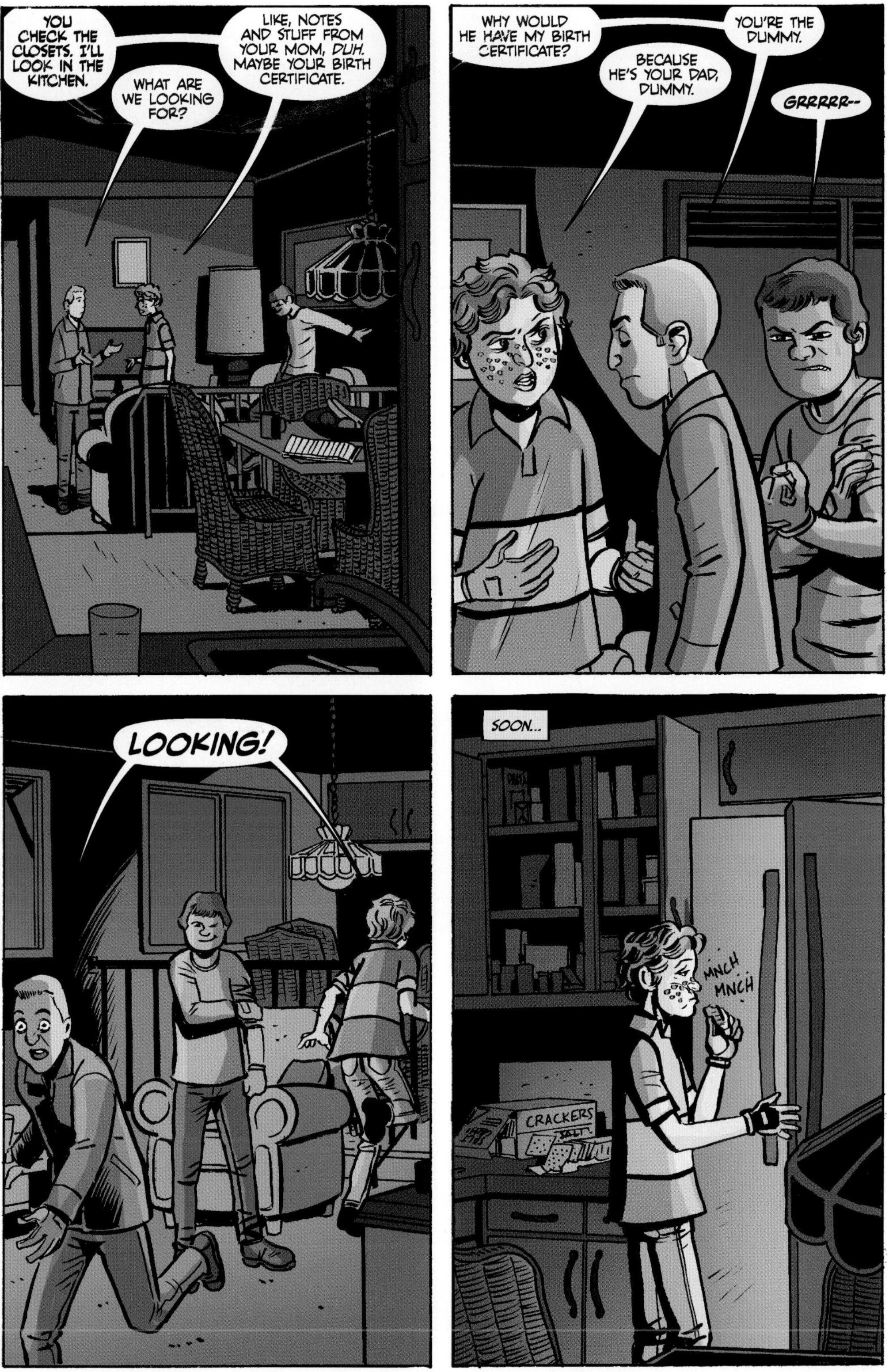
YOU CHECK THE CLOSETS. I'LL LOOK IN THE KITCHEN.
WHAT ARE WE LOOKING FOR?
LIKE, NOTES AND STUFF FROM YOUR MOM, *DUH.* MAYBE YOUR BIRTH CERTIFICATE.
WHY WOULD HE HAVE MY BIRTH CERTIFICATE?
BECAUSE HE'S YOUR DAD, DUMMY.
YOU'RE THE DUMMY.
GRRRRR--
LOOKING!
SOON...
CRACKERS
MNCH MNCH

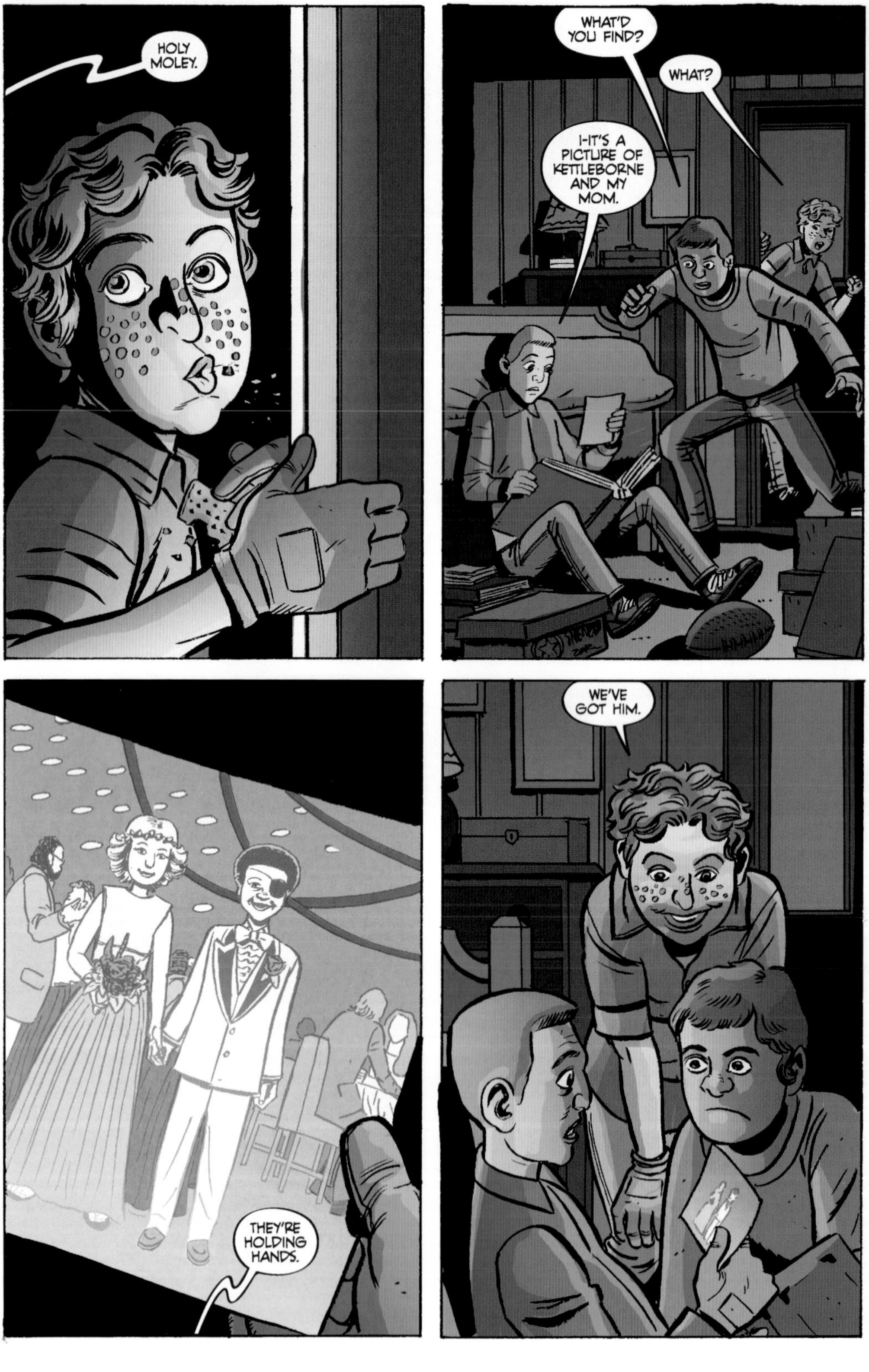
HOLY MOLEY.
WHAT'D YOU FIND?
WHAT?
I-IT'S A PICTURE OF KETTLEBORNE AND MY MOM.
THEY'RE HOLDING HANDS.
WE'VE GOT HIM.

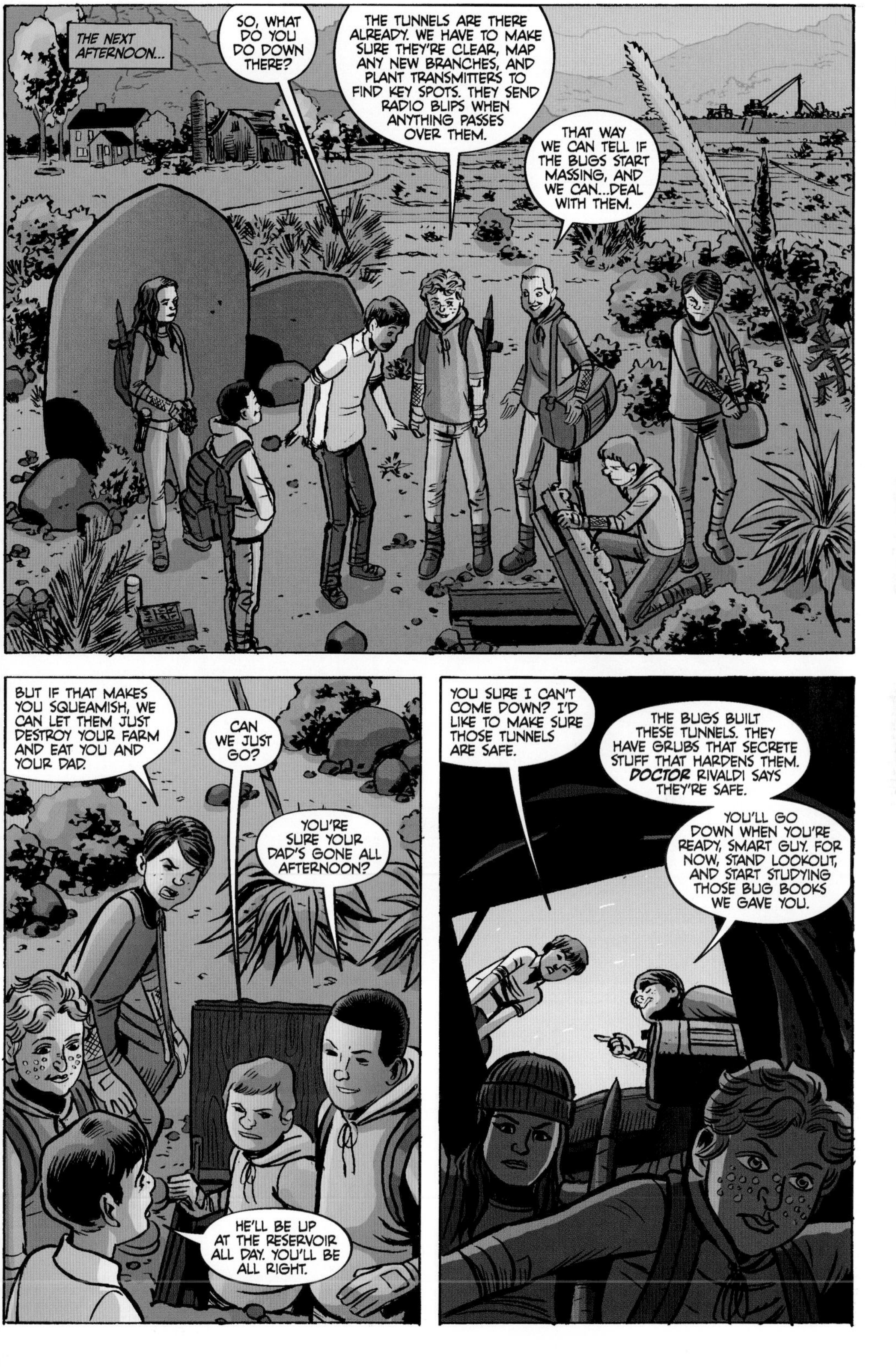
THE NEXT AFTERNOON...
SO, WHAT DO YOU DO DOWN THERE?
THE TUNNELS ARE THERE ALREADY. WE HAVE TO MAKE SURE THEY'RE CLEAR, MAP ANY NEW BRANCHES, AND PLANT TRANSMITTERS TO FIND KEY SPOTS. THEY SEND RADIO BLIPS WHEN ANYTHING PASSES OVER THEM.
THAT WAY WE CAN TELL IF THE BUGS START MASSING, AND WE CAN...DEAL WITH THEM.
BUT IF THAT MAKES YOU SQUEAMISH, WE CAN LET THEM JUST DESTROY YOUR FARM AND EAT YOU AND YOUR DAD.
CAN WE JUST GO?
YOU'RE SURE YOUR DAD'S GONE ALL AFTERNOON?
HE'LL BE UP AT THE RESERVOIR ALL DAY. YOU'LL BE ALL RIGHT.
YOU SURE I CAN'T COME DOWN? I'D LIKE TO MAKE SURE THOSE TUNNELS ARE SAFE.
THE BUGS BUILT THESE TUNNELS. THEY HAVE GRUBS THAT SECRETE STUFF THAT HARDENS THEM. DOCTOR RIVALDI SAYS THEY'RE SAFE.
YOU'LL GO DOWN WHEN YOU'RE READY, SMART GUY. FOR NOW, STAND LOOKOUT, AND START STUDYING THOSE BUG BOOKS WE GAVE YOU.

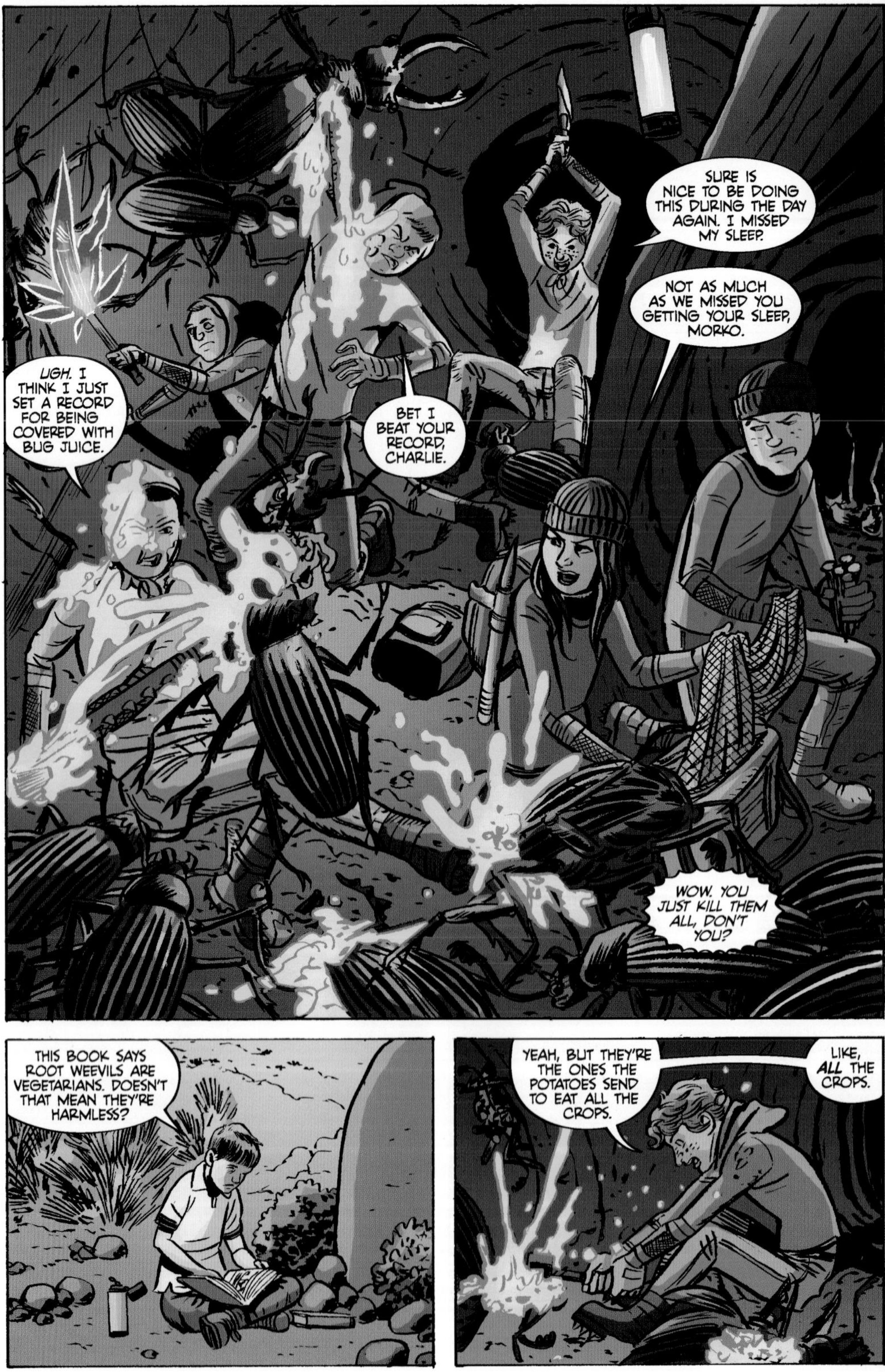
SURE IS NICE TO BE DOING THIS DURING THE DAY AGAIN. I MISSED MY SLEEP.
NOT AS MUCH AS WE MISSED YOU GETTING YOUR SLEEP, MORKO.
UGH. I THINK I JUST SET A RECORD FOR BEING COVERED WITH BUG JUICE.
BET I BEAT YOUR RECORD, CHARLIE.
WOW. YOU JUST KILL THEM ALL, DON'T YOU?
THIS BOOK SAYS ROOT WEEVILS ARE VEGETARIANS. DOESN'T THAT MEAN THEY'RE HARMLESS?
YEAH, BUT THEY'RE THE ONES THE POTATOES SEND TO EAT ALL THE CROPS.
LIKE, ALL THE CROPS.

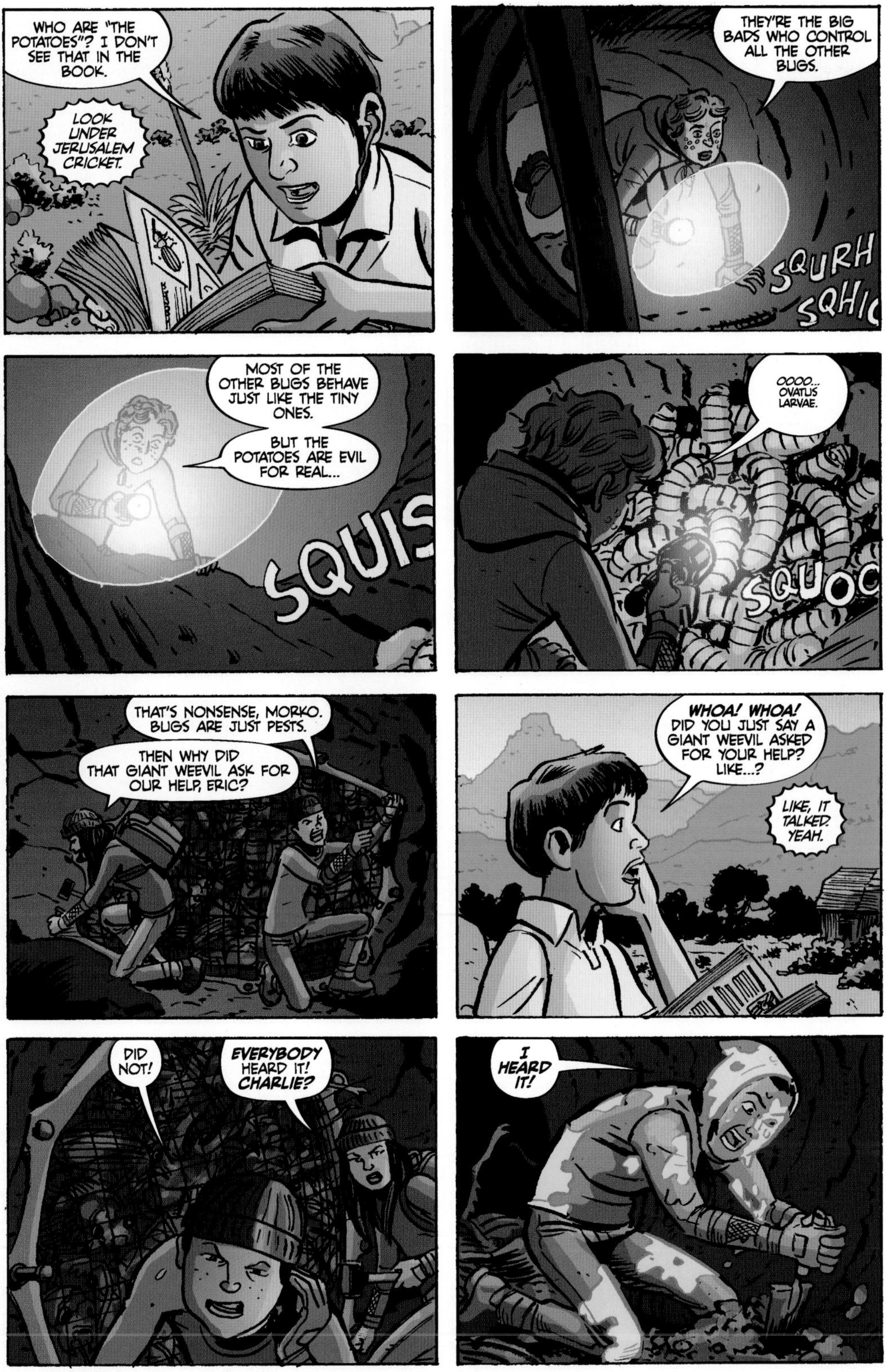
WHO ARE "THE POTATOES"? I DON'T SEE THAT IN THE BOOK.
LOOK UNDER JERUSALEM CRICKET.
THEY'RE THE BIG BADS WHO CONTROL ALL THE OTHER BUGS.
SQURH
SQHIC
MOST OF THE OTHER BUGS BEHAVE JUST LIKE THE TINY ONES.
BUT THE POTATOES ARE EVIL FOR REAL...
SQUIS
OOOO... OVATUS LARVAE.
SQUOC
THAT'S NONSENSE, MORKO. BUGS ARE JUST PESTS.
THEN WHY DID THAT GIANT WEEVIL ASK FOR OUR HELP, ERIC?
WHOA! WHOA! DID YOU JUST SAY A GIANT WEEVIL ASKED FOR YOUR HELP? LIKE...?
LIKE, IT TALKED. YEAH.
DID NOT!
EVERYBODY HEARD IT! CHARLIE?
I HEARD IT!

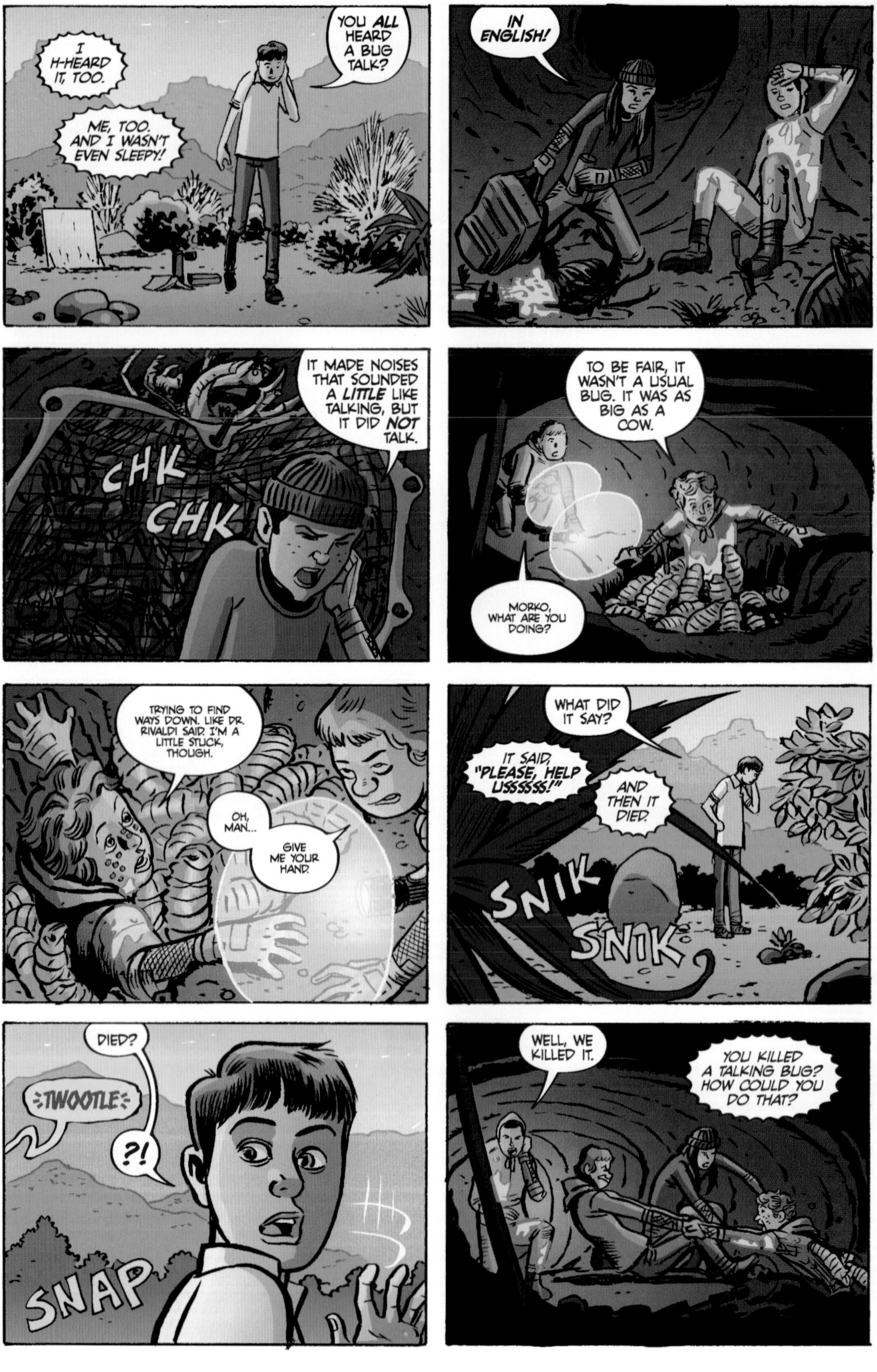
YOU ALL HEARD A BUG TALK?
I H-HEARD IT, TOO.
ME, TOO. AND I WASN'T EVEN SLEEPY!
IN ENGLISH!
IT MADE NOISES THAT SOUNDED A LITTLE LIKE TALKING, BUT IT DID NOT TALK.
CHK CHK
TO BE FAIR, IT WASN'T A USUAL BUG. IT WAS AS BIG AS A COW.
MORKO, WHAT ARE YOU DOING?
TRYING TO FIND WAYS DOWN. LIKE DR. RIVALDI SAID. I'M A LITTLE STUCK, THOUGH.
OH, MAN...
GIVE ME YOUR HAND.
WHAT DID IT SAY?
IT SAID, "PLEASE, HELP USSSSSS!"
AND THEN IT DIED.
SNIK SNIK
DIED?
TWOOTLE
?!
SNAP
WELL, WE KILLED IT.
YOU KILLED A TALKING BUG? HOW COULD YOU DO THAT?

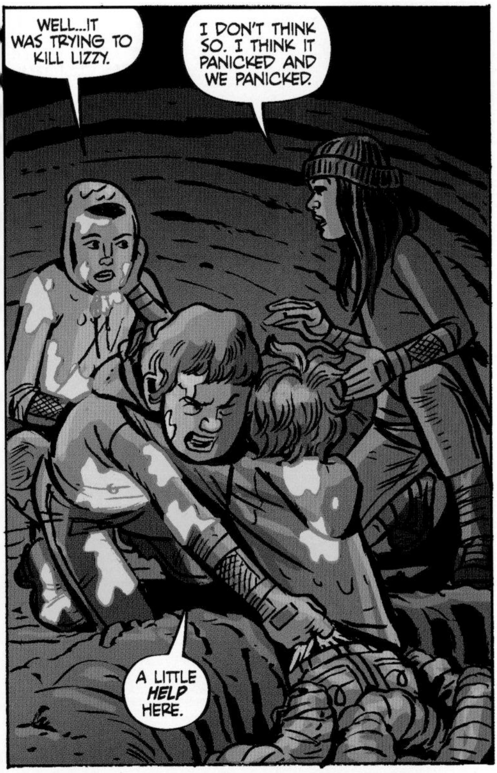
WELL...IT WAS TRYING TO KILL LIZZY.
I DON'T THINK SO. I THINK IT PANICKED AND WE PANICKED.
A LITTLE HELP HERE.

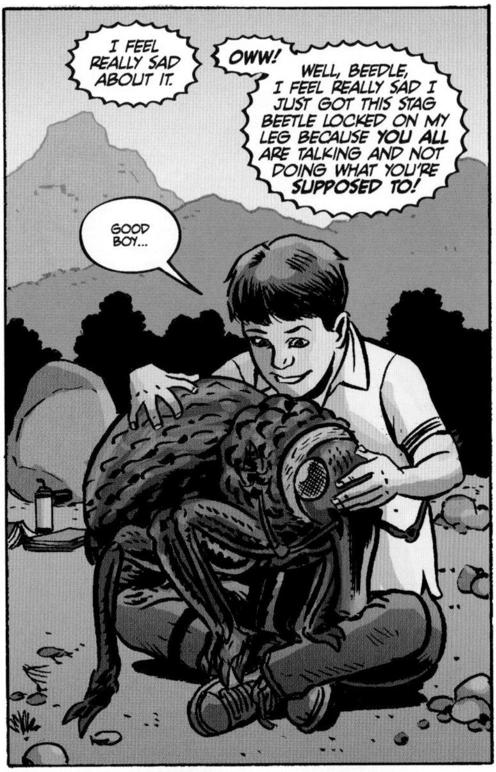
I FEEL REALLY SAD ABOUT IT.
OWW!
WELL, BEEDLE, I FEEL REALLY SAD I JUST GOT THIS STAG BEETLE LOCKED ON MY LEG BECAUSE YOU ALL ARE TALKING AND NOT DOING WHAT YOU'RE SUPPOSED TO!
GOOD BOY...

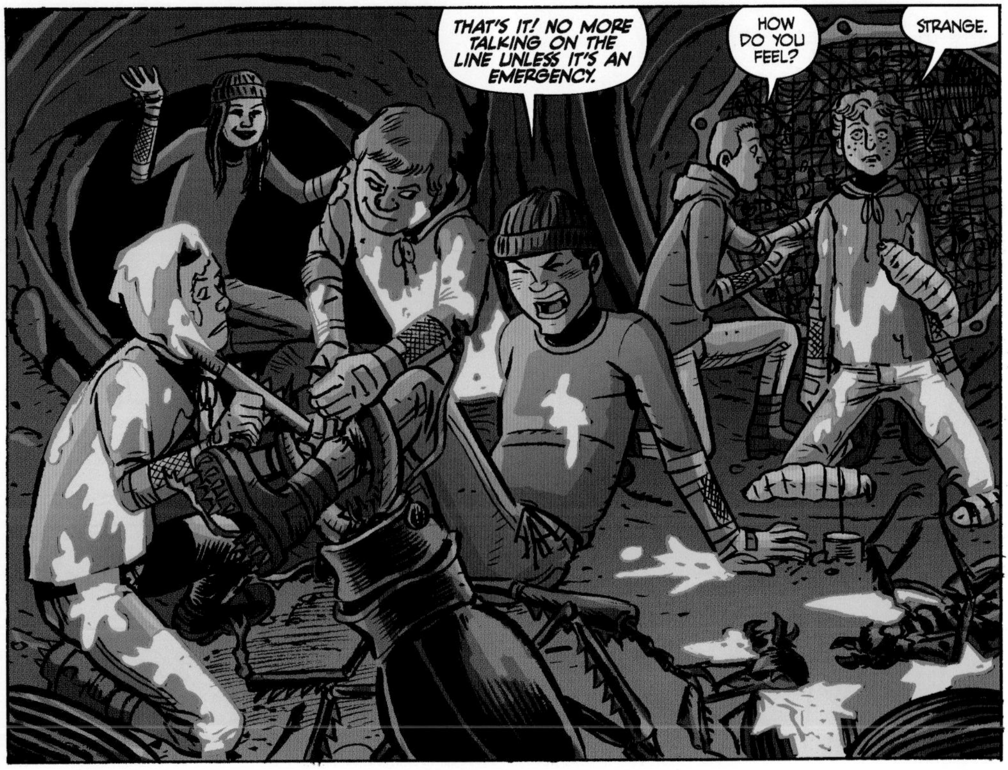
THAT'S IT! NO MORE TALKING ON THE LINE UNLESS IT'S AN EMERGENCY.
HOW DO YOU FEEL?
STRANGE.

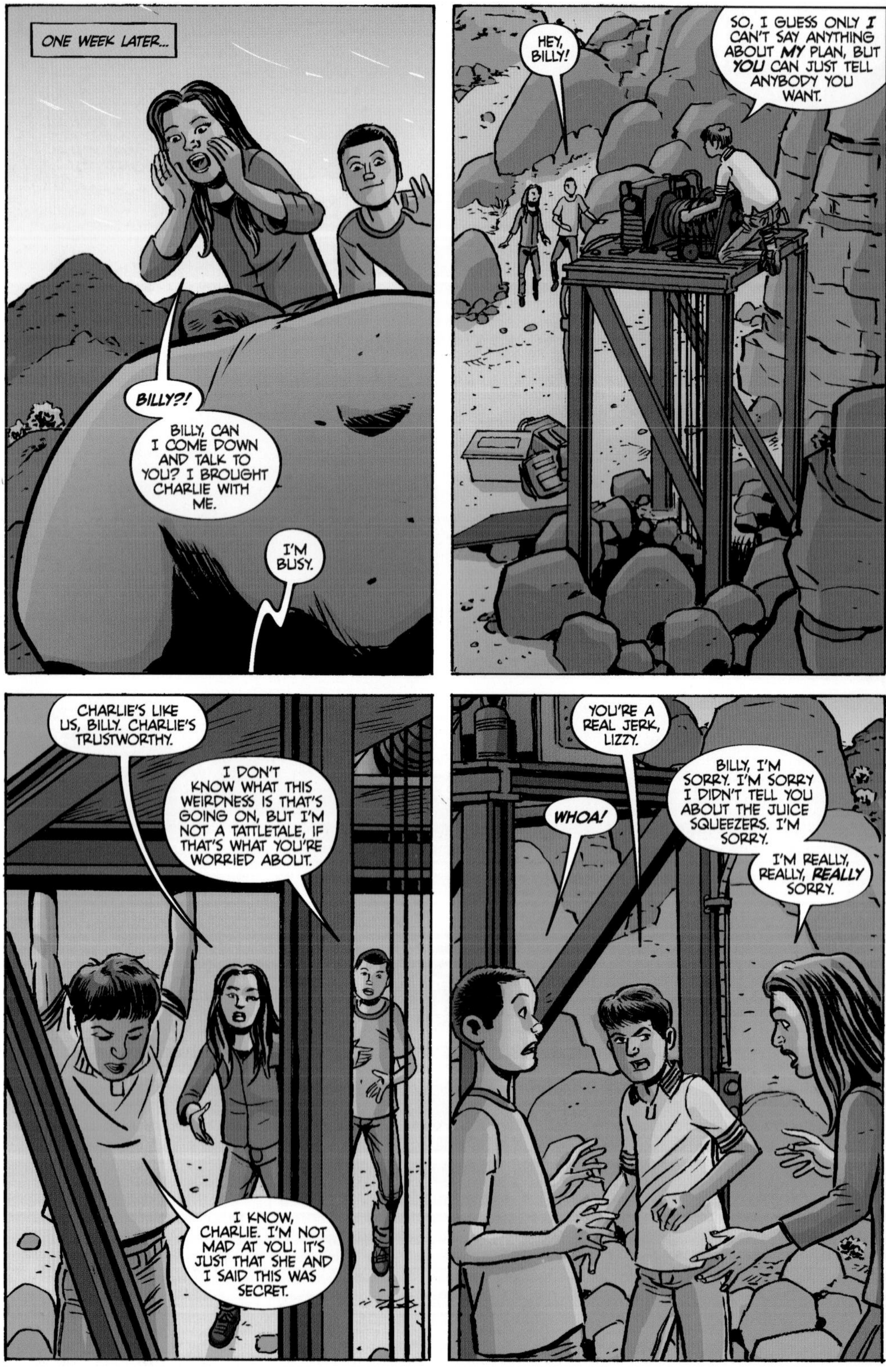
ONE WEEK LATER...
BILLY?!
BILLY, CAN I COME DOWN AND TALK TO YOU? I BROUGHT CHARLIE WITH ME.
I'M BUSY.
HEY, BILLY!
SO, I GUESS ONLY I CAN'T SAY ANYTHING ABOUT MY PLAN, BUT YOU CAN JUST TELL ANYBODY YOU WANT.
CHARLIE'S LIKE US, BILLY. CHARLIE'S TRUSTWORTHY.
I DON'T KNOW WHAT THIS WEIRDNESS IS THAT'S GOING ON, BUT I'M NOT A TATTLETALE, IF THAT'S WHAT YOU'RE WORRIED ABOUT.
I KNOW, CHARLIE. I'M NOT MAD AT YOU. IT'S JUST THAT SHE AND I SAID THIS WAS SECRET.
YOU'RE A REAL JERK, LIZZY.
WHOA!
BILLY, I'M SORRY. I'M SORRY I DIDN'T TELL YOU ABOUT THE JUICE SQUEEZERS. I'M SORRY.
I'M REALLY, REALLY, REALLY SORRY.

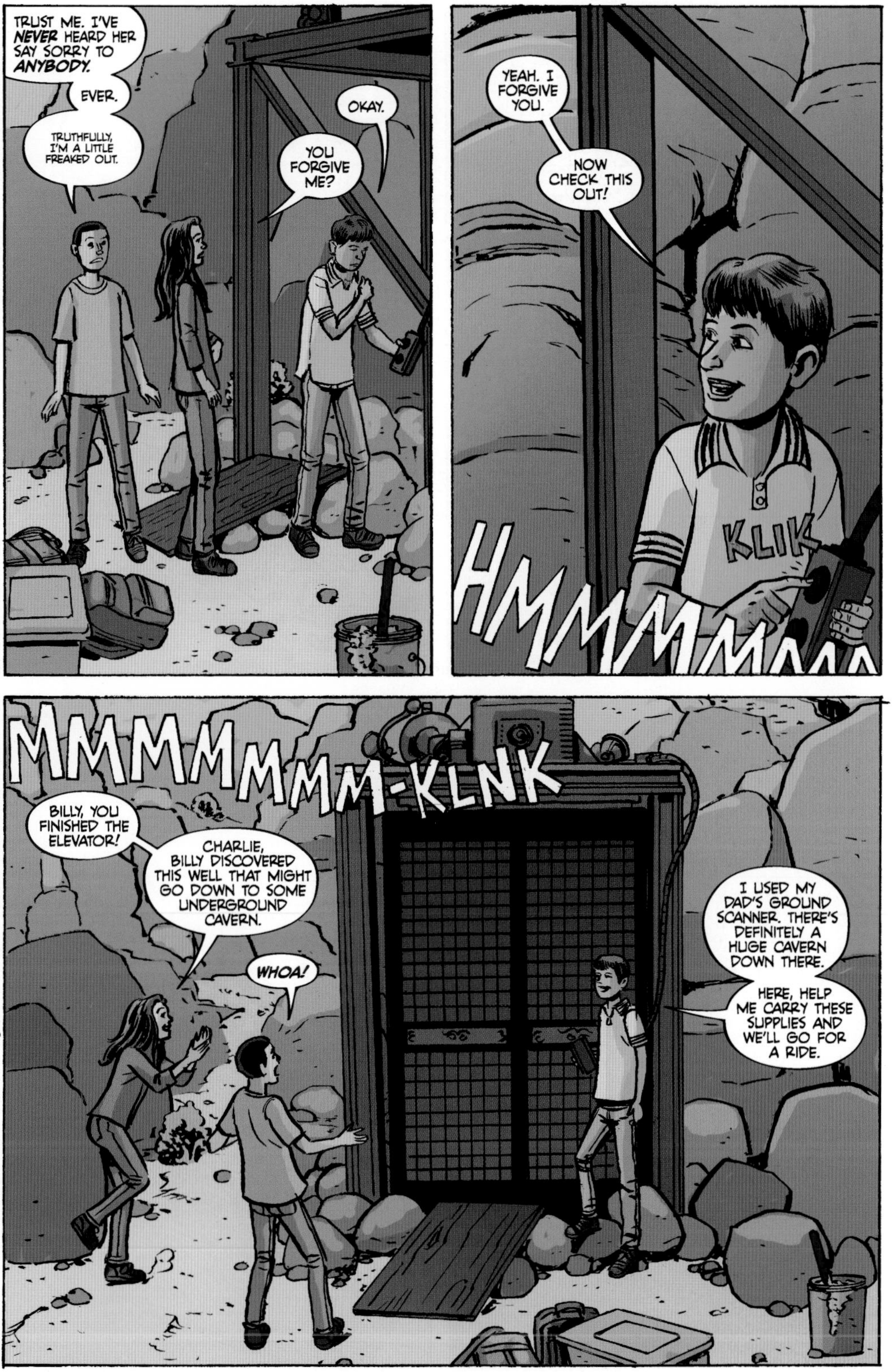
TRUST ME. I'VE NEVER HEARD HER SAY SORRY TO ANYBODY.
EVER.
TRUTHFULLY, I'M A LITTLE FREAKED OUT.
YOU FORGIVE ME?
OKAY.
YEAH. I FORGIVE YOU.
NOW CHECK THIS OUT!
KLIK
HMMMMMM
MMMMMMM-KLNK
BILLY, YOU FINISHED THE ELEVATOR!
CHARLIE, BILLY DISCOVERED THIS WELL THAT MIGHT GO DOWN TO SOME UNDERGROUND CAVERN.
WHOA!
I USED MY DAD'S GROUND SCANNER. THERE'S DEFINITELY A HUGE CAVERN DOWN THERE.
HERE, HELP ME CARRY THESE SUPPLIES AND WE'LL GO FOR A RIDE.

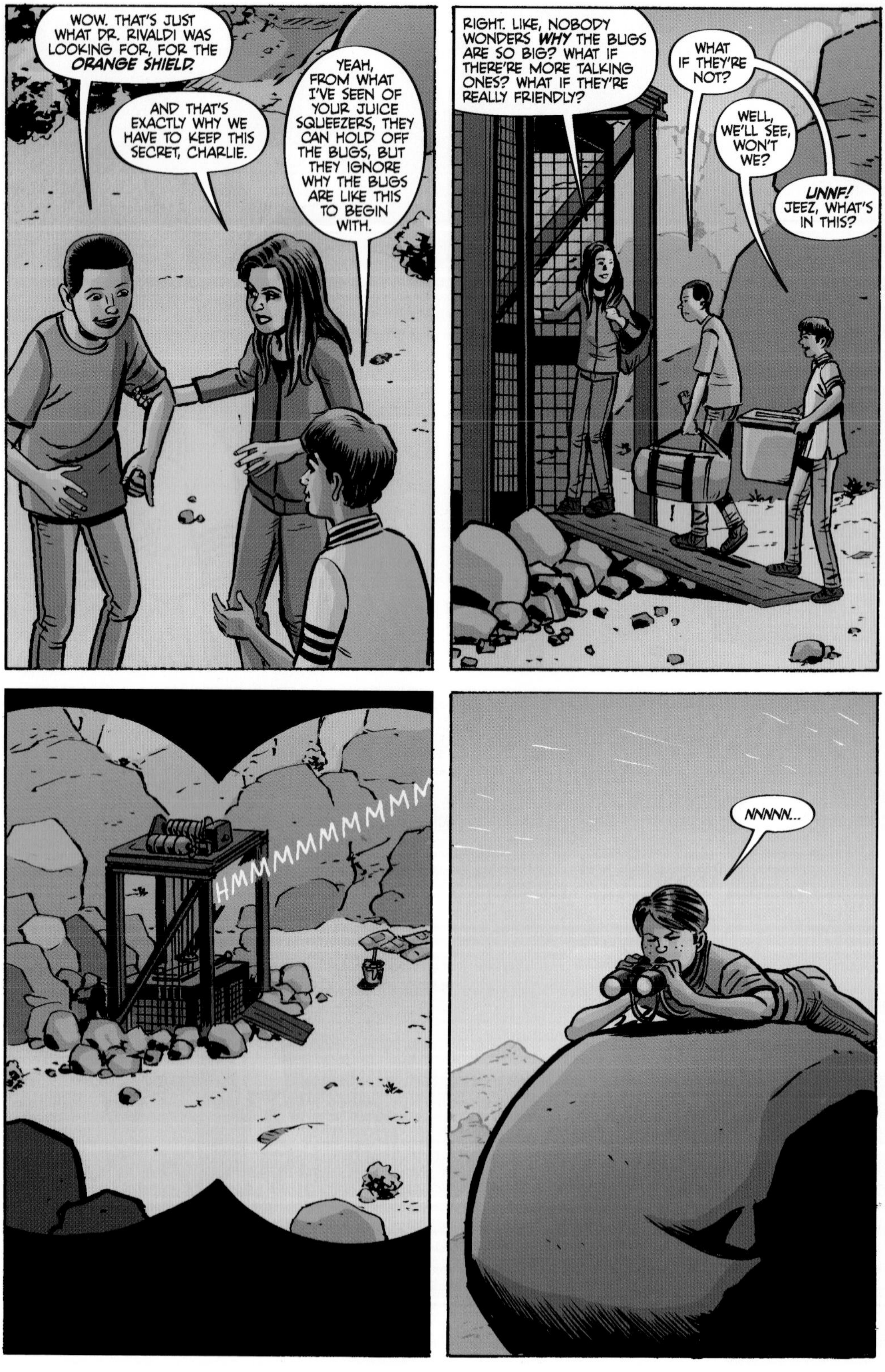
WOW. THAT'S JUST WHAT DR. RIVALDI WAS LOOKING FOR, FOR THE ORANGE SHIELD.
AND THAT'S EXACTLY WHY WE HAVE TO KEEP THIS SECRET, CHARLIE.
YEAH, FROM WHAT I'VE SEEN OF YOUR JUICE SQUEEZERS, THEY CAN HOLD OFF THE BUGS, BUT THEY IGNORE WHY THE BUGS ARE LIKE THIS TO BEGIN WITH.
RIGHT. LIKE, NOBODY WONDERS WHY THE BUGS ARE SO BIG? WHAT IF THERE'RE MORE TALKING ONES? WHAT IF THEY'RE REALLY FRIENDLY?
WHAT IF THEY'RE NOT?
WELL, WE'LL SEE, WON'T WE?
UNNF! JEEZ, WHAT'S IN THIS?
HMMMMMMMMMMM
NNNNN...

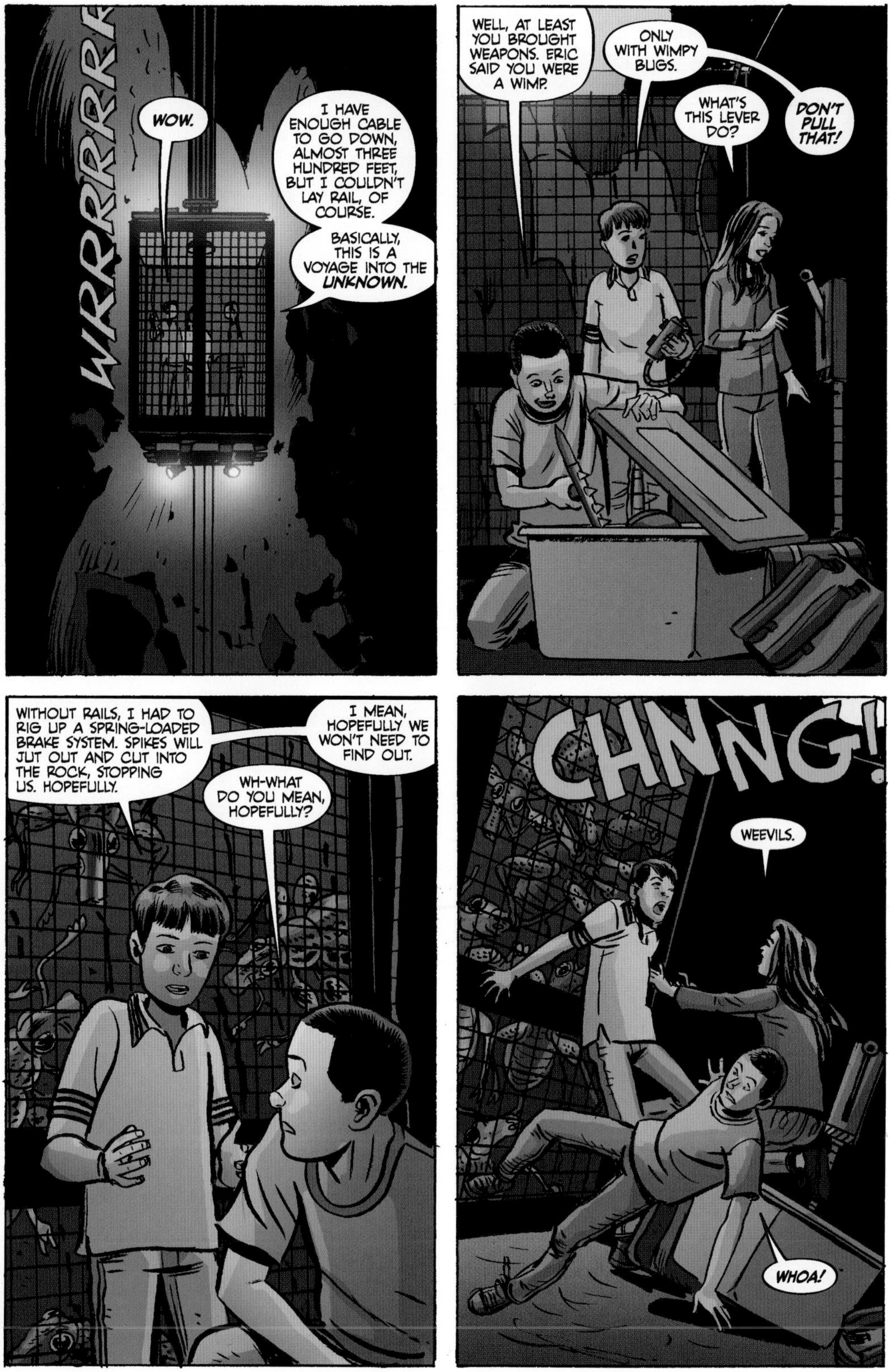
WRRRRRR
WOW.
I HAVE ENOUGH CABLE TO GO DOWN, ALMOST THREE HUNDRED FEET, BUT I COULDN'T LAY RAIL, OF COURSE.
BASICALLY, THIS IS A VOYAGE INTO THE UNKNOWN.
WELL, AT LEAST YOU BROUGHT WEAPONS. ERIC SAID YOU WERE A WIMP.
ONLY WITH WIMPY BUGS.
WHAT'S THIS LEVER DO?
DON'T PULL THAT!
WITHOUT RAILS, I HAD TO RIG UP A SPRING-LOADED BRAKE SYSTEM. SPIKES WILL JUT OUT AND CUT INTO THE ROCK, STOPPING US. HOPEFULLY.
I MEAN, HOPEFULLY WE WON'T NEED TO FIND OUT.
WH-WHAT DO YOU MEAN, HOPEFULLY?
CHNNG!
WEEVILS.
WHOA!

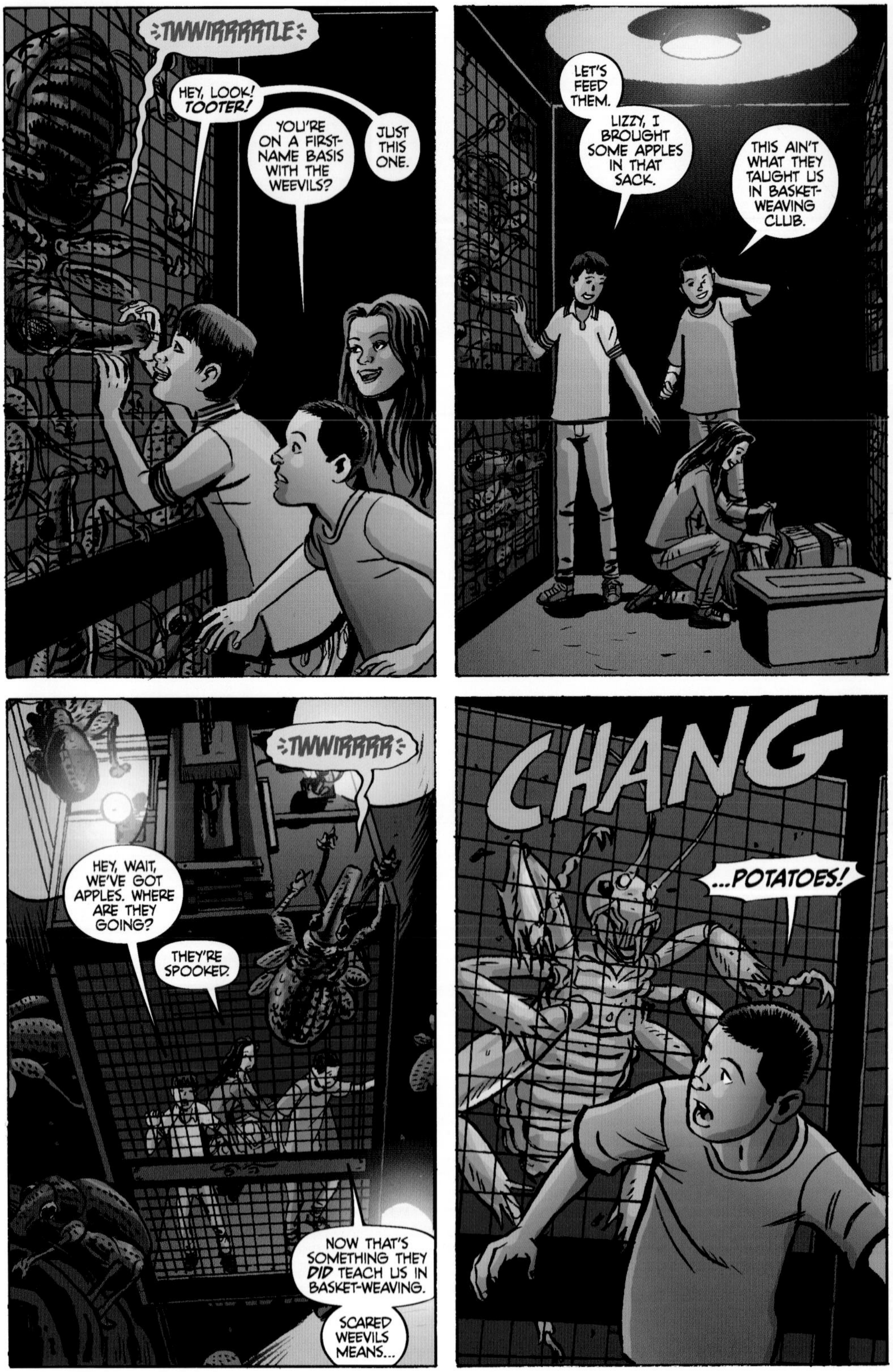
TWWIRRRRRTLE
HEY, LOOK! TOOTER!
YOU'RE ON A FIRST-NAME BASIS WITH THE WEEVILS?
JUST THIS ONE.
LET'S FEED THEM.
LIZZY, I BROUGHT SOME APPLES IN THAT SACK.
THIS AIN'T WHAT THEY TAUGHT US IN BASKET-WEAVING CLUB.
TWWIRRRRR
HEY, WAIT, WE'VE GOT APPLES. WHERE ARE THEY GOING?
THEY'RE SPOOKED.
NOW THAT'S SOMETHING THEY DID TEACH US IN BASKET-WEAVING.
SCARED WEEVILS MEANS...
CHANG
...POTATOES!

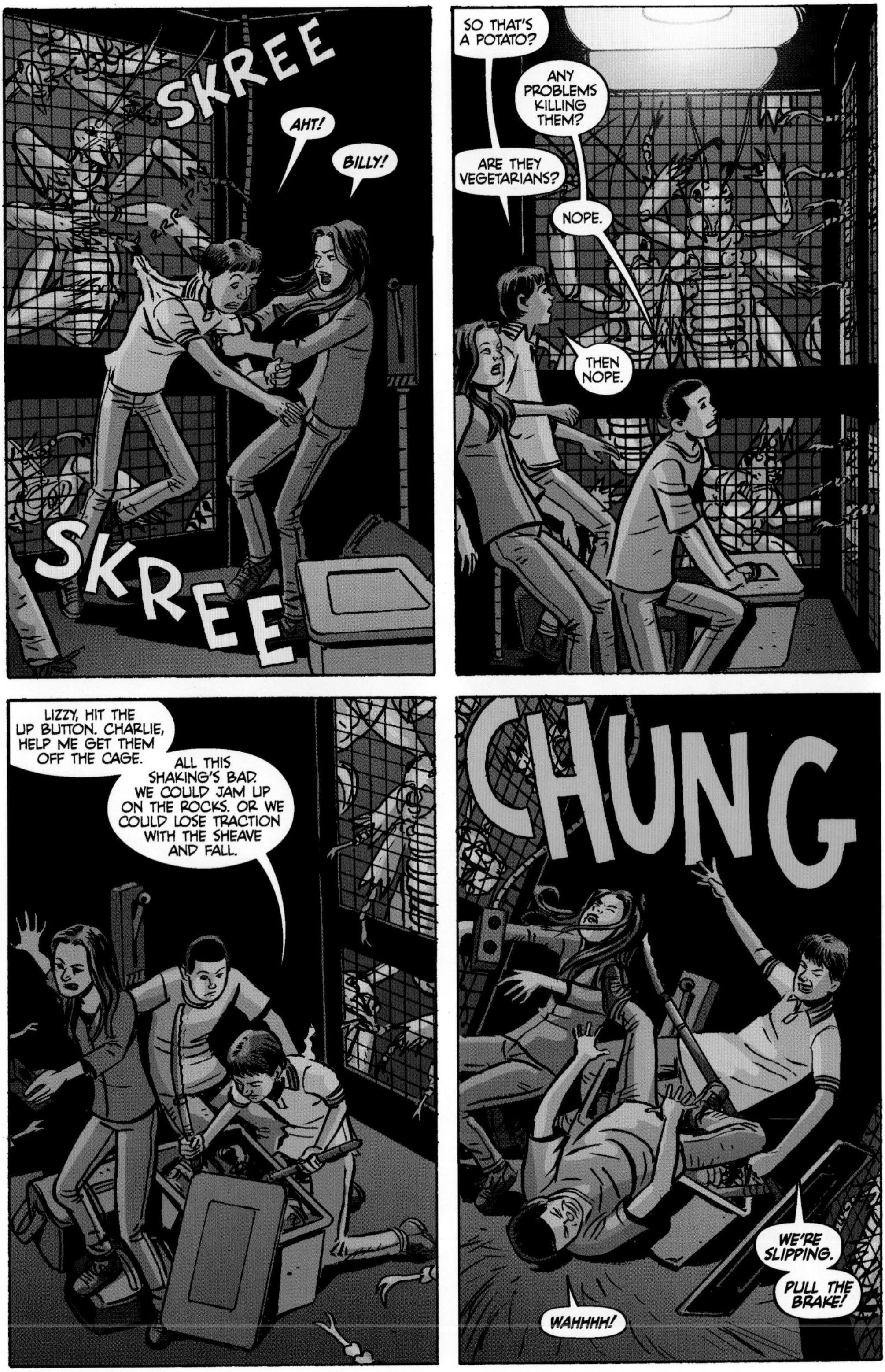
SKREE
AHT!
BILLY!
SKREE
SO THAT'S A POTATO?
ANY PROBLEMS KILLING THEM?
ARE THEY VEGETARIANS?
NOPE.
THEN NOPE.
LIZZY, HIT THE UP BUTTON. CHARLIE, HELP ME GET THEM OFF THE CAGE.
ALL THIS SHAKING'S BAD. WE COULD JAM UP ON THE ROCKS. OR WE COULD LOSE TRACTION WITH THE SHEAVE AND FALL.
CHUNG
WE'RE SLIPPING.
PULL THE BRAKE!
WAHHHH!

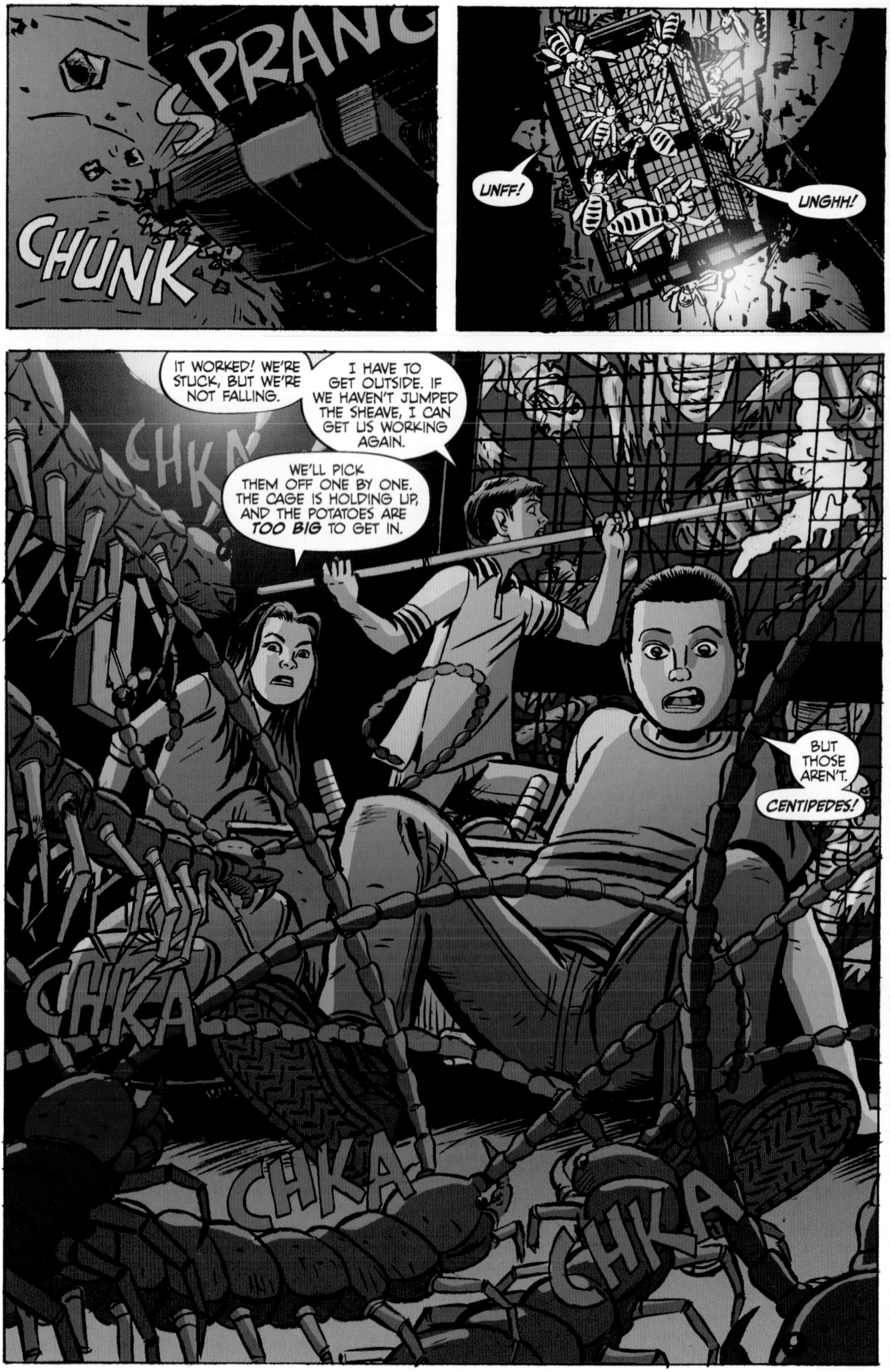
SPRANG
CHUNK
UNFF!
UNGHH!
IT WORKED! WE'RE STUCK, BUT WE'RE NOT FALLING.
I HAVE TO GET OUTSIDE. IF WE HAVEN'T JUMPED THE SHEAVE, I CAN GET US WORKING AGAIN.
WE'LL PICK THEM OFF ONE BY ONE. THE CAGE IS HOLDING UP, AND THE POTATOES ARE TOO BIG TO GET IN.
BUT THOSE AREN'T.
CENTIPEDES!
CHKA
CHKA
CHKA
CHKA

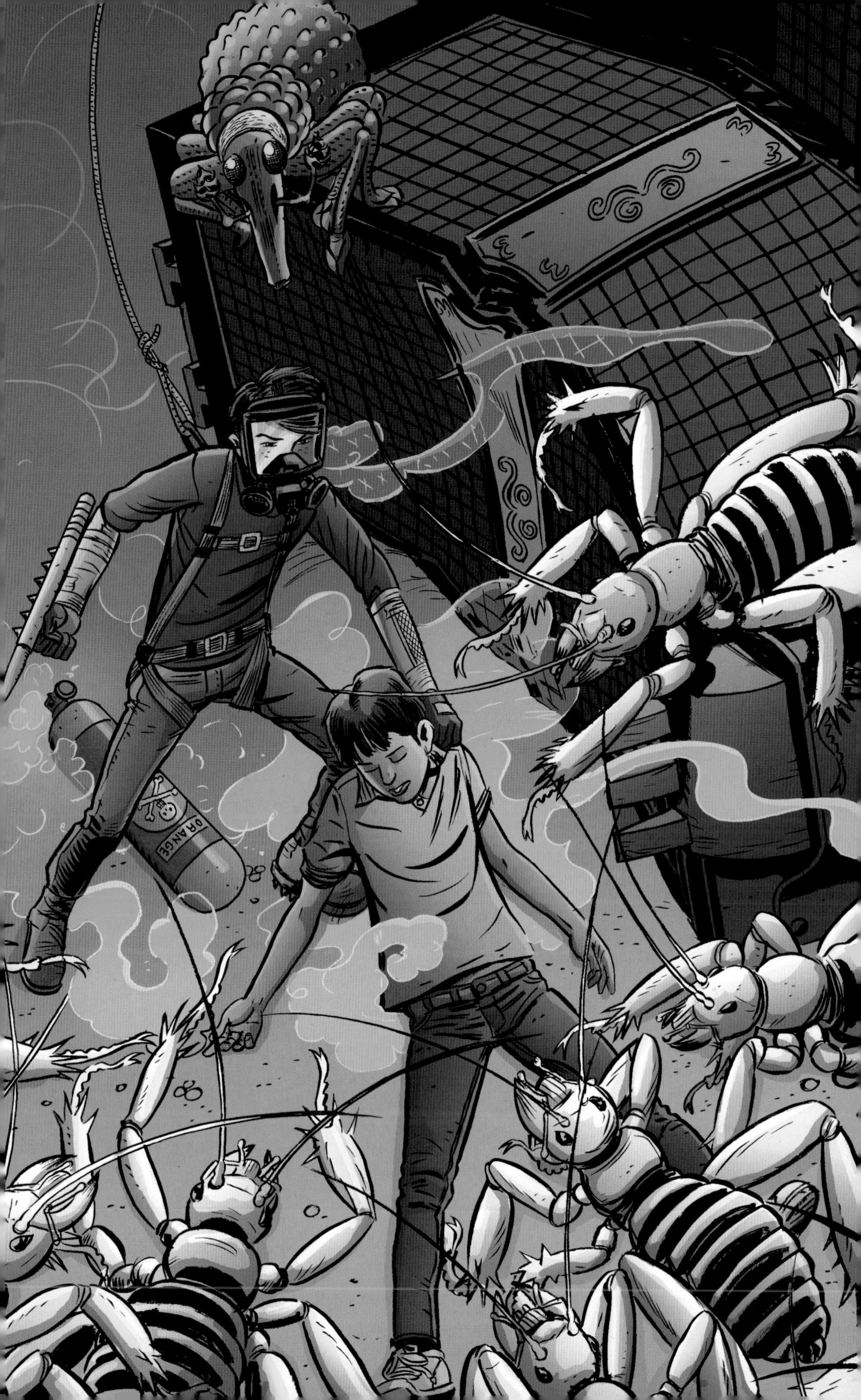
ORANGE

THE GREAT BUG ELEVATOR

PART FOUR: BUG CITY

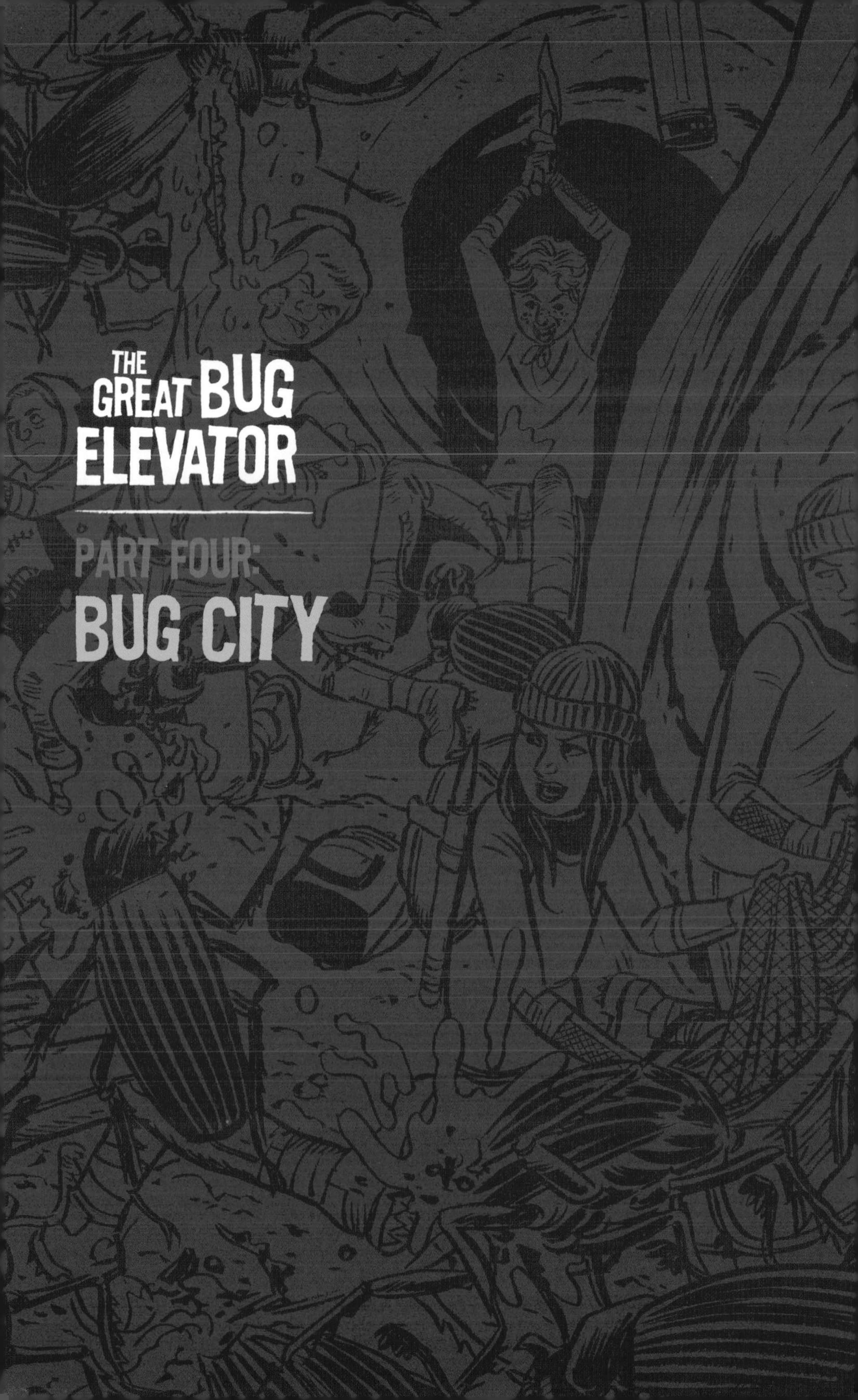

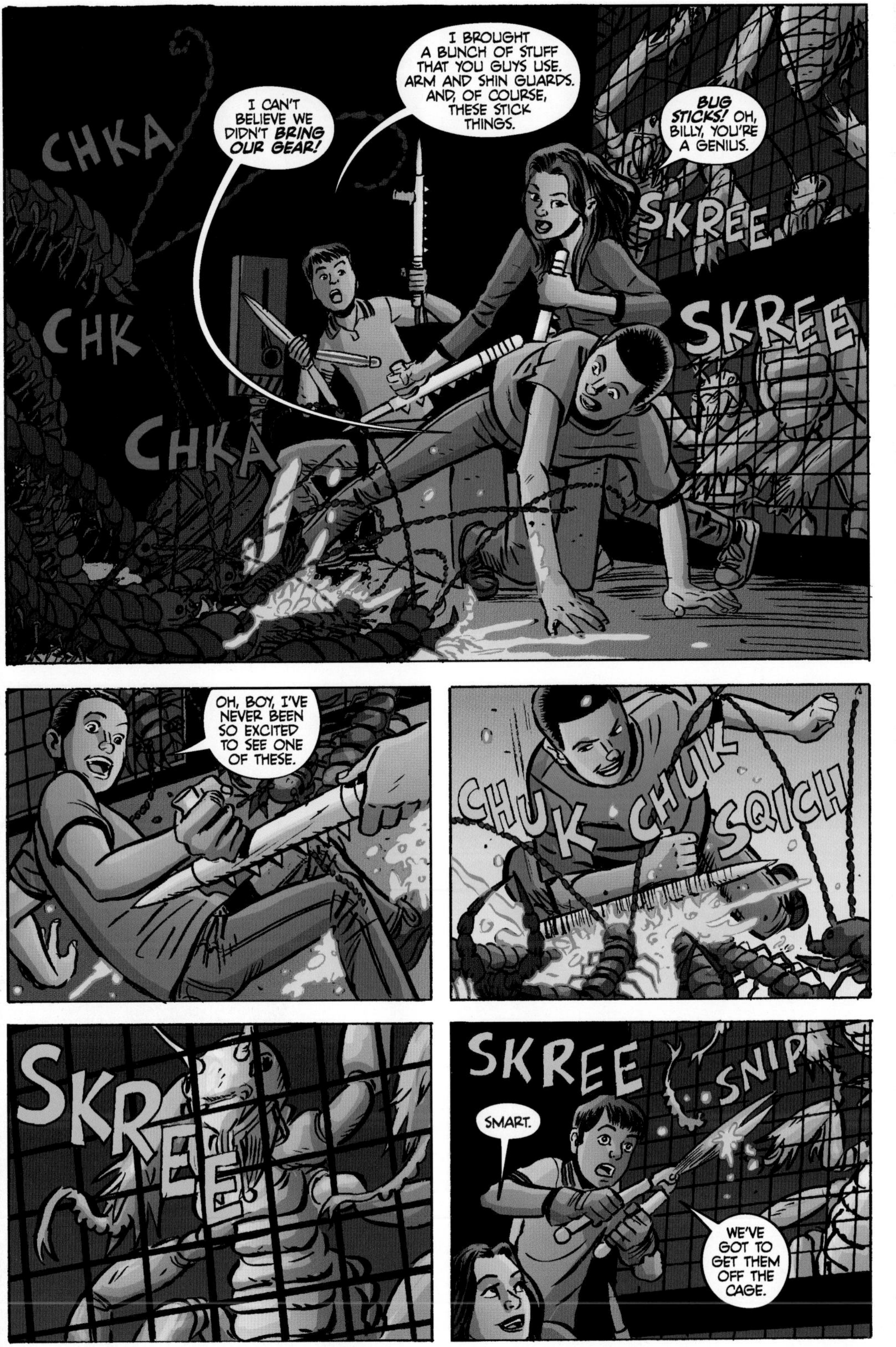
CHKA
CHK
CHKA
I CAN'T BELIEVE WE DIDN'T **BRING OUR GEAR!**
I BROUGHT A BUNCH OF STUFF THAT YOU GUYS USE. ARM AND SHIN GUARDS. AND, OF COURSE, THESE STICK THINGS.
BUG STICKS! OH, BILLY, YOU'RE A GENIUS.
SKREE
SKREE
OH, BOY, I'VE NEVER BEEN SO EXCITED TO SEE ONE OF THESE.
CHUK
CHUK
SQICH
SKREE
SKREE
SNIP
SMART.
WE'VE GOT TO GET THEM OFF THE CAGE.

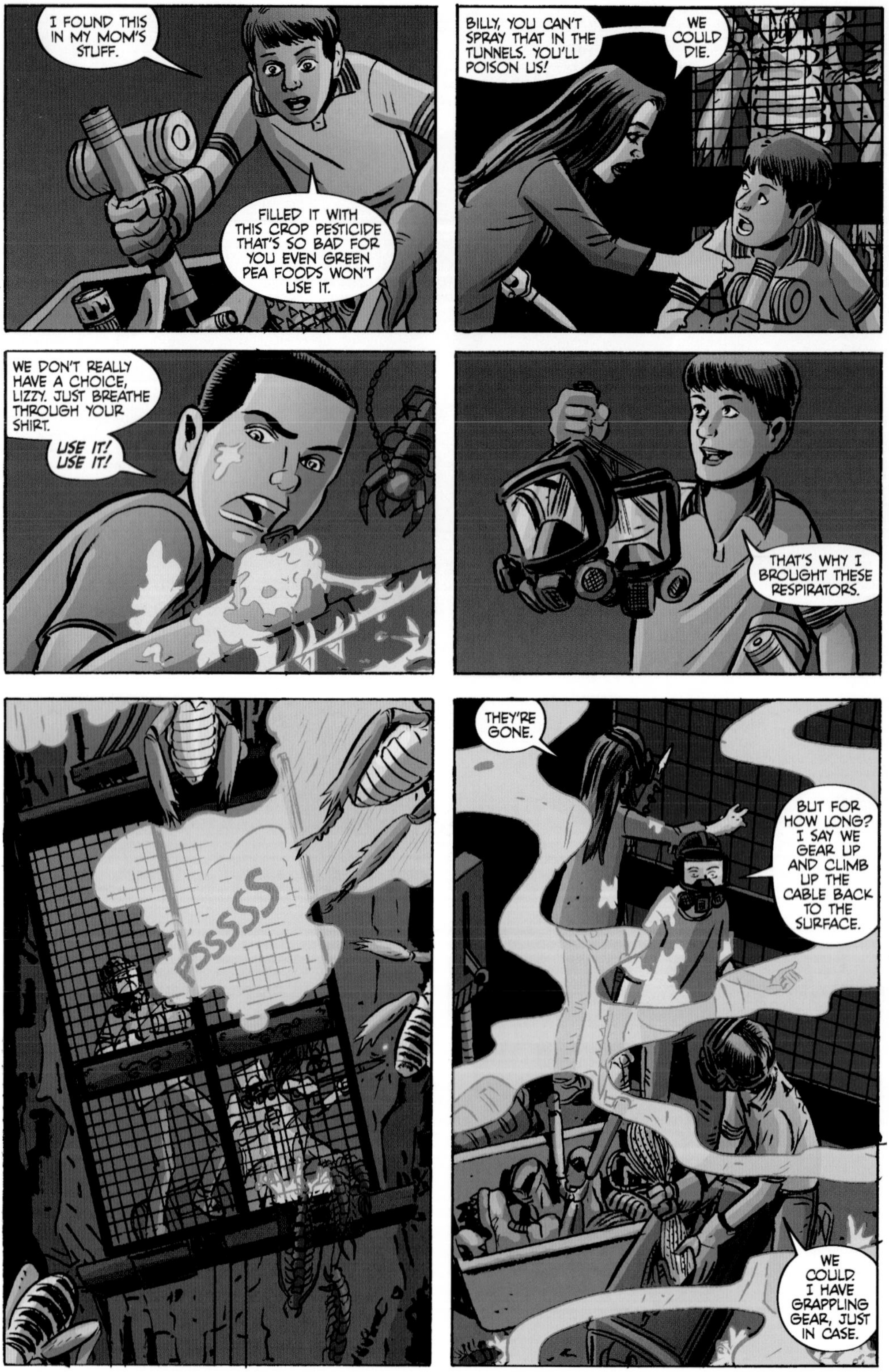
I FOUND THIS IN MY MOM'S STUFF.
FILLED IT WITH THIS CROP PESTICIDE THAT'S SO BAD FOR YOU EVEN GREEN PEA FOODS WON'T USE IT.
BILLY, YOU CAN'T SPRAY THAT IN THE TUNNELS. YOU'LL POISON US!
WE COULD DIE.
WE DON'T REALLY HAVE A CHOICE, LIZZY. JUST BREATHE THROUGH YOUR SHIRT.
USE IT! USE IT!
THAT'S WHY I BROUGHT THESE RESPIRATORS.
PSSSSS
THEY'RE GONE.
BUT FOR HOW LONG? I SAY WE GEAR UP AND CLIMB UP THE CABLE BACK TO THE SURFACE.
WE COULD. I HAVE GRAPPLING GEAR, JUST IN CASE.

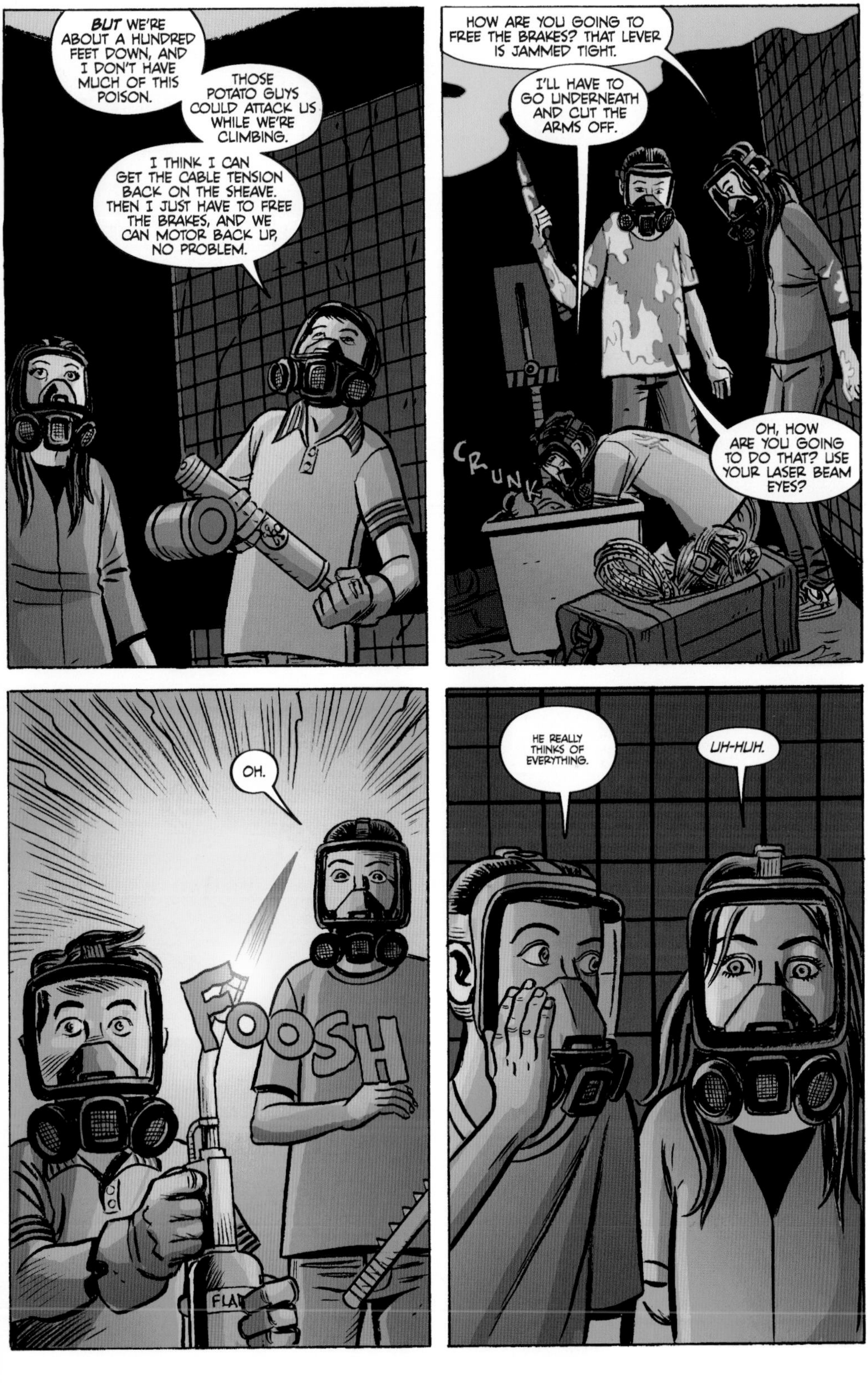

BUT WE'RE ABOUT A HUNDRED FEET DOWN, AND I DON'T HAVE MUCH OF THIS POISON.
THOSE POTATO GUYS COULD ATTACK US WHILE WE'RE CLIMBING.
I THINK I CAN GET THE CABLE TENSION BACK ON THE SHEAVE. THEN I JUST HAVE TO FREE THE BRAKES, AND WE CAN MOTOR BACK UP, NO PROBLEM.
HOW ARE YOU GOING TO FREE THE BRAKES? THAT LEVER IS JAMMED TIGHT.
I'LL HAVE TO GO UNDERNEATH AND CUT THE ARMS OFF.
CRUNK
OH, HOW ARE YOU GOING TO DO THAT? USE YOUR LASER BEAM EYES?
OH.
FOOSH
HE REALLY THINKS OF EVERYTHING.
UH-HUH.

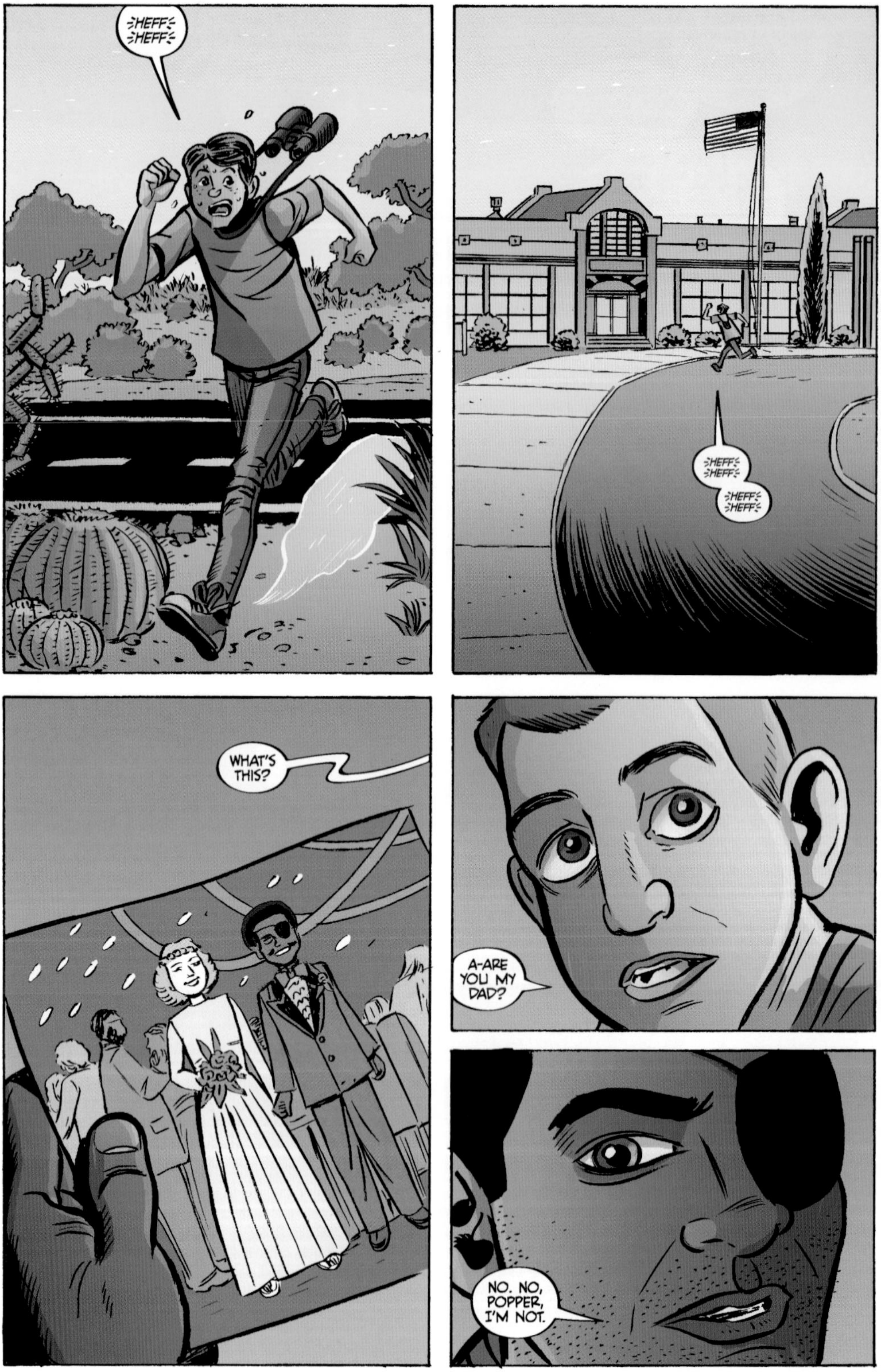
HEFF HEFF
HEFF HEFF
HEFF HEFF
WHAT'S THIS?
A-ARE YOU MY DAD?
NO. NO, POPPER, I'M NOT.

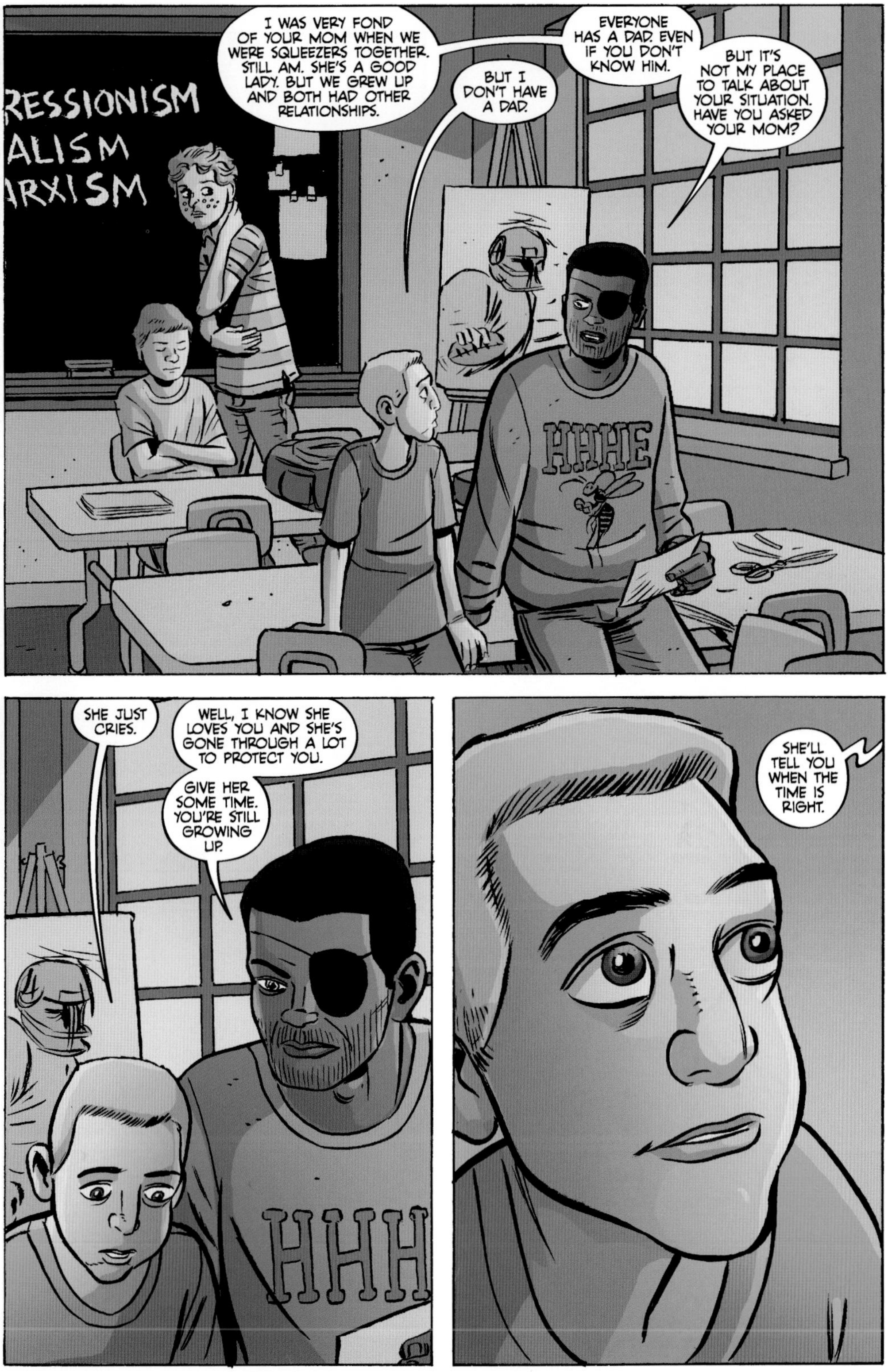
RESSIONISM
ALISM
ARXISM
I WAS VERY FOND OF YOUR MOM WHEN WE WERE SQUEEZERS TOGETHER. STILL AM. SHE'S A GOOD LADY. BUT WE GREW UP AND BOTH HAD OTHER RELATIONSHIPS.
BUT I DON'T HAVE A DAD.
EVERYONE HAS A DAD. EVEN IF YOU DON'T KNOW HIM.
BUT IT'S NOT MY PLACE TO TALK ABOUT YOUR SITUATION. HAVE YOU ASKED YOUR MOM?
HHHE
SHE JUST CRIES.
WELL, I KNOW SHE LOVES YOU AND SHE'S GONE THROUGH A LOT TO PROTECT YOU.
GIVE HER SOME TIME. YOU'RE STILL GROWING UP.
HHH
SHE'LL TELL YOU WHEN THE TIME IS RIGHT.

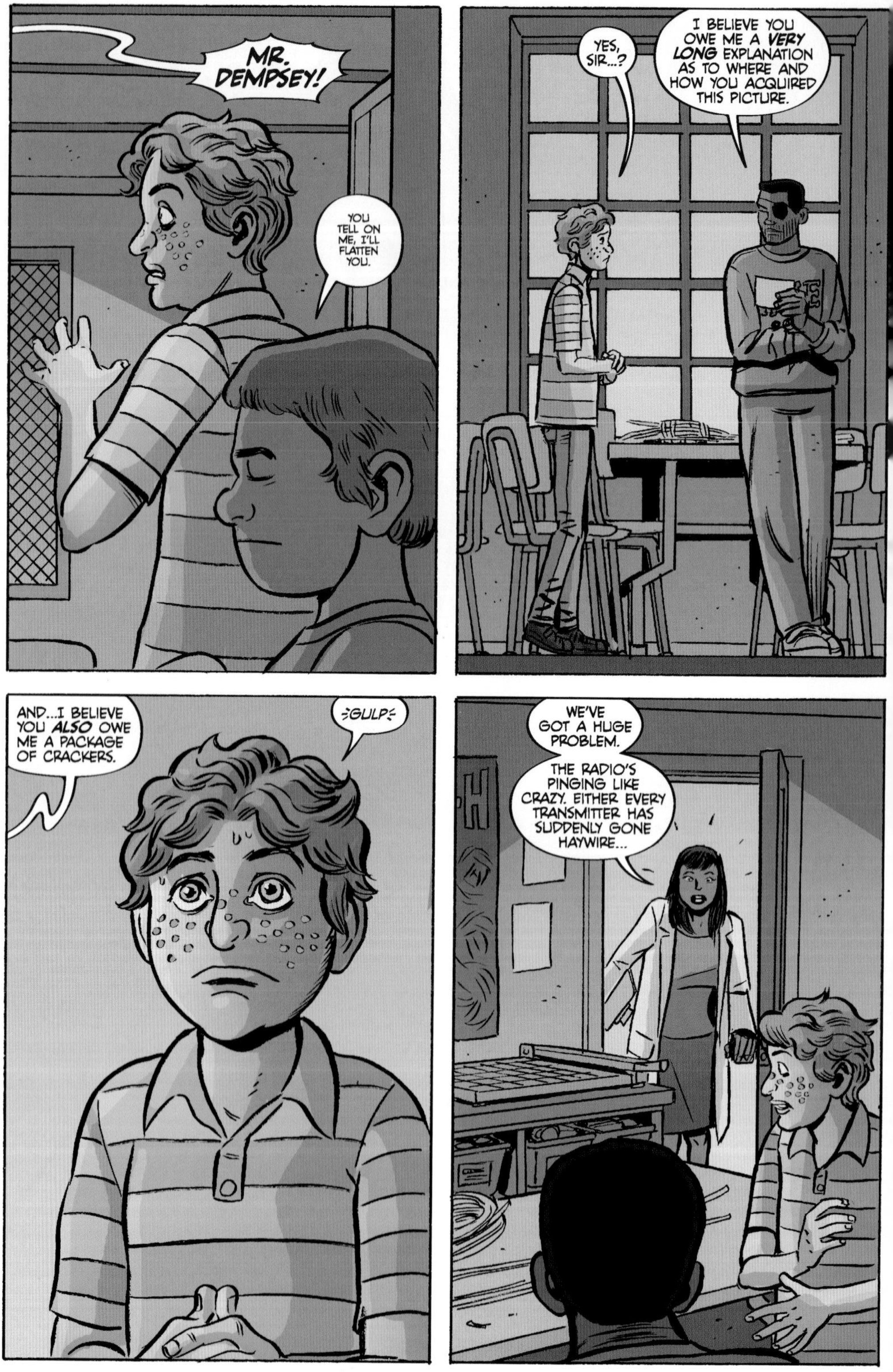
MR. DEMPSEY!
YOU TELL ON ME, I'LL FLATTEN YOU.
YES, SIR...?
I BELIEVE YOU OWE ME A VERY LONG EXPLANATION AS TO WHERE AND HOW YOU ACQUIRED THIS PICTURE.
AND...I BELIEVE YOU ALSO OWE ME A PACKAGE OF CRACKERS.
GULP
WE'VE GOT A HUGE PROBLEM.
THE RADIO'S PINGING LIKE CRAZY. EITHER EVERY TRANSMITTER HAS SUDDENLY GONE HAYWIRE...

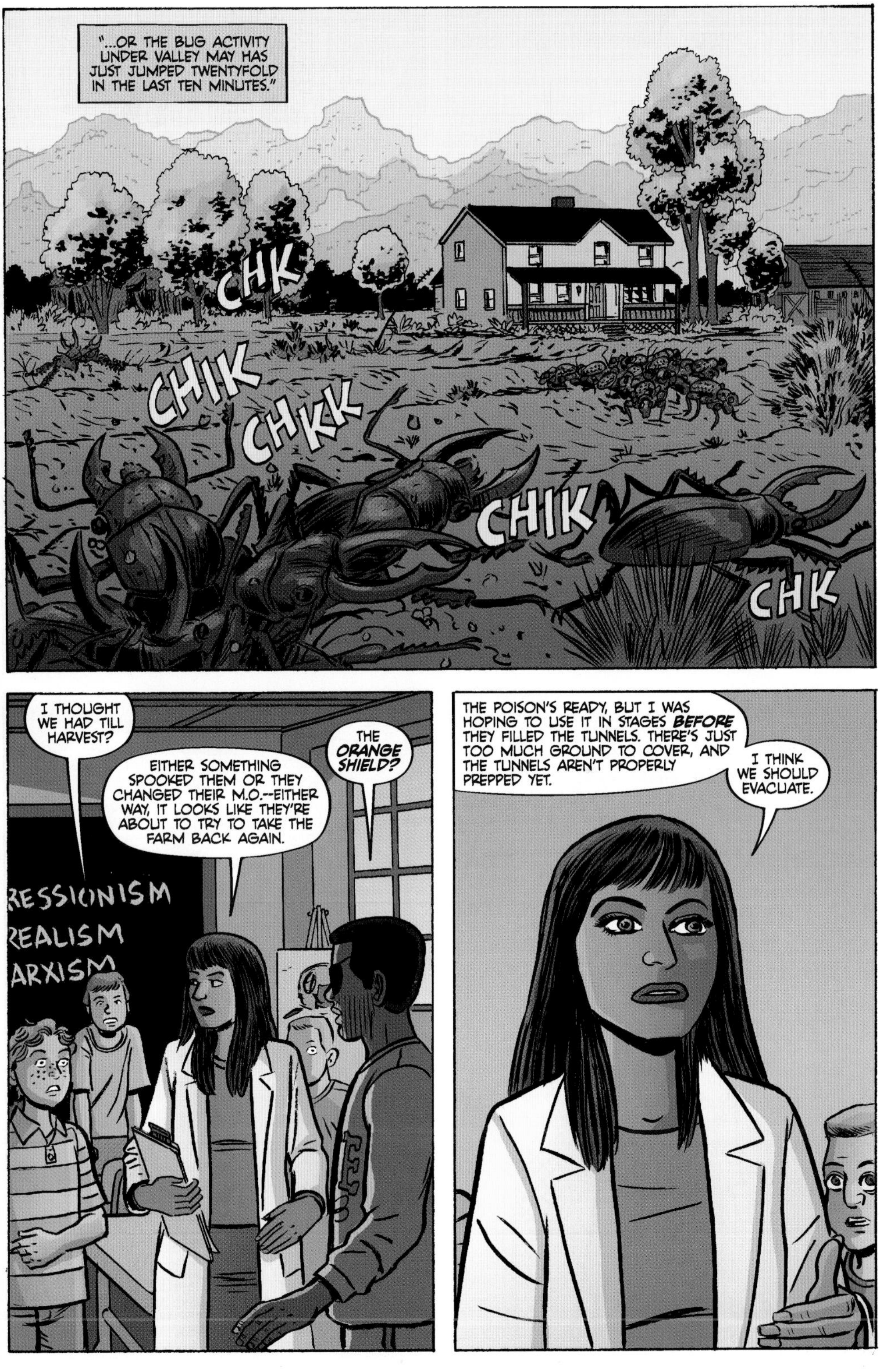
"...OR THE BUG ACTIVITY UNDER VALLEY MAY HAS JUST JUMPED TWENTYFOLD IN THE LAST TEN MINUTES."
CHK
CHIK
CHKK
CHIK
CHK
I THOUGHT WE HAD TILL HARVEST?
EITHER SOMETHING SPOOKED THEM OR THEY CHANGED THEIR M.O.--EITHER WAY, IT LOOKS LIKE THEY'RE ABOUT TO TRY TO TAKE THE FARM BACK AGAIN.
THE *ORANGE SHIELD?*
RESSIONISM
REALISM
ARXISM
THE POISON'S READY, BUT I WAS HOPING TO USE IT IN STAGES *BEFORE* THEY FILLED THE TUNNELS. THERE'S JUST TOO MUCH GROUND TO COVER, AND THE TUNNELS AREN'T PROPERLY PREPPED YET.
I THINK WE SHOULD EVACUATE.

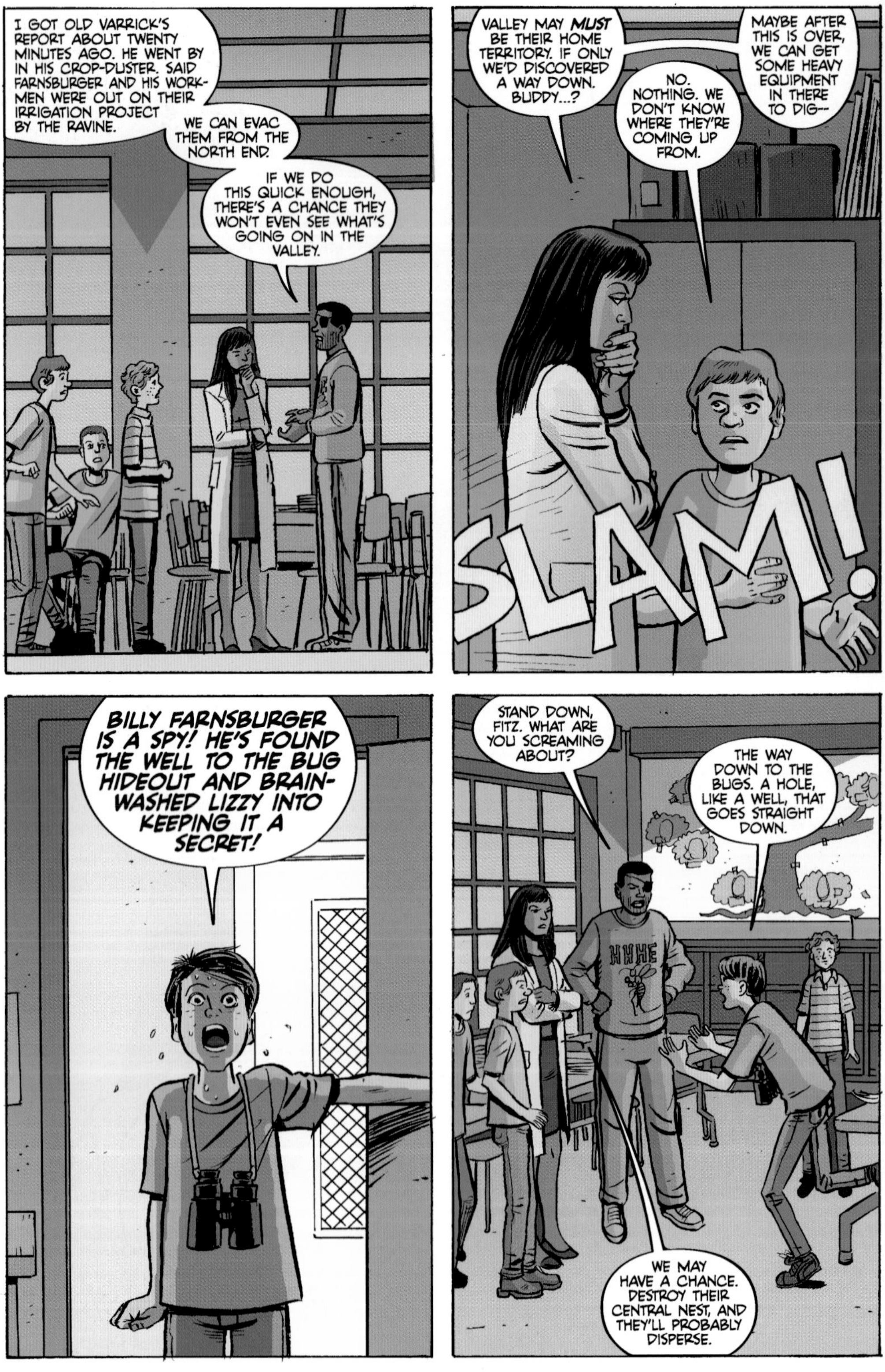
I GOT OLD VARRICK'S REPORT ABOUT TWENTY MINUTES AGO. HE WENT BY IN HIS CROP-DUSTER. SAID FARNSBURGER AND HIS WORK-MEN WERE OUT ON THEIR IRRIGATION PROJECT BY THE RAVINE.
WE CAN EVAC THEM FROM THE NORTH END.
IF WE DO THIS QUICK ENOUGH, THERE'S A CHANCE THEY WON'T EVEN SEE WHAT'S GOING ON IN THE VALLEY.
VALLEY MAY *MUST* BE THEIR HOME TERRITORY. IF ONLY WE'D DISCOVERED A WAY DOWN. BUDDY...?
NO. NOTHING. WE DON'T KNOW WHERE THEY'RE COMING UP FROM.
MAYBE AFTER THIS IS OVER, WE CAN GET SOME HEAVY EQUIPMENT IN THERE TO DIG--
SLAM!
BILLY FARNSBURGER IS A SPY! HE'S FOUND THE WELL TO THE BUG HIDEOUT AND BRAIN-WASHED LIZZY INTO KEEPING IT A SECRET!
STAND DOWN, FITZ. WHAT ARE YOU SCREAMING ABOUT?
THE WAY DOWN TO THE BUGS. A HOLE, LIKE A WELL, THAT GOES STRAIGHT DOWN.
HHHE
WE MAY HAVE A CHANCE. DESTROY THEIR CENTRAL NEST, AND THEY'LL PROBABLY DISPERSE.

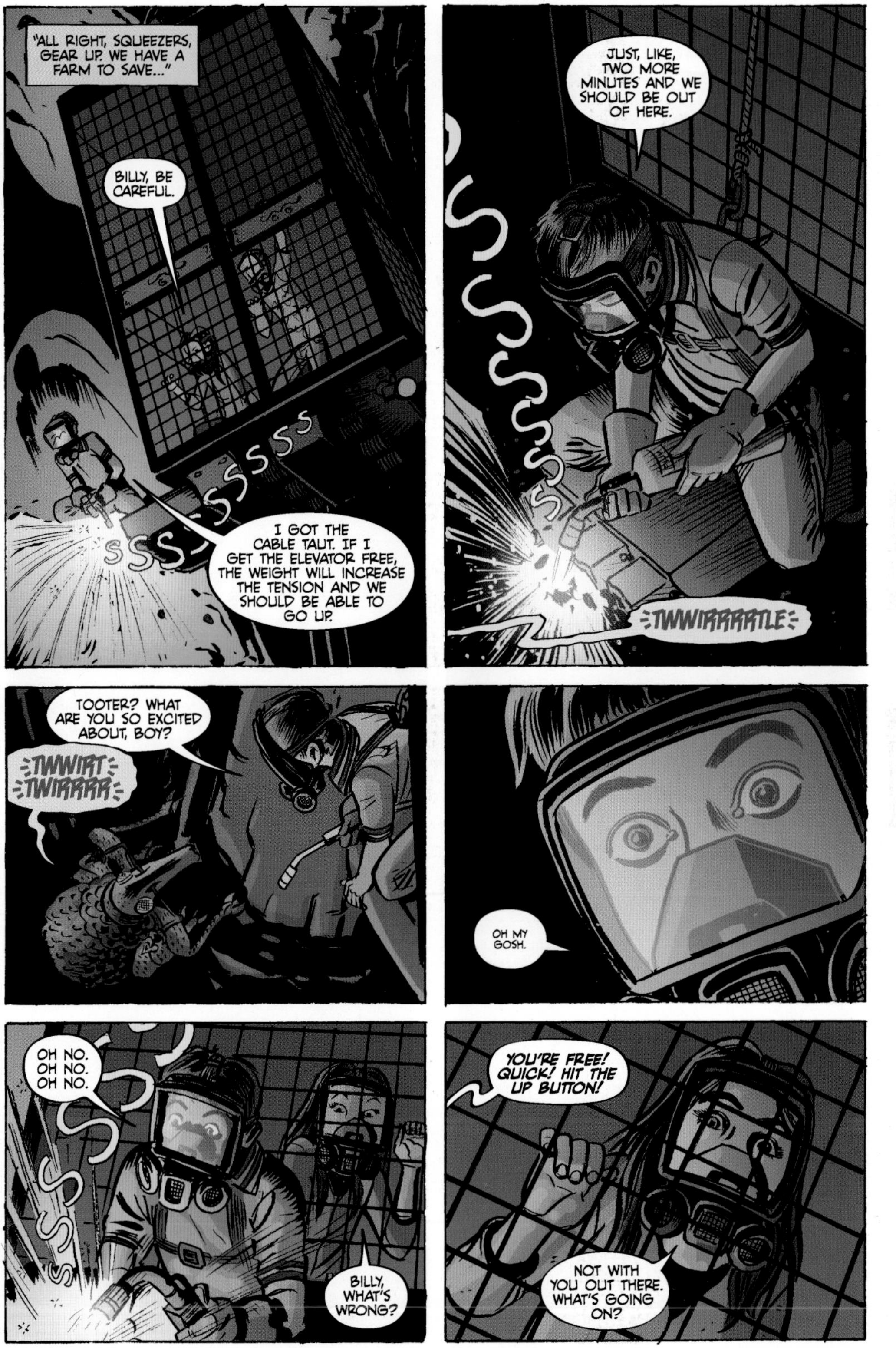
"ALL RIGHT, SQUEEZERS, GEAR UP. WE HAVE A FARM TO SAVE..."
BILLY, BE CAREFUL.
SSSSSSSSSS
I GOT THE CABLE TAUT. IF I GET THE ELEVATOR FREE, THE WEIGHT WILL INCREASE THE TENSION AND WE SHOULD BE ABLE TO GO UP.
JUST, LIKE, TWO MORE MINUTES AND WE SHOULD BE OUT OF HERE.
TWWIRRRRRTLE
TOOTER? WHAT ARE YOU SO EXCITED ABOUT, BOY?
TWWIRT TWIRRRR
OH MY GOSH.
OH NO. OH NO. OH NO.
BILLY, WHAT'S WRONG?
YOU'RE FREE! QUICK! HIT THE UP BUTTON!
NOT WITH YOU OUT THERE. WHAT'S GOING ON?

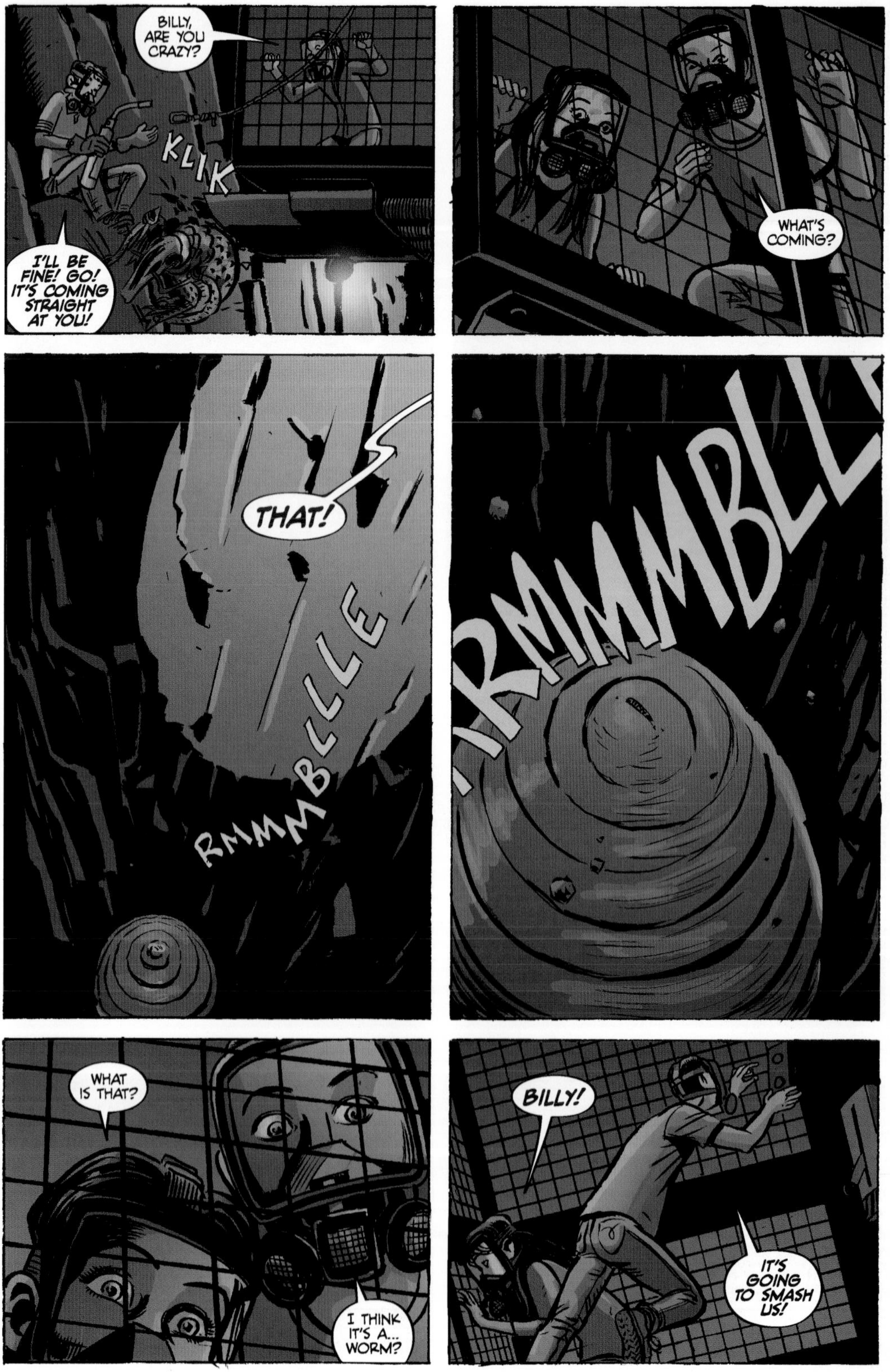
BILLY, ARE YOU CRAZY?
KLIK
I'LL BE FINE! GO! IT'S COMING STRAIGHT AT YOU!
WHAT'S COMING?
THAT!
RMMMBLLLE
RMMMBLLE
WHAT IS THAT?
I THINK IT'S A... WORM?
BILLY!
IT'S GOING TO SMASH US!

KLIK

GNNNN...

MMMMBLI

HMMMMMMMMM

WWWWW!

RRRMMBLE

WWWE'RRE GGGONNAAA DDDIEEEE!

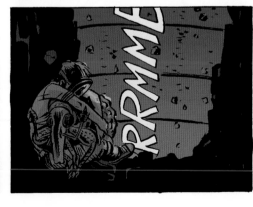

RRRMME

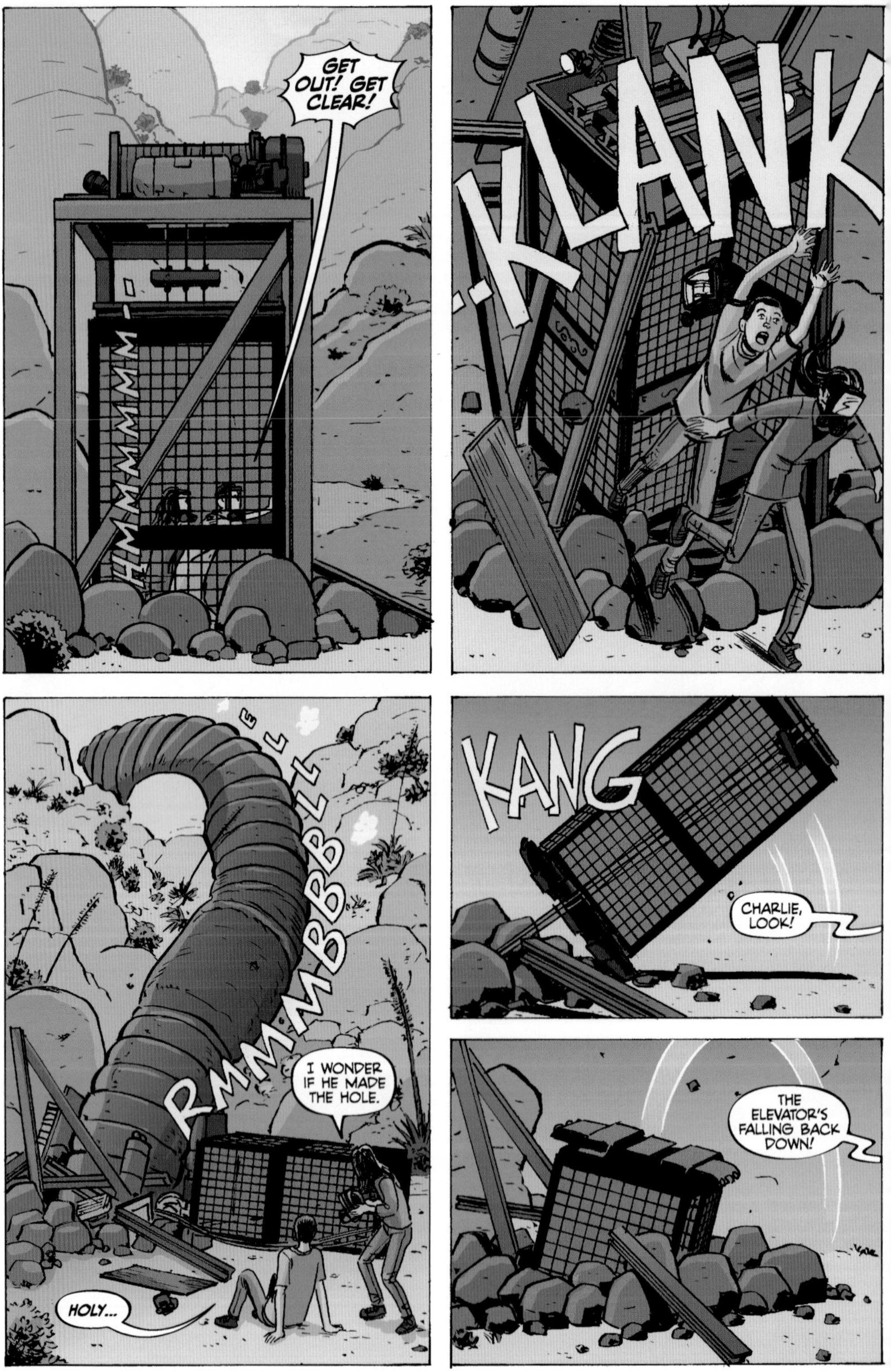
GET OUT! GET CLEAR!
HMMMMMM-
KLANK
KANG
CHARLIE, LOOK!
RMMMMBBBLLLE
I WONDER IF HE MADE THE HOLE.
HOLY...
THE ELEVATOR'S FALLING BACK DOWN!

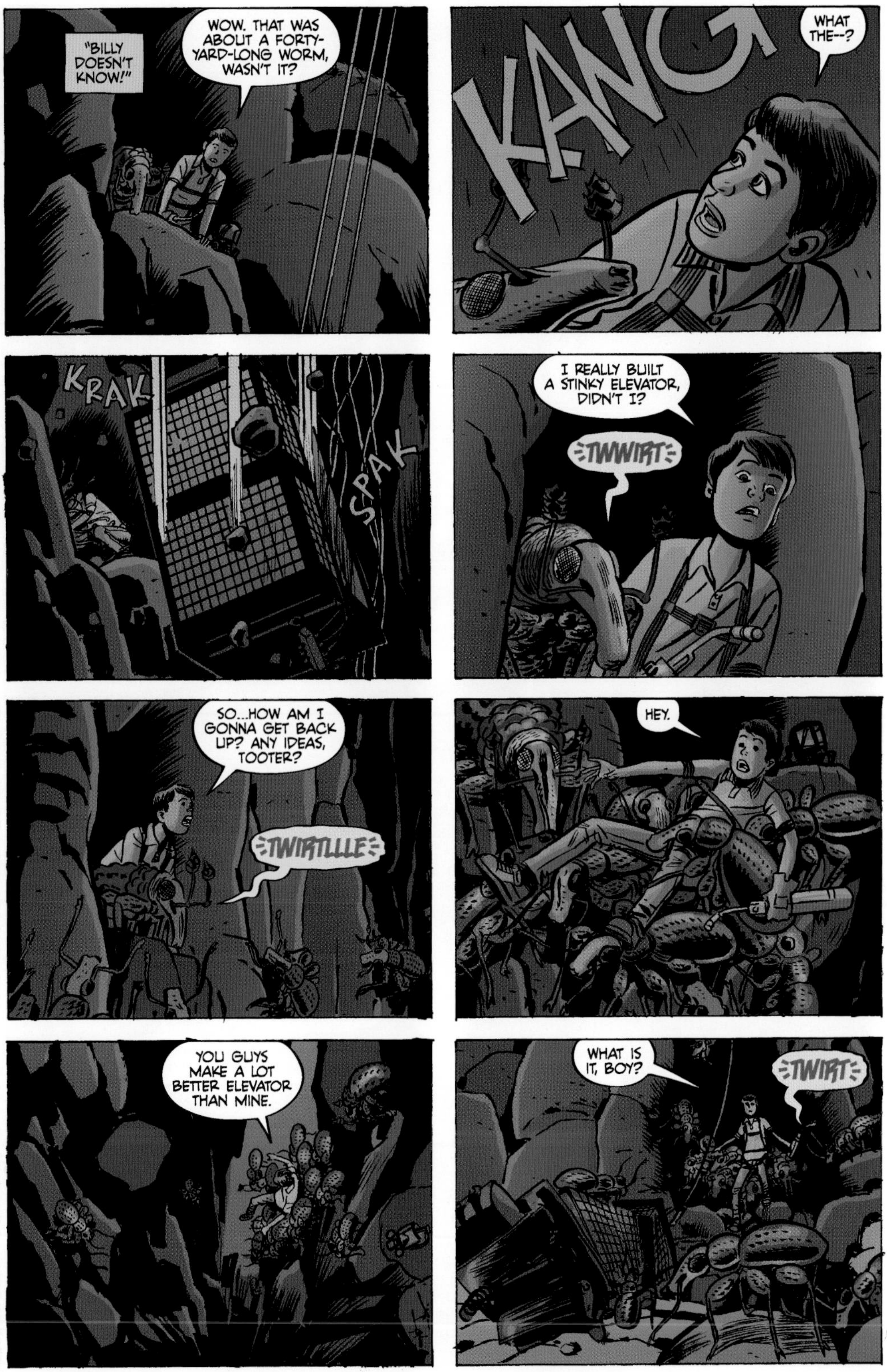
"BILLY DOESN'T KNOW!"
WOW. THAT WAS ABOUT A FORTY-YARD-LONG WORM, WASN'T IT?
KANG
WHAT THE--?
KRAK
SPAK
I REALLY BUILT A STINKY ELEVATOR, DIDN'T I?
TWWIRT
SO...HOW AM I GONNA GET BACK UP? ANY IDEAS, TOOTER?
TWIRTLLLE
HEY.
YOU GUYS MAKE A LOT BETTER ELEVATOR THAN MINE.
WHAT IS IT, BOY?
TWIRT

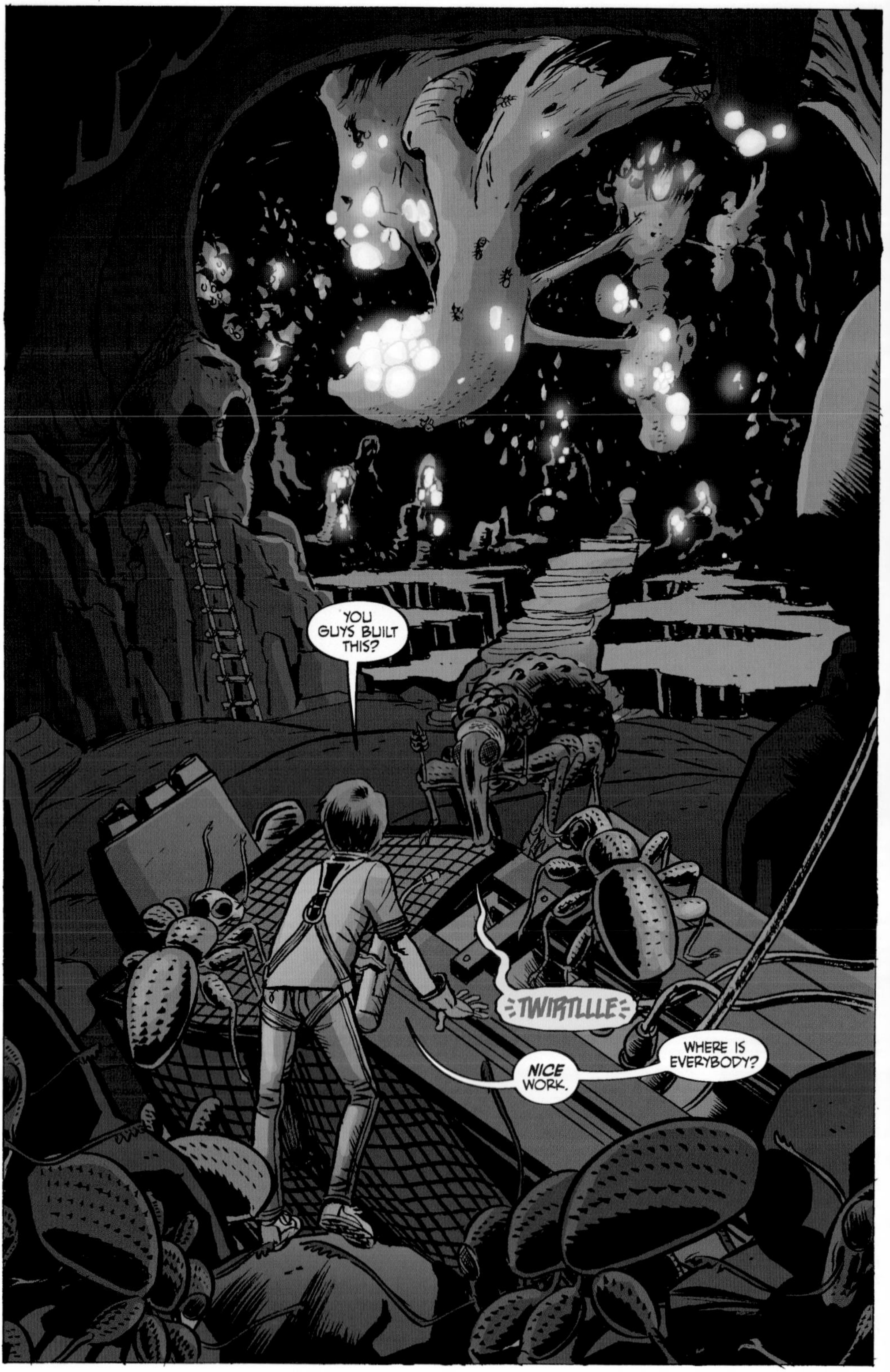
YOU GUYS BUILT THIS?
TWIRTLLLE
NICE WORK.
WHERE IS EVERYBODY?

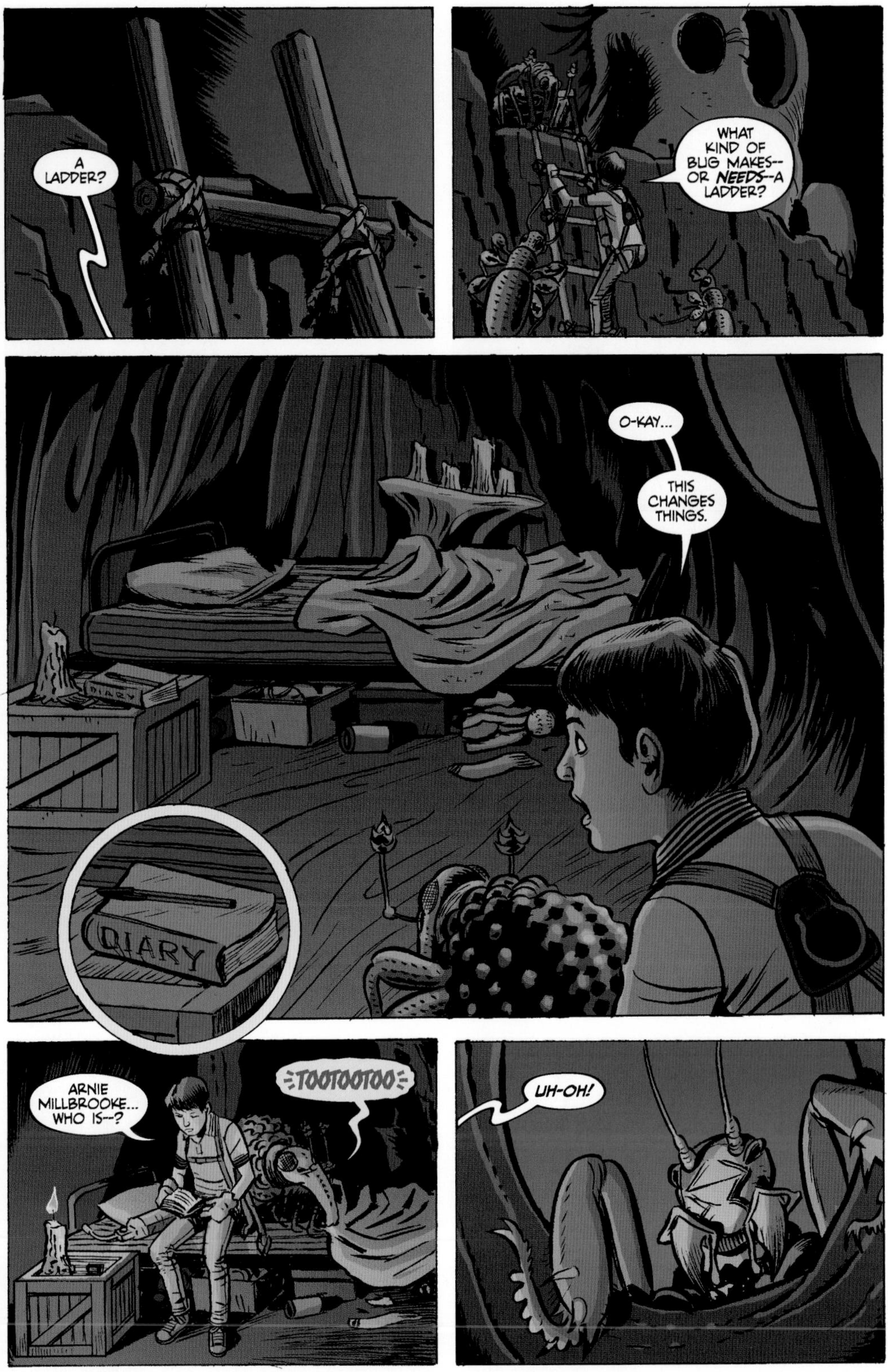
A LADDER?
WHAT KIND OF BUG MAKES-- OR NEEDS--A LADDER?
O-KAY...
THIS CHANGES THINGS.
DIARY
DIARY
ARNIE MILLBROOKE... WHO IS--?
TOOTOOTOO
UH-OH!

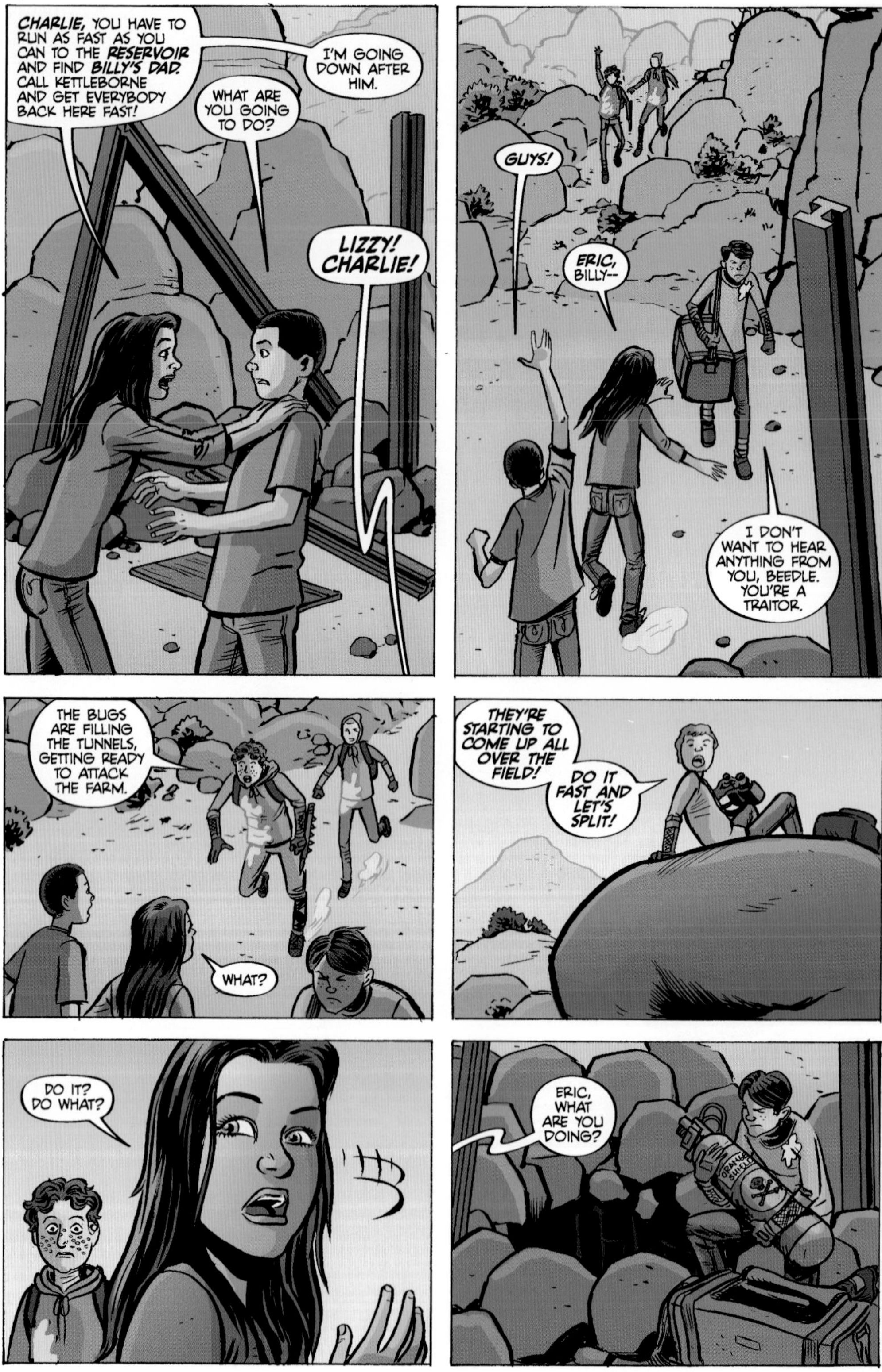
CHARLIE, YOU HAVE TO RUN AS FAST AS YOU CAN TO THE RESERVOIR AND FIND BILLY'S DAD. CALL KETTLEBORNE AND GET EVERYBODY BACK HERE FAST!
WHAT ARE YOU GOING TO DO?
I'M GOING DOWN AFTER HIM.
LIZZY! CHARLIE!
GUYS!
ERIC, BILLY--
I DON'T WANT TO HEAR ANYTHING FROM YOU, BEEDLE. YOU'RE A TRAITOR.
THE BUGS ARE FILLING THE TUNNELS, GETTING READY TO ATTACK THE FARM.
WHAT?
THEY'RE STARTING TO COME UP ALL OVER THE FIELD!
DO IT FAST AND LET'S SPLIT!
DO IT? DO WHAT?
ERIC, WHAT ARE YOU DOING?
ORANGE SHIELD

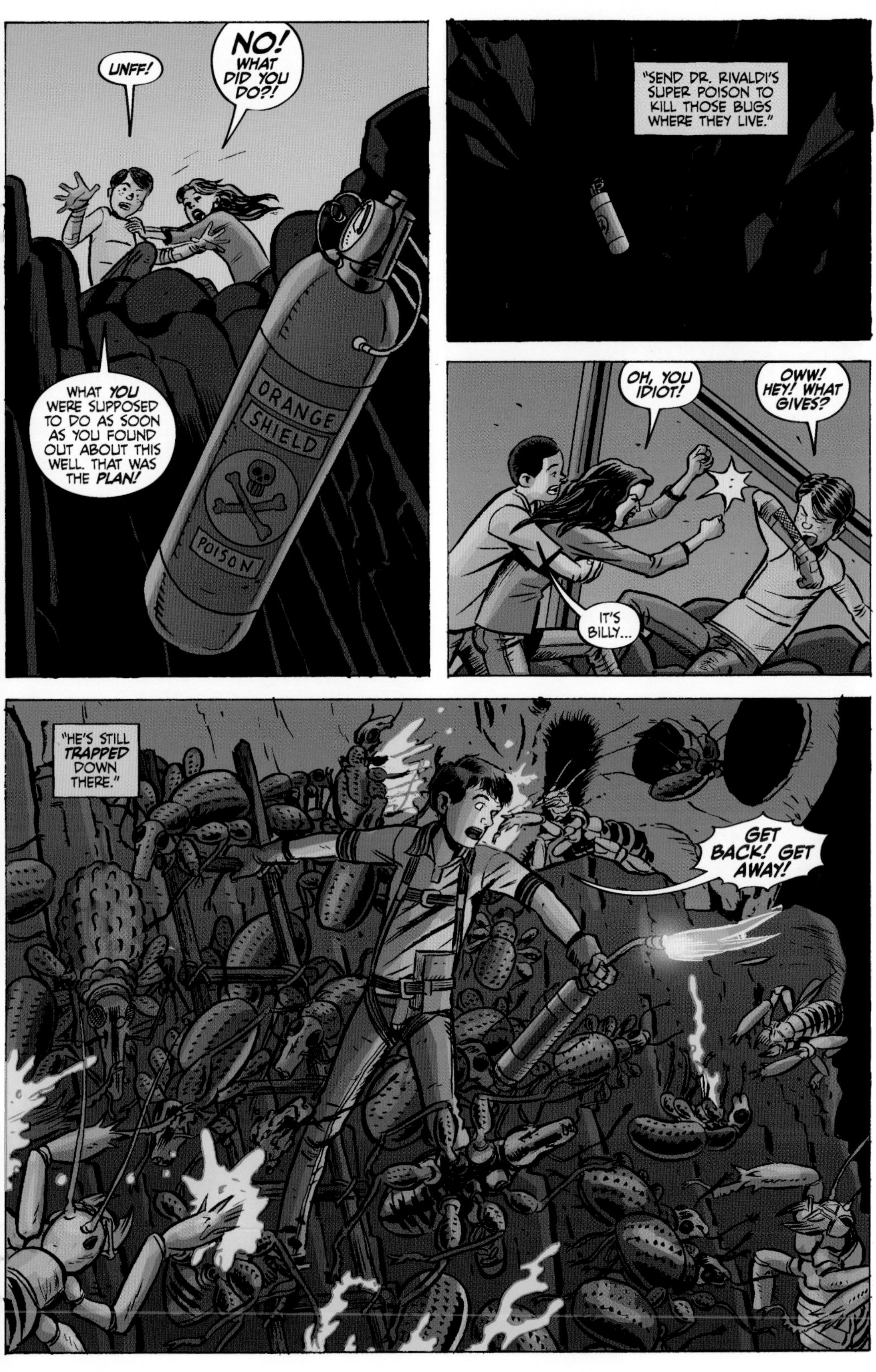
UNFF!
NO! WHAT DID YOU DO?!
WHAT YOU WERE SUPPOSED TO DO AS SOON AS YOU FOUND OUT ABOUT THIS WELL. THAT WAS THE PLAN!
ORANGE SHIELD
POISON
"SEND DR. RIVALDI'S SUPER POISON TO KILL THOSE BUGS WHERE THEY LIVE."
OH, YOU IDIOT!
OWW! HEY! WHAT GIVES?
IT'S BILLY...
"HE'S STILL TRAPPED DOWN THERE."
GET BACK! GET AWAY!

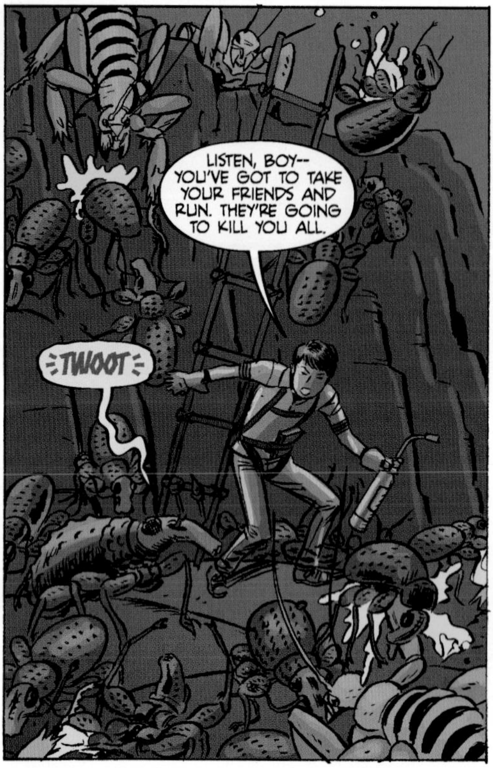
LISTEN, BOY-- YOU'VE GOT TO TAKE YOUR FRIENDS AND RUN. THEY'RE GOING TO KILL YOU ALL.
TWOOT

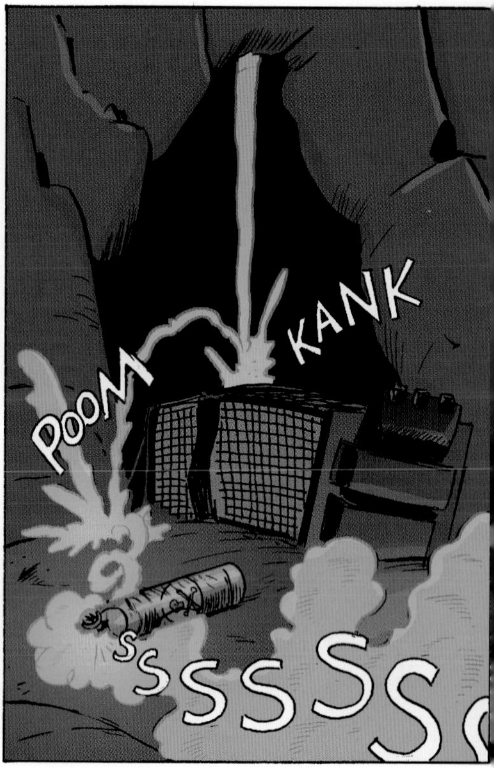
KANK
POOM
SSSSSS

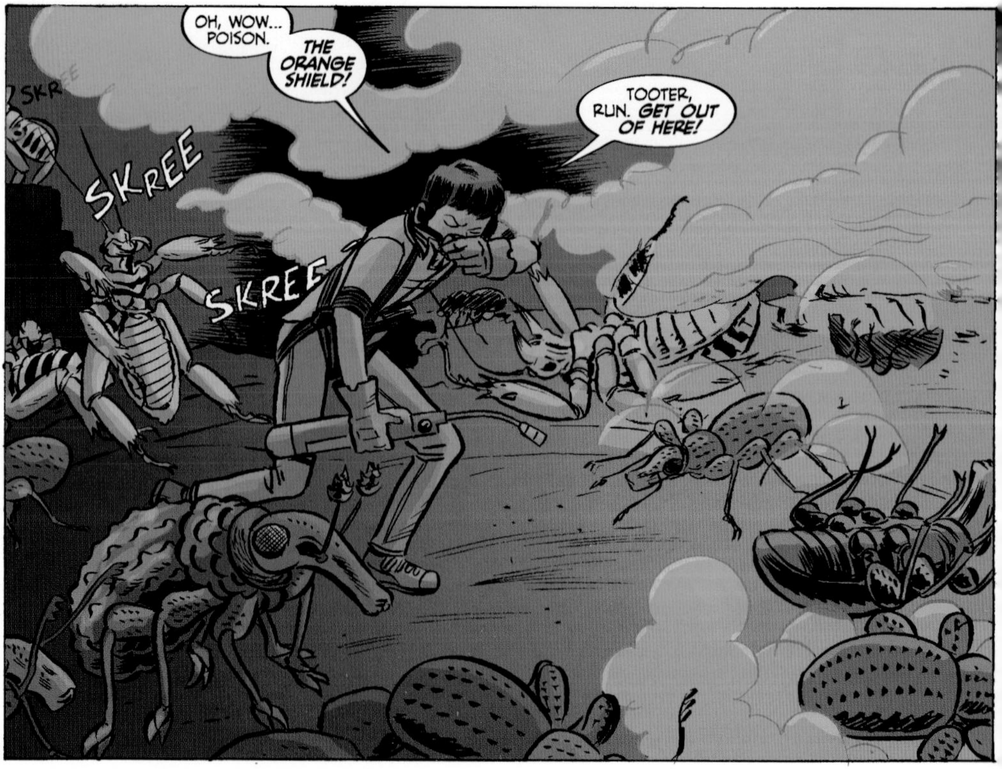
OH, WOW... POISON. *THE ORANGE SHIELD!*
TOOTER, RUN. *GET OUT OF HERE!*
SKREE
SKREE

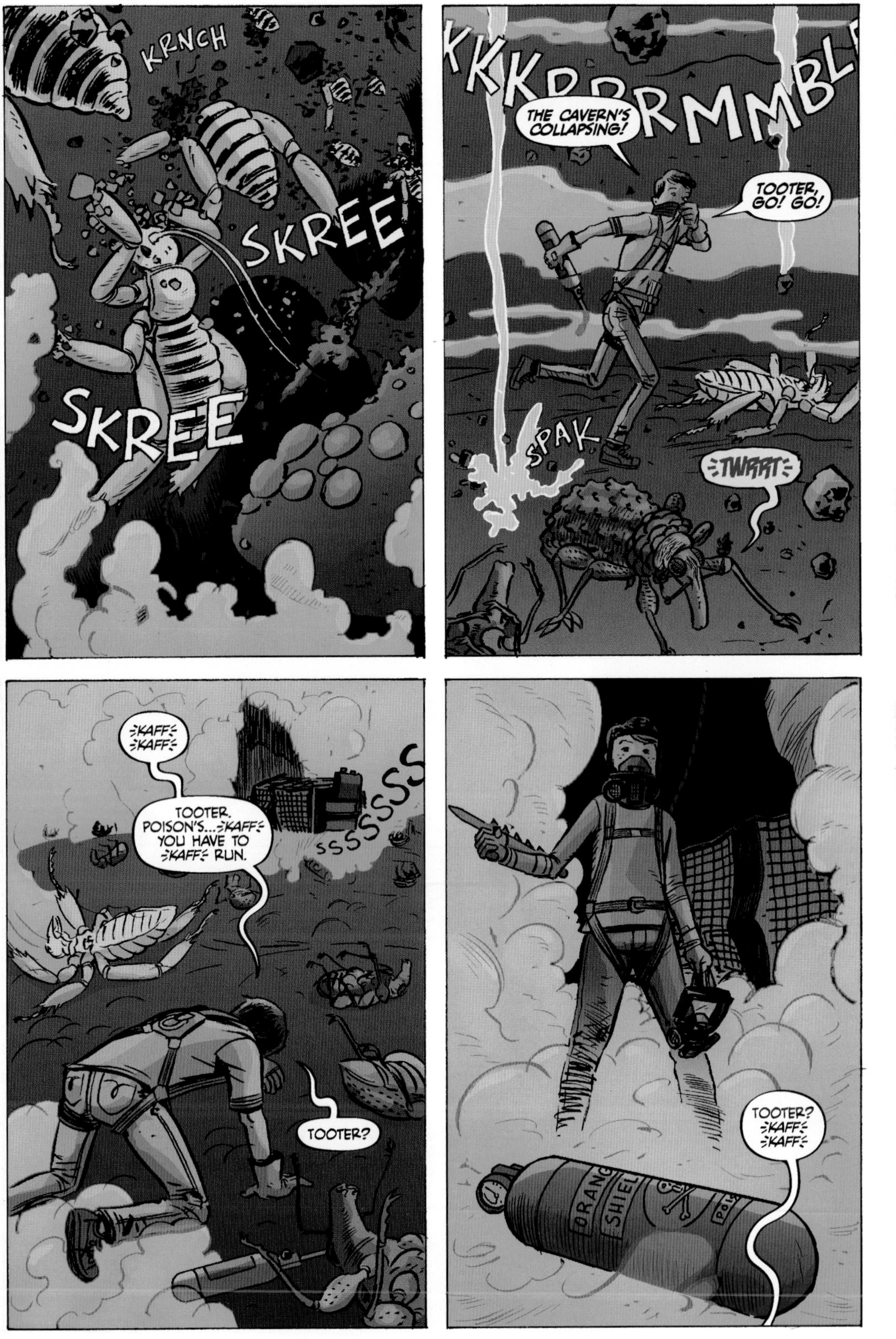
KRNCH
SKREE
SKREE
KKKRRRMMBL
THE CAVERN'S COLLAPSING!
TOOTER, GO! GO!
SPAK
TWIRRT
KAFF KAFF
TOOTER. POISON'S... KAFF YOU HAVE TO KAFF RUN.
SSSSSSSSS
TOOTER?
TOOTER? KAFF KAFF

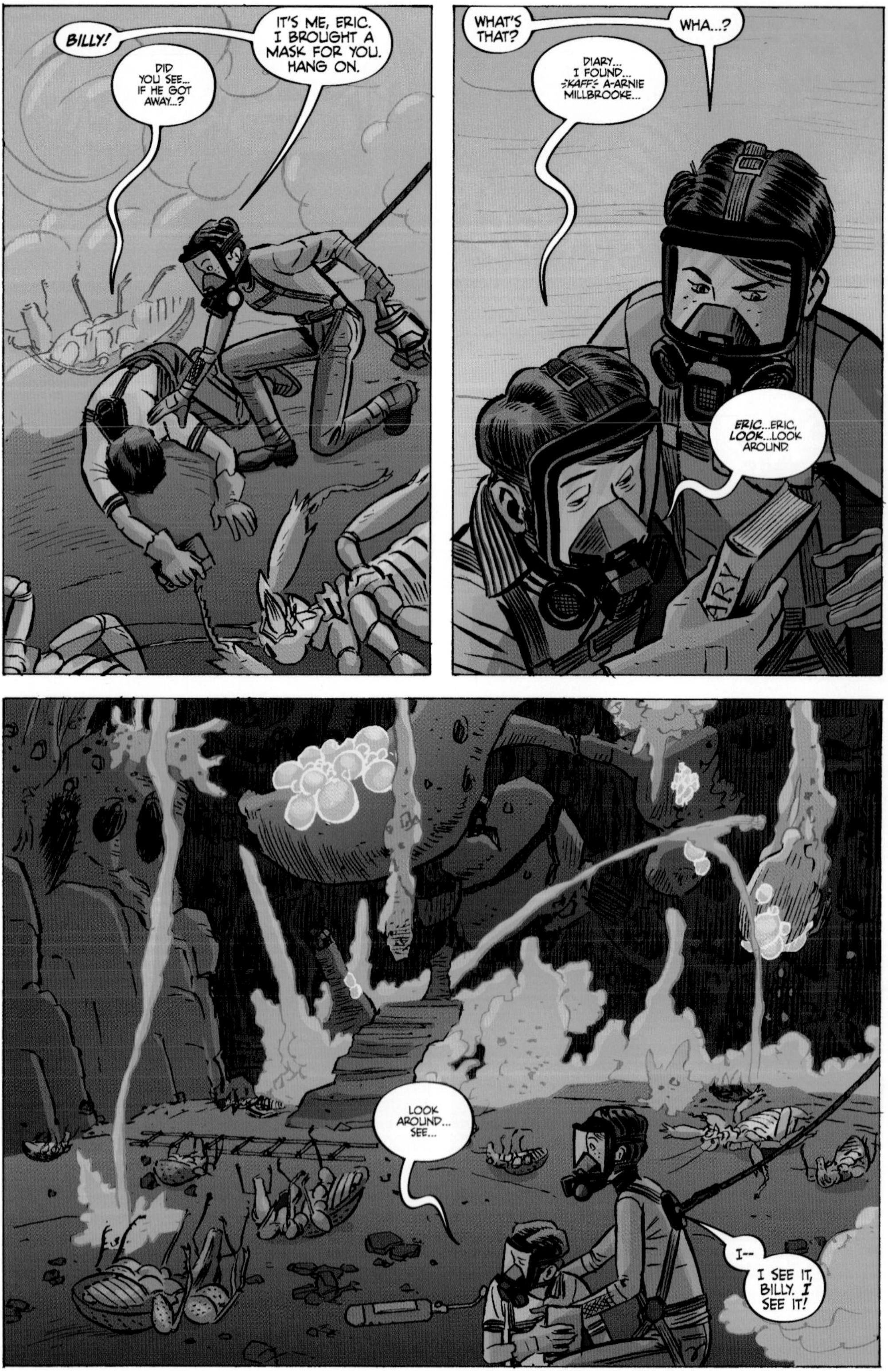
BILLY!
IT'S ME, ERIC. I BROUGHT A MASK FOR YOU. HANG ON.
DID YOU SEE... IF HE GOT AWAY...?
WHAT'S THAT?
WHA...?
DIARY... I FOUND... ≈KAFF≈ A-ARNIE MILLBROOKE...
ERIC...ERIC, LOOK...LOOK AROUND.
LOOK AROUND... SEE...
I--
I SEE IT, BILLY. I SEE IT!

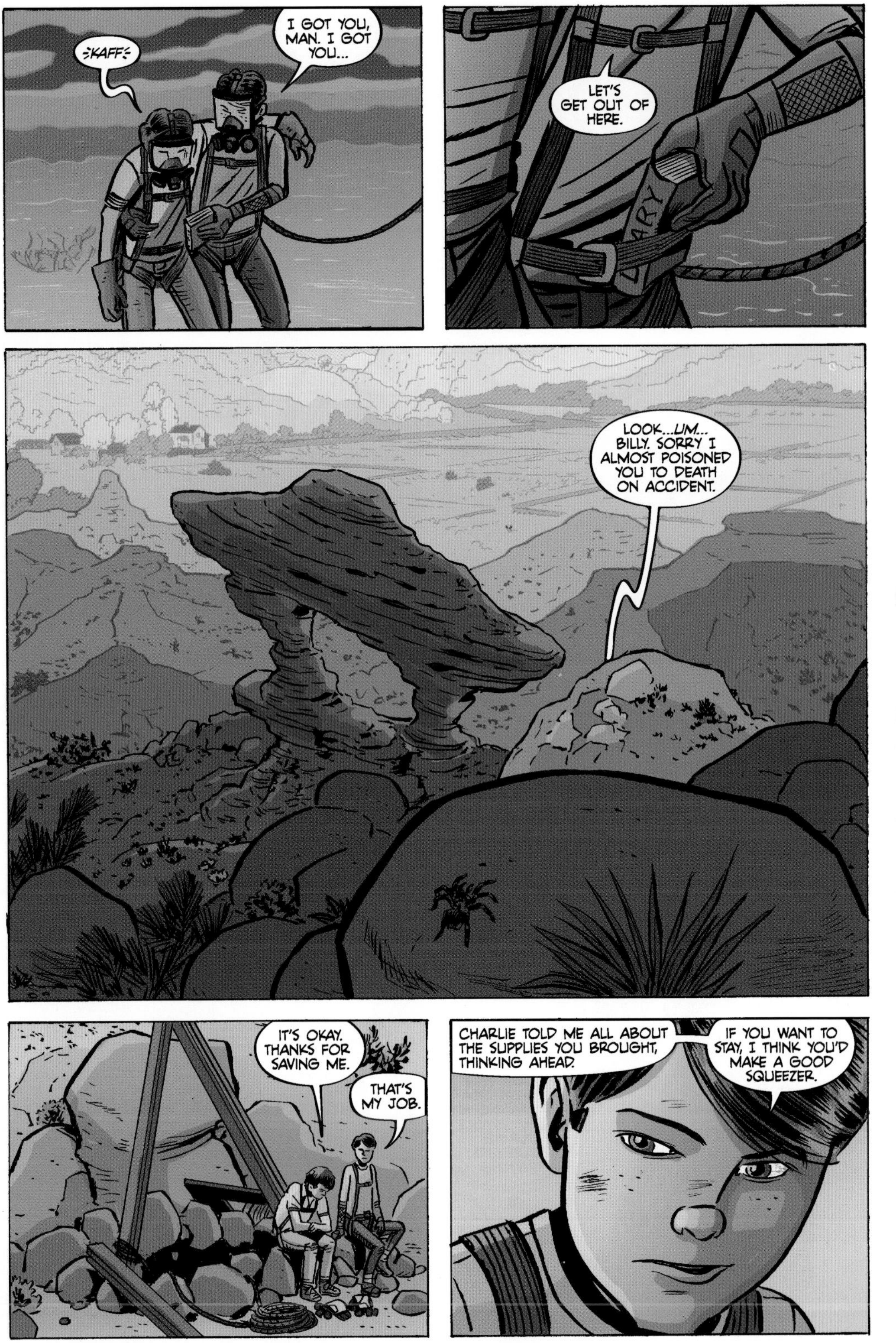
KAFF
I GOT YOU, MAN. I GOT YOU...
LET'S GET OUT OF HERE.
LOOK...UM... BILLY. SORRY I ALMOST POISONED YOU TO DEATH ON ACCIDENT.
IT'S OKAY. THANKS FOR SAVING ME.
THAT'S MY JOB.
CHARLIE TOLD ME ALL ABOUT THE SUPPLIES YOU BROUGHT, THINKING AHEAD.
IF YOU WANT TO STAY, I THINK YOU'D MAKE A GOOD SQUEEZER.

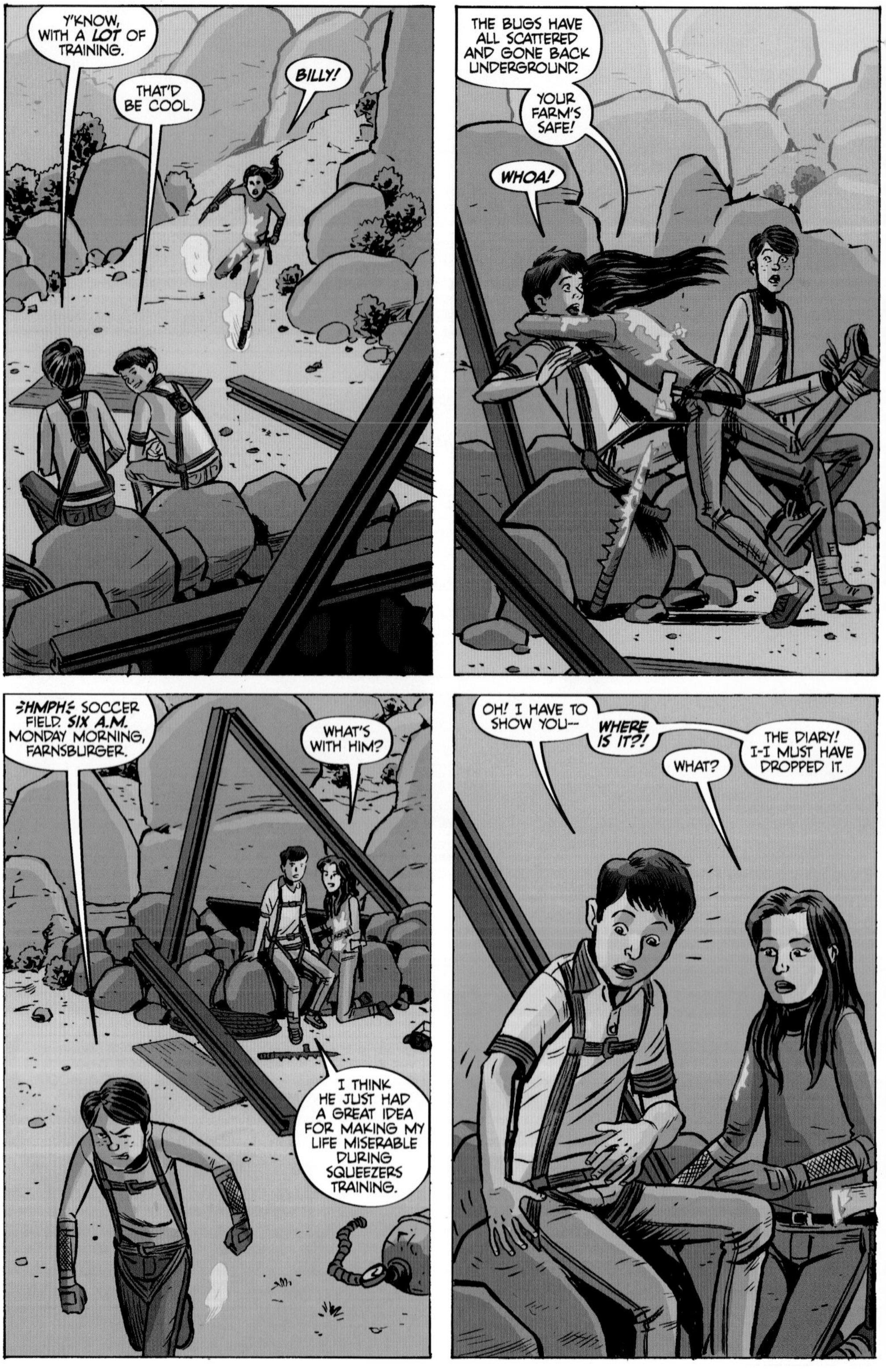

Y'KNOW, WITH A LOT OF TRAINING.
THAT'D BE COOL.
BILLY!
THE BUGS HAVE ALL SCATTERED AND GONE BACK UNDERGROUND.
YOUR FARM'S SAFE!
WHOA!
HMPH! SOCCER FIELD. SIX A.M. MONDAY MORNING, FARNSBURGER.
WHAT'S WITH HIM?
I THINK HE JUST HAD A GREAT IDEA FOR MAKING MY LIFE MISERABLE DURING SQUEEZERS TRAINING.
OH! I HAVE TO SHOW YOU--
WHERE IS IT?!
WHAT?
THE DIARY! I-I MUST HAVE DROPPED IT.

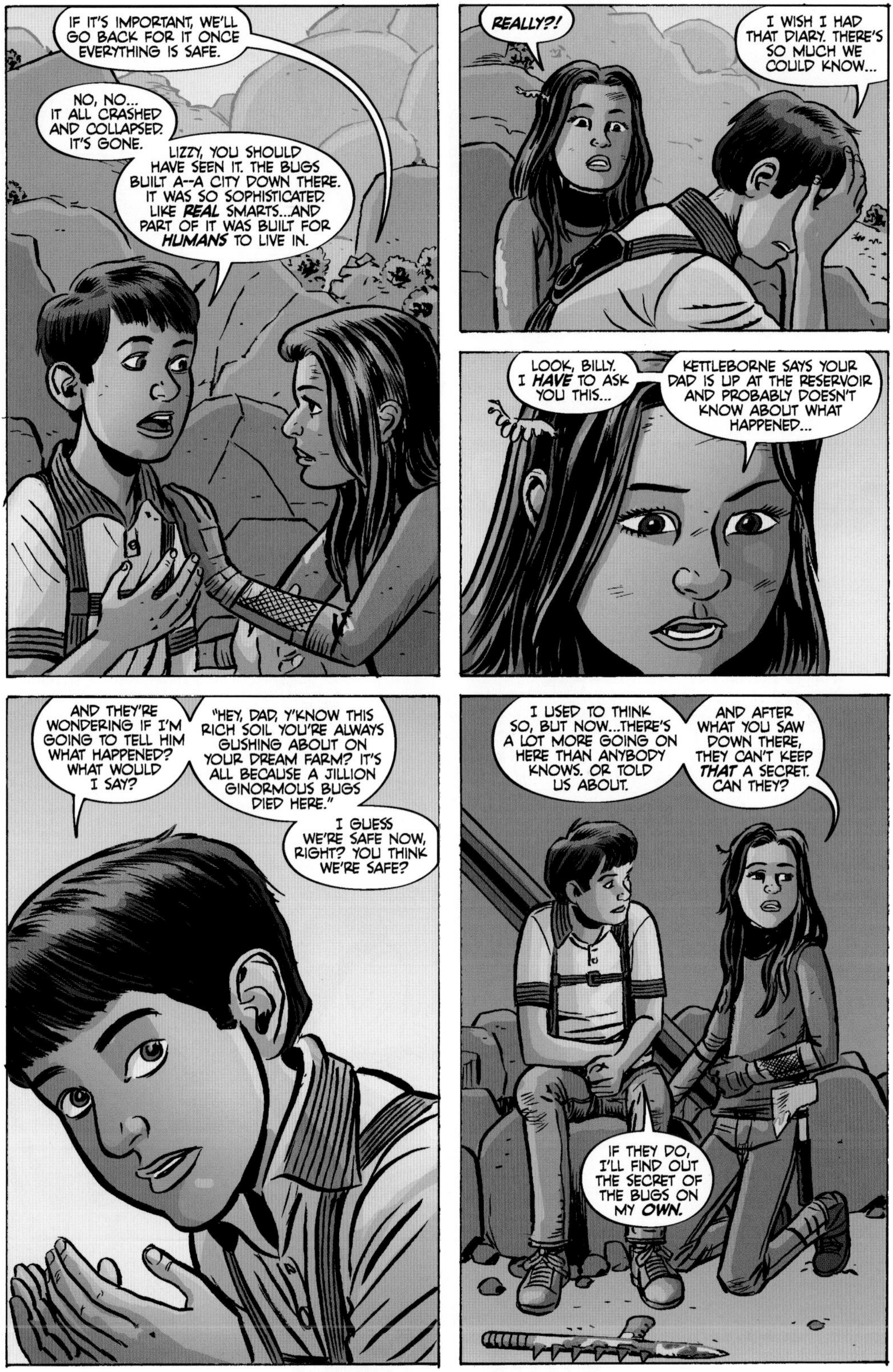
IF IT'S IMPORTANT, WE'LL GO BACK FOR IT ONCE EVERYTHING IS SAFE.
NO, NO... IT ALL CRASHED AND COLLAPSED. IT'S GONE.
LIZZY, YOU SHOULD HAVE SEEN IT. THE BUGS BUILT A--A CITY DOWN THERE. IT WAS SO SOPHISTICATED. LIKE REAL SMARTS...AND PART OF IT WAS BUILT FOR HUMANS TO LIVE IN.
REALLY?!
I WISH I HAD THAT DIARY. THERE'S SO MUCH WE COULD KNOW...
LOOK, BILLY. I HAVE TO ASK YOU THIS...
KETTLEBORNE SAYS YOUR DAD IS UP AT THE RESERVOIR AND PROBABLY DOESN'T KNOW ABOUT WHAT HAPPENED...
AND THEY'RE WONDERING IF I'M GOING TO TELL HIM WHAT HAPPENED? WHAT WOULD I SAY?
"HEY, DAD, Y'KNOW THIS RICH SOIL YOU'RE ALWAYS GUSHING ABOUT ON YOUR DREAM FARM? IT'S ALL BECAUSE A JILLION GINORMOUS BUGS DIED HERE."
I GUESS WE'RE SAFE NOW, RIGHT? YOU THINK WE'RE SAFE?
I USED TO THINK SO, BUT NOW...THERE'S A LOT MORE GOING ON HERE THAN ANYBODY KNOWS. OR TOLD US ABOUT.
AND AFTER WHAT YOU SAW DOWN THERE, THEY CAN'T KEEP THAT A SECRET. CAN THEY?
IF THEY DO, I'LL FIND OUT THE SECRET OF THE BUGS ON MY OWN.

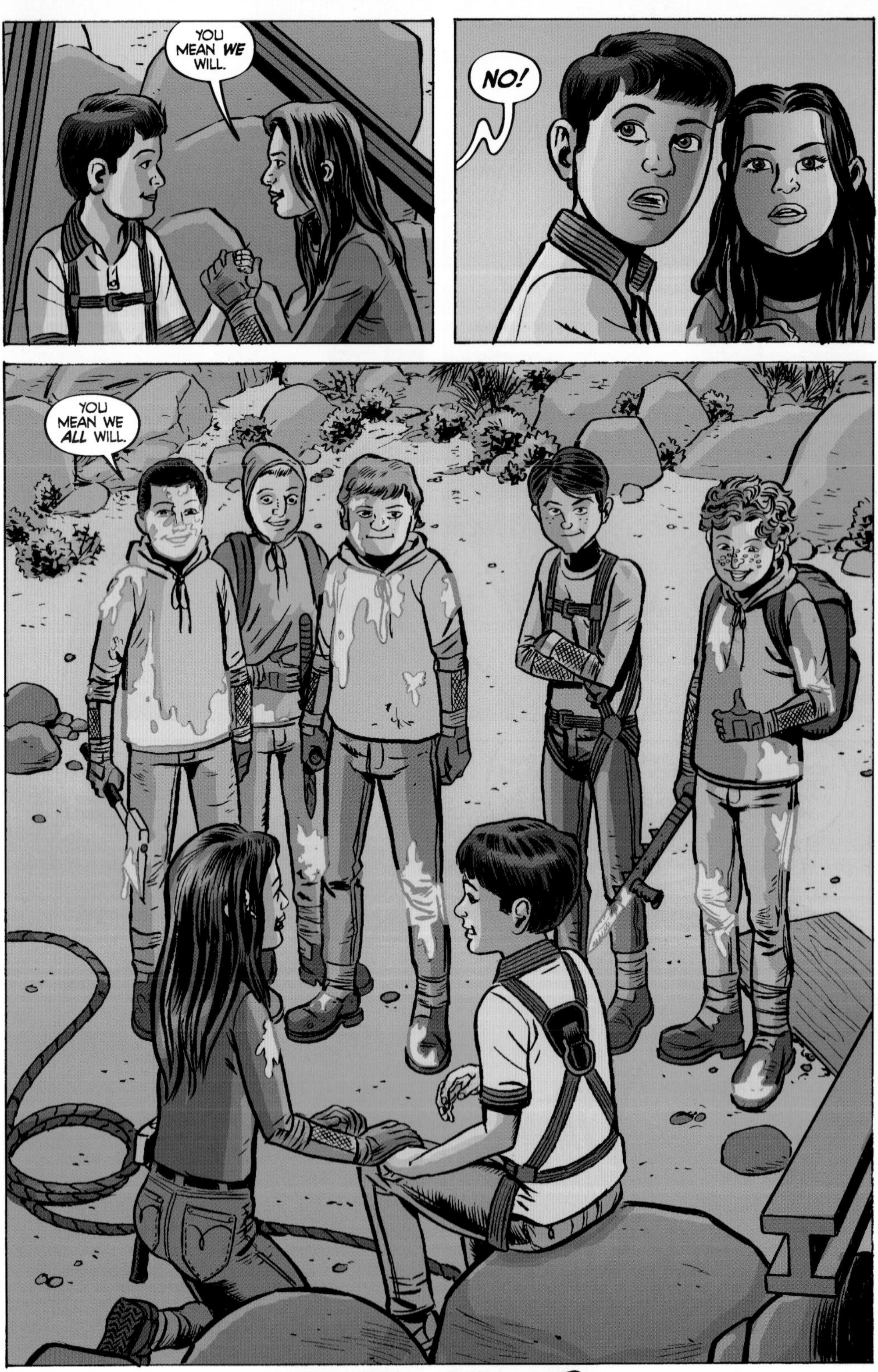
YOU MEAN *WE* WILL.
NO!
YOU MEAN WE *ALL* WILL.

THE END...?

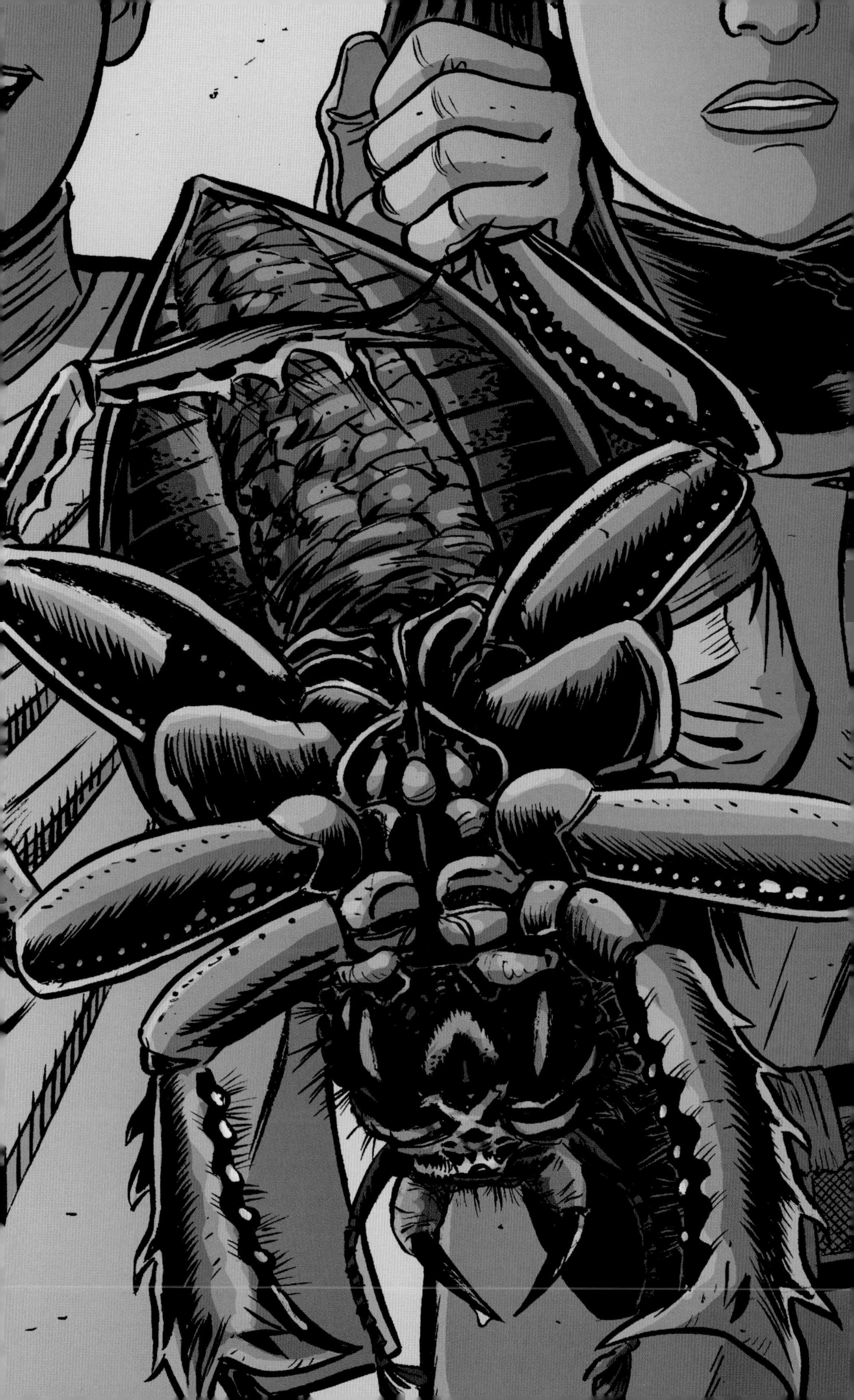

ANTS IN YOUR PANTS: A JUICE SQUEEZERS TALE

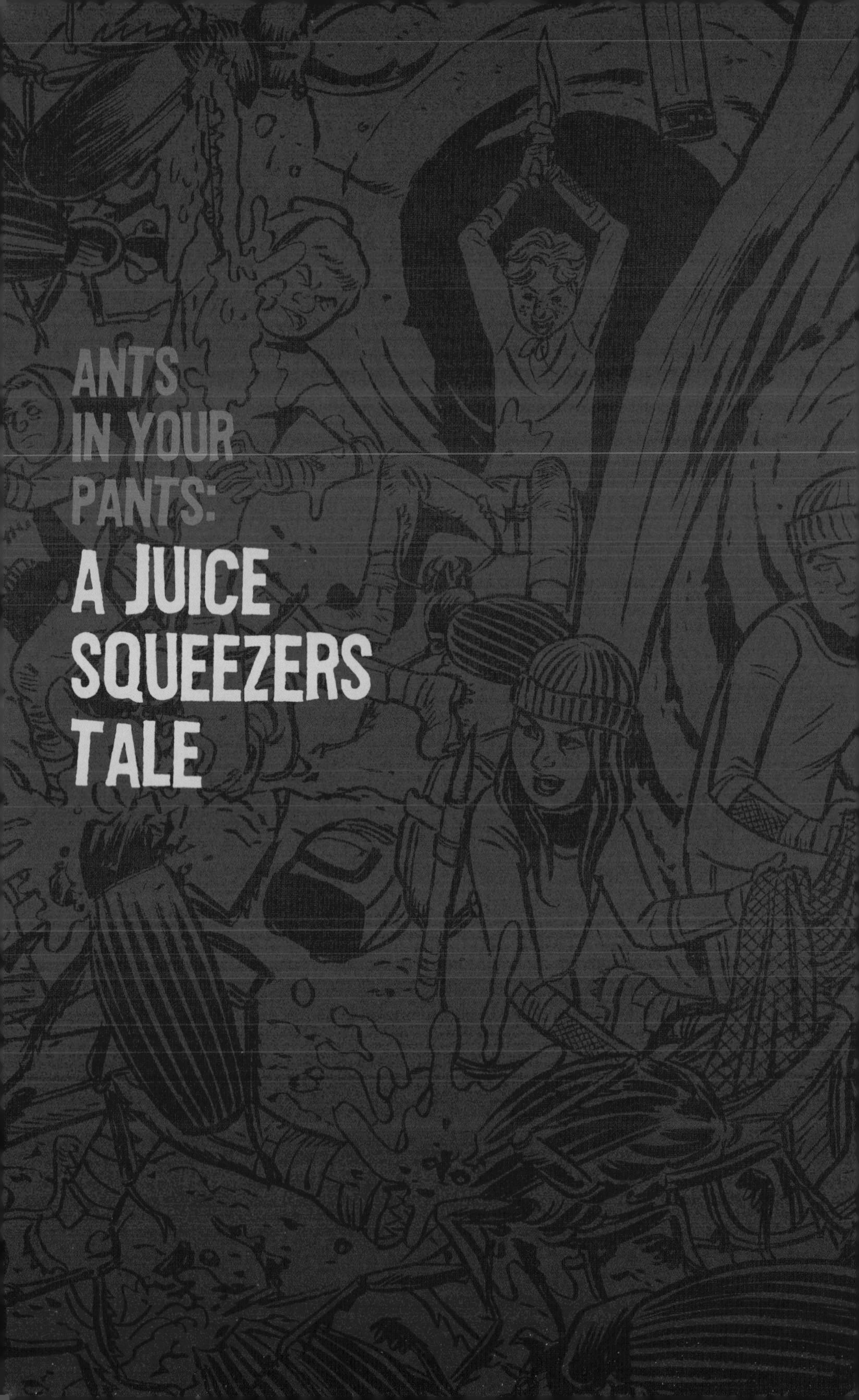

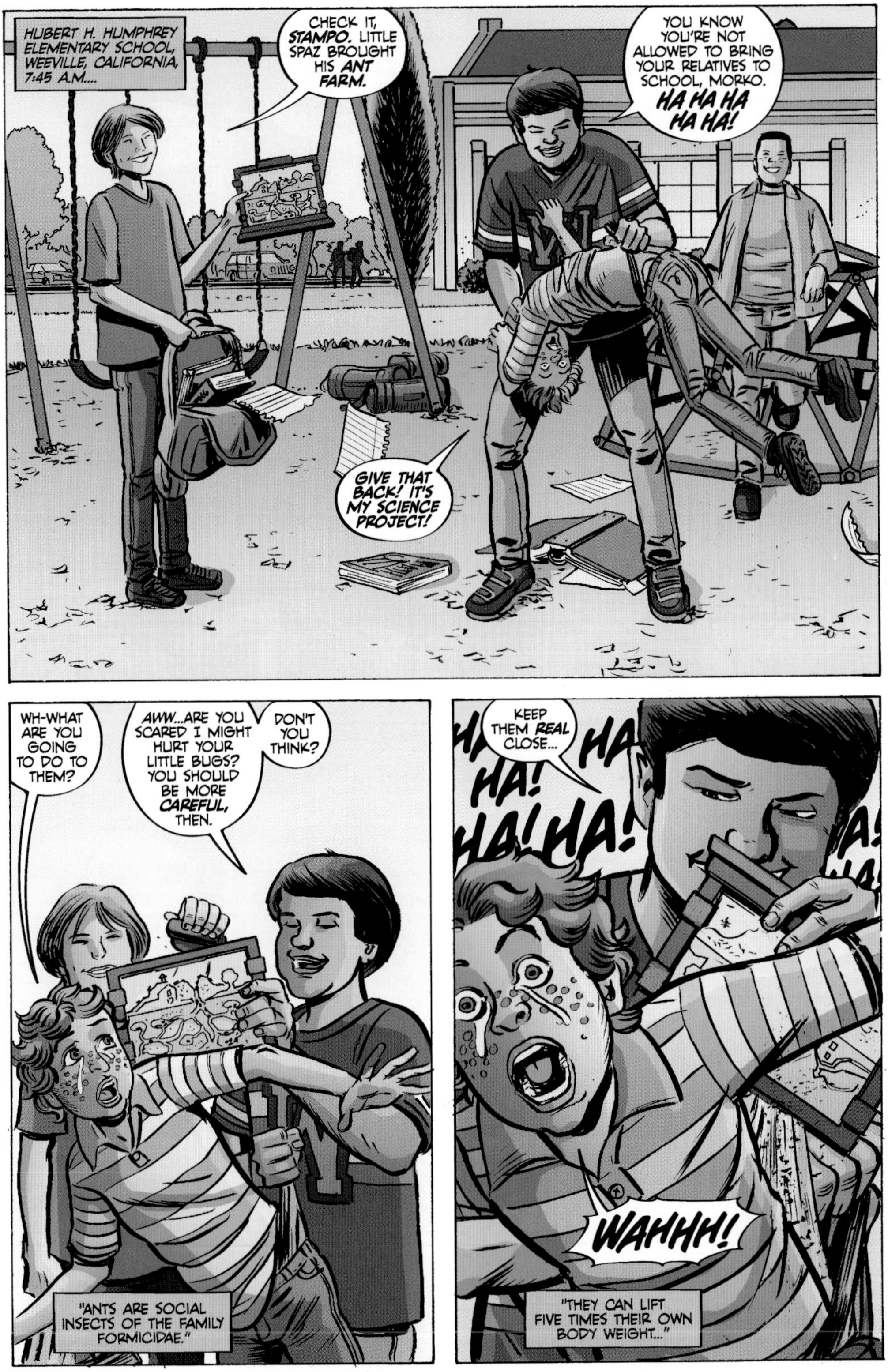

HUBERT H. HUMPHREY ELEMENTARY SCHOOL, WEEVILLE, CALIFORNIA, 7:45 A.M....
CHECK IT, STAMPO. LITTLE SPAZ BROUGHT HIS ANT FARM.
YOU KNOW YOU'RE NOT ALLOWED TO BRING YOUR RELATIVES TO SCHOOL, MORKO. HA HA HA HA HA!
GIVE THAT BACK! IT'S MY SCIENCE PROJECT!
WH-WHAT ARE YOU GOING TO DO TO THEM?
AWW...ARE YOU SCARED I MIGHT HURT YOUR LITTLE BUGS? YOU SHOULD BE MORE CAREFUL, THEN.
DON'T YOU THINK?
"ANTS ARE SOCIAL INSECTS OF THE FAMILY FORMICIDAE."
KEEP THEM REAL CLOSE...
HA HA! HA! HA!
WAHHH!
"THEY CAN LIFT FIVE TIMES THEIR OWN BODY WEIGHT..."

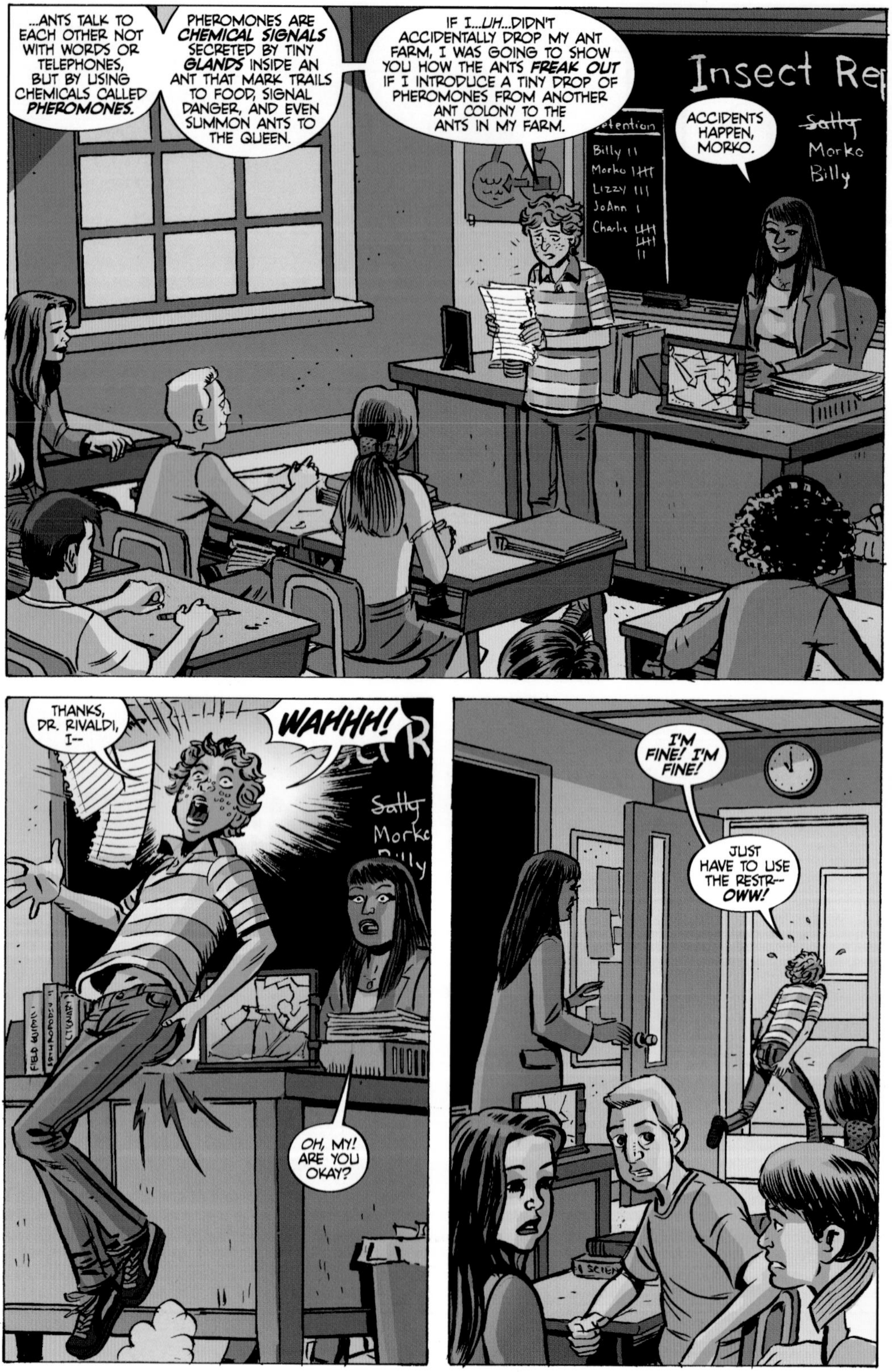
...ANTS TALK TO EACH OTHER NOT WITH WORDS OR TELEPHONES, BUT BY USING CHEMICALS CALLED *PHEROMONES.*
PHEROMONES ARE *CHEMICAL SIGNALS* SECRETED BY TINY *GLANDS* INSIDE AN ANT THAT MARK TRAILS TO FOOD, SIGNAL DANGER, AND EVEN SUMMON ANTS TO THE QUEEN.
IF I...*UH*...DIDN'T ACCIDENTALLY DROP MY ANT FARM, I WAS GOING TO SHOW YOU HOW THE ANTS *FREAK OUT* IF I INTRODUCE A TINY DROP OF PHEROMONES FROM ANOTHER ANT COLONY TO THE ANTS IN MY FARM.
ACCIDENTS HAPPEN, MORKO.
THANKS, DR. RIVALDI, I--
WAHHH!
OH, MY! ARE YOU OKAY?
I'M FINE! I'M FINE!
JUST HAVE TO USE THE RESTR-- *OWW!*

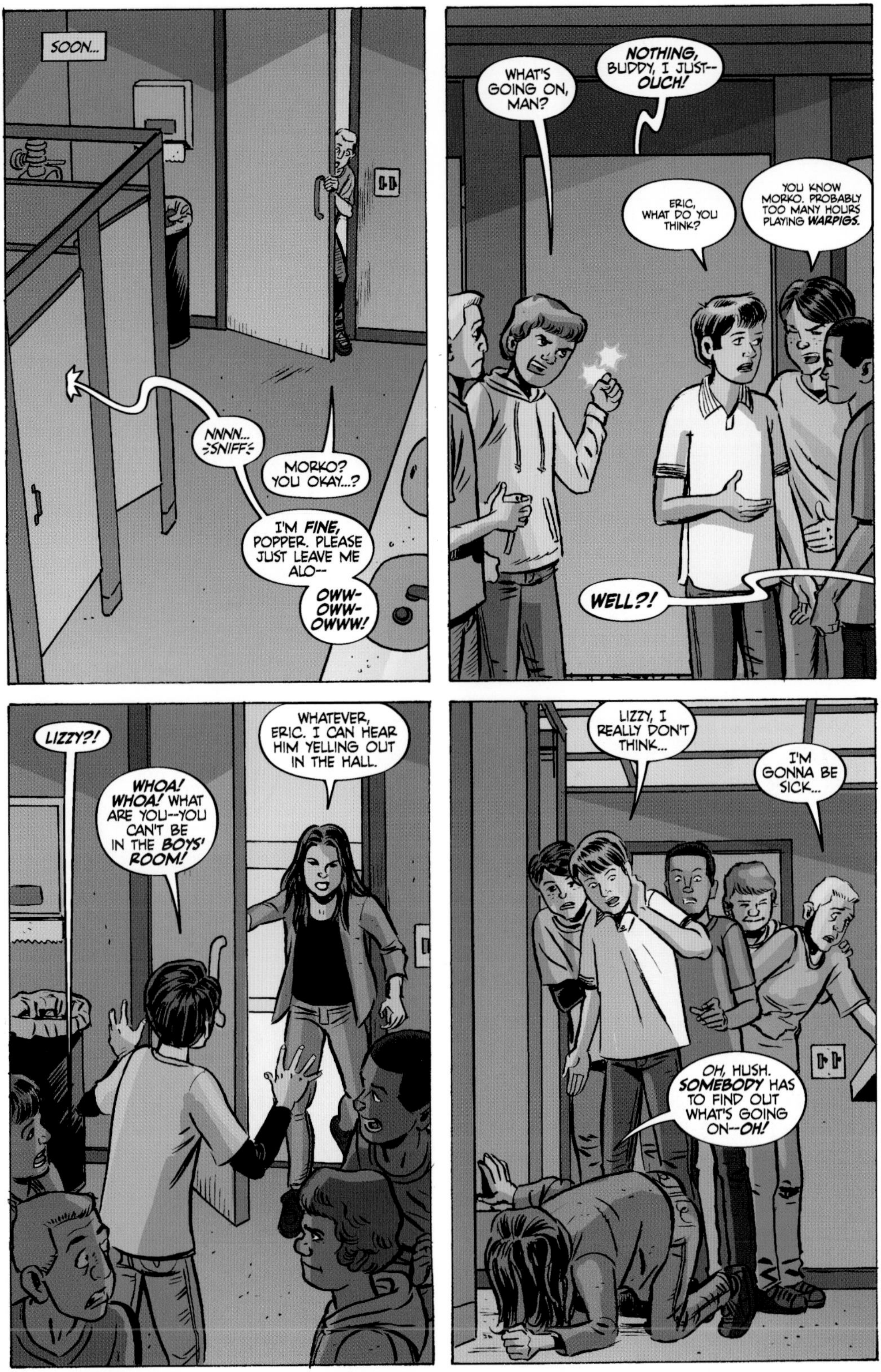
SOON...
NNNN... ≶SNIFF≶
MORKO? YOU OKAY...?
I'M FINE, POPPER. PLEASE JUST LEAVE ME ALO--
OWW-OWW-OWWW!
WHAT'S GOING ON, MAN?
NOTHING, BUDDY, I JUST-- OUCH!
ERIC, WHAT DO YOU THINK?
YOU KNOW MORKO. PROBABLY TOO MANY HOURS PLAYING WARPIGS.
WELL?!
LIZZY?!
WHOA! WHOA! WHAT ARE YOU--YOU CAN'T BE IN THE BOYS' ROOM!
WHATEVER, ERIC. I CAN HEAR HIM YELLING OUT IN THE HALL.
LIZZY, I REALLY DON'T THINK...
I'M GONNA BE SICK...
OH, HUSH. SOMEBODY HAS TO FIND OUT WHAT'S GOING ON--OH!

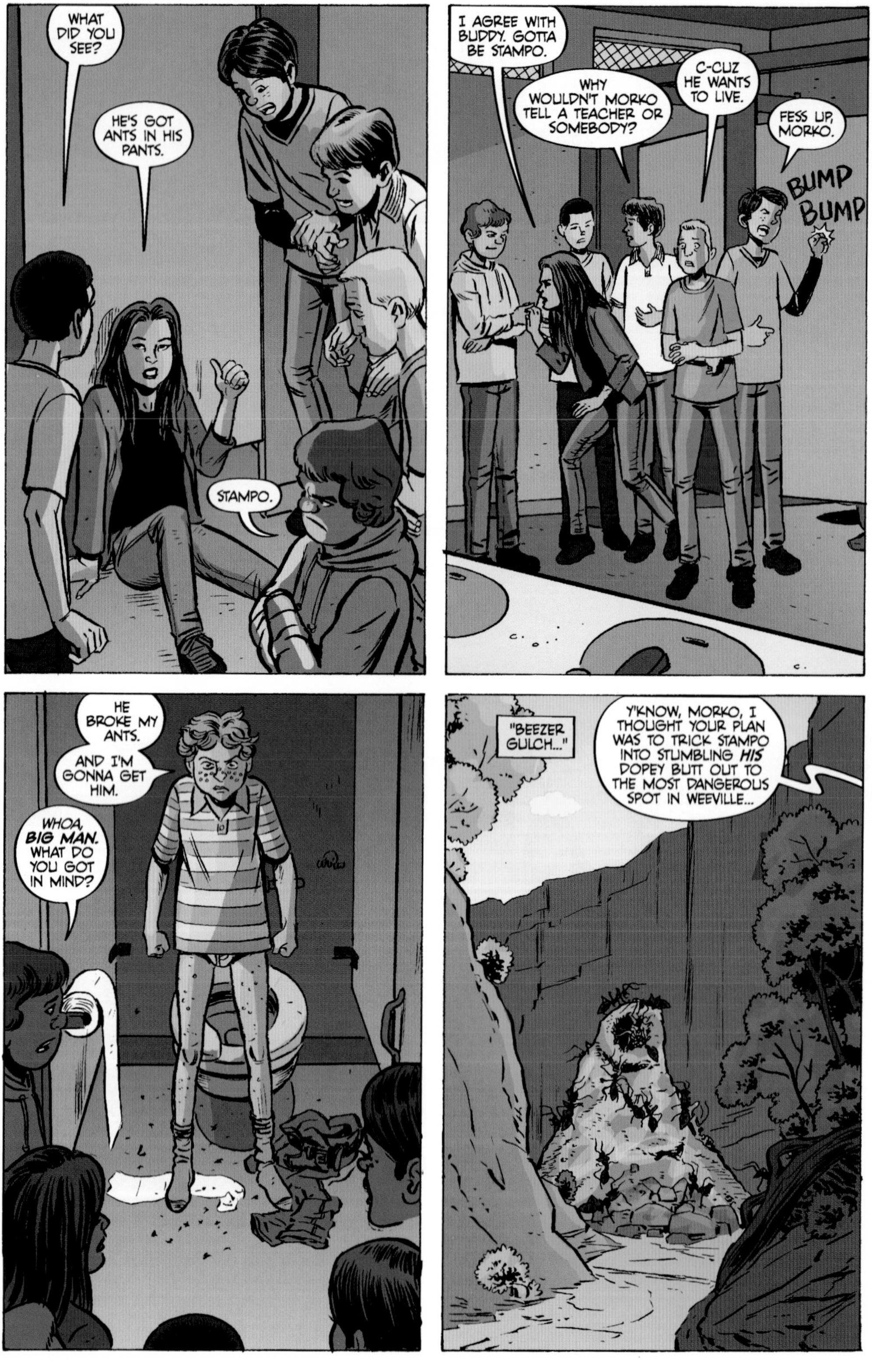
WHAT DID YOU SEE?
HE'S GOT ANTS IN HIS PANTS.
STAMPO.
I AGREE WITH BUDDY. GOTTA BE STAMPO.
WHY WOULDN'T MORKO TELL A TEACHER OR SOMEBODY?
C-CUZ HE WANTS TO LIVE.
FESS UP, MORKO.
BUMP BUMP
HE BROKE MY ANTS.
AND I'M GONNA GET HIM.
WHOA, BIG MAN. WHAT DO YOU GOT IN MIND?
"BEEZER GULCH..."
Y'KNOW, MORKO, I THOUGHT YOUR PLAN WAS TO TRICK STAMPO INTO STUMBLING HIS DOPEY BUTT OUT TO THE MOST DANGEROUS SPOT IN WEEVILLE...

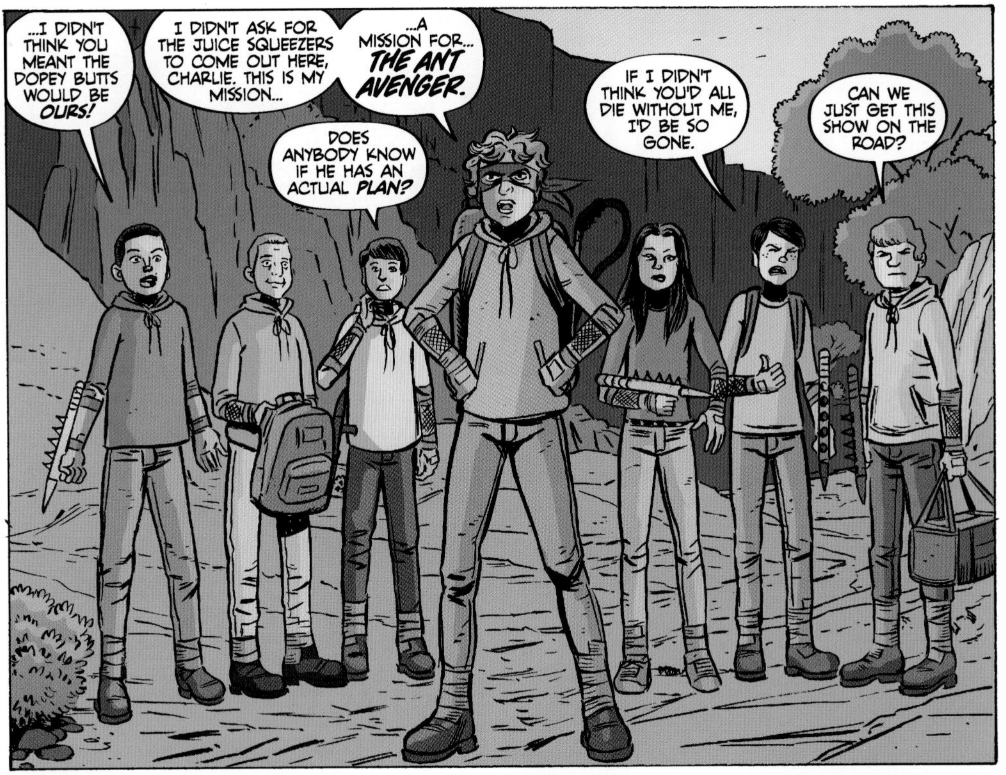
...I DIDN'T THINK YOU MEANT THE DOPEY BUTTS WOULD BE OURS!
I DIDN'T ASK FOR THE JUICE SQUEEZERS TO COME OUT HERE, CHARLIE. THIS IS MY MISSION...
...A MISSION FOR... THE ANT AVENGER.
DOES ANYBODY KNOW IF HE HAS AN ACTUAL PLAN?
IF I DIDN'T THINK YOU'D ALL DIE WITHOUT ME, I'D BE SO GONE.
CAN WE JUST GET THIS SHOW ON THE ROAD?

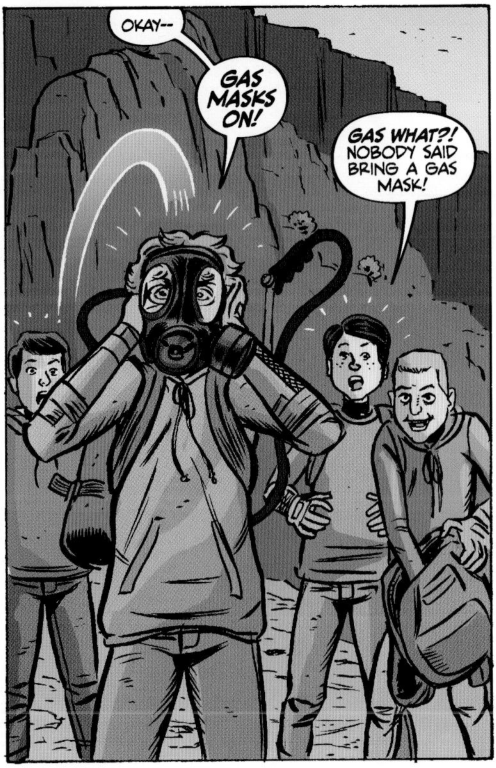
OKAY--
GAS MASKS ON!
GAS WHAT?! NOBODY SAID BRING A GAS MASK!

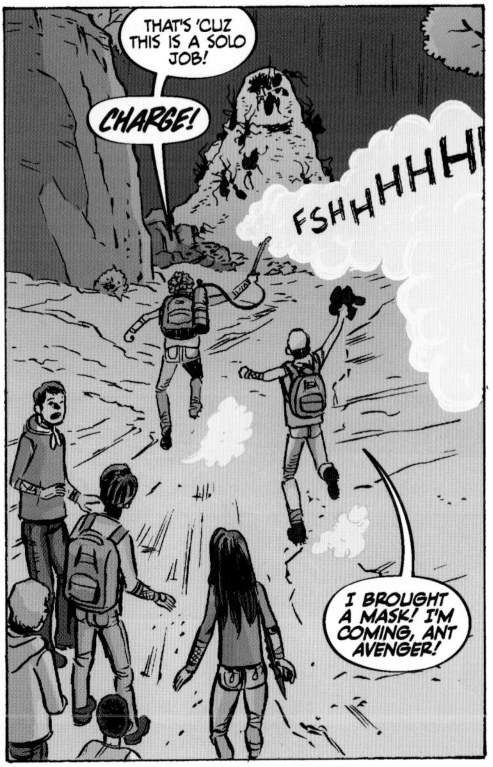
THAT'S 'CUZ THIS IS A SOLO JOB!
CHARGE!
FSHHHHHH
I BROUGHT A MASK! I'M COMING, ANT AVENGER!

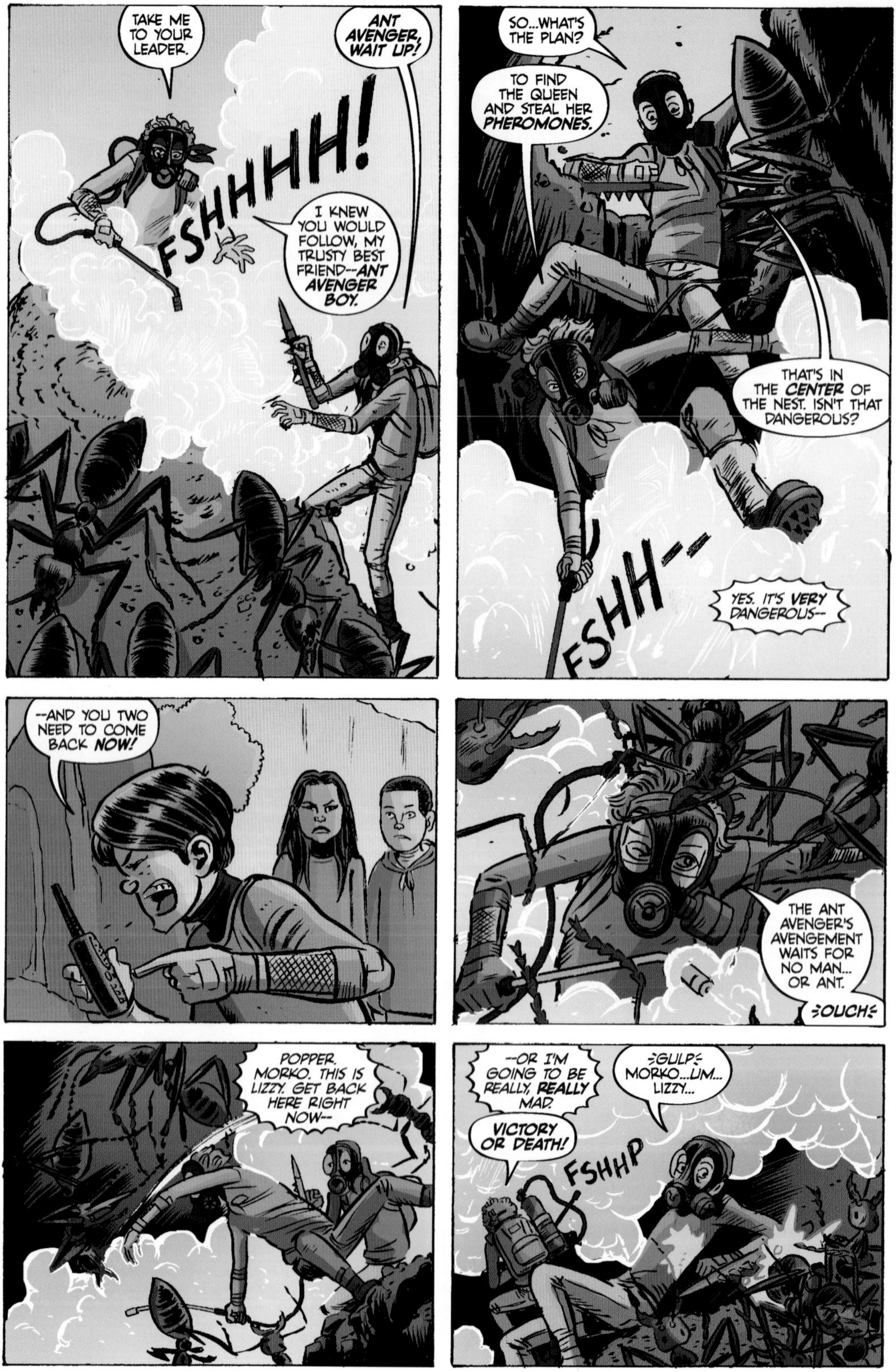
TAKE ME TO YOUR LEADER.
ANT AVENGER, WAIT UP!
FSHHHHH!
I KNEW YOU WOULD FOLLOW, MY TRUSTY BEST FRIEND--ANT AVENGER BOY.
SO...WHAT'S THE PLAN?
TO FIND THE QUEEN AND STEAL HER PHEROMONES.
THAT'S IN THE CENTER OF THE NEST. ISN'T THAT DANGEROUS?
FSHH--
YES. IT'S VERY DANGEROUS--
--AND YOU TWO NEED TO COME BACK NOW!
THE ANT AVENGER'S AVENGEMENT WAITS FOR NO MAN... OR ANT.
OUCH
POPPER. MORKO. THIS IS LIZZY. GET BACK HERE RIGHT NOW--
--OR I'M GOING TO BE REALLY, REALLY MAD.
GULP MORKO...UM... LIZZY...
VICTORY OR DEATH!
FSHHP

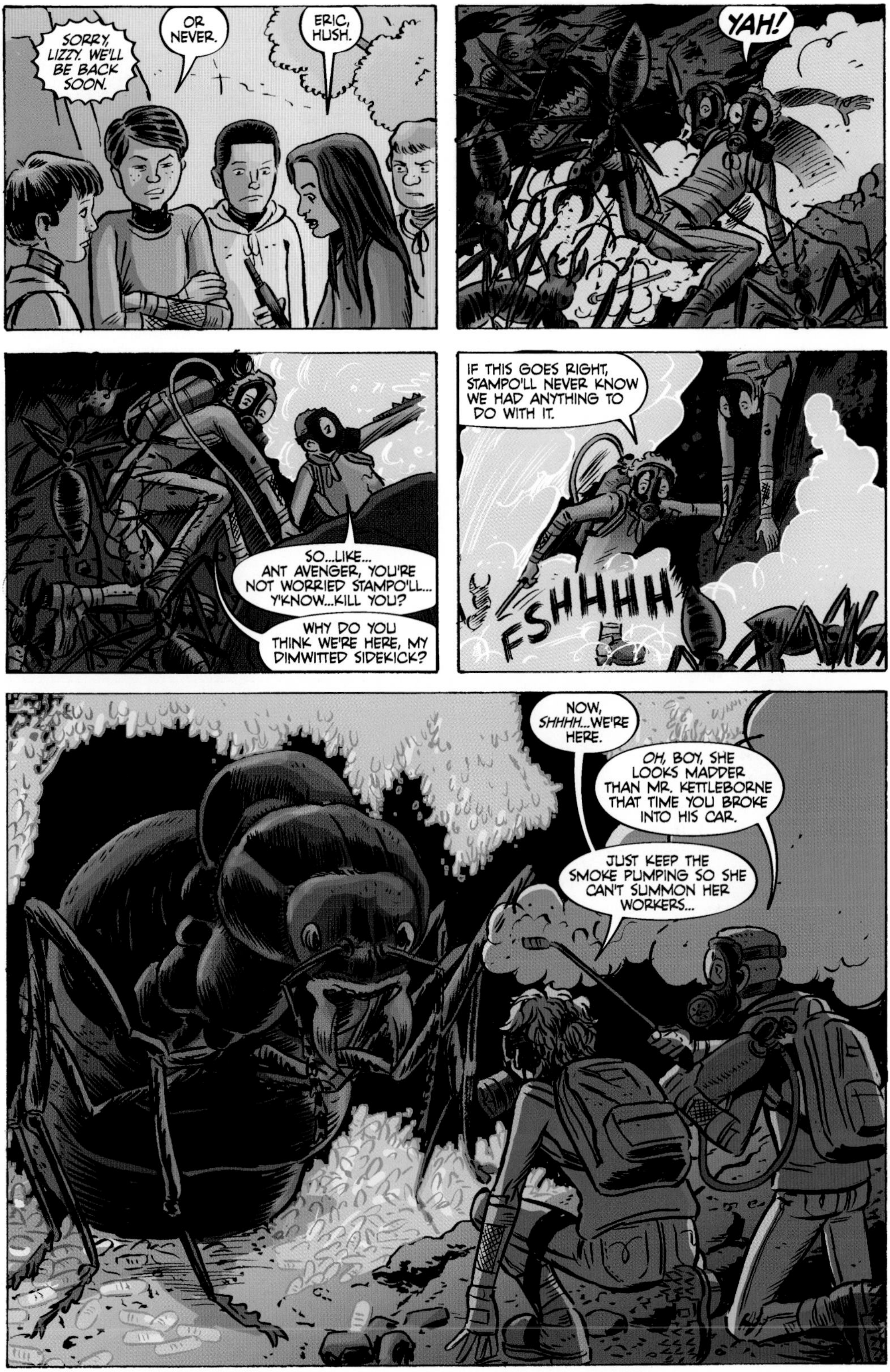
SORRY, LIZZY. WE'LL BE BACK SOON.
OR NEVER.
ERIC, HUSH.
YAH!
SO...LIKE... ANT AVENGER, YOU'RE NOT WORRIED STAMPO'LL... Y'KNOW...KILL YOU?
WHY DO YOU THINK WE'RE HERE, MY DIMWITTED SIDEKICK?
IF THIS GOES RIGHT, STAMPO'LL NEVER KNOW WE HAD ANYTHING TO DO WITH IT.
FSHHHHH
NOW, SHHHH...WE'RE HERE.
OH, BOY, SHE LOOKS MADDER THAN MR. KETTLEBORNE THAT TIME YOU BROKE INTO HIS CAR.
JUST KEEP THE SMOKE PUMPING SO SHE CAN'T SUMMON HER WORKERS...

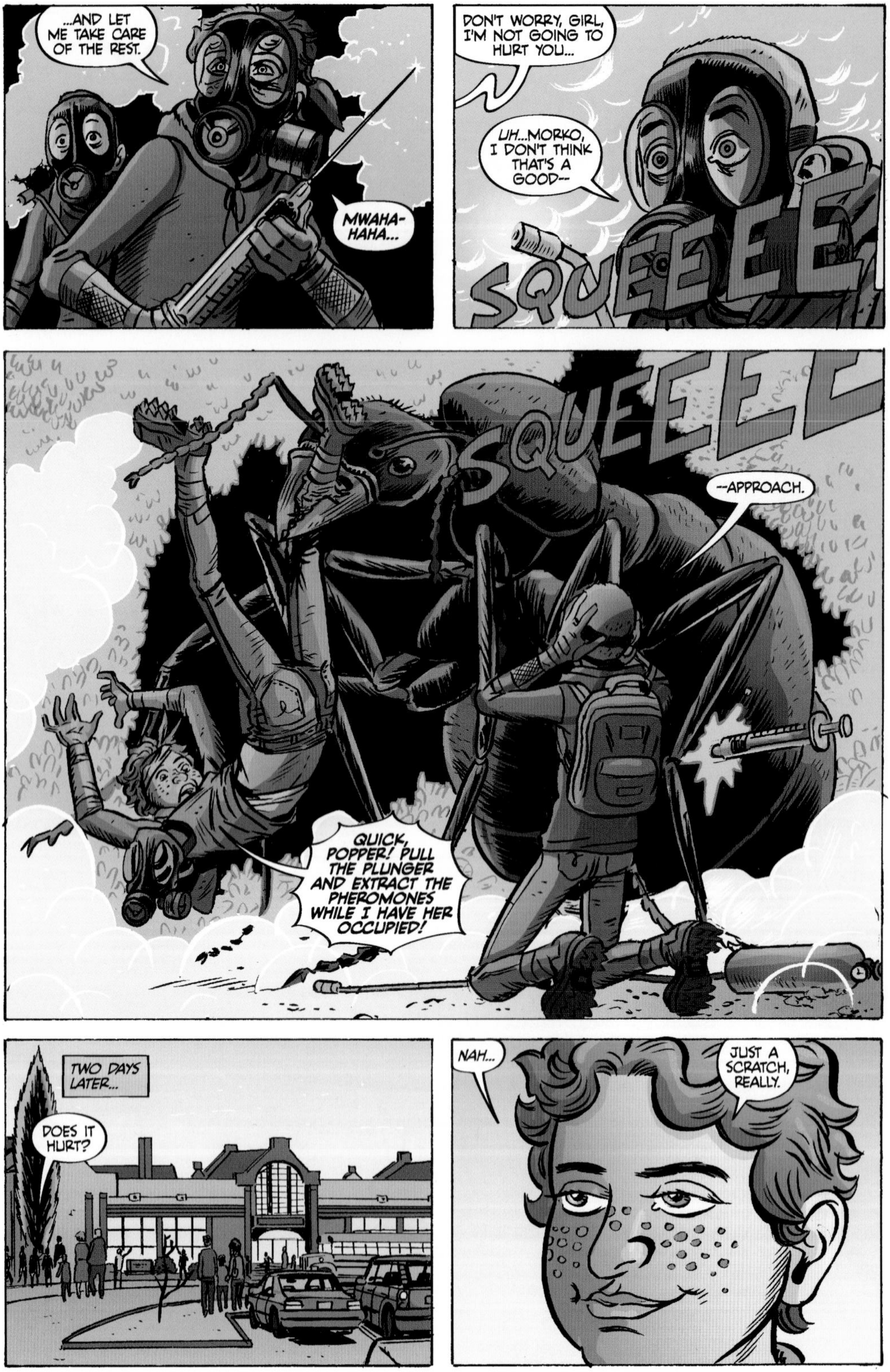
...AND LET ME TAKE CARE OF THE REST.
MWAHA-HAHA...
DON'T WORRY, GIRL, I'M NOT GOING TO HURT YOU...
UH...MORKO, I DON'T THINK THAT'S A GOOD--
SQUEEEE
SQUEEEEE
--APPROACH.
QUICK, POPPER! PULL THE PLUNGER AND EXTRACT THE PHEROMONES WHILE I HAVE HER OCCUPIED!
TWO DAYS LATER...
DOES IT HURT?
NAH...
JUST A SCRATCH, REALLY.

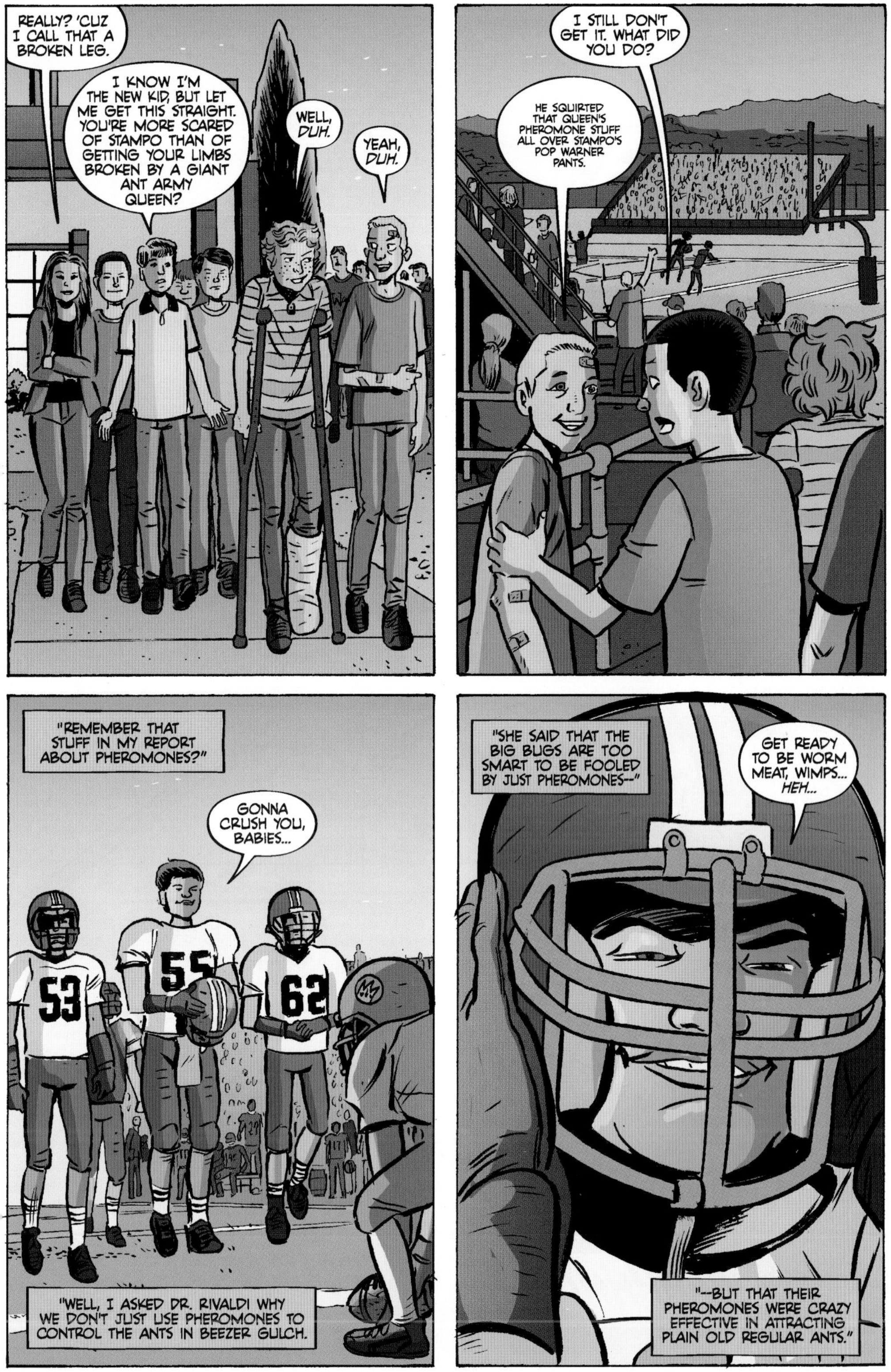
REALLY? 'CUZ I CALL THAT A BROKEN LEG.
I KNOW I'M THE NEW KID, BUT LET ME GET THIS STRAIGHT. YOU'RE MORE SCARED OF STAMPO THAN OF GETTING YOUR LIMBS BROKEN BY A GIANT ANT ARMY QUEEN?
WELL, DUH.
YEAH, DUH.
I STILL DON'T GET IT. WHAT DID YOU DO?
HE SQUIRTED THAT QUEEN'S PHEROMONE STUFF ALL OVER STAMPO'S POP WARNER PANTS.
"REMEMBER THAT STUFF IN MY REPORT ABOUT PHEROMONES?"
GONNA CRUSH YOU, BABIES...
"WELL, I ASKED DR. RIVALDI WHY WE DON'T JUST USE PHEROMONES TO CONTROL THE ANTS IN BEEZER GULCH.
"SHE SAID THAT THE BIG BUGS ARE TOO SMART TO BE FOOLED BY JUST PHEROMONES--"
GET READY TO BE WORM MEAT, WIMPS... HEH...
"--BUT THAT THEIR PHEROMONES WERE CRAZY EFFECTIVE IN ATTRACTING PLAIN OLD REGULAR ANTS."

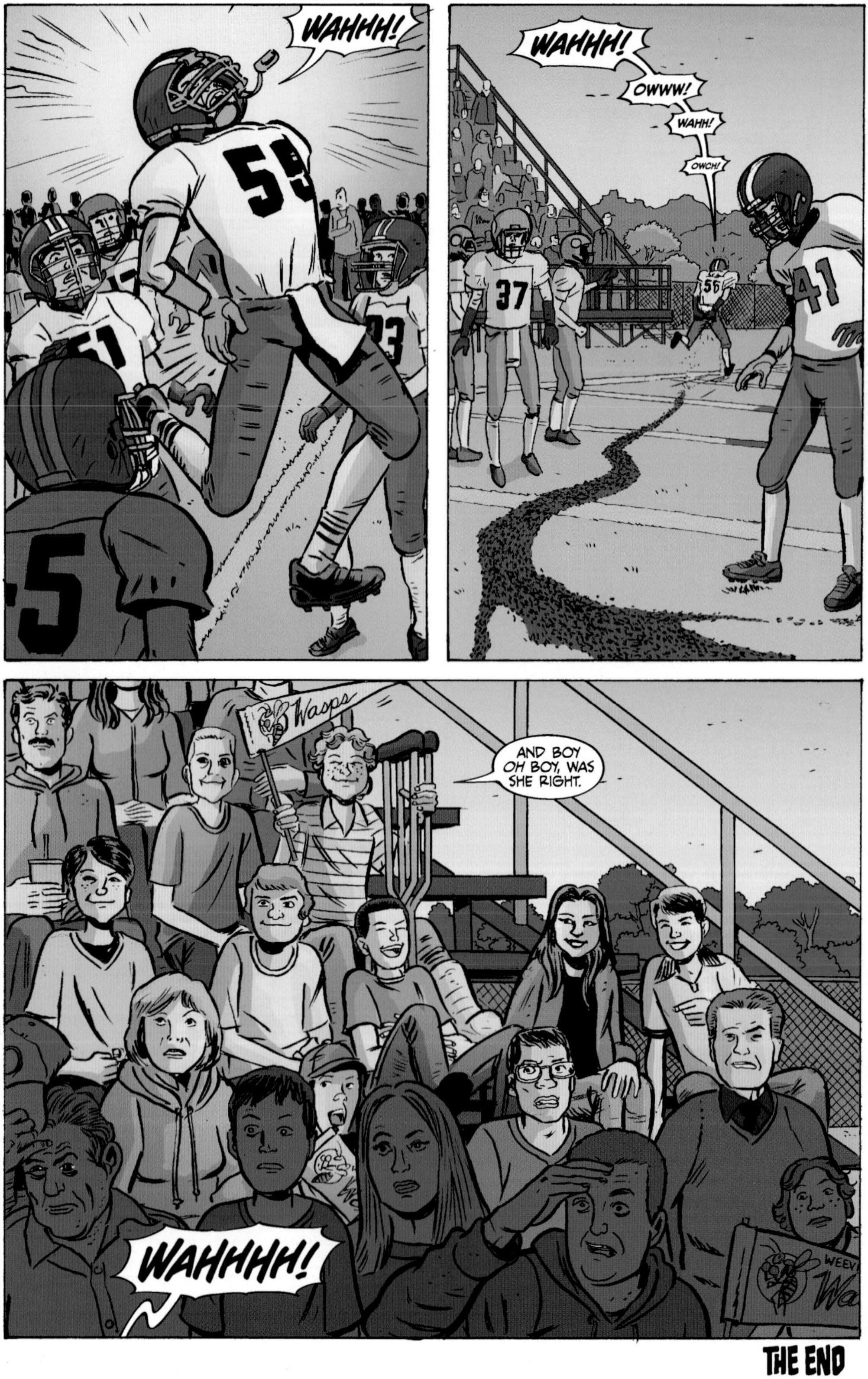
WAHHH!
WAHHH!
OWWW!
WAHH!
OWCH!
Wasps
AND BOY OH BOY, WAS SHE RIGHT.
WAHHHH!

THE END

BUGS BEWARE!

THE Juice Squeezers™

ARE HERE!

TOUGH KIDS KICKING INSECT BUTT!

Collect all the Juice Squeezers for more kids versus giant bugs action than you can handle!

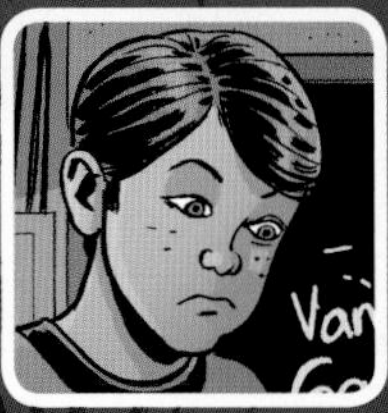

Fitz

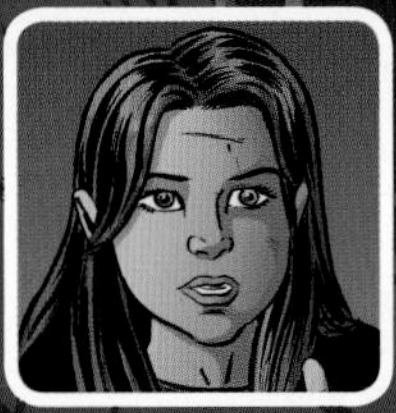

Beedle

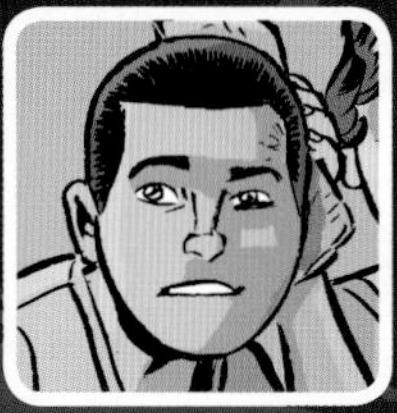

Patton

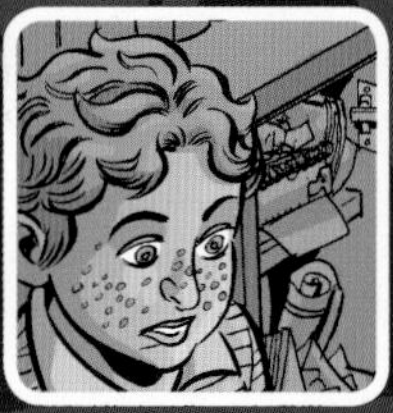

Morko

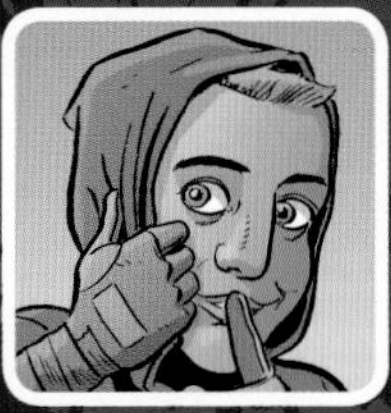

Popper

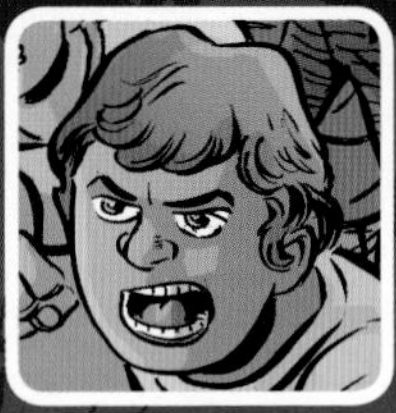

Buddy

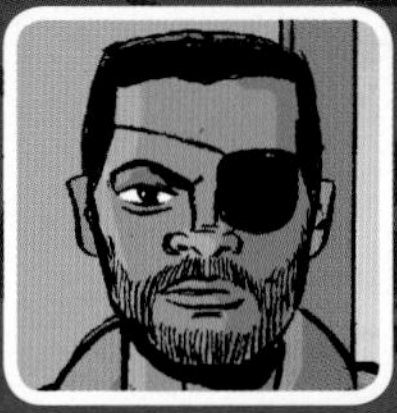

Bug Eye

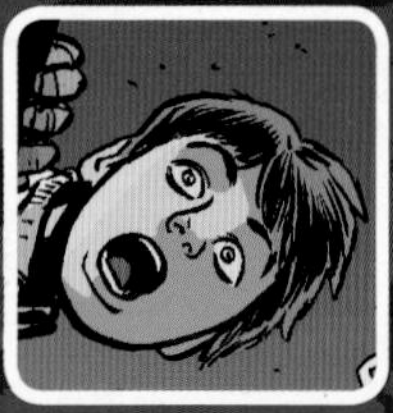

Farnsburger

Clip and save for your Juice Squeezers Command Files

JUICE SQUEEZER # 001

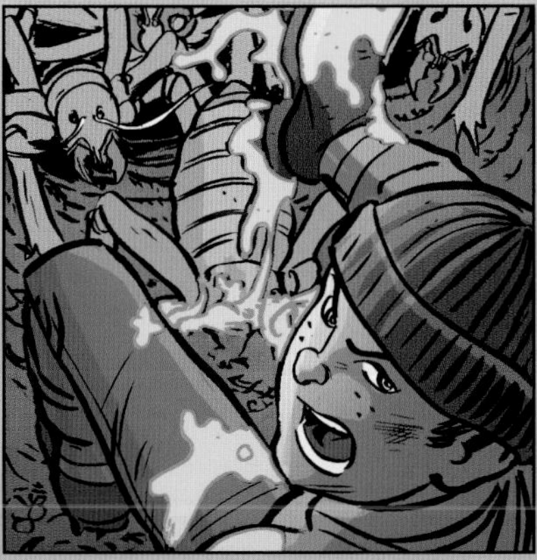

Name: Eric Fitz
Rank: Field Captain
Height: 4'3"
Weight: 72 lbs

Specialties: Bossing the Squeezers around, drill sergeant attitude

Weapon of choice: Bug stick

Eric Fitz may act like a jerk from time to time, but that's only because he understands what's at stake. Taking his role as the Juice Squeezers' field captain in their war against the giant bugs who live below their town very seriously, Eric's tough and great at what he does, showcasing strong leadership in the heat of bug battle.

"Practice hard and stay focused and there's not a centipede or potato bug you can't crush!"

JUICE SQUEEZER # 002

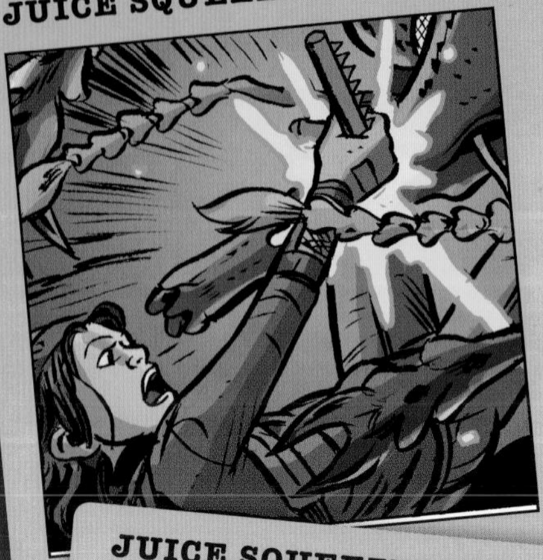

Name: Elizabeth "Lizzy" Beedle
Rank: Intelligence Officer
Height: 4'2"
Weight: 71 lbs

Specialties: No-nonsense attitude, gathering intel, first aid, asking the important questions
Weapon of choice: Shovel

The heart of the Juice Squeezers squad, Lizzy Beedle is smart, sharp, cool, tough as nails, and cute as all get out. The only girl in the group, Lizzy doesn't take any guff from anybody and when she gets mad she'll cut off her nose to spite her face. Bugs fear her anger, but Lizzy also is the only Squeezer who wonders what's behind this bug epidemic.

"Doesn't matter if you're talking bugs or boys—they could all use a swift kick in the butt!"

JUICE SQUEEZER # 003

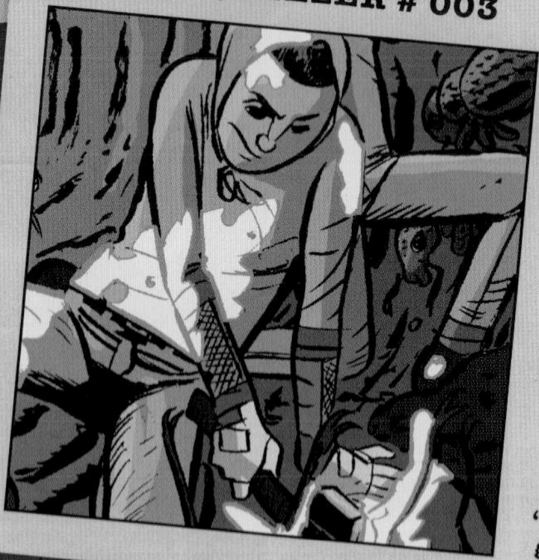

Name: Charles "Charlie" Patton
Rank: Morale Officer
Height: (Just a hair over) 4'
Weight: 64 lbs

Specialties: Thinking on his feet, new Squeezer outreach, jokes in the heat of battle
Weapon of choice: Hatchet

Always ready to crack wise, Charlie Patton is the clown of the group. He may be the most personable member of a group of kids who spend more time in tunnels than in the classroom, but he doesn't let his fun-loving attitude get in the way of his bug-squishing duties! When it comes to Squeezer reliability, the gang know Charlie's always got their backs! Plus, he's distantly related to famed WWII general George Patton, so . . . that has to be good, right?

"Let's finish squishing these centipedes so we can get home and play *World of Warpigs!*"

JUICE SQUEEZER # 004

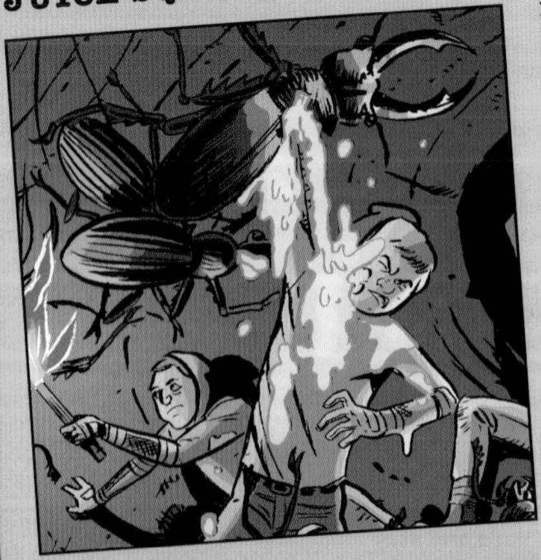

Name: Buddy (Yeah, just Buddy. What's it to you?)
Rank: The Muscle
Height: 4'1"
Weight: 70 lbs

Specialties: Hand to hand combat, intimidation, stealth infiltration
Weapon of choice: Bug stick (or his fists)

Buddy's size may not show it, but he's one Squeezer that you don't want to mess with! An easygoing kid of few words, Buddy's slow to anger, but when he gets there, watch out. The Squeezers' resident heavy hitter is the first to roll up his sleeves in defense of a friend, and while his reach might not be long, you don't want to end up on the wrong end of one of his knuckle sandwiches.

"Yeah, I've wrestled a dung beetle before. No big deal."

USAGI YOJIMBO™

Created, Written, and Illustrated by Stan Sakai

AVAILABLE FROM DARK HORSE COMICS

Book 8: Shades of Death
$14.99 | ISBN 978-1-56971-259-7

Book 9: Daisho
$14.99 | ISBN 978-1-56971-292-4

Book 10: The Brink of Life and Death
$14.99 | ISBN 978-1-56971-297-9

Book 11: Seasons
$14.99 | ISBN 978-1-56971-375-4

Book 12: Grasscutter
$16.99 | ISBN 978-1-56971-413-3

Book 13: Grey Shadows
$14.99 | ISBN 978-1-56971-459-1

Book 14: Demon Mask
$15.99 | ISBN 978-1-56971-523-9

Book 15: Grasscutter II
$15.99 | ISBN 978-1-56971-660-1

Book 16: The Shrouded Moon
$15.99 | ISBN 978-1-56971-883-4

Book 17: Duel at Kitanoji
$16.99 | ISBN 978-1-56971-973-2

Book 18: Travels with Jotaro
$15.99 | ISBN 978-1-59307-220-9

Book 19: Fathers and Sons
$15.99 | ISBN 978-1-59307-319-0

Book 20: Glimpses of Death
$15.99 | ISBN 978-1-59307-549-1

Book 21: The Mother of Mountains
$15.99 | ISBN 978-1-59307-783-9

Book 22: Tomoe's Story
$15.99 | ISBN 978-1-59307-947-5

Book 23: Bridge of Tears
$17.99 | ISBN 978-1-59582-298-7

Book 24: Return of the Black Soul
$16.99 | ISBN 978-1-59582-472-1

Book 25: Fox Hunt
$16.99 | ISBN 978-1-59582-726-5

Book 26: Traitors of the Earth
$16.99 | ISBN 978-1-59582-910-8

Book 27: A Town Called Hell
$16.99 | ISBN 978-1-59582-970-2

Book 28: Red Scorpion
$17.99 | ISBN 978-1-61655-398-2

Space Usagi
$17.99 | ISBN 978-1-56971-290-0

Usagi Yojimbo: Yokai
$14.99 | ISBN 978-1-59582-362-5

The Art of Usagi Yojimbo
$29.95 | ISBN 978-1-59307-493-7

47 Ronin
Written by Mike Richardson
$19.99 | ISBN 978-1-59582-954-2

The Adventures of Nilson Groundthumper and Hermy
$14.99 | ISBN 978-1-61655-341-8

AVAILABLE FROM FANTAGRAPHICS BOOKS
fantagraphics.com

Book 1: The Ronin
Book 2: Samurai
Book 3: The Wanderer's Road
Book 4: The Dragon Bellow Conspiracy
Book 5: Lone Goat and Kid
Book 6: Circlesw
Book 7: Gen's Story

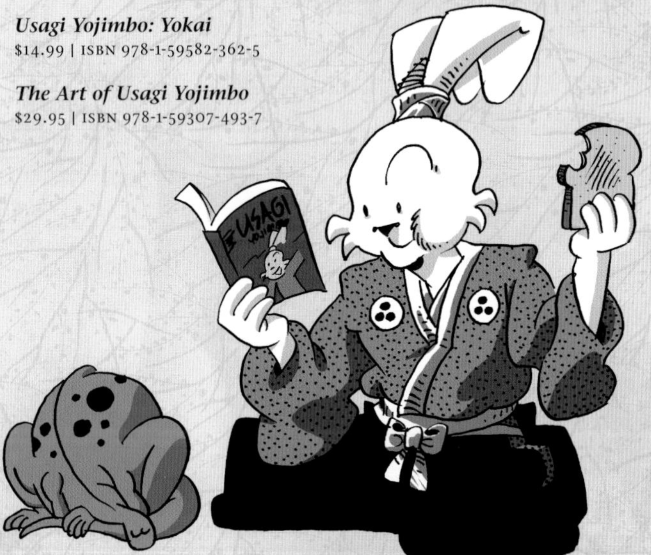
USAGI
YOJIMBO

AVAILABLE AT YOUR LOCAL COMICS SHOP OR BOOKSTORE
- To find a comics shop near your area, call 1-888-266-4226. For more information or to order direct:
- On the web: DarkHorse.com •E-mail: mailorder@darkhorse.com
- Phone: 1-800-862-0052 Mon.-Fri. 9 A.M. to 5 P.M. Pacific Time. *Prices and availability subject to change without notice.

DISCOVER THE ADVENTURE!

Explore these beloved books for the entire family.